FROM MIGRANTS TO REFUGEES

For Brian

CONTENTS

Abbreviations · ix
Acknowledgments · xi

Introduction · 1

PART I. THE MAKING OF MIGRANTS

1   Tracing a Boundary: Cultural Connections and Mandate
    Separation · 23

2   Canalization and Control: Unbounded Migrants · 43

3   Developmental Disappointment: Continuities in Late Colonial
    and Early Independence Ngara · 57

PART II. THE MAKING OF REFUGEES

4   Developmental Refugees: The Politics of Rwandan Refugee
    Settlement in Ngara District, 1959–1969 · 77

5   Citizens and Refugees: The Politics of Refugee Aid · 95

6   Conflicting Sovereignties: Competition at Mwesi Refugee
    Settlement, 1963–1970 · 113

PART III. THE MAKING OF CITIZENS

7   Of "Natural" Citizens and "Natural" Illegality: *Ujamaa*, *Magendo*,
    and Naturalization in Ngara District, 1970–1984 · 139

8   Competition and Backstabbing: The International Response to the
     Rwandan Refugee Crisis, 1994–1996 · 158

9   Of *Génocidaires* and Humanitarians: The Rwandan Refugee
     Emergency in Ngara District · 176

     Conclusion: The Business of Nationalism and
     Humanitarian Aid · 193

     Notes · 205
     Bibliography · 285
     Index · 301

ABBREVIATIONS

BCCU	Bugufi Co-operative Union
BNCU	Bukoba Native Co-operative Union
CCM	Chama Cha Mapinduzi
DC	District Commissioner
DWS	Department for World Service, Lutheran World Federation
EAC	East African Community
IFRC	International Federation of Red Cross Societies Archives
IMF	International Monetary Fund
LRCS	League of Red Cross Societies
LWF	Lutheran World Federation Archives
NA	British National Archives
NAM	British Army Museum Archives
NGO	Nongovernmental Organization
NPA	Norwegian People's Aid
OAU	Organization of African Unity
PMC	Permanent Mandates Commission
RADER	Rassemblement Démocratique Rwandais
RC	Regional Commissioner

RPF	Rwandan Patriotic Front
SILABU	Sisal Labor Bureau
TANU	Tanganyika African National Union
TC	Trusteeship Council
TCRS	Tanganyika Christian Refugee Service
TNA	Tanzanian National Archives, Dar es Salaam
TNA-Mwanza	Tanzanian National Archives, Mwanza
TTB	Tanganyika Tobacco Board
UDSM	University of Dar es Salaam Archives, East Africana Collection
UNAR	Union Nationale Rwandaise
UNHCR	United Nations High Commissioner for Refugees Archives
WCC	World Council of Churches
WFP	World Food Program
WLP	West Lake Province
WLR	West Lake Region

ACKNOWLEDGMENTS

It truly takes a global village to write a transnational local history. From New York to Atlanta, Geneva to Dar es Salaam, Ngara district back to New York, my village has been populated with the most exceptional people whose utmost generosity and indefatigable support transcend the descriptive bounds attributable to any one language.

At Emory University my graduate adviser, Clifton Crais, taught, motivated, encouraged, rallied, and inspired me. Clifton has had endless patience, reading an unending deluge of chapter drafts, revisions, and emails—always responding with insightful comments and questions. It is rare to find a mentor with such integrity and compassion, and I am grateful for his continued guidance. Kristin Mann has been a fountain of support, spending countless hours talking with me about writing, teaching, and living. Kristin's attention to detail and analytical skill greatly improved the chapters of this book. Kara Moskowitz has been a sounding board, colleague, cheerleader, and close friend throughout this process. Kara generously read several chapters in different stages of their creation. Her comments and friendship are deeply appreciated.

This work would not be possible without Joseph Rwagaba and the entire Rwagaba family. Joseph introduced me to Ngara district, becoming a brother and mentor in the process. The whole Rwagaba family warmly welcomed me as their own in every district of Tanzania to which this project led me. In particular, I would like to thank Thadeus, Leonia, Shangwe, and Bernard Rwagaba for welcoming me into their homes and for their continued love and support.

My time in Ngara was spent working directly with my research assistant Bernard Gwaho, who labored tirelessly to locate remote village elders and aid workers throughout the district. Bernard endured long interviews, terrifying car rides, and unending questions with patience and grace. Bernard's friendship and assistance were invaluable.

In Ngara, our neighbors Everready Nkya and his brilliant young daughter Everbright were constant sources of support and friendship. Everready is dearly missed, and we joined the whole Ngara district in mourning his sudden and tragic passing. Beyond his tireless work to improve the lives of many Ngarans, Everready provided an optimistic glimpse of how humanitarian aid can indeed be humanitarian.

During research work in Dar es Salaam and since, Lilian and Winnie Kokubanza Kiobya provided a home away from home. Lili and Winnie took us in as family, providing unending conversation, happiness, love, and sustenance.

Archival staff in Geneva and Tanzania went above and beyond to help me locate sources, some more obscure than others. I thank the archivists at the United Nations High Commissioner for Refugees (UNHCR), the Lutheran World Federation (LWF), the International Federation of Red Cross and Red Crescent Societies (IFRC), the Tanzania National Archives at Dar es Salaam and Mwanza, and the British National Archives. The Tanzanian Commission for Science and Technology (COSTECH) graciously granted me a research permit, for which I owe Opportuna Kweka a great deal. At LWF, Bernard Hitzler gave me much encouragement and provided a healthy dose of optimism for the long road ahead. I would also like to thank the late Egil Nilson, Michael Hyden, Isaac Laiser, Duanne Poppe, Bernhard Staub, and Peter Tyler for their time and support. Tony Waters generously supplied contacts and advice throughout the research and writing process. I am grateful to Tony and to Brian Neldner for their time during interviews and for enabling the pathways to my research.

I have been privileged to benefit from the expertise and creativity of an ever-growing network of scholars and friends, collaborators and mentors—too many to thank here. My thanks in particular to John Aerni-Flessner, Angelika Bammer, Marie Berry, Jennie Burnett, Husseina Dinani, Liz Fink, Dave Glovsky, René Lemarchand, Peter Little, Deo Mwapinga, David and Catherine Newbury, Pamela Scully, Jessica Reuther, Muey Saeturn, Marcia Schenck, Nathan Suhr-Sytsma, Thaddeus Sunseri, Meredith Terretta, Joanna Tague, Sarah Watkins, Mari Webel, and Christian Williams. Richard Roberts welcomed me to Stanford University as an acting assistant professor in 2014 and has been a fountain of guidance and invigorating critique ever since.

My intellectual home since 2016 has been the History Department at Hunter College. Words fail to describe the warmth, friendship, and solidarity I have received from the amazing scholars there. As chairs, first Mary Roldán and now Donna Haverty-Stacke have had unending patience in their support and encouragement of this project and my career. Manu

xii · Acknowledgments

Bhagavan, Eduardo Contreras, Elidor Mëhilli, Jonathan Rosenberg, and Iryna Vushko (now at Princeton) welcomed and inspired me. Jonathan, Eduardo, and Elidor also graciously commented on various versions of the manuscript.

Initial dissertation research funding was provided by the Institute of International Education Graduate Fellow/Fulbright Hays Doctoral Dissertation Research Award and the Laney Graduate School, Emory University. Subsequent funding for both research and writing was generously supplied by Stanford University; the Professional Staff Congress of the City University of New York (PSC-CUNY); the Faculty Fellowship Publication Program, CUNY; the Presidential Faculty Advancement Award, Hunter College; and a Faculty Research Fellowship, Hunter College.

I was fortunate to have the opportunity to test various versions of this book's chapters at many lectures, workshops, and conferences around the world. The chapters that follow have been refined from presentations at the Institute of African Studies at Emory University, the Center for African Studies at Stanford University, the CUNY Mellon Faculty Diversity Career Enhancement Initiative, the "Rethinking Refuge" workshop in Berlin, and the German Historical Institute, among others.

Earlier versions of chapter sections appeared in the *Journal of African History*, *International Journal of African Historical Studies*, and the edited volume *Refugee Crises, 1945–2000* published by Cambridge University Press. Many thanks to all those who commented on these prior versions.

Elizabeth Ault, my editor at Duke University Press, has been incredibly patient throughout the editing process—the majority of which took place during these long years of COVID-19. My thanks to Elizabeth and to her editorial associate Benjamin Kossak for all their help and understanding. Writing and editing alone do not make a book whole, so I must express my appreciation for Matthew Bandurchin's diligent work creating the maps for this volume. My sincerest gratitude to the two anonymous reviewers whose comments and suggestions vastly improved the final quality of this work.

My dearest friends endured long absences and frantic phone calls— never knowing whether to expect laughing or crying. So many thanks to Karl Bendorf, Julie Brown, Mary Carroll, Megan Dumas, the late and dearly missed Richard Feirstein, Stephanie Hundt, Lauren Kretz, Rebecca Kumar, Julie Niedzialkowski, and Jessie van Wijk for sanity-checking and providing emotional support along the way.

Of course, none of this would have been possible without the bedrock support from my family: my brother Adam Rosenthal and his wife, Eunhee

Kim-Rosenthal, my lovely in-laws Rod Guerrierro and MaryAnn Slaven, and my cousins Viki and Zachary Quick. My parents, Peter and Sandy Rosenthal, have been unwavering pillars of love and encouragement. They have long endured my long absences and unending historical rants with poise and affection. One final grudging acknowledgment must go to that swell guy Brian who handled all the documentation, travel logistics, security, finances, boredom, and white-knuckle driving but not proofreading. His typical response, "I was literally there, I already know what it says," sums him up succinctly, and it is to him that this book is dedicated.

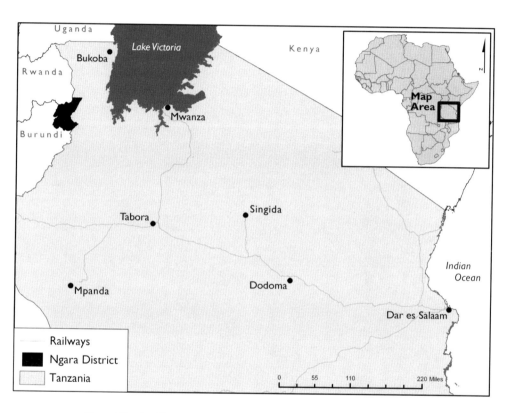

MAP 1. Ngara District, Tanzania. Created by Mathew Bandurchin.

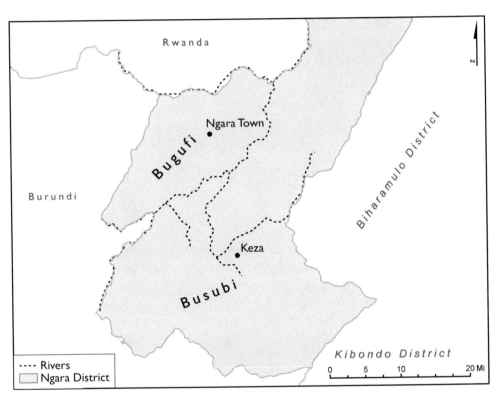

MAP 2. Precolonial Chiefdoms, Ngara. Created by Mathew Bandurchin.

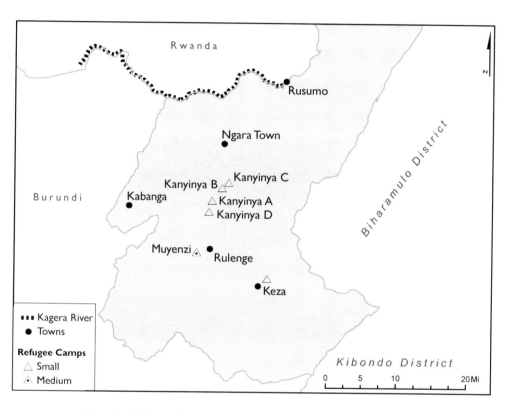

MAP 3. Rwandan Refugee Camps and Main Settlements in Ngara, 1960s. Created by Mathew Bandurchin.

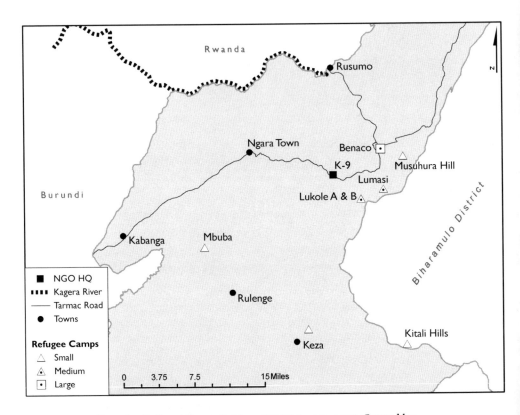

MAP 4. Rwandan Refugee Camps in Ngara District, 1994–1996. Created by Mathew Bandurchin.

INTRODUCTION

Who Qualifies to Be a Refugee? Who Was Barn [*sic*] to Be a Refugee?—Who Has the Right to Be Not a Refugee?
—Lazarus Mezza

Over a twenty-four-hour period beginning on April 28, 1994, the most rapid refugee exodus ever recorded took place.[1] More than 150,000 Rwandans, fleeing the violence of genocide and civil war, crossed the Rusumo Bridge into Ngara district, Tanzania. During the next two years, Ngara became host to one of the largest refugee camps in the world. As aid agencies and media outlets descended on this remote area of Tanzania, they, and the refugees they sought to aid, became crucial elements of the identity politics of the district, a politics embedded in Ngara's long history of migration. For hundreds of years, migrants from Rwanda and Burundi had settled in Ngara, forging cultural, political, and economic linkages throughout the region. It was only in the 1960s, however, with the advent of decolonization and the creation of the first Rwandan refugee camps in Ngara—when national and international actors called such migrants *refugees* for the first time—that the connections among these populations gave way to a politics of difference.

The long and varied presence of humanitarian aid to a specific sector of the Ngaran population—Rwandan refugees—has deep implications for Ngarans as well as for how we understand the history of humanitarian aid and nation-state formation in Africa. Examining this history yields insights into changing international geographies of control and regulation and their effects on local notions of citizenship, nation, and "others." International aid meant to subdue and control the segment of the Ngaran population labeled Rwandan refugees was often unsuccessful. However, rather than the failures or successes of such programs, this book focuses on the evolving political concepts and competing topographies of authority and control that produced refugee encounters in Ngara district, as they did throughout the decolonizing world. It also reveals the seminal role that Africans played, as aid workers, hosts, and refugees, in the evolution of refugee policies.

There are two general categories of people who live in Ngara district: those who are Tanzanian citizens and those who are not. Ngarans have an unmistakable pride in their Tanzanian identity, a sense of belonging to a history born of the nation's first president, Julius Nyerere, and the ideals he represented. Perhaps the pride stems from a memory of what people hoped the nation could be—a nostalgia rooted in a legacy of promised development and equality. And yet, there are few signs of development in the district, and rampant inequalities exist between those with connections to the government and those without. Everyone is aware of the corruption endemic to governance in Tanzania—it is an accepted part of life in Ngara. Moreover, state officials' repeated promises to deliver on development goals have remained dramatically unfulfilled. Ngarans remember the bitter hardships that followed the government's failed *ujamaa*, or forced villagization, in the 1970s and 1980s. Many people speak of the violence of *ujamaa*, vividly recalling the state agents who burned their homes and forced them to move to state-run villages. The reach of the state within Ngara has not always been benevolent or reliable, just as it has often been absent.

Driving northwest from the southern tip of Lake Victoria in Tanzania to Ngara district, one passes through a flat land dotted with foothills and forests. Suddenly, on entering Biharamulo district in the Kagera region, the hills get bigger, the slopes steeper. By the time one enters Ngara district, the hills and plateaus have become massive, the drive a constant struggle against gravity. Soon the landscape is covered with the wide green leaves of banana trees, which cluster around each mud and concrete house. The scenery is typical of the African Great Lakes region, an area populated by people who share similar cultures, languages, and political traditions.

There are Tanzanians in Ngara who cannot speak Kiswahili, the mandated national language, while fluency in Kisubi and Kihangaza, the languages of the district's former chiefdoms, abounds. Ngarans frequently violate state immigration laws, passing across the international borders to Rwanda and Burundi to conduct trade illicitly and to visit friends and family. Linguistic similarities facilitate this circulation of people and goods, as do cultural connections rooted in the precolonial and colonial traditions of the Great Lakes region. And yet Ngarans in Tanzania hold fast to a Tanzanian identity, particularly when referring to the "others" who live and work in the district.

"That person is Rwandan," my research assistant, Bernard Gwaho, would whisper to me as we drove along the main street of Ngara town. Ngarans

2 · Introduction

frequently reference Rwandans by noting the problems they cause in the district. Rwandans and, to a lesser extent, Burundians in Ngara district are not considered Tanzanians. They are viewed with suspicion and, occasionally, fear. In a place where the Tanzanian state has so obviously failed to achieve its promises, in a district that exists on the margins of the nation-state and remains economically and culturally nestled within a regional community, how have people come to identify with the Tanzanian nation-state?

This book analyzes the history of how the "nation" came to be actualized in the popular imaginations of people living on the border of the Tanzanian nation-state. I am concerned with the processes through which the people of the Busubi and Bugufi chiefdoms of Ngara district became Tanzanians—how the borders of a colony were operationalized to become the boundaries of a state and a citizenry. The presence of Rwandan refugees and the actions of international humanitarian organizations were integral to the ongoing process of national identity formation in Ngara. I argue that transnational aid to Rwandan refugees in Ngara unfolded as part of a broader project of nation-state formation and regulation—one that deeply affected local narratives of community and belonging.

While *From Migrants to Refugees* is geographically centered in Ngara district, it is also a history of the creation and maintenance of the world of nation-states during and after decolonization. During the late colonial and early independence eras, Ngara became a testing ground for novel forms of migrant containment and, later, refugee aid as the Rwandan refugee crises of the 1960s and 1990s offered humanitarian agencies new opportunities to experiment and expand their operations in sub-Saharan Africa. Ngaran history is thus entwined with that of the international humanitarian community, a group of people and organizations that created the bureaucratic category of "refugee," and with the actions that led to the sedimentation of this identity for those who live along the borders of the nation-state.

In our current historical moment, it seems that refugees are everywhere: in the news, in academia, and in politics. Refugees as a discursive group are demonized by some, exalted by others. Similarly, host communities are valorized or victimized in the press and academic literature. This book does neither. Rather, I show that host communities in Ngara responded to the refugees in their midst from the 1960s through the 1990s in myriad ways, including with generosity, with animosity, and with prejudice. As the postcolonial era progressed, however, it was the figure of the official refugee—the dangerous person who needed to be controlled in internationally funded refugee camps—that became the "other" against which Ngarans came to define themselves as Tanzanians.[2] Rwandan refugees never appear in this book as a homogeneous group, except as they were configured in international and national discourses. The refugees in this book comprise a diverse group of peoples, with all the attendant political and economic rivalries inherent to *agentive individuals*, a fact that international refugee agencies were unable and, as self-described apolitical agencies, unwilling to comprehend. It was in this part of the African Great Lakes region that transnational initiatives, beginning with the League of Nations, emerged to control the political futures of migrants. And it was in response to the politics of the local people who became citizens and refugees in Ngara that such initiatives evolved into the global governance regime on display today.

The following chapters reveal the hard reality of who gets resources and why in the world of humanitarian aid. It is a history of who mattered to aid agencies and the state, and who did not, in a peripheral region that neither colonial nor postcolonial governments cared much about. Some Ngarans resented the aid given to those labeled Rwandan refugees, others profited from working with aid agencies, and still others were indifferent. None could ignore, however, the changes that aid agencies and refugees brought to Ngara district over the last sixty years. While scholars have written about the Rwandan refugee crisis following the genocide in the 1990s, until now, there has been no comprehensive study of the history of migration and asylum in the area. This book reveals how shared histories and cultures between Rwandans and Ngarans gave way to separate sovereign nation-states, both politically and ideologically, during the twentieth century.

Scholarship on the Edge

Ngara district falls on the western edge of Tanzania, just within the triangle of borders that demarcate the nation-states of Burundi, Rwanda, and Tanzania under international law. The district's landscape, as seen from the ground, consists of large hills and valleys that extend relentlessly past state boundaries. Today, as in the past, Ngarans are aware of the borders that separate Tanzania from its neighbors.[3] Rather than preventing travel, this knowledge serves as a conduit for the widespread circulation of people, animals, and goods in the area.[4] Regional laborers, traders, and herders, as well as entire sports teams, cross state boundaries daily. Borders, then, cannot be conceived of as barriers for Ngarans. Rather, during the second half of the twentieth century, there developed what Paul Nugent and A. I. Asiwaju

4 · Introduction

have called the "mental space" of "difference between communities across the line."[5]

In his study of autochthony and belonging in contemporary Africa, Peter Geschiere writes that "it is high time . . . for a return to the topic of nation building," particularly since we have "surprisingly few studies of what nation-building meant on the ground."[6] For Geschiere, current politics and violence around notions of belonging cannot be divorced from the "specific trajectories that nation-building took" during moments of decolonization.[7] And, as Frederick Cooper has shown, the nation-state was only one of many political forms possible in Africa during decolonization.[8]

To understand how different versions of nation and citizenship gained traction locally, it is necessary to examine how people came to imagine their place in the world and who they came to include and exclude within that imagined space. In other words, we have to denaturalize what Agamben calls "the trinity of state-nation-territory."[9] And if historians are to take seriously the challenge of analyzing the processes of nation building, we have to acknowledge a discursive population that has remained in the shadows of historical writing—the figure of the refugee.

New discursive formations of the refugee emerged alongside those of the nation-state. Only a decade prior to Tanzanian decolonization, events in postwar Europe had propelled the leaders of the great powers to create a system of global governance based on a notion of inviolate, sovereign nation-states.[10] In 1951 a definition of *refugee* became solidified in international law for the first time.[11] Concurrently, nation-state representatives developed an international apparatus to police and "aid" those rejects of the nation-state system whose unauthorized migration was "a threat to territorial security."[12] These events occurred on the cusp of decolonization, itself a refugee-generating project that separated the "natural" inhabitants of new states from those who did not belong.[13]

During the Cold War, great powers and leaders in Geneva, New York, and Africa became intent on maintaining the boundaries of the colonial state within the nation-state form.[14] Those borders of the colonial state that had remained largely "operationally nonexistent" for the majority of their history needed to be actualized.[15] This domestication of borders became crucial to nation building and "the creation of novel sources of legitimizing political membership."[16] Such actualization was necessary to begin with, however, because the model of the sovereign nation-state did not comfortably align with realities on the ground. Indeed, in their travels, Ngarans and Rwandans blurred the lines of borders and thus citizenries, which are assumed to be natural and permanent under the sovereign nation-state system. The fact that some Rwandan refugees were able to self-settle in Ngara during decolonization, while others were forced into internationally controlled camps, underscores the gap between the idea of the nation-state, with its well-defined borders, citizenries, and "others," and the much more entangled, contingent, and "slippery" categories of refugee and citizen.[17]

However, although scholars have increasingly called attention to the role of refugees in the processes of nation-state formation, we know little about the relationship between refugees and nation building during decolonization.[18] Historians have been slow to examine the significance of refugee experiences.[19] This "structural" exclusion of refugees from the historical canon, according to Tony Kushner, is due to historians' emphasis on "continuity of presence rather than temporariness, flux and statelessness."[20] Yet historians have interrogated topics of migration and instability in relation to issues such as slavery, colonialism, labor, and development. Particularly in the African Great Lakes region, where migration myths legitimize political claims, historians have explored migration and change in cultural, economic, and political contexts.[21] Scholars have also examined the histories of border regions in Africa, exploring their historical roots as well as more contemporary economic patterns.[22] It is therefore peculiar that the role of refugees in African history has been neglected until recently, as historians are uniquely situated to counter dominant representations of displaced people that often strip individuals of history and agency.[23]

Just as historians have excluded refugees from their purview, scholars of forced migration studies have neglected history.[24] History was not included among the "novel multi-disciplinary approaches" advocated by early proponents of refugee studies.[25] This inattention to the longer histories of refugee populations is due, in part, to forced migration studies' early emphasis on the immediate humanitarian concerns of refugee populations, as well as the influence of aid policies and agendas.[26] However, as scholars in this field are beginning to note, history is integral to understanding current refugee crises.

Writing on the conceptual deficits in forced migration studies, Philip Marfleet posits that "forced migrations have a long half-life," affecting later forced migrations as well as myths of belonging and citizenship.[27] For Marfleet, understanding recent refugee crises necessitates analyzing historical context and precedent. Such studies are of particular importance in northwestern Tanzania, where scholars examined the 1994 Rwandan refugee crisis almost entirely without reference to previous refugee crises.[28] Scholarly inattention to the longer history of refugees and aid in the region obscures not only past interactions and regional connections between Ngarans and refugees, but also the evolving and formative relationships among aid agencies and states.

Recent historical scholarship on refugees illustrates the seminal role that such groups played in the formation of nation-states.[29] This literature reveals that the creation of the nation-state in early modern Europe depended on new techniques of territorially "fixing people and places."[30] The displacement of "others" who did not fall within accepted (re)definitions of national citizenries was critical to nation building, as "people *rejected* by the new nations were in fact integral to them."[31] Such rejections often entailed violent processes of mass displacement, and these movements were most visible in border areas—where populations at the geographic edge of one vision of nationalism encountered those expelled from another. And, as Mbembe and Randall note, this "polarization with regard to culture and identity," which is so intrinsic to nationalism, becomes most visible within the space of the refugee camp.[32] Historical inquiries into refugees are therefore integral to understanding ongoing processes of nation-state territorialization.[33]

Rwandan refugees first entered Ngara district in 1959, just as the international community began to pay attention to refugees in sub-Saharan Africa. Examining the improvisation of policy and implementation occurring during and since the 1960s—the "watershed period," when attempts to control the movement of people became "inescapably global"—is crucial to understanding how and why the current international refugee regime operates as it does and how it affects sites of aid implementation.[34] It was precisely during, and as a consequence of, decolonization of the "third world" that transnational bureaucracies such as the United Nations (UN), United Nations High Commissioner for Refugees (UNHCR), and Lutheran World Federation (LWF) widened their mandates and programs to intercede in the regulation of African borders. Created in part to control and stabilize nation-state boundaries, UN agencies became major donors and administrators of refugee aid. In so doing, they became entangled with identity politics on the ground.

There has been a relative dearth of historical scholarship on Ngara district, yet political analyses have flourished.[35] The peripheral location of the district, in terms of both the Tanzanian state and the wider region, has likely contributed to this lack of historical attention.[36] However, shifting our gaze to the edge of historiography, to the peripheral places outside the central

Introduction · 7

kingdoms and places that are more easily accessible and prone to attract attention, reveals much about the social, political, and economic processes that created the center. And, as David Newbury notes, peripheral status is always bestowed by outsiders and is therefore subject to change.[37]

The Rwandan genocide is not the focus of this book, yet it looms over much of the relevant history. The genocide is glimpsed in the blithe divisions that came to demarcate who became Tanzanian and who became Rwandan—and in some cases, who would live and who would die sixty years after British and Belgian representatives first marked the border's course. More concretely, the genocide and its aftermath came to Ngara in the form of the refugees who entered the district in 1994, including those who had perpetrated, witnessed, and suffered the genocide in Rwanda. Much has been written about the arrogance and shortcomings of the international community during the Rwandan refugee emergency in the Great Lakes region.[38] However, no work takes into account the long history of migration and refugee hosting in Ngara. Through such an analysis, the evolution of international refugee policy, itself rooted in the region's colonial migrant containment camps, becomes clear.[39] In tracing this lineage, I reveal the competing sovereignties that dominated refugee camps in Ngara, both during decolonization and during the 1990s. Transnational, national, regional, local, and refugee actors all competed to control the political futures of refugees in Ngara. These legal, ethical, and political confrontations resulted in distrust and animosity. Such conflicts also exposed the basic contradictions of a refugee system that claims jurisdiction over refugees' lives while simultaneously proclaiming itself to be outside of politics.[40]

Sovereignty is, more than anything, an ideal that never matches the power realities in national and international spaces. As an idea, it has many components: that states control their borders, which are clearly defined; that the sovereign holds a monopoly on violence within its borders; that the nation-state is recognized as a legitimate and equal member of an international community; and, perhaps most important, that other nation-states agree not to interfere in the internal operations of sovereign states. At all these levels, the concept of sovereignty is threatened by lived realities (most famously, by the fact that no state exerts complete control over its borders or the use of violence therein).[41] At the international level, the makeup of the UN Security Council, with its five permanent members, privileges the power of some nation-states over others. In other words, if the end of empires and the division of the world into separate, connecting nation-states were the beginning of something new (as Kelly and Kaplan assert), that

8 · Introduction

new world order would be filled with unequal sovereignties. Nation-states with more economic and military power have frequently impinged on the internal affairs of those with less power. Humanitarian and development organizations similarly intercede in the legal and economic spaces of "less-developed" nations. So perhaps it is best to understand sovereignty as a "set of claims"—directed both internally over a demarcated space and citizenry and outwardly within the international arena.[42]

Similarly, citizenship, like any identity, is linked more to emotion than to a fixed concept of rights and duties. The creation of a citizenry out of a colony centers on the building of a shared identity—based on loyalty to an "imagined community."[43] Ideally, citizens have certain rights derived from their birth within a national family, one that is married to the political bureaucracy of a state (including the right to peace, the right to a certain standard of living, and the right to political participation—to name a few). These rights are balanced by the citizens' duties to the nation-state: to pay taxes, to obey laws, to be loyal. And yet, like sovereignty, these are not absolutes but ideals that citizens negotiate in their lived, everyday experiences, just as negotiations over who belongs in a nation evolve over time.

Ngaran history reveals that the image of the nation-state, its benevolence and its power, can clash with lived realities but still hold political-ideological sway. Indeed, the failure of the territorial sovereignty of the Tanzanian nation-state—its inability to control its long borders—created practical, physical, and ideological effects that helped shore up the idea of the postcolonial nation among those living along its margins. The failure to contain migrants, in the form of refugees, and their movements led to the imposition of an international humanitarian and legal community that was frequently at odds and in contest with the power of the new state, locally and nationally. However, as refugees were contained and made into a privileged "other" within internationally funded and run refugee camps, the notion of regional closeness gave way to a perception of national strangers—a notion that slowly percolated through Ngaran communities. As this process unfolded, another failure of the new state became clear—its inability to protect the livelihood of its citizenry. As a result, Ngarans continued and increased their illicit trading across international borders, thereby sustaining themselves and their communities when the state could not. These tangible rifts at the margins actually helped the center to hold.

Overall, this was a process of becoming a perceived nation and a citizenry—one in which the rights of the citizen often conflicted with the realities of life in Ngara. The process was aided by the failures of new nation-

Introduction · 9

states in the region: failure of the Rwandan state to protect and control its borders and new citizens (the rejection of some clarified an ethnically defined citizenship for the rest); failure of the Tanzanian state to control its borders and protect citizens' livelihoods; and failure of the humanitarian community, which attempted to control migrants and national laws. Ironically, the very unevenness of state power in Tanzania helped instill some ideas about the duties of the citizen—who turned away from the violence linked to regional affiliations and toward a perceived benevolent and peaceful central government. The duty to work hard and develop the nation was present, if not the rights that would have made this possible (e.g., the right to clean water, education, democratic representation). These duties of the citizen did not extend to obeying all the laws of the new state—whose failures necessitated their transgression. But it did extend to the idea of being Tanzanian, an idea embodied in the conflicting failures of the local, national, and global regimes.

The Colonial Origins of Refugee Aid: The Refugee and Human Rights

In attending to the history of Ngara and identity formation, this work analyzes not only the critical role of refugees in Ngaran political imaginations but also that of the agents and agencies that worked to control migration and actualize colonial borders under the auspices of the postcolonial nation-state. Ngaran history therefore contains traces of the long evolutionary process that led to a humanitarian system devoted to aiding, segregating, and protecting refugees. Such a history reveals the colonial origins of refugee protection, as well as the fraught link between human rights and the sovereign world of nation-states, as represented by the United Nations. As a former UNHCR official said of the challenges involved in protecting Syrian refugees, "Humanitarian work is not supposed to be political, but the reality is political."[44] This book delineates the ways in which aid to Rwandan refugees has shaped this humanitarian politics.

To understand the evolution of this politics, it is necessary to examine the long history of regional circulation and shared histories across what became an international border. Separated from the Belgian mandate of Ruanda-Urundi following World War I, as described in chapter 1, Ngara district became part of the Tanganyika Territory, a mandate colony governed by the British under the oversight of the newly constituted League of Nations. Paradoxically, under colonial rule, regional integration only increased as people ignored the newly delineated international borders to migrate into Ngara. Men from both colonies also traveled north to work in Buganda, thereby

10 · Introduction

ignoring colonial labor opportunities to the east in Tanganyika. As shown in chapter 2, the British responded by attempting unsuccessfully to direct and "canalize" migration in the Tanganyika Territory, creating the first migrant control camps in the region. In its efforts to manage and control migration in Ngara district, the colonial government utilized a discourse of protection, a rhetoric that elided the economic motivations of such measures.[45] This humanitarian language itself had a long history, rooted in the "civilizing mission" that empires had long used as an excuse to extend their control over people deemed less civilized. Thus, the "advent of humanitarianism" and the "tension between . . . compassion and repression" are not late twentieth-century adaptations, as Didier Fassin contends, but are deeply rooted in the logic of colonialism.[46]

When the League of Nations' system of global regulation collapsed during World War II, it was followed by a rhetoric of paternalistic development as the territory became a British "trustee" under the newly formed United Nations. What both the mandate system and the trust system had in common was the ranking of colonial possessions according to European logics of civilization. With decolonization, the United Nations, and its great-power leadership on the Security Council, became the arbiter of a new object of protection: the nation-state system.[47] Unregulated circulation within this system came under the auspices of a new organization, the United Nations High Commissioner for Refugees (UNHCR), formed in 1950. The global governance initiatives of migrant control started during imperialism therefore continued and evolved during the postcolonial era in the form of the United Nations and its refugee agency.

The UNHCR emerged to accommodate and protect refugees in Europe after World War II; however, the violence of decolonization quickly turned the organization's attention to sub-Saharan Africa. From the beginning of the UN's refugee protection initiatives, there existed a distinction between refugee protection in the "developed" states of the North and that in the global South. In the North, refugees generally underwent asylum hearings as individuals. In the South, refugees were admitted as groups, placing incredible economic burdens on host states that were themselves engaged in nation-building projects.[48]

In many ways, the UNHCR and the nation of Tanzania grew up together. The agency's interventions in northern Africa began only a few years prior to the first influx of refugees in Ngara. For the next sixty years, the UNHCR would work intensively in sub-Saharan African nations. It was in Tanzania that the UNHCR experimented with a new solution to the problem of refugees.

As a senior UNHCR official noted in 1963, "I think that the Rwanda refugee situation will offer us a welcome opportunity to find out in practice what the office can usefully do" to aid refugees.[49]

In some ways, the UNHCR itself functions as a state, with its large bureaucracy, standard operating procedures, and legislative section devoted to implementing the 1951 Refugee Convention and the 1967 Protocol.[50] However, instead of appealing to and relying on a citizenry or tax base for its functioning, the UNHCR is accountable only to its external donors, which do not directly experience the effects of the agency's operations. Additionally, although its legal base confers a mandate to protect refugees, the human rights questions implicit to the idea of humanitarian aid were explicitly separated from the UNHCR's mandate and left within the realm of citizens' claims on nation-states.[51] Like the UN itself, the UNHCR was created not to secure a just or equal world but rather to maintain the sovereignty of a network of independent states.[52]

It is perhaps more accurate to understand the power wielded by the UNHCR, in its dealings with both host states and refugees, as a police function. The "problem" of refugees threatens the world of sovereign nation-states.[53] The three durable solutions created by the agency to address the refugee problem testify to this function. All three solutions (repatriation, integration in a first asylum country, and resettlement in a second asylum nation) are predicated on the idea of "settling" the refugee, of extracting the individual's and group's anomaly within the world of nation-states by recasting the refugee as a returnee and settler, thereby upholding the trinity of nation, territory, and citizen.[54] In this way, the organization maintains the international status quo ante, on the surface at least.[55]

In the post–World War II era of nation-state formation and refugee regulation, other agencies with separate, yet ostensibly parallel, interests began providing refugee relief as well. In Tanzania, the major agency involved in refugee aid from the 1960s through the early 1990s was the Tanganyikan Christian Refugee Service (TCRS). The history of this agency, its successes and failures, and its dynamic and, by 1996, tumultuous relationship with the UNHCR reveals how the policies and implementation of transnational refugee aid have changed over the past half century. The TCRS's archival and oral testimonies demonstrate that the international refugee community has altered its approach to balancing the protection of human rights and the achievement of institutional interests over time, with the latter becoming increasingly important in the realm of transnational refugee aid.

12 · Introduction

In the context of refugee camps, claims of sovereignty are frequently in conflict, as different groups seek to assert their own legitimacy and control over refugees' lives and the camps where they live. The legal apparatus created to govern refugees' lives exists simultaneously at the nation-state and transnational levels, which can lead to ambiguity, resentment, and confusion. On the ground, a host of representatives actively attempts to govern refugees' lives: local, state, and transnational actors all impose bureaucratic categorizations, expectations, and promises.[56] What is singularly missing from this analysis is the fact that refugees themselves are political actors and subjects in their own right. As refugees contemplated their political futures in Ngara, they frequently came into conflict with the local, national, and transnational officials who sought to order their lives. Humanitarian governance is thus not a straightforward endeavor but one shot through with competition and resistance, processes that contour both host and refugee notions of citizenship and belonging.[57]

In the absence of any clear demarcation of protection responsibilities within the international community (for both states and aid agencies), relief agencies have inconsistently called for the protection of populations based on their own evolving "willingness to be accountable."[58] More cynically, humanitarian agencies have invoked human rights discourse to legitimize interventions and to discredit those who obstruct and criticize their actions.[59] This book reveals the distinct difference between *humanitarianism* and *humanitarian aid* by historicizing the strategic interests underlying the business of aid interventions. From the League of Nations to the post–Cold War UN regime, I reveal the continuity with which humanitarian discourse has obscured economic and political motives.[60] As Scalettaris notes, the term *refugee* does not define "a relevant sociological group"; it reveals more about "the system that produced the label" than the people it refers to.[61] This system built on earlier colonial incarnations of migrant control to segregate those deemed "in need" of relief from the "natural" inhabitants of Ngara, thereby furthering the construct of the nation-state within Ngaran notions of belonging.

Deconstructing Refugee Aid

Over the past twenty years, scholars have examined the aid apparatus predominantly from the viewpoint of institutional discourse and policy analysis, revealing the depoliticizing discourse of aid institutions and the international politics that inform refugee policies.[62] We know much less about how humanitarian institutions function on the ground. Scholarship on international assistance has cited the need to "study up" aid institutions, as policies and practices cannot be divorced from the people who form and implement them.[63] However, to date, few works address the experiences of those who give, negotiate, and experience aid.[64]

It is through representation, and representatives, that transnational policies become entwined with circumstances at the site of policy implementation (the local). The linguistic metaphors scholars use to describe and analyze refugee organizations tend to revolve around such tropes as *agency, organization, state,* and *bureaucracy.* What often gets lost is the almost too obvious fact that organizations are made up of people, of individuals.

By "deterritorializing" the nation-state—thinking of the past and the present beyond taken-for-granted categorizations—scholars utilize notions such as contingency, affect, and heterogeneity.[65] This scholarship can also be applied to our understanding of humanitarian organizations and actions. It is in the testimony of organizational representatives that historians begin to understand the process of aid policy implementation.[66] Humanitarian aid was, and continues to be, a confusing and even contradictory business involving states, host populations, donors, recipients, and aid representatives. Policies and budgets created in Geneva and New York are filtered through national, regional, and local government and aid agency officials. In the process, agency representatives are almost constantly confronted with unexpected events and challenges, forcing them to improvise in the field. Such actions have consequences for future aid policies as well as for the inhabitants of the field itself.

How does the aid project look different if we privilege the voices of individuals in the voluntary, state, and refugee bureaucracies?[67] Instead of one UNHCR, refugee group, or state, we are confronted with myriad individuals involved in policy negotiation and implementation at several levels, each with their own perceptions, biases, and agendas.[68] In doing so at a particular time and place, such as northwestern Tanzania during and after decolonization, actions become de-situated from the corporatized space of the UNHCR, the state, and refugees.[69] The resulting history is a messy entanglement of individuals and their ideas, personalities, and influences on outcomes and policies.[70] Such analysis reveals the pivotal role of refugees and host communities in not only the processes of nation-state formation but also the evolution of humanitarian policies.

14 · Introduction

Methods

I was interviewing a man in Keza village in Busubi when he brought out a thick iron chain. This man was at least sixty years old, had lived his entire life in Ngara, and had walked to our interview without shoes, but he *had* brought the chain. Speaking Kisubi, he explained that slave traders had used this chain to enslave his grandfather and take him to the United States. It is extremely unlikely that a man from this part of Africa would have ended up as a slave in America. What was I to do with this information? Did this lapse in accuracy, which came at the end of our interview, discredit the hour preceding it?

Working with oral histories requires care. Perhaps this man's story about his grandfather had more to do with current perceptions of American hegemony or the visibility of an African American US president with family links to eastern Africa. What the chain signifies for me is the importance of taking subjectivity into account, both my own and that of those I interview. This is particularly important when considering how more recent events, such as the 1994 Rwandan refugee crisis, affect people's memories of earlier instances of migration and identity.

This work is based on more than one hundred interviews conducted in Ngara district, in addition to archival research in international and national archives.[72] In Ngara, I conducted interviews in 2012 with the assistance of Bernard Gwaho, my research assistant, who helped me ask questions in Kiswahili, Kisubi, and Kihangaza, the three local languages.[71] Bernard was more than an assistant; he became integral to my research process. I wanted to know how Ngarans had understood different forms of migration since the late colonial era, so Bernard helped me find people to interview throughout the border villages in the two subsections of Ngara: Busubi and Bugufi. Through his contacts, I was also able to interview village and town leaders throughout the district. We spoke with men who had been village officials during the first Rwandan refugee influx in the 1960s, as well as those who led villages during the massive Rwandan refugee emergency in the mid-1990s. We interviewed former lorry drivers who had transported migrant laborers to Buganda during the 1950s and economic migrants who had returned to Ngara, to an imagined "home," during decolonization. I met men and women who had never left their district and families that had traveled all over Tanzania and occasionally the world. I never forgot that I was an outsider.

In Ngara I am *mzungu* (white), in a place where white connotes not only a stranger but also suspicion and opportunity. In the villages where I conducted many of my interviews, my skin color provoked excitement, curiosity, and occasionally outright fear. As an American expatriate armed with a car, a *mzungu* partner, and a research assistant, how would I understand what the people I talked to were trying to explain? Was it hubris to believe that I could?

Most of these interviews were conducted either in people's homes or in village centers. To get there, Bernard, my partner Brian, and I traveled on roads that were little more than cattle paths, often walking the final kilometers through the bush to reach a homestead. The district continues to suffer from a lack of infrastructure, particularly in the Busubi area to the south. The banana groves that cover the landscape always seemed to extend more in the direction of Rwanda and Burundi, across the invisible borders of the district, than east across the mountains to the rest of Tanzania. On family *shamba* (farms), respondents often pointed out the border's location just over the hill or across a field. On the rough roads, we frequently came across day laborers who crossed the borders to work in Ngara.

Bernard assisted in identifying many of the people I interviewed, each individual then locating friends and acquaintances who lived in the area and might be interested in speaking with me. This "snowball" research technique was essential, particularly in identifying elders who remembered the late colonial period and decolonization. I also relied on the advice of Father Lazarus, a priest in Rulenge, who has lived and worked in Busubi since the 1950s. Another invaluable resource was *Bwana* Rwagaba, who worked with international agencies aiding Rwandan refugees during both the 1960s and the 1990s.

It was difficult for me to conduct interviews in Busubi, where the state and the UNHCR had settled Rwandan refugees during the 1960s and again in the 1990s. Brian and I resided in Ngara town in Bugufi, in a shipping container left over from the 1994 refugee emergency on the TCRS compound. To get to Rulenge, we had to travel over an alarmingly steep and curving "road" to reach villages such as Muyenzi, Keza, Kanyinya, and Mbuba— the places that became refugee settlements and later *ujamaa* villages. Even though I had fastidiously arranged my research documents and residency permits, my first days in Busubi were spent with the subward government administrator arranging my interviews and listening in on them. Luckily, the administrator seemed to grow bored with our work and was reluctant to travel the long distances along poor roads to many of the interview sites.

To show my appreciation, and to acknowledge that many of my informants had forgone work (agricultural or other) to meet with me, I always

16 · Introduction

paid them. The remuneration was usually 5,000 Tsh, the equivalent of about US$3 at the time and a substantial sum to many Ngarans.[73] I waited until the end of the conversation to offer money, after asking whether the interviewee had any questions for me. Occasionally, respondents would ask me to help them buy sugar or coffee. More common were questions about how I could help the people of Ngara who suffered from a lack of *maendeleo*, or development. When I asked what Ngara district needed to "develop," answers usually included access to clean water and to electricity and, perhaps most frequently, the ability to send their children to school. I responded honestly, admitting that I was not there to help, nor did I have the means to do so. I felt it was important to make no promises, revealing my own incapacity and deficits—a frustration that endures.

This work is also based on innumerable conversations I had in Ngara over soda or *pombe* (beer), bought locally or illegally or made in homes. Some of these conversations were later recorded as interviews. I was lucky to make friends in the district, although my privileged position was never far from my mind and undoubtedly affected the stories I was told. At times, extended families sat nearby during my interviews—excited to see *wazungu* (plural of *mzungo*) and equally excited to hear the memories of their elders. I was sometimes met with hostility, particularly by some female elders who no doubt wondered what I was doing on their *shamba* and rejected my privilege by choosing to reveal little of their lives. It was difficult to find older women to interview in the district's more remote areas, particularly in Busubi, where local administrators and others questioned what utility their memories could have. I was often treated as an informal man due to my white skin and monetary advantages—it always raised eyebrows when I asked to interview women about their experiences, as well as when I attempted to help the women of the households we visited cook or serve meals. Younger women, those who had lived through and worked with aid agencies during the Rwandan refugee emergency, however, were more eager to speak with me, likely due to generational differences in how women are perceived and the increasing number of women entering the formal workforce as teachers and aid workers.

In addition to interviews, I conducted research in seven archives. In Geneva, I examined the archives of the primary refugee agencies active in Ngara over the last sixty years. These holdings provided invaluable materials, including letters and reports from field officers in Ngara to their various headquarters in Geneva. Such holdings revealed the often experimental nature of refugee policies, as policymakers and practitioners confronted unforeseen problems

Introduction · 17

with often emotional and chaotic responses. These documents also revealed the limitations of aid agencies that were unable to consider host communities' needs due to their strict mandates.

Research in the Dar es Salaam and Mwanza branches of the Tanzanian National Archives and the British National Archives added important colonial, state, and African voices to the examination of the transnational production of borders and refugee aid. These collections revealed the chaotic and arbitrary creation of the international border between Ngara and Rwanda (then Ruanda-Burundi). I also discovered letters from colonial officials that expressed concerns over uncontrolled labor migration in this area, concerns that led to the first migrant containment schemes in Ngara.

By juxtaposing oral histories with archival material, I reveal the discrepancies between official visions in London and Geneva and realities on the ground. This attention to local and transnational gazes, and the distance between them, produces new insights into key questions of agency and responsibility in humanitarian action. It also provides a holistic account of how historical identities shifted as transnational agents divided the Ngaran population into locals and refugees over the course of the twentieth century.

The Road to Nation Building

The following chapters untangle how Ngarans came to conceptualize themselves as Tanzanians, despite the cross-border circulation of people in this region and the disappointments of independence. Crucial to this process of ideological nation building was the parallel process by which Rwandan migrants became refugees in Ngara. This is the story of how the people of Ngara district came to see themselves as part of a nation-state. It is a history of migrants who became citizens and migrants who became refugees. It is also a history of the colonial, national, and transnational agents who endeavored to aid, protect, and rule refugees over time.

The politics of difference that refugees came to represent in Ngara can be understood only in light of the regional ties Ngarans shared with Rwandans during the precolonial and colonial periods. Part I (chapters 1, 2, and 3) traces the haphazard construction of international borders and explores migration and development during the precolonial, colonial, and early postcolonial eras in Ngara district. These chapters argue that regional circulation and affiliations increased during this time, as Ngarans and their neighbors in Ruanda-Urundi utilized time-tested strategies of migration to navigate the changes brought by colonial and postcolonial rule. This deep history of

18 · Introduction

migration and cross-border cultural and economic connections is essential to understanding the effects of refugee movements and humanitarian aid examined in subsequent chapters.

Part II (chapters 4, 5, and 6) analyzes the processes through which Ngarans began to see themselves as Tanzanians, despite their historical connections to the Great Lakes region and the disappointments of independence. I argue that by segregating Rwandan refugees and giving them preferential aid in refugee camps—aid that refugees frequently subverted—Ngarans began to view Rwandans as inimical to Tanzanian nationalism. Further, this section reveals the competing sovereignties at work during decolonization as various groups attempted to control and rule Rwandan refugee camps.

Part III (chapters 7, 8, and 9) argues that citizenship in Ngara became predicated not only on one's place of birth, but also on one's relationship to international organizations. As Ngarans continued to migrate across the region and progressively adopted the mantle of "Tanzanians," local leaders denied refugees who had lived in internationally run refugee camps access to citizenship. The section ends by exploring the contradictory effects of the Rwandan genocide and refugee emergency in Ngara district, which produced both extreme hardship and novel opportunities for Ngarans, while simultaneously cementing local attachments to the Tanzanian nation-state.

Throughout this work, I show that, at the Ngaran edge of the African Great Lakes region, the evolution of transnational techniques of border control translated into containment policies for tens of thousands of people who were transformed from migrants to refugees by independence. At the edges of the colony, authorities struggled to be relevant to a population on the move. During decolonization, new transnational entities emerged to alter the balance of power and the meaning of identities in the region. Throughout the period I examine, the borders created by the League of Nations and the region's colonizers remained. In the decades that followed decolonization, people, goods, and ideas continued to flow, illegally and unabated, across the borders. And yet the border became a potent signifier of identity for Ngarans who became Tanzanians during a time when Rwandans became refugees.

Introduction · 19

PART I
THE MAKING OF MIGRANTS

1. TRACING A BOUNDARY

CULTURAL CONNECTIONS AND

MANDATE SEPARATION

It must have been an interesting sight: two men—one Belgian, one British—pointing to imaginary lines down a river to delineate which land, and therefore which people and resources, belonged to which colony.[1] Such borders came to define the limits of the colonial state and, later, the nationality of the peoples who lived therein. These borders had their start in colonial and, increasingly, transnational visions, which were both unable and unwilling to grasp the complexities of life in this part of the African Great Lakes region.

The settlement of the borders between the Belgian mandate of Ruanda-Urundi and the British mandate of Tanganyika took more than twenty years and involved myriad colonial and international officials, as well as the local porters who accompanied the *wazungu* responsible for demarcating the boundaries of each territory. The Europeans would have been accompanied by a handful of African laborers, men who likely considered themselves Banyambo and had lived in an area previously called German East Africa.[2] The river that was the center of *wazungu* attention that day, sometime during the year 1931, was the Kagera River—the waterway that remains the dividing line among the states we today know as Rwanda, Burundi, and Tanzania.[3]

The fact that colonizers delineated their colonies by drawing arbitrary borders that divided peoples, cultures, and geographies—lines that haunt the governments and peoples of postcolonial states—is not surprising or new. Much scholarship has been devoted to understanding the careless lines drawn across maps, often by men in distant centers of power who would never set foot in the areas they delineated.[4] Particularly in Africa, scholars have studied how far-off businessmen-cum-imperialists created borders that separated populations, resources, and trade routes.[5] The border created between Ngara district in Tanzania and areas in Rwanda and Burundi was just such a product.[6] Similar histories, languages, climates, economic relationships, productive activities, cultural traditions, and trading routes linked, and continue to link, this part of northwestern Tanzania with areas in present-day Rwanda, Burundi, and Uganda.[7]

How are borders made, and when do they become active markers of place and boundaries of difference? When and how do they become solidified in the imaginaries of populations who have never before experienced such divisions? During the period examined in this chapter, colonial officers created two types of boundaries in the area known as Ngara district. The first was the international boundary that separated the two mandate colonies of Ruanda-Urundi and Tanganyika Territory. The Paris Peace Conference following World War I divided the area—formerly part of German East Africa—into the Belgian mandate of Ruanda-Urundi and the much larger British mandate of Tanganyika. The Belgians and the British were to govern their mandates under the auspices of the League of Nations, with international as well as colonial oversight of the new borders and their inhabitants. The second boundary was seemingly more mundane: it separated Ngara—that is, the populations that lived in the Busubi and Bugufi chiefdoms—from Biharamulo district. In 1947 Ngara was officially separated from Biharamulo, becoming a colonial administrative district in its own right.[8] Once Ngara became an official administrative district of the Tanganyika Territory, it became subject to more direct colonial administration. Ngarans, however, remained relatively unaffected by the bordering processes occurring around them.

But all this becomes important later in the story. To understand the meaning of that first ambiguous border and how it came to be a marker of identity as well as international power, we must first understand the lives of Ngarans prior to the mandate system of the League of Nations and why it came into being at all.

24 · CHAPTER 1

In 1920 the League of Nations created a system of mandate states out of the former German and Ottoman Empires, the losers of World War I. The winners of the war divided up the former empires among themselves, ostensibly creating a type of guardianship—a "sacred trust"—by which the advanced nations would tutor these "backward" areas in the ways of modernity and, eventually, self-governance. In Africa, the former German colonies were divided among the French, British, and Belgians.[9]

The mandate system represents a formative moment in the evolution of international law, setting an ill-defined finish line by which African territories would learn enough of Western civilization to enter the world as sovereign, independent states. The mandates also thrust many of these territories into turmoil as they instilled new regimes and often required new borders, as many of the former German colonies were divided between more than one mandate authority.[10] Specifically, the division of German East Africa between British and Belgian authorities required, for the first time, a legal division between the areas that became the Tanganyika Territory and Ruanda-Urundi.[11]

As international law scholar Antony Anghie posits, the mandate system created a "new set of technologies" established, on the surface at least, to "protect" the colonized and, through a "system of international tutelage," to assist them to join the world of sovereign nation-states.[12] However, the League of Nations and its successor organization (the United Nations) retained "the practices of cultural subordination and economic exploitation" inherent to colonialism, a way of ranking and ruling the non-Western world that still plays a role in international affairs.[13] As the international institution designed to promote the welfare of "native" peoples during the late colonial period, the League of Nations was the template for later international organizations dedicated to developing and protecting the non-Western world. An enduring tension exists between the rhetoric of such institutions and the ethnocentric cultural and economic projects of their constituent members. These conflicting agendas at the heart of global governance efforts come to light in the areas that became Ruanda-Urundi and Ngara during the colonial period, as transnational policies meant to "protect" the people of the region obscured the motivations and effects of colonial and league policies.

Image, law, and *imaginary* are key words to understanding the opening scene of this chapter. It is the image of the middle (or *thalweg*) of the river that colonial officials concerned themselves with—an image that had traveled all the way to the political centers of the relevant imperial powers and to the international arbitrating entity of the time: the League of Nations. It was

Tracing a Boundary · 25

therefore in Brussels, London, and Geneva that the image of the *thalweg* of the Kagera River became inscribed in law as an international border. And it was among the people and spaces around the Kagera River that this inscription proved itself over the decades to be imaginary—a legal fiction, a physical boundary in name only.

Origin Stories

I was sitting in an office in Rusumo, just across the border from Rwanda in Ngara district and within sight of the Kagera River, when I first interviewed Daniel Izabaro.[14] Once a small town on the border, Rusumo had recently grown along with the new East African Community (EAC), an economic cooperative agreement that resulted in an exponential rise in transit along this crucial artery between Rwanda and Tanzania. My research assistant Bernard and I had arrived in Rusumo to interview residents about the history of Bugufi, the former chiefdom in this part of Ngara. Daniel claimed to be related to Chief Balamba II, the last Bugufi chief. He was happy to answer my questions about the origins of the chiefdom and told me how members of the Rwandan royal family, in search of land and pasture, had crossed the Kagera River and founded Bugufi long ago. Just one week later, during a different interview, a lifelong resident of Bugufi informed me that the first chiefs of Bugufi had come from Burundi.[15] Other interviewees claimed that the founders of Bugufi had no relation to the kingdoms of Rwanda and Burundi. We had encountered the same diverse responses during our interviews on the origins of the chiefdom of Busubi in the district's south. Similarly, when I asked people whether they were familiar with the Bacwezi—the semimythical polity that gave rise to the kingdoms of Rwanda and Burundi—most claimed ignorance.[16] But then again, the Bacwezi have come to be associated with witchcraft, and those who acknowledged knowing the word stressed that they were Christians and that the Bacwezi were just "local spirits." The fact that the Bacwezi are known at all indicates that these chiefdoms in Ngara once had origin myths similar to those of their larger neighbors, which is the best I can deduce. Those with direct knowledge of the chiefdoms' founding are long gone, and the elders I spoke to did their best to pass on their knowledge through the veil of memory.

When do we start the history of Ngara district? The beginning of any history is always a critical choice, one with political ramifications. Archaeologists, linguists, ethnographers, and historians have all tried to piece together the history of the African Great Lakes region, using everything from oral traditions to language itself. The results have been hazy, with scholars arguing fiercely about the origins of everything from cattle keeping to ethnicity—which are themselves linked. The question of ethnicity is particularly controversial: were ethnic groupings constructed prior to colonization, or were they created and imposed by various colonizers?[17] The answers become important and dangerous in an area that saw fierce ethnic violence during the twentieth century.

In Ngara, I interviewed more than one hundred residents in an effort to access the district's past. These oral histories are full of rich, often emotional, sometimes funny, sometimes tragic memories. They are recollections as told to me by farmers, pharmacists, teachers, aid workers, and others, some of them in their eighties or older. They are incredibly important and, like any archive, enormously flawed. These oral histories frequently contradict one another, as evidenced by the aforementioned discrepancies in the origins of the Bugufi chiefdom. What they unequivocally reveal, however, is a long, complex history of political, cultural, and economic exchanges among the people who came to live in Ngara and in Rwanda and Burundi.

The archival information, in contrast, was written almost entirely by those in the employ of the colonial state—people who had their own motivations and biases that deeply affected their writings and correspondence. These observations were themselves shaped by the rules governing correspondence among colonial administrators. At best, they give us a tiny glimpse into how people lived, worked, and thought in Ngara.

This chapter engages both types of histories to reveal the fissures as well as the connections between the peoples who would become Tanzanians in Ngara and Rwandans and Burundians across the international boundary created in the 1920s and 1930s. The Great Lakes region is a place of environmental and political diversity, one where understanding the context of local regions is crucial to conceptualizing how people imagined their places within the precolonial and colonial milieus. Even the powerful kingdoms of the area, such as the Rwandan Nyiginya dynasty, had their geographic reach challenged by strong regional, often autonomous polities that contested central state control. Nevertheless, European colonizers drew international boundaries that disregarded many of these semiautonomous regions in their attempts to delineate the two mandate states.

Colonial writers and officers understood the politics, economy, and culture of the Great Lakes polities through the lens of the Hamitic hypothesis, a dangerous and distorting theory that flows through the sinews of historical production in this region.[18] Based on interpretations of the Bible, the Hamitic hypothesis evolved to correspond to the imperialists' need to justify their actions, such as the slave trade and colonial rule. For the sake of simplicity, during colonization, the theory stated that all evidence of civilization—in particular, hierarchical societies—that Europeans found in Africa was the work of a superior race of people called Hamites, who were conveniently, if distantly, related to the Caucasian race. Immigrating from the Horn of Africa, the Hamites were thought to be intellectually and physically superior (in that they resembled Caucasians, with their greater height and slender noses), making them the natural rulers over the black Bantu populations. Hamites therefore linked advanced civilizations in Africa to the white race. However, Hamites remained inferior to Europeans due to their centuries of intermixing with black populations. The colonists therefore chose the Hamites to rule over Bantu Africans, albeit under varying models of European direction.

In this part of the Great Lakes region, Hamites came to be called *Tutsi*, a word that previously referred (generally) to rich cattle owners and those associated with local monarchies.[19] All others were called *Hutu*, a group of people the colonists deemed to be subservient and simple as well as aesthetically "blacker," given their wide noses, darker complexion, and shorter height.[20] Despite the obvious racial overtones and radical simplification of political, economic, and social history, much of colonial and subsequent historical writing on the region has been subjected to this distorted lens, making precolonial and colonial histories difficult to trust.

To make matters more complicated, many of the written sources on Ngara's history are muddled by the fact that they were written by the colonizers, often in conjunction with their ambitious local allies These written archives also include various versions of oral traditions. In societies without writing, such as those in the Great Lakes region, people developed other ways to access the past. Oral traditions, passed down from generation to generation, instructed populations in their history—including the formation of states and their rulers. In writing down these traditions, however, colonizers frequently distorted them to justify colonial claims to land and resources. We have evidence, for example, that members of the Rwandan court, who allied with German and later Belgian colonizers, embellished their oral traditions to prove that the precolonial Rwandan kingdom had control over a larger area than was actually the case. Belgian colonizers then advanced "rightful" claims to large land areas by referencing the historical narratives constructed by central Rwandan elites.[21] Though many of these claims have been contested, other colonially imposed histories, such as the Hamitic hypothesis in Rwanda and Burundi, came to be understood as fact.[22] In this sense, colonization attempted to disconnect people from their histories, a violence that continues to have stunning and tragic effects in the region.

It is perhaps more difficult to tease out the history of Ngara than that of other areas in the region due to its peripheral status in the archives and the contradictory writings and responses of those living in the district. We do know that during the precolonial period, the central-eastern Great Lakes region, which includes present-day Rwanda, Burundi, and northwestern Tanzania, underwent several waves of conquest and withdrawal. Ngara district was divided between the two former chiefdoms of Busubi and Bugufi (inhabitants of the former are known as Basubi, the latter as Bahangaza). We know that over a thirty-year period in the late nineteenth century, *Mwami* (king) Kigeri IV Rwabugiri of Rwanda embarked on a series of wars of expansion (sometimes referred to as cattle raids) into neighboring polities to the east and west.[23] Although the Rwandan state often conquered these regions, its presence and authority were neither all-encompassing nor lasting and frequently involved no more than paying tribute to the expanding Rwandan state.[24] Northeastern Burundi too shared "strong political, social and economic ties east to Bugufi."[25] However, the areas east of present-day Burundi seemed to enjoy regional autonomy from the central Rundi state, further confusing the precolonial lines of authority. Not much is known about this area during the nineteenth century, and records from the colonial period are scarce. Thus, only a mixture of oral interviews and colonial archives offers a brief glimpse of life in Ngara prior to colonization.

It is likely that during the precolonial era, Bugufi and Busubi, like many smaller polities in the region, engaged in various types of conflicts with the stronger, expanding states of Rwanda and Burundi. Whether outright wars or cattle raids, the chiefdoms probably experienced increasing political challenges from their neighbors, particularly during the late nineteenth century, when the centralized states in the region expanded. The late nineteenth century was also a time of epidemiological and ecological upheaval, as the region was ravaged by cattle diseases such as rinderpest and human diseases such as smallpox and jigger fleas.[26] These events devastated many polities in the region, laying the groundwork for the expansion of some and the collapse of others.[27]

Despite these political contests, which created shifting alliances and new areas of refuge (from Rwanda and Burundi into Ngara, and vice versa), cultural and familial links within the three areas endured.[28] Both Bugufi and Busubi were involved in vigorous trade with Rwanda and Burundi, as well as with states to the north such as the Bahaya. Similar languages and cultures facilitated trade among these shifting political groups, as the region's languages (Kihangaza, Kisubi, Kirundi, and Kinyarwanda) were mutually intelligible and widely spoken. Intermarriage among those in Rwanda, Burundi, Busubi, and Bugufi was also common—facilitated not only by trade but also by a shared culture that included similar religious rituals based on devotion to ancestors, cuisines rooted in the banana plant, and societies in which elite cattle herders developed clientele relationships with agriculturalists.

A favorite meal eaten in Ngara district is *matoke*. Made from mashed cooking bananas, which forms the base for piles of hot peppers, beans, and meat (for those who can afford it), *matoke* is a beloved mainstay that symbolizes the regional importance of bananas. Able to thrive on the steep slopes of the area's high hills and escarpments, banana trees are integral to life in the Great Lakes, now as they have been for centuries.[29] In addition to being used for food, the leaves are woven into mats, and the juice is fermented into *pombe* (beer). The wide green leaves of banana trees are evident throughout the area—as are the piles of bananas placed haphazardly on bicycles and trucks traveling to markets near and far. Along with Ankole cattle (distinctive cows with enormous sharp horns), goats, and other livestock, bananas are the basis of the region's economy.

One way to understand the relationship among precolonial polities in this region is to examine the writings of Bahangaza men during the colonial era. To explain why they required autonomy from Burundian king Mwambutsa, they wrote of the late nineteenth-century invasion of their country by Burundi. To evade capture, the Hangaza (Bugufi) chief fled to Gisaka, then a semi-independent kingdom within the Rwandan court's sphere of influence. It was in Gisaka that the Hangaza chief allegedly raised an army and took back rightful control of Bugufi.[30] Whether true or false, such writings indicate that shifting political alliances existed between what is now southeastern Rwanda, northeastern Burundi, and Ngara district.

Political alliances were likely facilitated by similar economic relationships, political organizations, and societal cultures that spread across the region. In all these territories, people measured wealth by the size of cattle herds, with the chief controlling the cattle of the polity.[31] In Ngara, as in Rwanda and Burundi, chiefs distributed cattle according to a tribute system whereby cattle were exchanged for goods and/or services, creating client relationships that crisscrossed the population, beginning with the chief.[32] In Ngara, the chief picked subdistrict chiefs (*batwale*) and landlords (*intole*) who distributed land according to this tribute system. *Batwale, intole,* and their tenants then paid *ngorole* (tribute) to the chief on a regular basis, and tenants also paid tribute to one or more *batwale* and *intole*. *Ngorole* could include services, beer, cattle, and later money. Banana beer played an important role in society, with regular payments of beer to *batwale* and the chief. The landlords and chiefs then shared their collected pots of banana beer with the nearby community, indicating that a symbolic form of redistribution between the political elite and the population was important to the functioning of society.[33] Checks on chiefly power also existed in the form of ritualists, known as *abatungwa*, who were responsible for maintaining the population's social health by communicating with ancestors and performing ceremonies.[34] And while the chiefs and their retinues were likely known as Tutsi, as they were in Rwanda and, to a lesser extent, in Burundi, they could probably move up (or down) in society by amassing (or losing) wealth in cattle.

Life in the present states of Rwanda and Burundi would have followed similar patterns, although by the late nineteenth century, there were more centralized states under the control of fewer members of the monarchy.[35] As the Rwandan state expanded, it increasingly centralized power in the hands of the monarchal elite: those called Tutsi. Despite these changes, some areas of present-day Rwanda retained political autonomy, and although social mobility decreased during this time, it was still possible for one to amass wealth and become Tutsi or for Tutsi to lose that title through economic losses.

It was at the Berlin Conference (1884–1885) that European statesmen decided that this central-eastern part of the African continent would come under German rule. At the time, this particular part of the African map was quite blank, and while rumors of hierarchical civilizations (thought to be ruled by Hamites) had reached the statesmen in Berlin via European explorers, little was known about them. Unlike the coastal areas where European and Arab trade had flourished for hundreds of years, few Europeans had dared to explore that part of Africa, so far from the safety of their forts and rivers. However, by the end of the century, the development of novel technologies such as steamships and Gatling guns, along with new defenses against tropical diseases such as malaria, enabled European explorers, missionaries, and armies to advance to the middle of Africa. Spurred by tales of newly found gold, diamonds, and other minerals in southern Africa, European statesmen and capitalists were eager to explore the possibilities of the interior. Then German chancellor Otto von Bismarck called the Berlin Conference to divide up the map and thus avoid European armed conflict over claims to African riches. The territory spanning the Swahili coast of

Tracing a Boundary · 31

contemporary Tanzania in the east to the mountains and plains of Burundi and Rwanda in the west became an entity called German East Africa.[36]

In their new colony, the German government and military were spread thin over a vast area, and its peoples and geography were largely unknown to the colonial government. There is little evidence of a German presence in Ngara district during the time it belonged to German East Africa.[37] When the British took control of the area following World War I, Ngara remained understaffed in comparison to the rest of the Tanganyika Territory.[38] Similarly, when the Belgians eventually took control of Ruanda-Urundi, in the far west of German East Africa, there were few colonial governors to be found. For those in Ruanda-Urundi and, to a lesser extent, in Ngara, much would change with the end of World War I and the creation of the transnational mandate system.

Making a "Good African": The "Sacred Trust" and the Mandate System

Following World War I, the victorious Allies formed the League of Nations.[39] Its principal function was to secure international peace after the heavy human and economic losses of the Great War. The Treaty of Versailles set the terms of the League of Nations' creation; however, it also stripped the defeated empires of their colonies. In the wake of competing claims to these territories and new questions about the role of empires, the European victors established a novel system to oversee the governance of these excised colonies. The League of Nations became the overseeing body of a new mandate system through which former German and Ottoman territories were distributed as a "sacred trust" to the victors. Article 22 of the league's covenant created this new framework for the management of redistributed colonies, stating that, for those "peoples not yet able to stand by themselves under the strenuous conditions of the modern world, there should be applied the principle that the well-being and development of such peoples form a sacred trust of civilization . . . the tutelage of such peoples should be entrusted to advanced nations who by reasons of their resources, their experience or their geographical position, can best undertake this responsibility."[40]

The idea that "advanced nations," due to their "resources," "experience," or "geographical position," were best suited to rule African peoples would be ludicrous if it were not so tragic. The nations entrusted with Germany's African colonies included Great Britain, France, and Belgium. Many of the "resources" of these nations came from their colonial holdings, whose raw materials had often been extracted through force and exploitation.[41] The resources of these nations, and so the fuel for their industrialization, had been accumulated largely at the expense of the peoples in the empires they controlled—hardly a glowing recommendation for entrusting these nations with the "tutelage" of the colonized. As for "experience," the three victors had just fought the bloodiest war yet known, leading to the destruction of a generation of European men and a legacy of violent conflict that they would inscribe among their African colonies. Last, in terms of "geographical position," they were located far from the mandate territories and in a completely different climate, meaning that they were unfamiliar with and unlikely to understand the environmental and cultural realities on the ground and therefore ignorant of the factors that might ameliorate the lives of their mandated populations.

The Allies then took it upon themselves to rank their former foes' territory according to their own rubric of civilization, placing themselves at the top, of course. The territories were then ranked according to their degree of advancement—or readiness for self-rule. The Middle Eastern territories thus became "A" territories, deemed ready to rule themselves with relatively little European aid. Most African territories received a "B" rating—meaning that they required substantial European tutelage until they would be ready to rule themselves at some distant, unspecified date. Germany's Pacific island territories and the area of southwestern Africa now known as Namibia were to be ruled as integral parts of the mandated state, as they were considered perpetually unable to govern themselves due to their underpopulation and geographic positions.[42] German East Africa was then split into two "B" mandate territories, with the majority of the area becoming the British mandate of Tanganyika and a smaller area becoming the Belgian mandate of Ruanda-Urundi. Having declared themselves to be the most civilized of all and thus in a position to tutor the rest of the world, the Allies ushered in a new era of international law—a bedrock that continues to influence international institutions.

Of course, there remained great ambiguity about what exactly the capability for self-rule entailed, as well as how a transfer in authority might take place. Moreover, a basic tension existed between the furthering of "native" economic development and that of the mandatory government's economic ambitions.[43] However, as long as the colonizers cloaked their exploitation and subjugation of the colonized in words like *development* and *well-being*, mandatory states could create policies that attempted to exert control over their new territories.[44] As the mandatory governments moved to improve their own economic positions, the "native" was "no longer to be conquered and dispossessed; rather, he was to be made more productive," with *productivity* defined by the mandatory governments themselves.[45]

The League Council, the League of Nations' executive body, then formed the Permanent Mandates Commission (PMC), which consisted of European colonial "experts" who were charged with overseeing the administration of the mandate territories. Mandate states were required to submit annual reports on their territories to the PMC, which then made recommendations. Unable to acquire information directly from populations living in the mandate territories, the PMC relied almost exclusively on the accounts of European colonial officials, furthering their cultural and political bias.[46] Although it had no formal power to sanction the mandate states or to directly observe conditions within the colonies, the league was imbued with one significant power: mobilizing and shaping European public opinion.[47] Thus, under the authority of the League of Nations and the PMC, the British Colonial Office began to speak about the well-being of the inhabitants of its mandated territory in new ways.[48] Though much of this discourse in Geneva, London, and Dar es Salaam never traveled in a meaningful way to the colonial locales, perceptions of African well-being became integral to the disposition of borders in the Great Lakes region.[49] In retrospect, many observers view the League of Nations as a failure, in that it did not prevent World War II; however, the organization did significantly affect colonial discourse during the interwar period.

To the mandatory administrations, the creation of fixed boundaries was a way to ensure legitimacy and authority over their holdings.[50] The space for international colonial claim making had shifted after the fall of Germany and the subsequent creation of the League of Nations. The establishment in Europe of a transnational body to arbitrate conflict, as well as the custodianship of mandate territories, meant that the definition and redefinitions of the border between northwestern Tanganyika and Ruanda-Urundi were, from their earliest iterations, subject to transnational oversight.

The colonial powers were aware of the links between populations on either side of the border they created. The Anglo-Belgian Boundary Commission, which met from 1922 to 1924, traversed the geographic space from "Lake Tanganyika along the Urundi-Ujiji (now Kigoma) Boundary through West Usuwi, Bugufi, and Central Ruanda to the Uganda Border."[51] The commission's notes frequently confused alleged ethnic groups, such as Hutu and Tutsi, with precolonial polities that would have encompassed both ethnicities, such as Barundi and Baha. The commission also frequently ascribed

34 · CHAPTER 1

characteristics to these ethnic groups, noting that the "Batutsi" were "very intelligent, arrogant and treacherous," as well as taller than other inhabitants.[52] In 1924 the process of creating unified Bahutu and Batutsi ethnic categories was far from complete. In lumping together an alleged ethnicity (Bahutu) with distinct geographic chiefdoms (Baha and Baswui), the commissioners revealed their ignorance of specific local cultures and politics, as well as their awareness of their general similarities. Such statements provide rich insight into the commissioners' lazy attitudes toward the people on either side of the boundary they were creating.

European deliberations over the territorial placement of the small polity of Gisaka indicate the extent to which the mandatory states were subject to new international perceptions of colonial "welfare" and, simultaneously, unconcerned with the opinions and loyalties of Africans themselves. Gisaka, where Bugufi chief Balamba I reportedly found refuge, is located in the southeast corner of present-day Rwanda, just to the north of Ngara district. In 1919 the Milner-Orts agreement, which separated British Tanganyika from Belgian Ruanda-Urundi, included Gisaka within Tanganyika due to its strategic location along the envisioned Cape-to-Cairo railway.[53]

Nevertheless, British control over Gisaka became a heated international issue in which PMC members' perceptions of "native interests" outweighed the loyalties and wishes of those who actually lived in Gisaka. The British had taken control of eastern Rwanda in March 1922; their initial occupation had been delayed as Belgian officials worked with allies in the Rwandan monarchy to increase the court's influence in this fertile area.[54] To members of the PMC and the international public, Gisaka's inclusion in Tanganyika had disregarded local African interests, which they believed were represented by the central Rwandan monarchy and thus Belgian rule. Motivated by international opinion rather than native interests, PMC members became convinced of the need to "restore" Gisaka to the Rwandan state and Belgian trusteeship. The inclusion of Gisaka within British Tanganyika thus "appalled a number of the League's strongest supporters and remained a serious embarrassment for the PMC."[55]

Ironically, Gisaka had existed as a separate kingdom until its conquest by *Mwami* Rwabugiri in the mid-nineteenth century, after which rulers in Gisaka continued to enjoy relative political autonomy. Following Rwabugiri's death, throughout the 1890s, and well into the twentieth century, the population of Gisaka revolted against central Rwandan court rule.[56] Moreover, after World War I, Gisakans flocked to British rule, perceiving the British as a bulwark against the tyranny of Belgian and Rwandan governance.

Despite this context, the PMC criticized Gisaka's inclusion in Tanganyika as "hardly justifiable" in terms of the "well being, good order and political stability" of the local African community.[57] The PMC then threatened the reproach of international public opinion to goad the British Colonial Office to cede Gisaka to the Belgians.[58] Following the actions of the PMC, on December 31, 1923, British officials began transferring the region, with its nearly half a million people, to Belgian control. The "return" of Gisaka was viewed as a public relations boon for the PMC. Great Britain also benefited, publishing the correspondence surrounding the boundary change as a command paper in order to receive credit from the international public for its territorial sacrifice in the name of safeguarding "the interests of the inhabitants."[59] Ironically, the inhabitants now found themselves under an increasingly brutal and racialized rule, which led to increasing migration east.

The transfer of Gisaka was only the first in a long series of border adjustments between the Belgian and British mandate territories. The Anglo-Belgian protocol of 1924 stated that the border between the Tanganyikan Territory and Ruanda-Urundi ran "along the midstream of the Kagera River from the Uganda boundary to the point where the Kagera River meets the Western boundary of Bugufi."[60] However, rivers are ever-changing landmarks, and the midstream of the Kagera is subject to fluctuation with the arrival of seasonal swamplands. As a result, the governor of Tanganyika, Sir Donald Cameron, proposed that the border be fixed, "not by the midstream of the river but by a series of beacons built on dry land in the proximity of the river—i.e. by a line traversing the river in several places."[61] The border would then be marked by beacons placed on river islands.[62] The proposal to shift the formal border between the two mandate territories led to years of bickering between Great Britain and Belgium over the placement of the boundary.[63]

While new humanitarian sentiments were growing in Geneva, the need to develop colonized populations according to their best interests was not always, or often, a motivation of international boundary commissions. Early discoveries of tin along the Kagera River, and the prospect of future economic windfalls, also informed border policy. Thus, a July 1928 letter from the acting controller of mines to the chief secretary of Dar es Salaam posited that "prospecting is active on both sides of the Ruanda-Irundi [sic] boundary. On the Tanganyika side tin has been found near the Kagera River in Bukoba District and the Ruvuvu River in Biharamulo District . . . the finding of tin is leading to applications for Water Rights which will affect . . . the boundary."[64] These comments reveal that economic interests and imperial

36 · CHAPTER 1

rivalries remained crucial to those who created and governed the mandates of Tanganyika and Ruanda-Urundi. In May 1931, after much correspondence and several surveys by both British and Belgians envoys, the mandatory states decided that a joint commission composed of members from each government would demarcate the boundary between Ruanda-Urundi and Tanganyika. The border was then drawn by an "imaginary line" connecting constructed beacons on dry land.[65] The surveyors placed boundary markers on inhabited islands, resulting in a change in colonial power, and eventually sovereignty, for the populations that lived on the many Kagera River islands.[66]

Article V of the Treaty Concerning a Modification of the Boundary between Tanganyika Territory and Ruanda-Urundi was finally signed in London on November 22, 1934, and became effective on May 19, 1938. The transfer of the Kagera River islands demonstrates the careless disregard of officials in London and Brussels. In so blithely dividing the populations there, Britain and Belgium ignored the cultural, economic, and social links connecting the region.[67]

The United Nations, Trusteeship, and *Mwami* Mwambutsa

Following World War II, the United Nations was created to replace the League of Nations. Under the UN, the mandate system was reformed into a system of trustee territories.[68] Outlined in chapters XII and XIII of the UN charter, the trusteeship system operated "much like its League predecessor"—continuing and augmenting the principle of a sacred trust underpinning the mandate system.[69]

Organizationally, the PMC was replaced by the UN Trusteeship Council (TC), which held its first session in March 1947. World War II had deeply affected the tenor of imperialism, in part due to the increasing condemnation of an international community that attributed the horrors of the war to unbridled racism.[70] The TC therefore had a more robust mandate than that of the PMC, as its members were required to visit the trust territories and could receive petitions directly from the populations therein.[71] As international criticism of colonialism increased after 1945, internal dissent both in the metropole and in the colonies also grew.[72]

The role of the United Nations and the TC was quickly put to the test in Ngara. In 1948, as a UN visiting mission passed through the northeastern part of Urundi, members were presented with a petition from the Rundi *Mwami*. Based on an alleged precolonial conquest of Bugufi, *Mwami*

Mwambutsa claimed that Bugufi was a traditional part of the Burundian state and appealed to the UN for its return. At first, the mission was inclined to accept Mwambutsa's point of view, as it seemed "that the disputed district clearly belonged to Ruanda-Urundi and the inhabitants appeared to be Barundi"; however, "some kind of consultation with the Bugufi population" was needed, "under the auspices" of the TC.[73]

Unlike events surrounding the transfer of Gisaka to Rwanda in the mid-1920s, the TC attempted to consult the people of Bugufi to discern their "best interests." However, the British government was well aware of the "dangers of frontier rectification under the auspices of the United Nations" and lobbied to keep the matter out of the hands of the TC.[74] For the British, the question of altering the boundary was not simply about Bugufi, an "area of brush invaded by tse-tse fly"; it had ramifications for contested borders throughout the empire, thereby threatening the disposition of imperial borders from Togoland to the Falklands.[75] To keep the question out of the hands of the increasingly anticolonial TC, and to avoid a plebiscite that would likely jump-start "'self-determination' methods" in other parts of the empire, the trustee governments agreed to send two representatives on a "confidential investigation" to Urundi and Bugufi.[76] Sir Alan Burns of Britain and Monsieur Pierre Ryckmans of Belgium then set out to determine the best interests of the populations involved, meeting with groups of people in both territories and indicating the extent to which the climate of international trusteeship had altered by the late 1940s.

The Bahangaza undoubtedly had much in common with the Barundi. Among all the languages of the Great Lakes region, Kihangaza is perhaps most closely related to Kirundi, and there was much trade and intermarriage between the peoples. Moreover, during the 1940s, increasing numbers of Barundi had settled in Bugufi to escape both the hardships of Belgian rule and population pressure in Burundi. The British government suspected that M. Schmidt, the Belgian resident of Urundi, had influenced Mwambutsa in his petition, likely desiring more land and greater power and revenue.[77] Nevertheless, in appealing to the UN, the *Mwami* showed political acumen—perhaps realizing that international opinion and approval from Geneva had influenced decisions regarding Gisaka's place along the Anglo-Belgian border.

Residents of Bugufi also understood the potential power of the TC, responding with outrage over Mwambutsa's claim in their own petitions to the UN and the British government. Some petitioners even suggested that parts of Burundi be returned to Bugufi, as the Europeans had mistakenly placed Bugufi land on the Belgian side of the mandate.[78] Many Bahangaza writers stated that Mwambutsa had bribed the Bahangaza elite to uphold his claim, so only criminals agreed that Bugufi had ever been part of Burundi. Balamba II himself seized on the power of international public opinion, writing a letter to the editor of the *Times* alleging the historical legitimacy of the Bugufi kingdom.[79] In the end, despite the "historical legitimacy" of Mwambutsa's claim, the TC decided that the interests of Bugufi would be best served in Tanganyika, where the majority of people wanted to remain. The Belgian representative went on to note that "the whole of the family relations . . . and the whole of the customary life of these peoples, in spite of the existence of a frontier has gone on as though there were no frontier. Family visits, payment of dowries," and other activities had continued despite the border's creation.[80] The utility of the border, so carefully delineated by the British and the Belgians, thus remained in question.

What Mwambutsa's petition reveals is an increasing tension between trust governments and the United Nations. The many petitions written to the TC and the British Colonial Office from Bugufi, both for and against Mwambutsa's claim, also demonstrate that a literate elite in the chiefdom understood the power dynamics at work in determining their political future, and they attempted to manipulate international opinion. The correspondence involved in the decision to keep Bugufi in Tanganyika also affirms the political and economic links that continued to exist across the border of the two trust territories well into the late colonial period. Perhaps most presciently, the frantic European correspondence over the Mwambutsa petition reveals a colonial obsession with borders and the fear that altering borders, even in this relatively unimportant part of the world, could lead to the unraveling of the whole endeavor. As this book moves toward decolonization and the creation of a world of sovereign nation-states based on such borders, the former colonizers will continue to place great importance on maintaining the status quo. Ironically, as revealed in chapter 2, they were unable to do so during the colonial era.

Colonial Rule

There would be dire consequences for those peoples living in the Belgian mandate of Ruanda-Urundi. While the British ruled Tanganyika through their native administrations and, in far-off places like Ngara, through the creation of native authorities (known as Tutsi in Ngara), they made no attempt to rule Tutsi any differently from the rest of the population. The same could not be said of the Belgians in Ruanda-Urundi. Belgian colonialism there took on a different pace and method than that of the British to the east. The Belgians utilized racial theories born of the Hamitic hypothesis to divide the population of Ruanda-Urundi into stratified ethnic groups: the superior Hamitic Tutsi and the inferior Bantu Hutu.[81] In the 1930s the Belgian colonial government issued all inhabitants of Ruanda-Urundi identification papers that labeled them either Hutu, Tutsi, or Twa.[82] Supposedly based on the ten-cow rule, whereby all males with at least ten cows were Tutsi, in actuality, everything from nose width to connections with European officials affected an individual's identification.[83] A person's identity in Ruanda-Urundi was now reduced to either Tutsi or Hutu, with little ambiguity and little possibility of social or economic mobility. Through these draconian laws, a "cohesion of oppression" came to exist, whereby Hutu identified themselves based on the ethnicity that allowed their oppression at elite Tutsi hands.[84] In this "halfway house" of indirect rule, Belgian colonizers closely supervised Tutsi chiefs.[85] Not all Tutsi chiefs agreed to the edicts of the colonizers, but many did so with zeal. In this densely populated colony, Hutu were forced to work for both chiefs and colonizers. Cultivation of coffee and tea was compulsory, and the punishments meted out for disobedience could be swift and brutal.[86] Famines often plagued the mandate state, as Belgian quotas of these cash-crop exports took precedence over local needs. In this context, many residents of Ruanda-Urundi looked for ways to better their living conditions, and many would find the answer by moving to the east— to Ngara district.

If the goal of colonial rule was profit, the method was divide and rule: a strategy by which a minority of Europeans ruled over a majority of natives. For the British, this translated to a policy known as indirect rule, whereby each tribe was ruled by native authorities.[87] First formulated in Nigeria as a way to rule the population on the cheap, indirect rule became the hallmark of British colonial policy in Africa. This strategy utilized ostensibly preexisting African polities in a project of self-rule that had "customary authorities" working with colonial officials. Chiefs amenable to European rule were recognized as "traditional rulers" who codified "customary law." Such customs, however, were often widely manipulated in the interest of colonial profit and control, increasing the power of chiefs to the detriment of other members of the population.[88]

The second main tool used by colonial states was taxation—a method to force the population into the wage economy, usually involving colonially inspired schemes such as mining or cash-crop production. Taxation was a way to control the population, which had been enumerated by the census, and to increase revenue for the colonial administration. Thus, "colonial conquest brought all the imperial instruments of state fixity—map, census, and tax"—to communities throughout Africa.[89] However, in Ngara district, as in so much of the colonial world, local residents found their own ways to navigate the changes wrought by the colonial state.

Conclusion

As seen in the debates over the "return" of Gisaka, the imperial disputes over minerals, and *Mwami* Mwambutsa's petition to the Trusteeship Council, the delineation of the border between Ruanda-Urundi and Ngara district was as haphazard as it was impossible to regulate. These same debates reveal how this peripheral area of the Great Lakes region became central to colonizers' anxieties about the relationship between imperial borders and control, as British administrators feared that altering one international border would lead to chaos along the empire's many contested boundaries.

The imperial debates around border making in Ngara signaled the birth of a specific type of global governance—one born within the League of Nations and later continued in the United Nations and its refugee agency, the United Nations High Commissioner for Refugees (UNHCR). Border making in Ngara thus illustrates the beginning of a transnational governance regime that cloaked the self-interested economic agendas of imperial powers in a discourse of dynamic notions of "development" and "best interest." As European agencies and governments attempted to delineate the political boundaries of Ngara, they became intertwined with local politics, a legacy that would continue throughout the second half of the twentieth century, as examined in the remaining chapters of this work.

Nevertheless, cultural, economic, and even political circulation continued unabated, despite the bickering over border placement between Belgium and Britain. While these international divisions would later prove decisive in determining citizenship, they also represented the hypocrisy of an international regime that proposed to protect its wards while remaining ignorant of their lives and eager to exploit their resources. In spite of the boundary making taking place around them, Africans in the region remained committed to determining their own futures, as evidenced by the migrations from Gisaka and Urundi to Ngara and the Bahangaza elites' petitions to remain under British rule. Such actions resulted from Africans' clear-eyed understanding of the advantages of life under British indirect rule—which was preferable to the more brutal and racialized rule imposed by the Belgians in Ruanda-Urundi. In the 1940s and 1950s such African agency would continue to compel people across the borders created by Europeans, to the consternation of colonial officials who could neither control nor understand the people who lived along the border.

Due to differences in colonial statehood, language, and the configuration of space itself, the people who lived on the west side of the Kagera boundary would eventually come to see themselves as Hutu and Tutsi.[90] To the east, in the area that became Ngara district, the people called themselves Bahangaza and Basubi, after the chiefdoms in which they lived and to which they owed tribute and allegiance. Over time, these people came to see themselves as part of an entity called Tanganyika and later Tanzania. Although Ngarans later came to identify themselves with the images first created in the centers of colonial and later state power, the same cannot be said of their understanding of the river that became the legal mark of division. This boundary of authority at the edge of the colonial state never deterred the migrants and the trade that had circulated through the eastern edge of the Great Lakes region for centuries. Through their physical trespasses across this border, the people who lived on either side of it proved fictive the notions of boundary and control that borders represent.

2. CANALIZATION AND CONTROL

UNBOUNDED MIGRANTS

Naming, delineating, and controlling colonial territories were important means of colonial rule, a rule that had one overarching goal: making money. For both Britain and Belgium, it was crucial that colonies at least be profitable enough that the colonial administration did not become a burden on British or Belgian taxpayers. In other words, the colonized had to pay for their own colonization. For the British Colonial Office, this meant installing a system of indirect rule, whereby a relatively small number of British officers oversaw a vast network of native authorities, who in turn administered specified areas.[1] New colonial regions and districts were theoretically made into static spaces where people's identities automatically matched their "tribal" affiliations, as decided by imperial cartographers.

Under this system, based loosely on the traditional authorities who had ostensibly ruled in the areas demarcated, native chiefs and their administrations were responsible for implementing colonial laws. The most important of these was the collection of taxes. The imposition of taxes, payable only in money, was used to force colonized populations into wage labor—often on colonial projects located some distance from the administrative district itself.[2] Thus, laborers were encouraged to migrate to work on projects supported by the colonial administration.[3] Colonial states used taxation, therefore, to impose a capitalist economy as well as to control the colonized by making them obedient to colonially inspired markets. Unfortunately for the Tanganyikan government, Ngarans were more interested in working within a regional economy steeped in cultural connections than in the market the state hoped to capture them in.

Boundaries codified by law are not the only methods of delineating space. As Liisa Malkki suggests, "both displacement and emplacement are seen as historical products, ever unfinished projects."[4] How, then, did Ngarans conceive of place, of colonial attempts to emplace and control them, during the colonial period? Through their own movements, Ngarans (re)made the space of the new district and the colony in which they lived.[5] If we imagine the borders of Ngara to exist less in colonial and international law and more in the place-making habits of its population, the borders of the district become fuzzy—extending east into the colony of Ruanda-Urundi and north into the area of Buganda in the British protectorate of Uganda.[6] There, Ngarans, along with laborers from Ruanda-Urundi, worked on Baganda plantations, harvesting cotton, coffee, and other cash crops. In Buganda they found an area that was similar in language, culture, and climate to their home areas. They also found a cash-crop system controlled by Baganda farmers rather than Europeans.

This regional circulation presented the European powers with a threat. The three territorial administrations (Ruanda-Urundi, Tanganyika, and Uganda) thus spent much time, energy, and money trying to understand and control the flow of migrant laborers into and out of Ngara district. European debates and policies around migration and border control in Ngara continually conflicted with these place-making patterns in the district and the region. As imperial powers increasingly attempted to control the movements and livelihoods of people in the district, they remained peripheral to local patterns of circulation. Ngarans did not ignore the colonial borders and edicts imposed on them; rather, they navigated those laws that they could not avoid—namely, taxation—by relying on time-tested livelihood strategies.[7] In seeking wage labor through regional migration, Ngarans and their neighbors entered a colonially imposed wage economy while simultaneously flouting the laws created to dictate the manner of their entrance—a process that would continue into the postcolonial period. Those who lived in Ngara district during colonialism thus constituted a population that, though subject to colonial laws, remained uncaptured by them.

Nevertheless, for the people of Busubi and Bugufi, the major change wrought by the colonial state was monetization of the local economy.[8] Over a few short decades, Ngarans found that, in addition to taxes and chiefly tribute, everything from bride wealth to building materials had been commoditized as well.[9] This presented a challenge to the people of the district, who now required money to participate in integral social and economic processes such as marriage, *shamba* (farm) maintenance, clan obligations, and poll taxes. Although the mechanisms and bureaucracy built by the colonial state to run and profit from the Tanganyika Territory rarely intruded on the lives of those who lived in far-off Ngara district, the need for money vastly changed how Ngarans lived and worked. The sheer number of men who walked and then rode lorries more than one hundred miles to work on Baganda farms in southern Uganda indicates the dramatic way people's lives were affected by colonization and the introduction of a monetary economy. The fact that this labor migration often took place in opposition to the policies of colonial agents indicates the extent to which people were still able to make their own choices while residing within the economic framework of the colonial state.

In the course of their labor migrations, men of the Tanganyika Territory, along with those of Ruanda-Urundi, continually circumvented the borders imposed by European policymakers. Despite the efforts that the Belgian and British had put into creating and ratifying the borders dividing the three territories of Ruanda-Urundi, Tanganyika, and Uganda, cross-border migrations increased during the late colonial period—to the chagrin of colonial officers. As efforts to control and "canalize" popular migration increased, illicit migration swelled. The British trustees eventually reverted to the burgeoning rhetoric of development in their attempts to control popular movements within and across this area of Tanganyika. Despite efforts to convince people that their "best interests" would be served by following British edicts and policies, migrants continued to find their own paths to navigate the changes imposed by the colonial government. Transcolonial attempts to demarcate the boundaries of this part of the Great Lakes region and to control popular migration therein then led to the creation of the first migrant containment camps in the area. Such camps became the theoretical precursors to the Rwandan refugee camps that transformed the landscape of Ngara district in the following decades.

"Feudal" Ngara

According to colonial authorities, uncontrolled migration out of Ngara district stemmed from its "feudal" makeup. However, for the British colonial state, life in Ngara district existed primarily as told by government sociologist Hans Cory. The son of a "Viennese musical family," Cory was "largely self-taught in . . . social anthropology," and his early interest in African songs and ceremonies led to his work for the Tanganyikan government, codifying and unifying the territory's customary laws.[10] During the 1940s and 1950s, Cory's writings on the chiefdoms of Bugufi and Busubi translated life on the ground to decision makers in Dar es Salaam and provincial headquarters in Bukoba, creating a picture of places that would be amenable to bureaucratic colonial intervention.[11] According to Cory, the chiefdom of Bugufi in the district's north was a backward "feudal" state, similar to those in the Bahaya territories to the north and in Belgian-held Ruanda-Urundi to the west. Similarly, Cory wrote that the Busubi chiefdom to the south (where he spent only a fortnight) was feudal in nature, but of a more benign kind. Thus, rather than an impersonal bureaucracy, it was the actions and words of a few people, and specifically one man, that shaped colonial policy in Ngara district. Many of Cory's reports were written at the request of district officials who knew little about the people living in the areas they governed and who desired to increase their authority and control.[12] Cory's conclusions, therefore, are suspect due to both his position as a sociologist in the service of the colonial state and the limited time he spent in Ngara.

This is not meant to suggest that Cory's intentions were bad or that he was unwilling to understand the patterns of life in Ngara. Rather, Cory was apparently motivated by a true sense of outrage at the native authorities in Ngara and by a genuine, albeit patronizing, compassion for the natives of the area—whom he often referred to as "primitive."[13] Perhaps because of his wide travels and many studies throughout Tanganyika, Cory was prone to making hasty comparisons and creating generalized solutions to the problems he encountered in Ngara. For example, the legal code he suggested for Ngara closely resembled the land laws he created for Bukoba.[14] The information that follows on the political structure of Ngara district during the colonial period must therefore be viewed in the appropriate context: a colonial project to exert control over a population perceived to be mentally and culturally inferior to Europeans.[15]

During the colonial period, Bugufi was the larger and better known of the two chiefdoms in Ngara.[16] The *boma*, or administrative center, first opened in 1929.[17] Numerous documents describe the leaders of both Bugufi and Busubi as Hamites, related in myth and/or ancestry to the Bacwezi.[18] Regarding Cory's use of the word *Hamite*, he subscribed to the typical colonial narrative of Great Lakes societies, which depicted the Tutsi as racially and intellectually superior "invaders" who had conquered the natives, or Hutu, of the region. Accordingly, Cory wrote, "The history of Bugufi is not much different from that of many other districts where a superior race like men of Hamitic origin subdued an indigenous inferior people like the Bahutu without fighting, just by being superior."[19] He attributed the continuance of the Hutu's "serf" attitude to the fact that they "came later and less intensively in contact with Europeans."[20] With these sentences, Cory reveals himself to be a typical colonial civil servant of the time, believing that all Ngara's ills stemmed from the "selfish" Tutsi overlords and that all prospects for progress emanated from European decrees and example. This problematic association of Great Lakes rulers with Hamites marks almost all colonial writings on the political, economic, and social facets of life in Ngara.

British colonial officials took their cue from Cory, describing both the precolonial and colonial politico-economic organizations in Ngara as "feudal," where a Tutsi aristocracy controlled all the land and the cattle and exploited the majority of the population.[21] In using the term *feudal*, these officials described a community of serfs and landlords, the former living in continual debt to the latter and in constant fear of losing their tenuous landholdings. Cory frequently disparaged these "traditional" land tenure rules, whereby the landholdings of squatters (as well as *umunhu wi intole*, or retainers/tenants) could be removed following the death or replacement of the *batwale* (subdistrict head).

Although Cory noted that "popular opinion" in Bugufi protected tenants and squatters from eviction, he did not explore the role of societal opinion and custom in limiting elite power in Bugufi.[22] And despite decrying the plight of the "serfs," Cory noted that "life for the Muhutu in Bugufi is not hell and that here as everywhere the natives sing and dance although they pay here tribute."[23] Disparities exist throughout Cory's writings on the Hutu in Bugufi, whom he described as "obedient" serfs. However, in other reports, Cory noted that eleven of thirty-one *batwale* in Bugufi were "bahutu," which complicates the image of the Hutu as obedient underlings in the Bugufi chiefdom.[24]

In contrast to Bugufi, Cory described Busubi as characterized, until the 1950s, by low population density and more harmonious relations between the Tutsi aristocracy and the Hutu peasantry.[25] According to Cory, the Subi chiefs were "men of Rundi stock." However, he also noted that some of the chiefs had arrived as hunters from Karagwe, and "the elephant hunters of Karagwe considered Busubi as their hunting ground. The importance of elephant hunting for the economy of a Chiefdom in the olden days was great."[26] In addition to the trade in goats and cattle from Burundi to Karagwe, with Basubi acting as middlemen, the importance of elephant hunting to Basubi chiefs indicates the chiefdom's involvement in regional long-distance trade.[27]

On the subject of Ngarans' mental intransigence, Cory complained that the Bahutu and Barundi in Ngara made it hard to help them, as "there is not a single complaint about ngorole or expulsion from holdings, services or tribute."[28] Cory continually lamented the unsavory land -tenure laws in Bugufi, which he blamed on the unscrupulous elite chiefs and their unquestioningly obedient serfs. Unsurprisingly, the question of native consciousness in Ngara district may not be well answered by looking at the colonial record, which is itself ambiguous. For example, according to Cory, the major factor in his description of the Bahangaza as a feudal society came from his assessment of the Hutu as unthinking, obedient serfs.[29] In other writings, however, Cory noted that some *batwale* were seen as just and good leaders by their subjects, while one leader who was not beloved kept "a bodyguard because he is afraid to be attacked by his people."[30] These comments indicate that the serfs were not always as blindly obedient as Cory claimed, and they cast doubt on Cory's conclusions about societal malaise in Ngara district.

Cory viewed the serfs' insecure land tenure as the prime reason for the Bahangaza's refusal to cultivate coffee as a cash crop (see chapter 3) and as a major factor in their increasing labor migration to Uganda.[31] He noted that few squatters were actually deprived of their land and that the *batwale* themselves refused to grow coffee, yet he insisted that because the Bahangaza could, in theory, be deprived of their land, this is what made them reluctant to invest time and energy in their plots.[32] This correlation between insecure land tenure and migration to Uganda and a reluctance to grow cash crops also failed to account for why the people in neighboring Busubi— where Cory described land as both plentiful and free—also refused to grow coffee and traveled to Uganda in numbers proportional to the Bahangaza migrants.[33]

The chiefs, through their influence and that of their subchiefs, certainly had much more of a presence in the daily lives of Ngarans than did the colonial government. Additionally, local people had no reason to trust a colonial government that had imposed taxes on them, as well as compulsory labor

48 · CHAPTER 2

on development projects.[34] Speaking with Ngarans today about past chiefs reveals an array of responses about Bugufi chief Balamba II and Busubi chief Nsoro, both of whom ruled during the 1940s and 1950s, when Cory conducted his research.[35] Though most people readily admitted that Balamba and Nsoro were "good chiefs," they were also quick to point out the drawbacks of the chieftaincies—particularly the everyday events that affected their or their parents' lives. These issues included the burdens imposed on local populations when the chief traveled, such as transporting the chief by carrying him in a chair, building rest stops and homes for the chief and his entourage, and bringing cattle to the chief.[36] People also noted with disgust the chief's possession of all the cattle in the chiefdom.[37] Oral interviews indicate that people were very conscious of the authoritarian and unfair nature of life under the chiefs, although they may have been reticent about sharing such information with colonial interlocutors.[38]

Without a doubt, however, Ngarans were acutely conscious of the problems the colonial state introduced into their lives, including the collection of taxes (*kodi*) by colonial agents. Many of those interviewed perceived an inaccurate division between the chiefs' work and that of the colonial government.[39] Thus, many people only remembered colonial agents collecting taxes, despite the fact that the chiefs' agents collected taxes for the government and a portion of those taxes went to the native authorities run by the chiefs.[40] Nevertheless, Ngaran anger over *kodi* tended to be directed toward the colonizers, not those who enforced colonial law. As one respondent noted, "Britain forced people to cultivate cash crops for their own industries, we got back very little money . . . whatever they did they did for themselves."[41]

The Color of Money: The Uganda Complex

Cory and other colonial officials who visited Ngara attributed much of the native "misery" to the growing number of male migrant laborers who traveled to Buganda during the late 1940s and 1950s.[42] As one colonial official wrote, the annual migration for work in Uganda "has constantly expanded, to the detriment of agriculture at home—Bugufi is constantly on the verge of a food shortage in spite of the fertility of its soil."[43] In addition to food shortages, migration to Buganda frustrated British attempts to develop agriculture in the district, presenting Ngaran officials with an "increasingly permanent" situation.[44] Colonial officials therefore expended much time and effort trying to curtail and control regional migration.[45]

For the men who undertook the long, often arduous journey to Uganda, there was often no other perceived viable choice. When asked why they did not work in Tanganyika, most former migrants replied that they had gone to Uganda because nobody had any money in Tanganyika, and working conditions there were poor, even slave-like.[46] Others replied that Tanzanians "had not discovered themselves."[47] In contrast, in Buganda, money could be earned, and eventually migrants might even own a plot of land.[48] Presciently, Ngarans understood that Buganda was in closer proximity than other areas of Tanganyika, both geographically and culturally. In contrast, areas to the east in the Tanganyika Territory had seemingly alien cultural traditions.[49]

Ngaran economic migration began in earnest in the 1920s, with men walking, usually in groups for protection, for months to reach Buganda. With the introduction of better roads and transportation around the 1940s, it became easier to reach Buganda and therefore provide for one's family, secure the money needed to marry, pay taxes, and, as one former migrant put it, have "life."[50] Money was also used to buy and maintain livestock, including cattle.[51] Additionally, men often brought back agricultural goods, such as seedlings, that were lacking in Ngara.[52] One respondent noted that by going to work in Buganda, he could escape paying taxes in Ngara.[53] The ability to purchase and consume *pombe* (beer) was also important to some.[54]

As a result, men in Ngara district, often accompanied by men from Ruanda-Urundi, made the long trek to Uganda to farm for African Baganda businesses.[55] Because work in Buganda (usually on cotton or coffee farms) followed the rhythms of the harvest, Ngaran men worked there for an average of seven to ten months, usually leaving Ngara at the beginning of the year. This migration was almost exclusively undertaken by men, although a few families traveled to Buganda.[56] Some families eventually acquired plots of land in Buganda, using their agricultural profits to sustain themselves and send their children to school.[57] Many remained in Uganda for several years, and some are still in Uganda today.[58] Ngaran labor migration also took on a generational dimension, with young men and boys often following brothers, fathers, and uncles to work on Baganda farms. A certain prestige developed around the journey to Uganda, and young men who returned home were considered social adults, eligible for marriage, in the eyes of most communities.[59]

While they were gone, most men arranged to have a family member or a male friend look after their wives, families, and farms.[60] Some wives whose husbands migrated to Uganda remembered that, *bila shaka* (without a doubt), the men were missed.[61] But for the most part, there were few problems for the families who remained behind, as communities and neighbors helped one another.[62] Only one woman claimed she received no help while her husband was in Uganda.[63] Often such arrangements were cyclical: when one migrant returned home, he would look after the families of those who had helped his family while he was away, even advancing travel money to those neighbors or family members.[64] Contrary to Cory's writings, few people remembered an acute famine in Ngara during this time, although many were quick to note that famine is a constant threat to life in Ngara.[65]

Many people from the Belgian colony of Ruanda-Urundi traveled through Ngara district on their way to work in Uganda, and some stayed in the district. According to respondents, it was relatively easy for such people to acclimate to life in Ngara.[66] Indeed, many of the interviewees did not seem to differentiate between Barundi, Banyarwanda, and Basubi or Bahangaza until decolonization and the arrival of Rwandan refugees in the late 1950s.[67] Many Ngarans recalled that people from Rwanda and Burundi passed through Ngara on their way to Uganda, while others stayed to work on local *shamba* and remained in the villages, often intermarrying with local people throughout the district.[68] Ngarans and migrants from Ruanda-Urundi often traveled the route to Uganda together. Once in Uganda, however, it was rare for people from Ngara district to work with individuals from Ruanda-Urundi.[69]

Canalization and Migrant Control

To the British colonial government, this migration represented an economic, medical, and social threat to the communities in Ngara district.[70] The governors of the Belgian and British territories tried unsuccessfully to control this unauthorized movement of migrants across the three colonies. Officially, British concern over such migration began in 1927, when the Tanganyikan government was asked to comment on a report by the director of the International Labour Office that noted the presence of spirillum-carrying ticks along the path traversed by migrants from the "Congo" and the threat posed by the spread of spirillum fever and dysentery among the local population.[71] In 1930 the labor commissioner of Uganda submitted a "scheme" to control incoming migrants and proposed the creation of "control camps" along the Ruanda-Urundi border to contain migrants entering Uganda from both Ruanda-Urundi and Tanganyika. Although the British government turned down this initial scheme due to concerns about offending Belgian officials, it became the forerunner of colonial migrant containment policies.[72]

In 1946 the three governments had their first official conversations about the need to "set up some administrative machinery to control and supervise these labour migrants and to improve the conditions of migratory labour with special reference to the social effects of such migration."[73] Annual meetings with representatives from the three territories, including members of labor and medical departments, then began in 1949. A report written by Major Orde-Browne, who had surveyed the migrant routes, noted:

> The obvious and traditional goal of their peregrinations in Uganda, where the local proprietors of the very considerable native plantations are well pleased to these wandering strangers. . . . In Tanganyika the movement has been more recent in origin, and the food factor has hitherto outweighed the desire for cash; there have in the past been serious crises owing to the . . . resources of the Territory being suddenly overstrained by a flood of semi-starving and frequently diseased immigrants. There is, however, a definite tendency of late to endeavour to utilise this source of labour, and the situation is growing rather more like that in Uganda.
>
> It will be obvious that large crowds moving to and fro entirely without control or supervision, let alone any sort of medical inspection, must present a permanent threat. . . . Proper control and supervision of this migratory movement is, therefore, absolutely essential to safeguard the health of the inhabitants of the neighbouring territories whatever the cost which may be involved.[74]

The circulation of Rwandan and Urundi migrants through Ngara district and into Uganda therefore posed problems, even a "permanent threat," for the Tanganyikan colonial state. The notion of "diseased immigrants" is found throughout the territory's archives. Although medical concerns over tuberculosis and other diseases may have been valid, it is likely that local attitudes toward Rwandan migrants found their way into official vocabularies as well.[75] As Orde-Browne went on to note:

> The tendency to travel from Ruanda-Urundi into Tanganyika is an old established one; the density of population and the periodical shortage of food are factors which have prompted movement on a scale which in some years has assumed very large proportions.[76] During the last twenty years there have been several of these large scale migrations causing grave embarrassment to the Tanganyika Administration and to the Medical Authorities. Numbers in thousands. A continuation of

this mass movement must sooner or later develop complications . . . clearly therefore, arrangements are required which will convert this annual movement from a liability into an asset; in other words, the conditioning camp system is indicated . . . the outstanding importance of the camp will be obvious, not only from the point of view of providing for labour requirements, but also as a valuable safeguard to the whole territory.[77]

The specter of such an uncontrolled "dire threat" to the health and society of Ngara led to colonial efforts to "canalize" the movement of migrants across the Tanganyika Territory and into Uganda by means of Orde-Browne's "conditioning camp system" network. The creation of borders and the introduction of monetization then led to the first type of migrant control in Ngara through the establishment of segregated camps in northwestern Tanzania. Among other things, such camps involved medical inspections and quarantine procedures before migrants were permitted to move on to their labor destinations. Such camps also aimed to sort the migrants according to colonial residency (to facilitate eventual repatriation), as well as to enable "careful pre-selection to ensure the natives' physical fitness and suitability."[78] As Orde-Browne noted, "This camp will be the first of its kind in Tanganyika and it will thus be in a measure experimental."[79] Such "experiments" in migrant management would be continued in the refugee era in Ngara.

At an interterritorial meeting held at Bukoba on July 6, 1949, officials concluded that "present measures of control were virtually useless" due to the "physical impossibility of controlling long boundaries." Therefore, the patrol of migrants' focal points of transit offered the best method of controlling the situation. This "canalization" of migrants was described as follows: "Control may be exercised by measures such as canalization within Tanganyika, mainly by attracting migratory labour to follow prescribed routes by the inducement of free or partially subsidized transport."[80]

In addition to the alleged "social welfare" benefits of these migrant camps, colonial officials hoped that the creation of "conditioning/acclimatization centres" would contribute "to the solution of the important problems of the low productivity and proneness to absenteeism of the African labourer."[81] The "protection of natives" and state-desired increases in "African" productivity were therefore blended in colonial proposals to control migrant labor in the region, revealing the tension within development programs meant to "lift up natives" and simultaneously increase the colonies' economic output. From the mid-1940s until decolonization (and beyond), both these goals targeted the "African himself" as a "primary site for development and change," in a discourse that simultaneously extolled the promotion of natives' well-being and masked the exploitative nature of colonial rule.[82]

Despite the building of canalization routes in the area, including the construction of roads, migrants from Ruanda-Urundi and Ngara continually circumvented, and even expressed hostility toward, both colonial officials and the controlled routes to Uganda.[83] As one official in the Uganda protectorate noted, "the immigrants are a suspicious people, who are note [sic] easily influenced and dislike being controlled."[84] As a result, officials contemplated building "containment camps" along the border with Ruanda-Urundi and Tanganyika, particularly in the "no man's land" of Ngara and Biharamulo.[85] Patrols along the Tanganyika border with Ruanda-Urundi were also suggested.[86] However, disputes over which territory should bear the financial burden disrupted plans for the creation of holding camps along the border.[87] Eventually, a control camp was built to house migrants at Bukoba, in addition to the conditioning camp at Kyaka ferry.[88]

The most popular routes for people traveling from Urundi to Uganda crossed through Ngara district. Additionally, increasing numbers of Banyarwanda, particularly from Kisaka district, made the journey south to Ngara before moving on to the Muwendo ferry and eventually the Kyaka ferry.[89] Often stopping for the night in the district and buying food along the way, migrants from the Belgian territories became common sights in Ngara district.[90] By 1951, an average of thirty lorries a week brought migrants from Rulenge, in Busubi, to Bukoba on the border with the Uganda protectorate.[91]

British frustration over the unauthorized and uncontrolled movement of migrants in northwestern Tanganyika also stemmed from the government's inability to take advantage of this labor pool within the Tanganyika Territory.[92] The state and various agencies had repeatedly tried to recruit Ngarans and migrants from Ruanda-Urundi to work in the territory. In an effort to better coordinate and control recruiting practices, the government enacted the Defense (Recruitment of Native Servants) Regulations in 1947. These regulations sought to control the unauthorized recruitment of natives by estate headmen and touts and redirect laborers to recruiters working for state-authorized projects, usually involving large-scale agriculture or mining. Under this regulation, only the acting labor commissioner (or district commissioner, if the migrants were to work within the district where they were recruited) was permitted to authorize labor recruitment.[93] However, these sanctioned recruiters were repeatedly unsuccessful in their attempts to recruit Ngarans and others to work within the territory, despite the erection of transit camps

54 · CHAPTER 2

by government-authorized private agencies, such as the camp operated by the Sisal Labour Bureau (SILABU).[94] At the SILABU "collecting center" in Ngara, workers were organized and then transported by lorry to Kahama (in contemporary Shinyanga district), where a large transit camp existed. Workers received medical examinations at this camp and were subjected to a two-week quarantine period against sleeping sickness. They were then transported by rail to their contracted labor destinations.[95]

Nevertheless, SILABU was unable to reach its recruiting goals, and in December 1955 it "closed its Office in the West Lake area . . . [as] recruiting within the Province, as was to be expected, was singularly unsuccessful." This desultory report noted that migrants from Ruanda-Urundi and Ngara moved through the Tanganyika Territory refusing recruiters' contracts, as "they were attracted by the freedom to go and return whenever they wished."[96] Similarly, the Tanganyika Sisal Growers Association (TSGA) was unable to meet its recruiting quota of five hundred people in the province.[97]

Conclusion

In a 1953 letter to Ngara's district commissioner, Hans Cory wrote, "The problems of Ngara have not been solved. But you are not the first District Commissioner to leave Ngara with a feeling of frustration, and I am afraid you will not be the last."[98] Cory was right. In the decades to come, Europeans would continue to enter Ngara intent on aiding the people and the migrants who lived in the district. As the following chapters show, they would continually be frustrated by the actions and reactions of those whose lives they hoped to affect.

After so much controversy over the placement of borders between Ruanda-Urundi and Tanganyika, it is perhaps not a surprise that the colonial powers were incensed to find that people largely ignored or took advantage of the new borders. Cross-border trade and circulation continued unabated, with neither colonizer able to control the long stretches of borderland between the two territories. Indeed, such migration had a long history. As early as 1900, residents of Gisaka fled drought and Rwandan court rule by moving to the east, a trend that continued following Gisaka's "return" to Belgium in 1924.[99] Rwandan migration then likely increased during and after the famine in southeastern Rwanda in the 1920s.[100] Demographic changes continued in Ngara during the 1940s, as large numbers of Barundi moved there permanently. Due to these migrations, from 1940 to 1948, the population of Ngara district nearly doubled—from 64,000 in 1940 to

112,000 in 1948.[101] Migrants from Ruanda-Urundi therefore elaborated on existing patterns of migration to extricate themselves from the brutality of Belgian rule.

This unauthorized migration only increased with monetization of the regional economy, a process the colonial states were unable to control. While the Belgians had hoped to use the densely populated area of Ruanda-Urundi as a labor reserve for their mining interests to the west in the Congo, they were continually dismayed by the circulation of migrant laborers to neighboring British colonies. Ngarans too were quick to seize new opportunities for labor migration in the region, albeit not the type the British had hoped for. While companies repeatedly tried to entice Ngaran migrant laborers to work in other parts of Tanganyika, the Bahangaza and Basubi insisted on remaining within the Great Lakes cultural zone, most often moving north to the Uganda protectorate for seasonal work.

From the 1920s to the 1950s, colonial rulers thus attempted unsuccessfully to control and direct the movements of people within and through Ngara district. Such efforts at containment and canalization led to the conditioning camps that were the theoretical, if impractical, forerunners of the refugee camps examined in the following chapters—camps that refugees often flouted. The containment camps intended to contain, sort, and diagnose migrants in the region, based on colonial residence and labor strength, would share some remarkable similarities with the refugee camps of the 1960s and 1990s. In both cases, colonial and postcolonial containment efforts were determined by a small number of agents who were either unable or unwilling to understand life in the district as perceived by its inhabitants—their major concerns were migrants' health and region of origin. As a result, perceptions of Ngarans' thoughts about politics, money, and identity were constrained by a developmental framework that was largely inapplicable to life in Ngara district. As the borders remained porous, people found ways to provide for themselves and their families outside of the imposed governmental framework by relying on time-tested regional circulations that belied the borders of the colonial state.

56 · CHAPTER 2

3. DEVELOPMENTAL DISAPPOINTMENT

CONTINUITIES IN LATE COLONIAL AND

EARLY INDEPENDENCE NGARA

Mwalimu (teacher) Nyerere. These were magic words. "He came to Ngara, you know?" "Chief Balamba went to school with him." "You know he was a teacher?" *Mwalimu*. I never asked directly about Julius Nyerere, limiting my questions to what and when development took place, and how independence affected Ngarans' lives. Yet there he was. Nyerere meant development. I asked one question over and over again: "Why did you stop going to find work in Uganda?" The answer: "*Mwalimu* Nyerere. He taught us to develop our own *shamba* [farms]. That instead of making money for others in Uganda, we could make money for ourselves. Develop ourselves. Develop Tanzania."[1]

Not everyone, of course, gave the same response. Some reported that they continued to work in Uganda after independence. A few went to avoid taxes.[2] Others said they waited to see whether Tanzania would "develop."[3] Always there is a certain friction in the archives, some recollections that deviate from the tenor and tone of the rest. Additionally, one cannot avoid and thus must account for the presence of nostalgia in oral interviews.[4] This is particularly true of Ngarans, many of whom deplore what they see as the corruption that descended on Tanzania following President Nyerere's departure from politics in the early 1980s. Nevertheless, the overwhelming majority of people I spoke with invoked the figure and the words of Julius Nyerere as they explained their decision to stop traveling to Uganda to work during decolonization. And in the words of Ngarans, he is never Julius Nyerere but Nyerere the teacher.

Few in Africa or Europe expected decolonization to occur in the manner or time frame that it did. The pace of decolonization is dizzying to behold more than half a century later, as are the continuities between the colonial and postcolonial periods. Given a past and present so replete with interlocking local, national, and transnational factors, we are forced to question the efficacy of neatly periodizing African history. Such reconsideration is particularly germane if we shift our view from the conference halls in Dar es Salaam, London, and New York to the hills of Ngara district.

Contradictions, disjunctions, and continuities marked the decolonization process in Tanganyika. Perhaps the most glaring continuity between the colonial and postcolonial eras was how government leaders thought of development and the methods they employed to achieve it. The late colonial and early independence years in Ngara in particular, and in Tanganyika in general, occurred in a postwar era of development planning and practice based on notions of progress rooted in modernization theory. This economic and political scholarship delineated a teleological model of history through which all economies and societies pass on their way toward development.[5] Like the League of Nations' ranking of A, B, and C mandates, the international community led by the Americans and Western Europeans understood development to mean the creation of industrial economies—in other words, that the final stages of progress and modernity were the creation of industrialized, capitalist economies modeled on their own. As a result, both British administrators and those in the early independence period believed that to achieve development and "catch up" to the Western world, local communities needed to evolve economically and politically. In terms of economics, both leaderships thought that centralized state management was necessary to transform local agricultural techniques and bolster the production of cash crops. Administrators of both governments also believed that for the territory to progress politically, traditional communities needed to be modernized through greater popular participation in local social-development and governance structures.[6]

58 · CHAPTER 3

Colonial and postcolonial leaders alike believed that technical solutions, such as the mechanization of cash-crop production and the introduction of new farming and husbandry techniques, were integral to but not sufficient for the territory's development. The state needed to additionally transform the habits and beliefs of the rural poor, who accounted for an overwhelming majority of the population. Development, therefore, had to be administered from the state's bureaucratic center, as local people could not be trusted to use government resources effectively. As Leander Schneider notes, Tanganyikan history from the late 1940s to the early 1970s was marked by the dominance of development as both a discursive justification for state authoritarianism and an extension of state power in local contexts.[7] Here, we glimpse a thread of continuity among all the bureaucracies this book analyzes (colonial, national, and transnational): the belief that local populations cannot be trusted to do what is "right" and therefore must be instructed in their own self-interests by properly educated "experts." The colonial development model therefore casts a lasting shadow over postcolonial aid and national projects alike.

This chapter compares officials' attempts to develop Ngara district in the late colonial and early independence eras, revealing blatant similarities and disappointing results. Both colonial and postcolonial leaders failed to deliver on promises to improve the district through educational and agricultural inputs. Both leaderships also retained a condescending attitude toward rural residents of Ngara. For Ngarans, postcolonial development initiatives in the district led, if anything, to more distrust of state development programs. Paradoxically, postcolonial development projects led to cross-border smuggling, as Ngarans continued to rely on regional economic strategies that bypassed the borders imposed by the colonial and then the postcolonial state. In the face of failed development initiatives, Ngarans engaged in illicit regional circulation, continuing to blur the boundaries meant to separate the district from Rwanda and Burundi.[8] These economic strategies would contrast markedly with the political divisions represented by the presence of refugees and refugee aid, discussed in the following chapters.

Development and Decolonization

Part of Britain's increased attention to and frustration with uncontrolled migration in Ngara stemmed from the lack of cash-crop cultivation in the district. The emphasis on cash crops was part of the British Empire's focus on development after World War II, when new development-related principles became pivotal to justify British colonial rule both at home and abroad.[9] In this sense, the word *development* underwent a dramatic shift in British colonial discourse. It no longer described simply the "best interests" or "economic progress" of the colonized. Colonial officials now believed that to prepare Africans for eventual self-rule, they needed to undergo a guided process to make their worldviews align with the economic, social, and political mores of Western civilization.[10] In many ways, the new development policies enacted after World War II were more invasive in Tanganyikans' everyday lives than earlier policies had been, as the colonial state sought to alter how people lived and thought.

Simultaneously, colonial development policy placed "complete faith" in the science of development.[11] Administrative solutions to the territory's "backward" economy included modernized cash-crop production—replete with seed trials and demonstration plots—combined with greater bureaucratic oversight to ensure that the population followed "expert" advice. Additional tools included village resettlement schemes and the modernization of African political beliefs and cultures.[12] Like the development principles described by Arturo Escobar and James Ferguson in the postcolonial era, these policies were flawed in that they emphasized technical, standardized procedures over the knowledge, interests, and particularities of local settings.[13] Interventions therefore failed to take into account local topographies of climate and geography, while creating models of homogeneous "backward" populations amenable to standardized solutions. The result was that expatriate "experts" degraded and ignored local knowledge and ambitions—a serious error, given that the inhabitants of an area are most likely to understand the vagaries of their respective locales and have their own ideas about what measures will improve their lives. Compounding these issues in Ngara, then as now, was a lack of government funding, as budgetary allocations reflected the district's peripheral position.

This new push for development was a product of the postwar world, where the very premise of empire was increasingly questioned. On the international stage, the end of World War II left a world dominated by the competing politics of the United States and the Soviet Union. American efforts to rebuild Europe and restrain the advance of communism led to unprecedented aid and economic reforms for a Europe that had been devastated by war. As the welfare state rose in western Europe, the United States and the Soviet Union embarked on a Cold War in which the political and economic allegiances of colonized peoples played pivotal roles.

The American public and leadership had long fostered concerns about the world of empires. Following World War II, US leaders called for a more benevolent, development-focused colonial state that would give colonized populations the tools necessary for self-determination.[14] As populations within colonial territories increasingly turned to nationalist movements to protest and expel colonial governments, American and Soviet criticism of European colonization swelled. Rebellions in India, Algeria, and Southeast Asia drew world attention to the plight of the colonized.[15] And, in the wake of what many viewed as a world war fueled by racial antagonism, international opinion questioned the validity of predominantly "white" rule over "colored" natives.[16]

Closer to home, many British citizens and their leaders grew frustrated with the costs of empire. And these costs were rising. As Frederick Cooper notes, African leaders often used European officials' words against them, demanding local reforms in line with the new social insurance policies enacted in Europe, reforms that the colonial state could ill afford.[17] In response to these complex pressures, the British inaugurated a new program of development that would, ostensibly, prepare Africans for self-rule.

Britain's 1940 and 1945 Colonial Development and Welfare Acts heralded what scholars have called the "second colonial occupation" of Africa.[18] These acts pledged more funding to develop Britain's African empire, a kind of development that required corresponding increases in expatriate manpower and infrastructure. In response to the 1945 act, colonial planners in Tanganyika drew up a ten-year development plan for the period 1947–1956.[19] A crucial goal of the ten-year plan was to increase the quality and quantity of the territory's cash crops, both to enhance the empire's profits and to improve the inhabitants' quality of life.[20] Propelled by the cash-crop boom of the early 1950s, European development experts penetrated the countryside with technological innovations such as plows and fertilizers.[21] Agricultural experts arrived in rural areas to educate Africans in the modern science of cash-crop production and soil conservation.[22] Because colonial planners thought of Africans as backward and "unwilling to accept modernization and change," officials made these new agricultural techniques mandatory and closely supervised farmers to ensure their compliance.[23]

Passive and active resistance to colonial farming techniques, many of which would later prove detrimental to agricultural production, led to the government's "focal point approach" after 1956.[24] Following this strategy, government officials chose and funded willing, often wealthy farmers to model development techniques. The logic behind the focal point approach

Developmental Disappointment · 61

was that as the locals saw the success of these model farms, they too would adopt modern techniques. In general, however, the strategy failed, as poor farmers viewed the focal point projects' success as stemming from the participants' prior wealth, rather than the modern techniques they used, which were too expensive to implement, in any event.

The "Man in the *Shamba*": Coffee as a Cash Crop in 1950s Ngara

To British administrators, the compulsory cultivation of coffee as a cash crop was the answer to Ngara district's poverty.[25] If Ngarans could be convinced, or forced, to remain in the district and cultivate coffee, they believed, the district would become profitable. Colonial officials understood the impediment to coffee's success in Ngara to be the district's "feudal" land laws, which encouraged migration, as well as Ngarans' lazy, backward production techniques. More accurately, the lack of coffee production was attributable to the burdensome bureaucracy, poor funding, and condescending attitudes of the district's governors and agricultural officers. The result was that Ngarans continued to migrate to Uganda, as their attempts at coffee production were continually frustrated.

Influenced by the success of coffee production in neighboring Ruanda-Urundi and Buganda and in the Haya areas to the north, the government aimed to make Ngara a center of coffee production.[26] However, coffee cultivation proved to be more haphazard in Ngara, largely due to insufficient funding, poor infrastructure (particularly roads), and colonial officials' inability and unwillingness to understand local needs and agricultural practices. Without a nuanced understanding of local conditions, the colonial state resorted to coercive policies, such as compulsory planting, to force Ngarans to cultivate coffee.[27] Such blunt policies led to ambivalence and occasional hostility toward coffee farming—reactions that colonial officials used as examples of the Ngarans' "backward" tendencies.

The development of coffee production in Ngara received sustained attention from the colonial government rather late in comparison to other areas of Tanganyika, and it was plagued by fits and starts. Coffee trials began in Ngara in the mid-1920s, but it was not until the mid-1950s that the government undertook sustained efforts to make the crop sustainable.[28] In 1931 officials had decided that intensive coffee planting would begin in Bugufi.[29] The district office then forced Ngarans to plant coffee plots, and those without suitable land "were compelled to start coffee plots on land belonging to others."[30] However, by 1953, "one quarter of Bugufi's coffee plantations" had been "abandoned."[31] As we have seen, government sociologist Hans Cory blamed the lack of coffee cultivation in the district on a lack of secure land tenure, which prompted Ngarans to migrate to Uganda for work. However, the Ngaran district commissioner apparently thought differently, noting, "it cannot be alleged that the primary purpose of the journey to Uganda is to earn allocation fees for land, which are only paid once." He went on to claim that migration to Uganda occurred due to "the high rate of bride-price and the demand for consumer goods," and he concluded that "what is significant is that there is little desire to earn needs through agriculture."[32] This last sentence is particularly telling, as Ngarans migrated to Uganda specifically to perform agricultural work. Aversion to agricultural work and land insecurity were thus insufficient explanations for Ngarans' reluctance to grow coffee as a cash crop.

A better reason for Ngara's lack of a robust coffee economy was inadequate funding for the district, in addition to the patronizing and coercive colonial administration, which many Ngarans viewed as untrustworthy.[33] One factor was the lack of consistent government assistance; the agricultural assistant assigned to Ngara was transferred in 1941, and according to Cory, "naturally the progress has been retarded since then."[34] The government then used native agricultural instructors to oversee the production of coffee. In Cory's opinion, the lack of cultivation in Ngara was the result of both absent male labor due to land tenure laws and the proclivities of the "natives," who could not be trusted to oversee coffee cultivation without "continuous control by a European Officer."[35] However, Cory noted in 1944 that even those Bahangaza who made "a considerable amount of money" from their coffee plots had "no love for their cash crop."[36] Thus, the disdain for coffee cultivation cannot be entirely explained by a lack of "proper" European supervision. It is more likely that colonial officials' coercive techniques and condescending attitudes affected Ngarans, who preferred to labor under African supervision in Buganda, where there were few *wazungu* overseers.

By the mid-1950s, however, attitudes in Bugufi were changing. As the district commissioner noted, "you can be sure that the African now has an excellent idea of the value of coffee today and none would abandon a healthy plot."[37] Many Ngarans had taken notice of the rising coffee prices during the early 1950s and expressed a renewed interest in cultivating the cash crop. Additionally, new cooperative societies flourished throughout the province and territory in the 1950s. In Ngara, the most important of these were the Bukoba Native Cooperative Union (BNCU) in Bukoba and the Bugufi Coffee Cooperative Union (BCCU) in Ngara. These cooperatives offered vital marketing

Developmental Disappointment · 63

opportunities for Ngarans, who had little direct access to the roads and markets necessary to sell their crops.

Nevertheless, to colonial officers, a major obstacle to the growth of cash crops in Ngara, and in the territory as a whole, remained the natives' lack of modern cultivation methods and poor attitude toward agriculture. According to the provincial agricultural officer for West Lake, its coffee crop had been static for thirty years due to "universally poor" standards of cultivation. He went on to write, "The big problem is how to put over to the cultivator these improved methods of cultivation."[38]

It seems, however, that the "big problem" was actually a lack of funding and manpower allocated to Ngara district, as well as British impatience for quick results. A close reading of the archives reveals that far from being resistant to modern techniques of coffee growing, by the mid-1950s, people in Ngara, and Bugufi in particular, were eager to participate in coffee seed trials and demonstration plots. What hampered coffee production in the district was therefore not a lack of effort or enthusiasm on the part of local growers.

Rather, the very development tools prescribed by the central government to fight imaginary laziness and resistance affected the pace of cultivation. To combat the perceived lack of discipline, modernization, and other issues, the government advocated the establishment of local coffee cooperatives that operated under the close control of the Agriculture Department.[39] The result was an underfunded and overzealous bureaucracy composed of "expert supervisors." The colonial administration also determined that coffee trials, organized around the focal point strategy, would serve as a model of success to local farmers.

Poor funding was exacerbated by the colonial state's emphasis on decentralization during the 1950s, as local institutions often had inadequate money to support extensive and efficient coffee production. Late colonial reforms intended to decentralize the state bureaucracy thus led to confusion and rivalries when it came to development funding.[40] The state's policy was for local native authorities (some of which had been "reformed" into village development committees) to work with the provincial commissioner and, when possible, for local cooperatives to enact development programs.[41] However, each organization in this equation expected the others to fund local projects, particularly as local native authorities and cooperative societies frequently ran at a deficit. The agriculture office's solution was to acknowledge the "enormous" local demand for coffee seedlings in Ngara while simultaneously suggesting that the cooperative reduce the number of seedlings and nurseries.[42] Many Ngarans who wanted to plant coffee were thus unable to do so due to a lack of seedlings.

Coffee trials also had to be recorded and supervised by field officers in the Agriculture Department. However, during the mid-1950s, there was only one properly trained field officer for Ngara, despite requests by the district commissioner and others for more staff.[43] And despite advocating for local cooperatives and participation, officials in the Agriculture Department closely monitored and supervised every decision made at the local level.[44] The process of creating and maintaining trial plots of coffee in Ngara was therefore as bureaucratically cumbersome as it was underfunded.

To the Agriculture Department, demonstration plots were essential to teach Ngarans to grow coffee through modern, approved methods. For example, the agriculture officer in Ngara spent much time and many resources discouraging the intermixture of bananas and coffee, a type of intercropping that Ngarans had practiced with success.[45] The accepted wisdom of the British "experts" was that such intercropping was detrimental to the coffee crop. This determination was as difficult to prove and enforce, as it was scientifically incorrect.[46] Furthermore, because the techniques the Agriculture Department insisted on had been designed for the territory as a whole, they were not adapted to the local climate and soil characteristics.

Another problem that plagued the development of coffee in Ngara was the district's location. With the province's main distribution center in Bukoba district, the lack of infrastructure in Ngara, particularly roads and mechanized vehicles, made the transport and marketing of Ngaran coffee very difficult.[47] The high cost of transport, when it was available at all, as well as inevitable delays often meant that coffee grown in the district never made it to government-approved buyers. Officials in Ngara noted that shipments from BCCU were beset with "perennial trouble."[48]

An overburdened and cumbersome bureaucracy, combined with a dearth of personnel, funding, and infrastructure, discouraged the bourgeoning interest in cash-crop cultivation in Ngara. Although some farmers sought opportunities for coffee production, the majority continued to migrate to Uganda to procure hard currency. This migration further hampered the growth of coffee production, as the women left in Ngara struggled to maintain their subsistence crops and their families' health, to the detriment of cash-crop cultivation. Those farmers who succeeded in growing coffee found that marketing their crops was easier, and more profitable, outside of state-imposed mechanisms of control, so they smuggled their coffee across the borders to Ruanda-Urundi and Uganda.[49] Ugandan buyers, in particular, paid higher prices for coffee in the late 1950s than their counterparts in the Tanganyika Territory. Ngarans therefore oriented their nascent coffee trade in the markets of the Great Lakes region.[50] Development, as it was conceived by colonial bureaucrats, had thus largely failed in the district—as it had throughout the territory and beyond.

Decolonization Considered

In the middle of the 1950s, something odd began to happen. In the summer of 1954, a United Nations Visiting Mission arrived in Tanganyika to tour the country and evaluate its progress in implementing the recommendations of the Trusteeship Council. In cities and villages, the mission came across people representing a new organization called the Tanganyikan African National Union (TANU). Many of TANU's members had western educations, and their leader, Julius Nyerere, was as charismatic as he was brilliant. It was at this moment that Julius Nyerere first entered the international stage. Nyerere charmed the members of the UN mission, as he would later captivate the entire UN General Assembly. A strange alliance began to take shape that summer between Nyerere, the organization that he chaired (TANU), and the UN mission. For the visiting mission, Nyerere and TANU became a tangible manifestation of the promise of Tanganyikan political development, of the potential for Africans to rule themselves.

The mission met members of the newly formed TANU at a "critical initial stage" of the organization's development.[51] Nyerere and other enterprising young Tanganyikans had recently formed TANU out of the Tanganyikan African Association (TAA).[52] Since its inception, TAA had championed the ideals of African empowerment and unity and an accelerated timetable for self-rule.[53] Although TAA had gained some rural support by championing local grievances against modernization techniques where the second colonial occupation was particularly robust, it never gained widespread popularity. Then, in 1954, a teacher from Lake Province named Julius Nyerere changed both the name and the image of TAA, creating TANU.[54]

Between 1954 and 1959, Nyerere made four trips to the United Nations. These international trips increased his reputation both in the territory and abroad. However, Nyerere realized that international pressure alone would not be enough to alter British policies.[55] Widespread support from the Tanganyikan people was also needed. The overwhelming popularity of TANU in the 1958 and 1959 elections solidified the organization's position as the vanguard of Tanganyikan politics. In part, these elections took place due to international

66 · CHAPTER 3

pressure; however, the support of the vast majority of Tanganyikans resulted from the popularity of TANU's mission of development and independence, as well as its strategic placement of political networks throughout the territory.[56]

As pressure mounted both inside and outside the territory, the British Colonial Office replaced Governor Edward Twining with Sir Richard Turnbull.[57] Turnbull had suppressed the Mau uprising in Nairobi, and he quickly took stock of the situation in Tanganyika.[58] The new governor recognized that the security forces in Tanganyika were too weak to be effective in the event of widespread civil disobedience. In addition, in Turnbull's estimation, "these chaps will be little more ready for self-government in fifty years' time than they will be in 15," which meant that it was in Britain's interest to accelerate the process of decolonization.[59] Given the poor prospects for development in the territory, Turnbull argued, it made more sense for the British administration to abdicate political control before local resentment of British rule threatened future economic partnerships.[60] Official independence occurred in December 1961.

Decolonization Experienced

The organization Nyerere had helped create won the overwhelming majority of votes in the 1959 and 1960 elections in Tanganyika, but it was slow to gain acceptance in Ngara.[61] Everyone remembers the day TANU was formed— it became a national holiday—but in general, Ngarans joined TANU rather late.[62] Although there were a few TANU programs (mostly educational) operating in Ngara, most Ngarans who joined TANU in the late 1950s and early 1960s did so because an elder male relative had previously joined.[63] Unfortunately, there is very little information on the number or distribution of new TANU members in the 1950s. The organization first took hold in urban spaces; then, as the 1950s progressed, it gained more rural support.[64]

In 1960 the first three-year development plan for independent Tanganyika was introduced. However, it was "largely a compilation" of existing programs prepared by the colonial ministries, with "no significant TANU contribution whatsoever during the preparation of the Plan."[65] Additionally, in preparation for independence, newly minted Tanganyikan governors adopted the administrative apparatus of their predecessors, thereby connecting the structure of the postcolonial state to its predecessor.[66]

When Prime Minister Nyerere took office in 1961, there was no guarantee that Tanganyika would become a peaceful country. In 1962 labor riots erupted, a military coup was attempted, and violence threatened to break out between African and Indian communities.[67] In addition, Nyerere and TANU had the overwhelming task of constructing a nation and a corresponding national identity for more than 120 different ethnic and subethnic groups in the territory. Nyerere needed to unite the country while simultaneously facing the fact that the very claims TANU had used to garner popular support could be used against a regime that was unable to deliver on its promises. In those first few years of independence, TANU leaders recognized that for national development to occur, the country needed foreign capital.[68] Unfortunately, after independence, such funds became difficult to come by. Nyerere and TANU were disappointed by British development aid, which, consisting of a £1 million development grant and an interest-free loan to cover the costs of expatriate workers, was less than anticipated.[69] Even worse, from 1963 to 1965, the real value of foreign development aid fell, and from 1965 to 1966, export price reductions led to the loss of around £25 million.[70] With dwindling funds, it was difficult to achieve the targets established by ambitious development plans.

Nevertheless, the archives provide evidence of hope and expectation in the district. With self-rule, Ngarans looked forward to a new future for themselves and their families—a future that would include access to better education and profitable cash crops. Many of these expectations were likely predicated on Nyerere's policies. He planned to forge a nation of economic equals, with economic restructuring erasing inequality between the poor and the wealthy. This would be socialism, Tanzanian style. There was a long way to go to achieve such results, however. Most Tanganyikans relied on subsistence farming, and due to drought, famine, and a drop in world prices for coffee and sisal, even those areas that did export cash crops experienced economic hardship. At the same time, Tanganyika had a growing population with a high proportion of children in need of education and sustenance. And, thanks to colonial reliance on expatriate development "experts," there was a severe lack of trained people. Indeed, in 1961 there were only twelve fully qualified doctors in the country, with a ratio of one doctor for every 875,000 people. Less than half the population was literate, and the average life expectancy was thirty to forty years.[71] In 1961 the vast majority of civil servants were expatriates.[72]

At the heart of Nyerere and TANU's development policy were the country's vast rural areas. At independence, 96 percent of the Tanganyikan population lived in rural areas, with two-thirds of the population living on only one-third of the land.[73] Administrators believed that interventions in rural agriculture—specifically, the cultivation of cash crops—were the key to development.[74] The government needed to instruct rural people in modern farming techniques; however, like its predecessors, TANU's manpower, funding, and knowledge of the territory's vast rural areas were lacking.

On the national level, Ngarans were quick to support and engage in the nation-building projects espoused by Nyerere. And yet, at the local level, Ngarans voted for rather conservative elements of society in the 1959 elections.[75] This outcome is consistent with how people felt about independence in the early 1960s. When asked how their lives had changed after 1961, most people responded that they had not changed at all. Though eager to develop their own farms after decolonization, many people continued to be unaffected, or even adversely affected, by development schemes in the early 1960s. Archival evidence points to worsening conditions in the district. There was an alleged famine during 1960 and 1961, likely rooted in the history of male migration to Uganda, as well as a lack of sufficient rainfall.[76] As a result, Ngarans struggled to find the resources necessary to feed their families.

Moreover, the "self-help" projects initiated by the Ngara District Council did not ameliorate poverty in the district. Lack of cooperation between local villages and the regional government, as well as poor funding, hampered these development initiatives. As the regional development commissioner noted, the start of self-help was all "wrong," as many projects began without proper consultation. Subsequent problems included poor building standards, impassable roads, and lack of infrastructure funding. The regional agriculture officer similarly expressed his "concern . . . at the apparent lack of liaison between the administration in Ngara" and the people it governed.[77] This inability of local and regional officials to coordinate and communicate with the people whose development they allegedly worked for continued throughout the 1960s and beyond.

The new government's approach to education would similarly disappoint Ngaran families. To meet the needs of the nation with limited resources, Nyerere and TANU made a difficult decision, prioritizing secondary schooling and university education for those few who were lucky and talented enough to be eligible. There was thus very little funding for education in Ngara, which had "one of the least developed primary school systems" in Tanganyika.[78] And primary education was what people living in Ngara district wanted perhaps more than anything.[79]

Those secondary schools that did exist were strategically placed around the country. This forced students who attended these schools to travel and interact with other people in Tanganyika, a deliberate nation-building strategy.

Developmental Disappointment · 69

Some Ngarans were able to attend secondary schools, but even for those who did not, travel within Tanganyika became a prominent feature of their lives.[80] Many Ngarans moved to cities like Mwanza to find work. All this travel contributed to a nascent social imagery in which Tanganyika became a reference for identity in Ngara district. This identity was further established by the decision to make Kiswahili the national language, although it is unclear how many people in the district actually learned or spoke the language at the time. Additionally, the 1963 abolition of the native authorities instilled a feeling of unity with other parts of Tanzania; rather than "hundreds of different leaders," there was only one leader: Nyerere.[81]

The "Man in the *Shamba*": Tobacco in Ngara, 1960–1968

The colonial state first attempted to introduce tobacco as a cash crop in Busubi in 1947.[82] However, it was not until independence that Ngaran farmers engaged in widespread tobacco cultivation. From 1960 to 1963, the number of tobacco growers in Ngara district increased from 32 to 2,022.[83] The rapid spread of tobacco cultivation in Ngara is a testament to the initial appeal of the new Tanganyikan institutions, particularly the state-supported societies that agreed to purchase and market tobacco on behalf of local farmers.

During the first years of independence, government officials frequently turned to cooperative societies and marketing boards to purchase and market small farmers' cash crops. Cooperative societies had existed during colonialism, but after independence, their number vastly increased.[84] These societies were organized from the central government down, generally with no knowledge of local contexts.[85] Additionally, illicit activities and a lack of funding hampered cooperatives' ability to fulfill their obligations to local farmers.[86]

In Ngara district, the government tasked various cooperative societies and marketing boards with setting the prices at which they would buy smallholders' tobacco prior to the harvest season. After harvest, representatives from these institutions would then collect villagers' crops at prearranged dates and locations. More often than not, however, prices and schedules were not followed—to the dismay of the district's tobacco farmers. Indeed, upon his 1963 arrival at the Nyamirembe Native Tobacco Board, tasked with purchasing tobacco from Biharamulo, Ngara, and Kibondo districts, the administrative secretary of the Kigoma region wrote that the board had no funds and was in a "desperate plight."[87] In his appeal for additional funding, the administrative secretary posited, "It is clear that unless the assistance now asked for is granted the Board will be unable to function effectively in the marketing of the present season crop. Furthermore this sad situation would so undermine confidence that untoward incidents could be expected from disappointed cultivators. . . . The requirement is Action NOW."[88] The secretary's call for urgency was not unfounded. In that same year, Ngaran farmers produced around thirty-three tons of tobacco for transport to Uganda. Of the approximately two thousand producers, only ninety had received payment by November 1963.[89]

Over the next three years, the government would place three different cooperative unions in charge of buying and selling Ngaran tobacco. These changes were due to the unions' ongoing failure to transport tobacco to Uganda (despite preapproved agreements), their "bad handling" of the crop, and the corruption (or "dirty tricks") of tobacco officials.[90] The high turnover in cooperative unions indicates the inconsistency and turmoil of tobacco marketing throughout the area.

Despite these issues and the warning of the Tanganyika Tobacco Board (TTB) that tobacco production "had not been functioning for about the last ten years [1956–1966]" in the area, local officials increased their efforts to expand tobacco cultivation in Ngara.[91] In 1966 the regional and district committees prepared a "full scale drive to increase [tobacco] production" in Ngara.[92] Officials noted that "farmers are enthusiastic to increase [tobacco] production," as long as they can be assured of better marketing institutions, prices, and grading methods.[93]

Such improvements would prove difficult, if not impossible, for the local and national governments to fund. During the tobacco harvest of 1967, the TTB refused to meet the price agreed on the previous year. Even worse, the persistent lack of infrastructure and staffing led cooperative agents to deviate from preestablished marketing schedules, and agents even refused to travel to Ngara. As a result, people in Ngara traveled long distances, sometimes for days, to preapproved market sites only to find them empty because the buyers had simply not shown up.[94]

By August 1967, the officer in charge (OIC) of the Ngara Agriculture Office wrote that farmers in the area "have lost hope" in their tobacco crop.[95] Ngaran farmers were discouraged by frequent delays and agents' reneging on purchasing schedules.[96] Frustrated by the lack of reliability and remuneration, which had become characteristic of state efforts to develop tobacco in Ngara, farmers increasingly bypassed state mechanisms for export, opting to smuggle their crops across the borders to Rwanda and Burundi.[97] As the OIC noted, "This is not their first time to be promised regarding tobacco marketing, and that is why they have decided to resume their illegal tobacco marketing."[98]

Despite all these disappointments and failures, in August 1967 the regional agriculture officer in Kigoma wrote that the TTB was still interested in encouraging tobacco in Ngara and that "no effort should be spared towards these ends."[99] And yet, barely a month later, the executive director of TTB "postponed indefinitely" any marketing efforts in Ngara and Biharamulo districts, as the expense of visiting the prearranged buying centers "exceed[ed the] total amount of money paid to growers."[100] Despite these difficulties related to logistics, corruption, and farmers' illicit trading, it was not until April 1968 that "alternative cash crops" were considered "for those areas currently dependent on tobacco as a main cash crop."[101]

In a repetition of colonial excuses, officials in Dar es Salaam blamed the failure of Ngaran tobacco on a poor-quality product grown by farmers whose "local cultures" stymied productivity. Officials did occasionally acknowledge the presence of environmental hazards, including plant diseases.[102] In so doing, however, they privileged a scientific interpretation of plant disease, one amenable to technical remedies such as pesticide spraying. While such measures may have been useful, they were also prohibitively expensive. By prioritizing a science of development, officials elided the political and economic developments necessary to the success of cash crops in Ngara district. For example, the prevalence of tobacco weevils was likely related to the long, unexpected delays between harvesting and marketing.[103] Such delays were caused by economic considerations that continued to underfund infrastructure and staff in Ngara—considerations that were often based on political priorities that allocated funds elsewhere.[104]

In the first decade of decolonization, then, Ngarans experienced little in the way of tangible improvements in their lives. Regional trade and smuggling continued across the borders of Rwanda and Burundi as the state continually broke promises of price guarantees and marketing assistance. Smuggling, however, was only one of the activities Ngarans participated in outside the confines of the new government's laws. In December 1963 the regional medical officer noted that due to the "complete breakdown of medical services in Ngara," the theft of drugs and the illegal administration of injections became common.[105] The police had trouble investigating these crimes due to the population's noncooperative attitude.[106] Illegal courts also cropped up throughout the region during the early years of independence.[107] Thus, the economic migrants who had returned to Ngara to enthusiastically

72 · CHAPTER 3

take up self-help projects and new cash crops were gravely disappointed by the absence of promised government assistance.

Conclusion

With decolonization, many Ngarans stopped traveling to Uganda for work and engaged in self-help projects and village development committees. This participation indicates a local awareness of, and enthusiasm for, the rhetoric of nation building espoused by the central government.[108] However, much of their work existed only on paper and in the promises of the new government—the majority of which went unfulfilled. People in Ngara who took part in development projects often found their efforts thwarted by cumbersome and paternalistic bureaucracies. The gap between local needs and state programs and promises led to Ngarans' refusal to conform to the flawed plans of both the colonial and postcolonial states. Ngarans then sought alternatives to the failed marketing and export programs of their new state within the regional economy, as they had before and would again.

The material nature of life in Ngara remained more or less the same during and after decolonization, as was amply expressed in interviews. Taxes still had to be paid, and land had to be cleared, planted, and harvested. The lack of schooling continued to be a problem, and parents still scrimped and saved to send their children to primary and, more rarely, secondary schools. Bush pigs and lions still menaced people's farms, as did outbreaks of sleeping sickness, due to the perennial lack of funding for bush clearance and tsetse fly removal. Malaria continued to threaten a population in need of health clinics and doctors. People still yearned for seeds to plant both old and new crops—seeds long promised but seldom delivered by either the colonial or the postcolonial government. And tellingly, both governments failed to provide the promised cash-crop improvements—in fact, the new government's failure in this respect exceeded that of the colonial government.

Although lived experiences at the local level belied governmental promises, the corruption and failure of regional organizations and officials did not necessarily affect Ngarans' views of the central government. They had pride in their new leader and hope for the future. Despite the largely unfulfilled promises of quality-of-life improvements, Ngarans were quick to praise the independence movement and the president who led it. While much of this feeling of nationalism had to do with the presence of refugees and aid agencies in the district, it also had to do with the ideology of the new central government—if not the seldom delivered pledges of development at the local level. In response to such failures, Ngarans once again turned to the economy of the Great Lakes region—smuggling cash crops across the borders of Rwanda and Burundi and, in the process, refusing to conform to development plans that could not meet their needs.[109]

It is difficult to periodize history. When did colonialism stop and independence begin? When, where, and to whom did it matter? The next part of this book explores how early independence policies attempted to secure people within geographies of control developed through particular notions of nationalism and progress. At the edges of the Great Lakes region, this translated into containment policies for tens of thousands of people who would be transformed from migrants to refugees. At the edges of the state, authorities struggled to be relevant to a population on the move. New transnational entities emerged from World War II and the displacement crisis in Europe to alter the balance of power and the meaning of development in the region. Throughout the years, however, the borders set by the Permanent Mandates Commission, the British, and the Belgians remained. In the decades that followed, people, goods, and ideas would continue to flow, unauthorized, across those borders. The themes analyzed in this first part will continue throughout the chapters to come: the legacy of a border never fully realized or denied; the creation of containment camps located at strategic boundaries, ignored and refused by people searching for a way of life other than that prescribed by authorities; and *development* as the byword of a government yearning for justification and control.

PART II
THE MAKING OF REFUGEES

4. DEVELOPMENTAL REFUGEES

THE POLITICS OF RWANDAN REFUGEE SETTLEMENT

IN NGARA DISTRICT, 1959–1969

Rwandans began trickling into Ngara district during 1959. These people were different from the migrant laborers who had come through the district in the past. They were women and elderly, men and children, leaders and civilians, farmers and herders. In the first few years from 1959 to 1962, they arrived in small groups from the Rwandan and Burundian sides of the Kagera River. There they paid local boaters or took a ferry to Ngara. Sometimes they swam. Occasionally, Father Van der Meeren of the Catholic mission in Rulenge would ferry people across the river. Many of these new arrivals were tired, hungry, and without friends. Others came with herds of cattle. Some lived with family and friends throughout West Lake Province (WLP), becoming in UNHCR parlance "spontaneously settled."

They moved throughout the area, occasionally remaining in villages such as Ntobeye, on the border of the Bugufi chiefdom and Rwanda. Others left the district entirely and found other Banyaruanda who had entered Tanganyika through Karagwe district. Many who came to Ngara had traveled south through Burundi first and then moved east to seek more advantageous living conditions.[1] A few even found their way across the new nation, settling in cities such as Mwanza and even Dar es Salaam. Most people stayed within WLP, however. In some places, such as the area that would become Missenye district, local leaders gave the refugees land to settle on. A web of connected Banyaruanda communities, varying in size from a few people to whole villages, sprang up throughout the province—as they were doing throughout the Great Lakes region.[2]

These refugees, as they would come to be called in Ngara, existed in the seams of decolonization and a burgeoning, often floundering, international aid regime. They represented the arrival of a new era in Ngara district, one in which the international and national often bumped against the local and regional. At a time when the nation-state was coming into existence in sub-Saharan Africa, refugees became actors and subjects in popular reimaginings of borders and identity. Such refugees also became instrumental to national development planning in Ngara district. As government officers sought to stabilize and centralize refugees in village settlement programs, they hoped the district and the nation would benefit from international refugee aid as well as Rwandan labor.

Concurrently, and in response to the perceived threat of unregulated refugee circulation, British officials increased their military presence along Ngara's borders. In attempting to police the borders of the new nation-state, they continued and enhanced the control measures for migrants begun during the colonial period. These efforts to control and stabilize migrants, now deemed refugees, continued through the first years of Tanzanian independence, indicating how colonial security forces attempted to securitize borders in the postcolonial and Cold War world—an effort that requires further study and complicates the neat periodization of African histories into "pre" and "post" colonial periods. Such actions also reveal how colonial anxieties around border control affected the treatment of the new nation-states' "rejects," who now became the objects of not only humanitarian but also military concern.[3]

Rwandan movements not only threatened the geopolitical stability of the Tanzanian state and the Great Lakes region, but also the development aims of national and international officials. International policymakers understood the refugees as a problem to be solved through villagization and settlement. Similarly, national leaders viewed Rwandan refugees through a lens of developmental opportunity. Both sets of officials conceived of refugees as passive actors to be controlled and utilized within carefully demarcated

78 · CHAPTER 4

development plans. As such, they elided the inherently complex, political, and diverse nature of refugee groups. Government and UNHCR officials then blamed all problems related to refugee settlement on a small group of refugee leaders seen as troublemakers, thereby occluding the very real political and material motivations of refugees' actions. In the midst of the Cold War and decolonization, the Tanzanian and British governments, as well as the myriad agencies involved in refugee aid, all had different political motivations for aiding (and securing) Rwandan refugees.

The Making of Rwandan Refugees

Near the end of Belgian colonization in Ruanda-Urundi, a group of educated Hutu gained power and recognition through the support of the Belgian political and military establishment as well as the Catholic Church. This group was led by Grégoire Kayibanda, a Hutu who advocated a political and social policy against the Tutsi (described as nonindigenous invaders from Ethiopia) and favored Hutu rule.[4] As we have seen, the Belgians had elevated a small portion of Tutsi monarchists to carry out Belgian law and reap the benefits of colonization. By the end of colonization, most Tutsi and Hutu held equivalent economic positions, but the prestige and power afforded a small Tutsi elite had angered the disenfranchised and brutalized Hutu population.[5] When some Tutsi leaders attempted to facilitate immediate independence in the mid-1950s, the Belgians switched their allegiance to the nascent Hutu elite.[6] The struggle over independence took place between these two unequally matched groups. Initial violence in 1959 resulted in the first wave of Tutsi exiles, some of whom left Rwanda to regroup and enable a Tutsi coup. From 1959 to 1964, about 150,000 Rwandan refugees fled into the neighboring states of the Great Lakes region and beyond.[7]

From across the borders of neighboring nations, some Tutsi leaders orchestrated raids into Rwandan territory, ostensibly to restore *Mwami* Kigeri V to power. Estimates of the number of incursions into Rwanda from asylum nations vary.[8] What is clear is that from 1960 to 1964, these armed cross-border raids resulted in violence and chaos within and without the new nation-state of Rwanda. This "exile politics" resulted in the deaths of small numbers of Hutu at the expense of tens of thousands of Tutsi, who were targeted by the regime in violent reprisals.[9] These raids, called *inyenzi* (cockroach) raids by the new Rwandan government—a dehumanizing term that would be taken up by callous regional and international actors— resulted in even more Rwandan Tutsi fleeing the state in search of safety.[10]

Developmental Refugees · 79

The people who came to be called Rwandan refugees in Ngara district traversed multiple boundaries. Most obviously, they moved across the borders of two colonies involved in accelerated moments of state creation. In so doing, they physically crossed a border created by European bureaucrats—one that people had traversed since time immemorial. By the end of the 1950s, however, colonialism in the Great Lakes region was coming to an end. The leaderships of the two new nations-states of Tanzania and Rwanda were actively involved in not just the demise of colonialism but also the creation of new national cultures and citizenries. In crossing into Ngara, Banyaruanda encountered a space of socialist ideas (if not always reality) about self-help, equality, and development. This space was populated by migrants, many of whom were returning to Ngara to assume the role of citizen-farmer—of Tanzanian.

Physically, the eventual containment of refugees within camps and settlements necessitated the crossing of an environmental boundary. The new government purposefully placed refugee settlements in wilderness areas—in the bush. By eventually moving into camps and settlements, Banyaruanda physically remade the landscape of Ngara district into one that was seemingly more at ease with national and international notions of development. With this movement, the refugees became crucial to development schemes for Ngara district, schemes that required governmental control over refugee labor and movement.

Most frequently, refugees crossed and contested the boundaries of authority in Ngara district. These included the borders of refugee settlements, district borders, and international boundaries of the rapidly decolonizing Great Lakes region. In their movements, refugees transgressed the national and international laws promulgated to make them stationary and subject them to transnational and national control. Time after time, national and international attempts to halt popular circulation in Ngara district were frustrated, as they had been in the past and would be in the future. However, for the first time, Rwandan regional circulation became construed locally and nationally as inimical to national progress and stability. Refugee circulation also provoked the ire of national and international actors, who resorted to increasingly draconian measures to control Rwandans in Ngara and Tanzania.

Thus, during their first few years of residence in Ngara, most Rwandans did not follow the commands of the various authorities involved in their so-called aid. Refugees moved throughout the region for a variety of reasons, including the maintenance and extension of business and family networks. Refugee circulation was also the result of individuals' and groups' commitment to make their own choices, particularly by comparing the quality of life in different areas. Most threatening to a Tanzanian state devoted to peaceful relations with its neighbors was some refugee leaders' ambition to replace the Parmehutu (Parti du Mouvement et de l'Emancipation du Hutu) regime in Rwanda with a Tutsi-led government.

Operation Book In

Roy Zandemar Stockwell, of Her Majesty's Special Branch, spent a year from May 1962 to April 1963 traveling the border between Ruanda-Urundi and Tanzania.[11] He was tasked with finding Rwandan refugees, a project that required long journeys by car and on foot, traveling for hours through the bush with local guides.[12] Once they were found, he reported the location, number, and status of the Rwandans, including how and when they had crossed into Tanzania. His mission, which began five months after Tanzania's official independence, was called Operation Book In.

What was this British officer doing in Ngara, a peripheral district in Tanzania, five months after independence? The presence of British military officials tasked with surveilling Rwandan refugees during the early 1960s in Ngara district tells us much about the politics of decolonization. The creation of nation-states in the Great Lakes region generated the first refugees there. The fact that these refugees were of such interest to the British military speaks to the perceived danger of refugee movements in these pivotal moments when political boundaries and responsibilities, as well as historical periods, are blurred.

For the British, Rwandan migrants threatened the harmony of the region—and indeed, the empire—at a time when the political futures of Tanzania, Rwanda, and Burundi were unknown. Certainly, the specter of the Congo crisis—the violence, instability, and communist threats following the independence of the Belgian Congo in 1960—loomed over the decolonizing world.[13] There were rumors among the British colonial elite that Rwanda, Burundi, or both would consider some sort of political or economic union with Tanzania—leading to unpredictability and perhaps violence in a territory with which the British hoped to remain economically allied.[14] In 1959 the future of Ruanda-Urundi was worryingly uncertain, with political violence escalating and rumors of communist influence over refugee groups growing. The British were even more concerned about the implications of large refugee groups in the Uganda protectorate and the Tanganyika Territory.[15]

Developmental Refugees · 81

As these migrations increased, so did British concern. In August 1961, on the eve of Tanzanian independence and elections in both Rwanda and Burundi, the British initiated Operation Book In. In part out of fear of armed refugees entering Tanzania, who would likely be followed by Belgian forces, the British government sent elements of the King's African Rifles (KAR) to northwestern Tanganyika, later augmented by police, field force units, and Special Branch detachments.[16] The British goal was to create a temporary "Border Province," which would include the districts of Kasulu, Kibondo, Kigoma, Karagwe, and Ngara, and to "maintain peace and good government in the border area by the orderly control of refugees and . . . the prevention of violation of the Tanganyika border with Ruanda Urundi."[17] The joint military-police-administrative force then set up headquarters in Ngara district, the nexus of the refugee presence in Tanzania.

This force, created to prevent the "violation" of borders, was to carry out reconnaissance of likely crossing points and control these areas "to the extent possible."[18] This need to defend the border through the surveillance and control of refugees had its origin in earlier attempts to canalize migrants in the region—attempts that had now evolved from migrant labor control to the control of noncitizens. These attempts signal the importance of border control to the maintenance of the sovereign nation-states ushered into being during decolonization.[19] Motivated not only by the fear of armed gangs but also by "reliable reports" that Rwandan Tutsi leaders were being trained by the communist-leaning Armée Nationale Congolaise (ANC) in the Congo, the force was also sent to prevent the spread of communism into Tanzania.[20] As with the creation of canalization routes and containment camps during the late colonial period, however, the members of Operation Book In would be unable to control migration across Tanzania's long, permeable border with Ruanda-Urundi.

To aid their efforts on the border, in 1959 and 1960 the British Trust government appealed to the Belgians to halt the flow of refugees or at least to participate in their care. It soon became clear that such help would not be forthcoming.[21] Fearing a loss of reputation in the United Nations, whose General Assembly now included an influx of newly independent African states, the British government was unsure how to proceed. As violence increased in Rwanda, and the Belgian Trust government seemed unable or unwilling to staunch the bloodshed, the British hoped that some sort of UN operation, possibly led by the newly independent African states, might intervene.[22] Regardless of the outcome, it was clear to both British and Belgian diplomats alike that in

82 · CHAPTER 4

the wake of decolonization, a "UN presence in this part of Africa" was likely "for many years to come."[23] On this point, they would be proved right.

The trickle of people showing up in towns and villages throughout WLP began to grow larger by late 1961 and early 1962, just as Tanzanians celebrated their official independence from Britain. To British and, later, transnational officials involved in aiding Rwandan refugees, as well as many scholars since then, the refugees were thought of as a coherent mass comprising an elite group of cattle herders. Aid workers identified these people as the Nilotic Tutsi—the tall, intelligent former leaders of Rwanda who were unfamiliar with agricultural work, as they had previously relied on their Hutu servants.[24] The diary of Stockwell, the British officer tasked with surveilling the border, tells a much more nuanced story.

From Stockwell's diary, we catch glimpses of poor and rich refugees alike, "straggling up the road from the border," many having walked as far as Kigali, the Rwandan capital. This is a story of not only Tutsi but also of Hutu, of those who had lived "much more civilized lives" and those whose lives had been "much more primitive" in Rwanda.[25] Some of these travelers had fled displacement camps in Rwanda, describing how government forces had attacked them one by one until they fled in terror, "practically starving" and in "broken families."[26] There were those who had crossed in canoes below Rusumo Falls and lived in small settlements "for many miles" along the Tanzanian side of the Ruvuvu and Kagera Rivers, a "pleasant, clean and friendly lot."[27]

The archives tell the stories of indigent refugees unwanted by the Burundian government, which forced them onto trucks headed for Tanzania. They were frequently joined by lorries hired by Church Missionary Society (CMS) missions in Burundi, which were unable to care for the refugees arriving in ever-increasing numbers.[28] Many of these trucks were then turned away at the border by a government unwilling to assume the expense of caring for so many poor and desperate people.[29] Some continued the journey to Tanzania on foot. We also glimpse Rwandan Tutsi and Hutu traveling north through Uganda and then south to Bukoba and Ngara, searching for the best opportunities.[30] We find traces of other individuals who traveled throughout the region, organizing military training and attacks against the new Rwandan state. What all these people had in common was not a singular way of life but their treatment as Rwandan refugees—as a people apart and in need of not only help but also control. This segregation would boost the development of a Rwandan identity forged not only in exile but also in encampment and therefore in difference.

Developmental Refugees · 83

Decolonization, Development, and the UNHCR: The Making of Rwandan Refugee Settlements

It is unclear at what point Nyerere and the new government determined that Rwandans constituted refugees and therefore potential beneficiaries of international aid.[31] On the one hand, some of the newcomers were in need of help. Many arrived with no food or livestock. Additionally, parts of Ngara experienced famine-like conditions in the early 1960s, and the increased population likely increased the burden on local farmers. On the other hand, the thousands of Rwandan refugees crossing the border presented Nyerere with a significant political problem. He wanted to show Rwanda and other independent African nations that Tanzania respected their sovereignty as new nation-states in control of their own borders and citizenries. He had to do this while living with the threat of refugee attacks into Rwanda across the hundreds of miles of unregulated borderland in WLP. Rwandan refugees were therefore an uncomfortable fit within Nyerere's open-door policy for refugees: as a strong supporter of Pan-African liberation movements in southern Africa, Tanzania would eventually welcome refugees and exile groups from those areas fighting for decolonization.[32] Rwandans, in fleeing a decolonizing African state, presented a different problem for Nyerere, one whose potential for militarization had to be controlled. Additionally, Nyerere feared that the refugees would spread ethnic violence into the "peripheral areas" of Tanzania.[33]

For Nyerere, development was a way to achieve nationhood, unity, and equality.[34] The goal of international aid bureaucracies, including the UNHCR, was much more modest: solving the refugee "problem" in one of three ways, with the applicable solution in Ngara being settlement and self-sufficiency. To achieve this goal, bureaucrats first needed to make the refugee population "legible" and amenable to containment and control.[35] As aid workers, government officials, and foreign military officers counted, registered, and situated refugees, they enforced an illusionary regime of control, one in which international and national authorities were frequently crossed.

If the ultimate goals of national development policy and those of the transnational aid community diverged, their ideas about the meaning of agricultural development and how it could be achieved were remarkably similar.[36] In essence, both national and international officials believed that by combining careful land use and refugee labor in scientific agricultural development programs, both the refugees and the land would become productive, thus helping to develop the new nation as a whole. The refugees would contribute the labor for these projects in return for rations and their own development. There was only one problem: many refugees were not interested in farming or in the development of Tanzania. Especially during their first few years of residence, many Rwandans believed that their stay in Tanzania was temporary. Additionally, many were Tutsi cattle herders who were reluctant to become farmers.[37] For those accustomed to farming, distrust of local authorities and inconsistent food and seed supplies made the often cited goal of self-sufficiency impossible to reach. It was in this context that the UNHCR first began aiding Rwandan refugees in Tanzania.

To understand why the UNHCR became so involved in the African Great Lakes region during decolonization, we need to examine the history of the agency itself. Today, it seems self-evident that the UN would create an agency responsible for protecting the world's refugees, but during the 1960s, the primacy and utility of the agency were anything but certain. The UNHCR was just one in a long series of temporary transnational agencies created since 1921 to ameliorate the plight of displaced people. The scope of these agencies' activities was usually delineated by geographic area and specified time frames, as in the case of Russian refugees after World War I. The end of World War II, however, ushered in a new phase of international aid to refugees. The devastation in Europe, and the corresponding displacement of millions of people, necessitated large-scale efforts to aid displaced populations.[38] The newly formed UN therefore created temporary agencies to protect, control, and repatriate millions of Europeans displaced by the war. The United States and United Kingdom, which largely funded these organizations, did so not only to help victims of the war but also to mitigate the threat of refugees, who were seen as mentally debilitated and dangerous. Displaced Persons camps were based on the military camp model, which underscored refugees' potential threat to the borders and ideologies of sovereign nation-states.[39] Simultaneously, a new Geneva Convention on refugees was ratified, defining refugees as temporally and geographically bound to events in Europe during World War II.[40]

Creation of the UNHCR was not popular among the new superpowers.[41] Until the early 1990s, the issue of refugees remained tangled in the politics of a new world order—that of the Cold War. The Soviet Union understood the UNHCR, like its predecessors, as a tool of the Western powers. In contrast, American policymakers perceived the whole UN system as subject to communist influence.[42] As a result, the United States promulgated its own institutions to aid and encourage flight from Soviet-controlled countries.[43]

US perceptions of the UNHCR as a tool of international politics began to change in the 1950s, particularly after the UNHCR's aid to Hungarian refugees fleeing the 1956 Soviet invasion.[44] The UNHCR reacted quickly and efficiently to that crisis, obtaining funds from Western governments eager to aid Hungarian refugees, whose flight they perceived as an assault on Soviet ideology. The first years of the UNHCR's existence were therefore marked by East-West tensions and subsequent political maneuvering in Europe.[45] By the end of the 1950s, however, the agency was faced with the first refugees created by decolonization in Africa. Soon, the decolonizing world, and sub-Saharan Africa in particular, became one of the UNHCR's main theater of operations.

New problems require new solutions and breed new possibilities. In this case, the first new refugee problem occurred in North Africa—where thousands of people fled anticolonial violence, and subsequent reprisals, in Algeria.[46] The situation was ripe for Soviet and American Cold War strategies of division. By providing aid to African refugees, the United States hoped to gain credibility and support among the fastest growing bloc of UN delegates, thereby facilitating its anticommunist agenda.[47] As the UNHCR's policies and funding expanded in the late 1950s, the High Commissioner used the "good offices" clause of the UNHCR statute to justify the expansion of programs beyond the original parameters.[48] From this brief history, we can discern the UNHCR not only as a humanitarian agency but also as a tool wielded by its funders for their own objectives. Although the agency would attempt to advance its own agenda over the next thirty years, it would continue to be hamstrung by the economic and political goals of its contributors.[49] In the African Great Lakes region during the 1960s, the agency encountered its first large-scale refugee crisis in sub-Saharan Africa, and due to the threat of communism in the region and the potential for violence, it piqued the interest of the great powers.[50]

In October 1961 the Tanzanian government first availed itself of the UNHCR's "good offices" to request funding to care for the more than six thousand Rwandan refugees then in Tanzania.[51] The League of Red Cross Societies (LRCS) too became involved in the effort to aid Rwandans in Tanzania. During the early 1960s, its main area of operations in sub-Saharan Africa was in the Congo, caring for both Rwandan refugees in the east and refugees along the Angolan border. However, as the situation for Rwandan refugees in the four main countries of asylum (Congo-Zaire, Burundi, Uganda, and Tanzania) worsened, LRCS operations bled into Rwanda and Tanzania.[52] The international community had a limited understanding of the political nature

86 · CHAPTER 4

of refugees, and both the UNHCR and the LRCS were devoted to predetermined, untailored "solutions" to the refugee problem.[53] Such technical solutions would fit poorly with the political and economic realities of refugee populations.

Simultaneously, leaders in Tanzania found themselves in a difficult spot vis-à-vis their promises of progress. As we have seen, development aid decreased following British decolonization, and there were few trained African civil servants in the country, forcing the government to rely on an expatriate staff that it could ill afford. In addition to the army rebellion in 1964, students had gone on strike in Dar es Salaam, and a communist revolution rocked the stability of neighboring Zanzibar.[54] The prospects for peace and prosperity seemed grim in a country with more than 120 different ethnic groups. Yet Nyerere and TANU held fast to a vision of a reorganized population that would work together to reclaim the land and so the future. The plan hinged on the country's vast tracts of seemingly empty land that, if populated, would lead Tanzania to increased productivity, industrialization, and achievement of that magical if ephemeral goal: development.[55]

Nyerere believed that only through economic and social development would his country become a nation. Development required manpower, however, and funds. In the sparsely populated and underfunded WLP, refugees and international refugee aid could perhaps solve these problems. And indeed, Rwandan refugees and international aid helped in the development of Ngara district. Particularly in the vermin-infested and tsetse fly–prone areas of Busubi, internationally funded refugee settlements contributed to the local economy, such as by clearing large tracts of land. However, Nyerere and the government envisioned that refugee settlements would operate as development villages—just like those voluntary development villages the state was attempting, unsuccessfully, to establish throughout the nation.[56]

Funding, labor, and development were all vital to the leadership's vision of what Tanzania should be. In many ways, the international community's ultimate goals for refugees in Ngara were similar to the national government's goals for Tanzania, including communities' achievement of self-reliance through self-help and farming. Economic equality was another shared goal, with each refugee having the same amount of land, seed, fertilizer, and supervision. In theory, the refugee camp would embody Tanzanian socialism on a small scale. However, as Nyerere discovered when he instituted *ujamaa* (forced villagization), the ideals of self-sufficiency, equality, and self-help require coercion and control. And often, induce resistance.

Developmental Refugees · 87

Self-Settlement and Absorption: The Making of Busubi, 1959–1962

In the early years of Rwandan arrival, many people in WLP shared whatever food and shelter they could afford. Tanzanian generosity to refugees is heralded in the literature, and from villages in Ngara and Biharamulo to those further north in Karagwe and Bukoba, many people were eager to help. Sharing similar languages and cultures, refugees often worked on local *shamba* and connected with earlier migrants as well as friends and families in the region.

Tanzanian officials viewed these newcomers through a lens of opportunity.[57] In 1959 and 1960 Bahangaza and Basubi still consistently left Ngara to work in Uganda. As a result, the few areas the colonial Agriculture Department had managed to clear of tsetse bush returned to wilderness.[58] Rwandan refugees represented a population of people who could help development in the district by settling, clearing, and farming the relatively depopulated areas of Ngara.

Since the colonial period, officials had expressed an interest in settling people in Busubi.[59] Those who lived in Busubi tended to reside in scattered areas between the swamplands and tsetse fly zones. The lack of infrastructure, particularly roads, forestalled governmental attempts at settlement, as had persistent male migration to Uganda. Moreover, the area was rife with dangerous animals such as lions, buffalo, and bush pigs. And as we have seen, the newly independent government's attempts to promote tobacco production in the area had failed, leaving behind broken promises and increased illicit trade.

In light of these ongoing issues, the leaders of Ngara and the region bemoaned the lack of development in the district. Roads were needed, as were clean water, hunters, and seeds. Nyerere had set up provincial development committees throughout the country, aiming to increase local self-sufficiency and land development. However, leaders who attended meetings of the WLP development committee in 1961 remarked that, without greater central government funding, it would be impossible to build the roads and distribute the materials necessary to enact the self-help programs the government deemed essential for development in Ngara.[60]

The newly arrived Rwandans were potential sources of manpower; they represented a chance to bring to fruition development schemes to eradicate tsetse flies and settle farmers, to make the land profitable and the people self-sufficient. Indeed, the settlement schemes envisioned for refugees mirrored the criteria for new development villages throughout the country.[61] And it could all be done with international funding. Nyerere himself sat in on a provincial team meeting in November 1961, during which the anticipated deficit for 1962 was reportedly raised from £400,000 to £2,000,000 and the leadership voiced their hope for additional international loans and grants.[62] At this same meeting, provincial officers discussed the donations received from the international community on behalf of Rwandans—a discussion aptly labeled in the official minutes "Position Regarding Development Projects."[63]

During the meeting, regional and national leaders referred to the Rwandans as "permanent settlers" who could be integral to the district's development. Thus, the provincial tsetse officer "expressed the hope that more settlers after the original group now proposed . . . would follow so that the area should be adequately occupied and the return of tsetse prevented." In this case, the deputy provincial commissioner noted that any additional settlers to Ntobeye should be locals, so as not to invite "inter-territorial incidents" by Rwandans.[64] Nevertheless, the notion of Rwandan settlers supplying much-needed development aid to Ngara district and to the broader region must have been in the air that day. The same deputy provincial commissioner later noted that "the area near Rulenge would prove satisfactory" for refugee settlement.[65]

Correspondence from the fall of 1962 indicates the local government's willingness to absorb the Rwandans into district development plans and thus into the Tanzanian nation-state.[66] Officials therefore invoked the ideals of the new nation when discussing the Rwandans' future. As the regional extension officer wrote to his superiors in Dar es Salaam, "I envisage a settlement which will encourage and enable the refugees to become useful Tanganyika citizens. . . . Furthermore the refugees will psychologically feel that they are Tanganyika citizens and be loyal to Tanganyika."[67] Clearly, many residents felt similarly, as evidenced by the outpouring of appeals from local people, and even chiefs, for clothing, rations, and seeds for the refugees in their areas.

However, from 1962 to 1964, the number of Banyaruanda entering Ngara and WLR grew exponentially.[68] The generosity of the local people could stretch only so far, particularly as Ngara itself experienced food shortages during 1960 and 1962.[69] Ngarans traveled to Burundi just to buy millet, a grain not usually favored in the area. The few resources provided by the international community to aid these newcomers rapidly became inadequate.[70]

Settling the Rwandans led to other problems as well. Some of the areas they attempted to settle were already overpopulated. And, more gratingly to a people doused in a national ethic of self-sufficiency and development, many perceived the refugees to be lazy, unproductive people. Protests from Bukoba town against the presence of the refugees became more common in official correspondence by 1962.[71] Complaints from residents and government officials throughout the region about the poor quality of refugee work became louder and more frequent.[72] As early as 1960, officials in Bukoba and Biharamulo complained to the central government that refugees were "unwilling to work" and were a "less industrious type who normally will not be easily settled."[73] To be fair, the refugees were not always able to work, as they were constrained by the seasonality of farming and local farmers' reluctance to employ refugees during the off-season.[74] Additionally, employment officers would not extend industrial (sisal) work to the newcomers, as few jobs existed for Tanzanians.[75] Tellingly, these constraints on refugee employment were rarely addressed in official correspondence.

Perhaps because of these issues, soon after Rwandans began to arrive in the region, the native authorities demanded a system to register aliens. As early as October 1961, the provincial commissioner requested each district to "telegram every Saturday (A) total refugees [in] your district (B) total refugees being sent [to camps] (C) total money expended."[76] This was the first salvo in an ongoing campaign to account for, and thus make legible, refugees in the region.

Muyenzi: From Reception to Settlement Camp, 1959–April 1963

In 1959 officials started to lay out a trading center at Rulenge in the Busubi area of Ngara. This area was already a center for the Catholic Church and would soon become the administrative center for ten thousand Rwandans.[77] It would be an experiment in development policy and refugee settlement.

The Muyenzi refugee settlement began as a transit camp in October 1961.[78] Government officials then hoped the refugees would stay in the area, clear the land, and become self-sufficient. Eventually, authorities transferred Rwandans residing in smaller camps to the larger, "permanent" settlements of Muyenzi in Busubi and Kimuli/Nkwenda in Karagwe district.[79] It is unknown how many Rwandans refused to go and evaded efforts to settle them in camps.

Of central concern to authorities was the possibility that refugee militarization would involve Tanzania in the violent and chaotic instability of the Great Lakes region. As a February 1963 telegram from the central government to the Ngara police noted, "President Nyerere [is] disturbed by [the] presence [of] inyenzi and other subversive elements" who attempted

90 · CHAPTER 4

the "violent overthrow" of the Rwandan government.[80] These mobile refugees were a potential threat to Tanzania's peaceful relations with its neighbors. Tanzanian concern over *inyenzi* groups in WLR extended beyond Rwandans in Ngara to those residing in neighboring countries as well. Following an incendiary speech by Milton Obote, the prime minister of Uganda, Second Vice President Kawawa asked officials to ensure that Rwandan refugees in Uganda did not enter Tanganyika, as it would be contrary to "its relationship with its independent neighbor." If any refugees did cross into WLR from Uganda, they were to be made "known" to government officials and "made to return."[81]

Despite its proximity to the border, the Muyenzi area seemed like a suitable place for the settlement of Rwandan refugees, as it was, "generally speaking . . . topographically, environimentally [*sic*] and ecologically similar to their own country."[82] Not everyone in the local administration agreed that Muyenzi would be a productive space for Rwandan settlement, however. The regional extension officer wrote that because of the area's remote location, in addition to the terrain's unsuitability for coffee production, the refugees would need to follow a rigorous and "fully intergrated [*sic*] farming system."[83] In light of these difficulties, the officer noted that it would be better for the government to settle the refugees outside WLR entirely. His suggestion went unheeded.

By November 1961, Rwandans had started building their own camp in the area.[84] In the fall of 1962, the government gave the refugees at Muyenzi some land for cultivation, in the hope that they would "farm communally."[85] However, they made only "spasmodic attempts at cultivation."[86] Nevertheless, local and national government officials hoped the refugees would be self-supporting by the end of 1962.

By November 1962, however, the refugees had not made any progress toward becoming self-supporting. Even worse, the population in Muyenzi had grown to seven thousand people, with the expectation that another three thousand to four thousand refugees from other areas would settle there.[87] Muyenzi was situated far from viable roads and administrative centers, so it was extremely difficult to obtain everything from petrol to paper and ledger books (for registering refugees).[88] Nevertheless, government officials began to demarcate plots of ten acres for each Rwandan family.[89] The demarcation and survey of settlement areas required an "estimated . . . 70 men per day for 4½ months at a rate of shs 2/75 per day" for the construction of about one hundred miles of internal roads, access roads, and waterways.[90] In addition, the government had reconnoitered eighty square miles of Ngara district in search of water sources.[91] These large projects were overseen by the Ministry of Agriculture and dependent on both governmental expertise and refugee labor.[92]

All this work had been carried out with national and international funding and had contributed to the area's legibility to the government, which did not even possess maps of the district. However, it had also been done with extreme reluctance on the part of the refugees who sporadically supplied labor to the various water and demarcation schemes. Local officials' frustration with the refugees can be glimpsed throughout the Tanzanian National Archives, particularly in correspondence regarding the provision of water. In June 1962 a field officer complained about the expansion of the Muyenzi camp beyond its original perimeters and the "appalling amount of human excrement" along the local stream, despite an adequate number of latrines. According to the officer, the refugees bathed and washed laundry upstream, "against the express instructions of the camp authorities."[93] Predictably, the drinking water at Muyenzi became polluted.

International agencies, such as the Food and Agriculture Organization (FAO), donated funds to supply the refugee settlement with adequate water. Not all local officials were happy about this aid, however. D. W. Edwards, the agriculture officer in charge, wrote that "not one of the settlement areas is seriously short of water." As for the £40,000 donated by the FAO for the provision of water, Edwards did "not consider that such a large sum of money is necessary and . . . it is out of proportion to the needs of the refugees."[94] Another official noted that many of the refugees' complaints were "exaggerated as to water supply and quite out of line with what local farmers can endure."[95] Poor conditions at Muyenzi during the previous rainy season added to the tension, as government officials complained about inadequate housing and delayed salary payment.[96]

Perhaps even more frustrating to the government was the refugees' refusal to follow orders and settle in the areas demarcated. Local and national officials blamed the lack of refugee cultivation on a few troublemakers, or *jumbes* (leaders). To increase refugee productivity and compliance, officials attempted to split up such individuals and send them to different settlements around the Muyenzi camp.[97] By March 1963, the Agriculture Department had demarcated more than fifteen settlement villages throughout the area around Muyenzi. However, in settlements such as Kanyina 1 and Mbuba 1, the refugees refused to stay and returned to the original camp.[98] Others refused to sleep in the new settlements, returning to Muyenzi each night.

Those individuals who refused to cooperate with Muyenzi authorities often had their *posho* (rations) withdrawn.[99] Government officials also responded by temporarily closing primary schools and dispensaries and by prohibiting mass gatherings. As a result, many individuals and groups began stealing from seed stocks in Muyenzi and beyond.[100]

While national and international actors tended to perceive the Rwandan refugees as pawns being manipulated by a few dangerous political leaders, others noted that the refugees did not constitute a homogeneous group.[101] Scholars who lived and worked in the settlements delineated the political, economic, and geographic tensions within the Rwandan community in exile.[102] Most leaders of the refugee group were part of the Union National Rwandaise (UNAR), which had been formed to contest, unsuccessfully, the 1961 Rwandan elections.[103] Despite this seemingly united refugee political elite, factionalism among leaders and divisions in the population were part of the political lives of refugees in all nations of asylum or exile. In Ngara, such political divisions involved a "traditional conservative Tutsi elite," who had benefited from the political power of the *Mwami* and the royal clan, and those "educated Tutsi" who were in favor of democratic reform.[104] Both leaderships favored repatriation and a restoration of the monarchy; however, the extremists advocated a policy of armed attack, while moderate leaders had more faith in peaceful repatriation and a power-sharing agreement, ostensibly under the auspices of the United Nations. These two sides coalesced, particularly from 1960 to 1963, over the question of dispersal. Both groups desired to remain together for "both physical and psychological security" in the face of governmental efforts to disperse the population.[105]

There were also distinct economic inequalities within the refugee group, which included Hutu as well as Tutsi. Wealthy refugees were able to obtain cattle from Sukumaland and Burundi.[106] Most of the group's leaders had gone to secondary school and spoke French, the language of the colonizers, indicating a high level of education and likely prior economic wealth.[107] These individuals had the skills aid groups looked for when seeking people to work with. Within the refugee group there were also teachers and doctors, businessmen and laborers. Indeed, the group as such referred more to an imagined collective history of pastoral rule than actual equality. When refugees voted for their leaders, they largely chose individuals they were familiar with, those who had been in charge in Rwanda.[108] Moreover, the refugees were "severely starved of accurate information about decisions being taken for or against them in different national and international fora."[109] This,

Developmental Refugees · 93

combined with inadequate rations, water, and clothing, made it relatively easy for leaders to aggravate popular fears and utilize nationalism, nostalgia, and even threats to manipulate the population.[110]

Conclusion

By 1963, there were more than ten thousand Rwandans living at the Muyenzi refugee camp and an unknown number living elsewhere throughout the district and region.[111] While many of these individuals settled with friends and family, it is likely that a majority came to live in the state-sanctioned refugee camps. These people were of interest to various authorities for different reasons. For the British military, they had to be counted and monitored because their transgression into Tanzania represented a potential threat to the efficacy of colonial borders in a decolonizing world.[112] They were also potential harbingers of violence and communism, both of which threatened British interests in the region.[113] Ironically, while state sovereignty is "closely tied" to the domestication of borders, here we see a former colonial power intimately involved in the surveillance and maintenance of boundaries—revealing the incomplete nature of independence during the early years of decolonization.[114] As the second largest contributor to the UNHCR, Britain's concern likely contributed to the agency's focus on Rwandan refugees, which increased throughout the 1960s in all four neighboring countries of asylum.

To the new Tanzanian government, these refugees were a developmental opportunity, one that brought much-needed international money and manpower to an underfunded district. In contrast, local government officials viewed the refugees as a privileged group—one that received international funding and amenities, such as water sources, far above what local Ngarans could claim. They were also an increasingly stubborn group that did not accede to officials' demands for resettlement throughout the refugee villages they had so carefully positioned around Muyenzi.

The refugees themselves were of course not a coherent group, although they looked that way to the various authorities who counted and directed them. Next we turn to refugee actions, as the process of refugee settlement became more contentious at Muyenzi in the 1960s—a time that brought international actors, funding, and frustration to Ngara as never before.

5. CITIZENS AND REFUGEES

THE POLITICS OF REFUGEE AID

On a night in April 1963, approximately six thousand men, women, and children, including many infirm and sick individuals, gathered what belongings they could carry and began walking from the Muyenzi refugee camp in Ngara to the Rwandan refugee settlement at Kiamba, just over the Burundi border. It was a thirty-mile trek without shelter, food, or water. The group was met at the border by Burundian soldiers, who refused them entry. The UNHCR office in Burundi similarly refused to provide rations to the refugees.[1] This much is known. But why did so many people undertake such drastic and seemingly spontaneous measures to leave Tanzania? Why, at that moment, did Burundi become a place of opportunity, or refuge, in the minds of so many Rwandans? The answers to these questions, gleaned from several archives, reveal much about how refugees understood the world of Muyenzi and how they, in turn, were perceived by the various authorities in their lives. As mutual suspicion and miscommunication infused encounters in Ngara, refugees increasingly found themselves pitted against aid workers, local agencies against transnational organizations, and Ngaran host communities against a refugee "Other."

This chapter reveals the conflicts among local and national officials, refugees, and international aid agencies over who would control refugee aid and how. *Collision* is an apt word to describe the early efforts of the UNHCR, the Red Cross, and the Tanzanian government to help and settle the refugees. Chaos was present as well, and confusion. Reading the archives of the four different institutions that were primarily involved with refugee settlement—the Tanzanian government, UNHCR, LRCS, and Tanganyikan Christian Refugee Service (TCRS)—yields four different versions of events. This is particularly true when examining the Rwandans' April 1963 exodus from the Muyenzi settlement. Each archive presents a different version of the various agencies' policies, refugees' motivations, and local politics in Ngara district. By putting these archives in conversation with one another and with the narratives of those present in Busubi at the time, it becomes possible to discern a more nuanced story of refugees as actors with differing motivations and hopes.

As various authorities jostled over the creation, maintenance, and authority structure of the refugee settlements, they continually collided with the political dynamics within the refugee community. At the local level, this led to resentment against the international aid agencies that contested local officials' authority and intelligence. In so doing, the aid agencies continued a colonial legacy of condescending development—one that threatened the flow of aid to the district. The ensuing correspondence reveals that, at this moment in the early 1960s, the central government prioritized international aid over local and regional expertise. The result would be an embarrassing failure at Muyenzi refugee camp—one the central government would struggle to rectify in its future contestations with the international aid community.

The chapter closes by revealing the processes by which the nation began to be actualized in the popular imaginations of those who lived on the edge of a space that was becoming Tanzania.[2] Ngarans began to identify as Tanzanians during the process of decolonization, a time when local political identities congealed around internationally reified categories of the refugee and the citizen. It was during this process that the border first became relevant to popular conceptions of identity in Ngara—as Ngarans began the process of perceiving themselves as belonging within the Tanzanian nation-state rather than within Great Lakes regional communities. The various nomenclatures used by Ngarans and officials to describe Rwandans in

96 · CHAPTER 5

Ngara reveal that Rwandans did not necessarily enter the district as refugees. Rather, during decolonization, they came to discursively and legally embody the concept of refugee through the contested process of settlement and aid.

State development planners, international aid agencies, and Rwandan refugees arrived in Ngara district as the Great Lakes region was undergoing a traumatic process of decolonization. As different versions of nationalism and "progress" collided, the presence of these three groups led to conflicts over security, identity, and development. However, as Rwandans resisted and subverted the programs enacted to make them stationary and profitable members of the state, they were increasingly perceived as threats to the Tanzanian nation. As many in Ngara began to perceive Rwandan refugees as both violent and lazy, they also reified a particular version of Tanzanian citizenship, one that existed more in ideology than in reality.

During decolonization, the Tanzanian state advocated a form of African socialism based on equality and a particular notion of African traditions. Pivotal to this policy was the idea of a culture of shared resources and self-help. Tanzania would be united through the language of Kiswahili. The 1962 demise of chieftaincies in Tanzania was welcomed by many Basubi and Bahangaza, who celebrated the end of chiefly tribute and looked forward to the social equality promised by Nyerere and TANU.[3] The Tanzanian state was far from a coherent entity in the early 1960s, but for many in Ngara, the idea of Tanzania and Tanzanian development became something to be proud of and to rally around.[4] And, despite the eventual failure of government projects in the district, many Ngarans were hopeful in the early 1960s. They had expectations of progress and, perhaps most important, given events in neighboring states, of a peaceful transition to independence.

The rhetoric of nation building in neighboring Ruanda-Urundi was much different. As we have seen, the struggle over independence in Rwanda occurred between two different visions of nationalism: one that discursively empowered Hutu as "true" Rwandans, and one that sought to restore the Tutsi monarchy and/or Tutsi leadership to power. Violent decolonization in Ruanda-Urundi not only resulted in the first large wave of late colonial–early postcolonial refugees but also presaged how interethnic violence could forestall a peaceful transition to independence. Many Ngarans are quick to laud the fact that violence did not engulf their new nation-state, that the "peaceful" nature of decolonization in Ngara stands in stark contrast to that of their neighbors to the west. Such musings clarify how Ngarans absorbed the rhetoric of central state actors, even while experiencing resentment and

Citizens and Refugees · 97

disappointment at the failed programs enacted at the district and regional levels.[5] Into this burgeoning appreciation of the discourse of self-help and familyhood came another factor: the international organizations that spent hundreds of thousands of dollars separating and aiding Rwandan refugees in refugee camps. The perception of Rwandans as privileged "Others" who did not appreciate all they had been given furthered the process by which Ngarans began to see themselves as part of a Tanzanian community, even as their lived experiences of illegal cross-border trade and bureaucratic incompetence revealed the weaknesses of the new nation-state.[6]

Flight from Muyenzi

During early April 1963, Ngara's agriculture officer sent a telegram to the provincial commissioner that read, "Nearly 95% of Refugees have ran away. Not known whether will come back. Please advise if whether the work of survey and dermacation [sic] will continue."[7] This was the heart of the problem for the local government. The expensive and painstaking process of laying out *shamba* (farms) and villages for the refugees had been, once again, interrupted. Perhaps even worse, the refugees had left the controlled area of the camp. Joseph Kato, the survey chairman of WLR, wrote a missive to his supervisor describing the events in April:

> For the month and some three days I stayed at Muyenzi it was hard to get labourer as the Refugees was not prepared to work as ordered by the Government. . . . The first week of this month there came the Field Force Team to get hold of the Refugee Jumbes or leaders who were making troubles and take them to other areas in Tanganyika. After they have been removed from the Camp, the . . . Refugees packed up their belongings and run out to Burundi. Where they were also kicked back by the Police of Burundi. They are now back at the Camp again finding their huts pulled down by Caterpilla of P.W.D.[8]

Kato's report illustrates how many local officials in Ngara understood April's events. Throughout the state and international archives, the notion that a few *troublemakers*—a term synonymous with refugee leaders—were influencing the general population is widespread.[9] At first, national administrators perceived the troublemaker problem as relatively easy to fix: separating the refugee leaders from the rest of the population would remove the impediments to refugee cooperation. Such excision was handled by the field force police, who rounded up and jailed most of the leaders in Muyenzi,

98 · CHAPTER 5

along with their families. With this removal, however, the vast majority of refugees in Muyenzi did not fall in line and cooperate with local authorities; instead, they attempted to flee the country. Part of the problem was that in labeling residents of Muyenzi troublemakers and refugees, the government ignored their evolving political identity as Rwandan citizens. In so doing, officials elided the political fears and ambitions among the Muyenzi population.

Traces within the national archives offer a different understanding of events from that articulated in local and regional correspondence and meeting minutes, one where food shortages, miscommunication, and fear fueled refugee behavior. Camp correspondence from 1962 and 1963 indicates acute food shortages in Muyenzi.[10] Lack of food was exacerbated by poor conditions on the one road in the area, which hampered the delivery of internationally donated food.[11] The settlement officer also withheld rations to punish families that refused to move from the central camp at Muyenzi to the disparate settlements.[12] Additionally, clothes donated by the international community were slow to arrive in Muyenzi and were inadequate for the refugees' needs. Foreshadowing problems to come, a camp officer lamented the Red Cross volunteers' poor handling of clothing distribution in September 1962. In this case, the lack of communication and organization among camp administrators, Red Cross volunteers, and refugees led to a "near riot" and resulted in "a pronounced feeling of bitterness amongst the refugees that unfair (unorganised) distribution had favoured a few and not satified [sic] the many truly needy cases. This is another instance where [if] the matter [had] been referred to me first indiscipline could have been avoided and an equitable distribution affected."[13] Additionally, refugees complained about Mr. Kambanda, the government-appointed leader of Muyenzi camp, and asked that he take "no part" in the organization of the villages around Muyenzi. In response, the district commissioner (DC) explained that Kambanda was "a leader who could teach good discipline especially to the Refugee Camp which was more or less like a military Camp."[14] The fact that the DC equated the refugee camp with a "military" establishment indicates that the local government viewed the refugees as a threat to be controlled and disciplined, rather than potential citizens to be absorbed and cared for.

Further complicating the version of events found in government archives is a letter written by Oxfam employee Rachel Yeld, the sociologist who worked with the government in Muyenzi camp.[15] Yeld's views were largely ignored by both governmental and transnational administrations. She alleged that the refugees' flight stemmed from endemic miscommunication and distrust between the government and the refugees. The April 1963 letter states that on numerous occasions local officials threatened to forcibly return the refugees to Rwanda, and that they never explained the proposed move to settlements. Furthermore, the government arrested the communities' leaders and their families without any explanation. The result was mass panic. Leaderless, confused, and afraid, the refugees decided to walk to Burundi. Yeld describes the thirty-mile trek as a desperate and arduous journey undertaken by people who had not received any rations for more than a week. She went to Burundi herself to try to explain the situation to the authorities and the UNHCR. She claims that the settlement commandant at Muyenzi burned the refugees' huts so they would be forced to move to the new settlements upon their return. When the refugees, out of options, did go back to Muyenzi, the commandant withheld medical care, transportation, and rations until all family members had moved to the new settlement villages. Due to these actions, two children died of malnutrition and exhaustion.[16]

Yeld's account certainly makes us more sympathetic to the Rwandan population in Muyenzi. Exacerbated by miscommunication and the possible threat of a forced return to Rwanda, refugee reluctance to move to outlying settlements seems understandable. Rather than being lazy, as local officials repeatedly stated, these people feared a process they did not understand. In this version of events, the refugees at Muyenzi counted on their leaders for information, and when government officials jailed these "troublemakers," the people were confused and frightened, feelings that were heightened by rumors of a forced return. In light of these events, it becomes easy to empathize with the Rwandans. Their flight to Burundi becomes less a political protest born of ingratitude and more a desperate move to regain some sense of control and safety in a confusing and malevolent world. Or so Yeld's letter would have us understand it.

Return to Muyenzi, April 1963–August 1964

Following the departure of the refugees in April 1963, the government stopped surveying and demarcating outlying settlements. The camp commander then "bulldozed or burnt" the vacated structures so that "there should be little likehood [sic] of them settling in that area [the central Muyenzi camp]." From this point on, the commander would allow the refugees to settle only on the government's "planned basis."[17]

Despite these renewed efforts to control the circulation of refugees, their unauthorized movements outside camp boundaries continued. As the field

100 · CHAPTER 5

officer for Muyenzi reported in May 1963, it was "rather impossible to control the movements" of refugees.[18] By July, the refugees had not cultivated the expected amount of land. The field officer's monthly report for June noted that the refugees feared being "removed to other places"; and that those refugees with connections to Rwandan communities elsewhere believed they would be leaving for Rwanda "very soon."[19] Their "will to work" was "poor" in terms of house building, and their refusal to sow maize continued.[20] Additionally, it was extremely difficult to keep track of the refugees, as some individuals registered multiple times with Muyenzi authorities, and others did not register at all.[21]

It is in this context that the Tanzanian government reached out to the UNHCR to find a suitable voluntary agency to administer the Rwandan refugees in Ngara district.[22] In the tripartite contracts the government signed in 1963 with the UNHCR, LRCS, and later TCRS, the division of responsibility for refugee development programs was clear. The state would provide the land; the international aid organizations, led by the UNHCR, would provide the funding; and the implementing agency would supply the camp administration and supervision.[23] In June 1963 the government signed its first tripartite agreement with the UNHCR and LRCS. The agreement gave operational responsibility to the LRCS, under the oversight of both the government and the UNHCR. As would become usual in these agreements, the government maintained responsibility for security and police activities within the refugee settlements. The agreement covered an operation planned for August 1, 1963, through June 30, 1964, with the aim of making the refugees at Muyenzi "self-supporting" by the end of that period.[24] Reports by the LRCS speculated that the government wanted an outside agency to take over the care of Rwandan refugees for three main reasons: the lack of government funding, the fear of damaging Tanzanian relations with Rwanda, and the "psychological impasse" between local authorities and refugees, such that "most of the Tanganyika officials involved seem to be 'fed up.'"[25]

The period of LRCS aid to Rwandan refugees in Ngara was to be a disaster in terms of refugee settlement in Muyenzi, revealing the mistrust and condescension with which transnational and local staff viewed each other.[26] A 1964 report by LRCS staff describes the agency's initial efforts with remarkable honesty. It notes that when the LRCS first began aiding Rwandan refugees in Tanzania, the organization had "little or no experience of resettling refugees."[27] Moreover, because LRCS officials viewed the operation as a typical relief action, they "underestimated the technical, political and psychological difficulties" they would face.[28] Additionally, because the LRCS was

Citizens and Refugees · 101

committed to providing emergency aid, officials refused to plan operations for longer than six to eight months at a time.[29] Staff later saw this as a crucial mistake because a minimum input of eighteen months was needed to effectively settle refugees. Another problem was the lack of LRCS personnel with the requisite local knowledge or "special qualities" needed to administer the settlement.[30]

The archives of the LRCS give us insight into the processes by which Rwandans became refugees locally. According to those who worked for the LRCS in Ngara (most of whom were expatriates), the key reason the refugees did not become self-supporting was the mutual distrust between the refugees and local government officials. The Red Cross archives elaborate on this distrust by discussing a "climate of terror" in the Muyenzi refugee camp, where the local police were interested in neither the welfare of the refugees nor harmony in the camp.[31]

One of the reasons for the antagonism between local officials and refugees appeared to be the behavior of local business elites in Ngara district. According to a January–July 1964 LRCS report, business leaders and politicians in northern Ngara viewed the permanent settlement of refugees in the south as a threat to their "majority and hegemony" in Ngara.[32] Staff noted that these politicians had the "ear" of the area commissioner, who was a "jealous," "difficult character . . . of very little intelligence."[33] This may have been why Ernst Rohner, an LRCS delegate, reported in June 1963 that the local government had arbitrarily moved refugee villages after the start of cultivation, disrupting the harvest as well as refugees' permanent settlement.[34] Delegates later decided that the area commissioner was not fit for service and spoke with the central government about having him removed, thus embedding themselves in a local politics with which they were, at best, unfamiliar.

If LRCS staff understood the local administration in Ngara through a lens of distrust, even contempt, members of the local administration understood LRCS staff to be incompetent and arrogant. Reports from the local branch of the Agriculture Department reveal the frustration of individuals whose experience and expertise were frequently ignored, to the detriment of refugee development. "I regret very much to note," wrote the officer in charge of the Ngara agriculture office, "that the Red Cross Authorities have either not sought our advice, neglected them or not cared about it," resulting in a land shortage in the refugee settlements.[35]

The LRCS administration, led initially by Knud Dahl, had determined that the government's decision to disperse the refugees in Muyenzi to disparate settlements would divide families, as well as those who were "naturally

102 · CHAPTER 5

inclined to work together." The LRCS's solution was to regroup the refugees to instill a "feeling of confidence."[36] This "solution" incensed the local agriculture officer, who wrote of a "complete stoppage of cultivation due to what I would call 'DISARRANGEMENT' instead of arrangement or regrouping of refugees as the Red Cross Authorities call it. Due to this regrouping refugees have put cultivation aside—the time cultivation is mostly needed—and are mostly engaged in building in their new village sites, besides this, this regrouping has brought in the same CONGESTION we had at Muyenzi and Nyarutiti early this year."[37]

Other local officials described the LRCS's regrouping of refugees as a "sorry affair."[38] The administrative secretary of WLR, R. K. Makao, noted that the Ministry of Agriculture had done an excellent job demarcating the original settlements and observed, "It is really very annoying to see that their advise [sic] is not followed."[39] The local agriculture staff also wrote that "the fact that we are merely advisers to the Red Cross Authorities has caused some embarrassment on the side of our staff and little or no work is being done as few refugees will listen to [us] . . . they have been bade to disregard whatever our staff say."[40] Further, according to local staff, the regrouping of refugees under the LRCS's direction led to conditions of "grossly over crowded" areas that lacked the necessary land for self-sufficiency.[41] This regrouping also caused almost "the complete destruction of the time, money and energy used in planning the land."[42] Moreover, "disturbances . . . have arisen between the Area Commissioner and the Red Cross," in which agriculture staff "have unjustly been accused."[43] As a result, the local officer in charge withdrew his staff from the refugee settlements. Local government workers thus found themselves actively pushed to the margins of planning for the refugees, a situation that likely echoed experiences under the colonial regime.

On the UNHCR side, a report written by Deputy High Commissioner Sadruddin Aga Khan to the Ministry of Agriculture noted:

On resettlement, the Red Cross delegate reported that he was regrouping some of the tiny settlements in the outlying areas into larger and more sensibly planned villages. Here again he had been occasionally hampered in his work by the local agricultural officers, who had reversed his arrangements on their own initiative. No one knew exactly where the orders had come from since both the Regional and the Area authorities had received copies of the "memorandum of Understanding" which clearly stated that administration was under the

Citizens and Refugees · 103

control of the Red Cross. It can be seen from the above that the chief delegate of the Red Cross felt that his efforts would be seriously obstructed unless the Tanganyika Government was able to control the local authorities. . . . The D.H.C. was somewhat upset to discover that the excellent co-operation between the United Nations, the Red Cross and the Tanganyika Government at the upper levels was apparently being undermined at the local level. It was appreciated that . . . the problem of the Ruanda refugees was an international one.[44]

This letter from the deputy high commissioner led to a maelstrom of accusations and denials from the local agriculture office and meetings with the LRCS, which in time noted that "there is no friction over the Ministry's policy or staff and our own administration."[45] What is interesting is the language used by Aga Khan, who would soon become high commissioner, and the reaction it caused both nationally and locally. The issue was that "orders" had been reversed on the ground, thereby threatening that part of the tripartite agreement that placed the LRCS in charge of administration. The fact that the agriculture office had staff on the ground in Busubi for two years prior to the LRCS's arrival is ignored in this version of events. Rather, the "international" nature of the "problem of the Ruanda refugees" is highlighted, thus requiring international efforts and simultaneously eliding the very local conditions and regional context of refugee settlement. Lastly, Aga Khan mentions that cooperation at the "upper levels" can be "undermined at the local level." This certainly would have alarmed many members of the Nyerere administration because with cooperation came funding. The central government therefore acted quickly to mitigate the issue by coordinating meetings with local agriculture staff and the LRCS and forwarding Aga Khan's report to the agriculture office and district offices. Such actions revealed friction between local and national officials, with the latter prioritizing transnational concerns over local concerns.

The one thing the local administration and the LRCS seemed to agree on was the detrimental "mentality" of the refugees. By the beginning of 1964, the LRCS was "wondering what sort of scheme it can implement," given the "narrow" attitude toward settling the refugees.[46] As for the agriculture office in Ngara, the December 1963 monthly report noted that "the hope for Rwandans being settled is getting very meagre," and "what used to be termed 'interference by the local Agricultural staff' . . . was merely concocted to make us scape goats," as the LRCS authorities "have anticipated the failure of their plan." This same report noted the strained relationship between the area com-

104 · CHAPTER 5

missioner and LRCS authorities, as well as an increase in "political activities" among the refugees, with the result that no cultivation had occurred; indeed the refugees had even uprooted some banana shoots in protest.[47] The lack of refugee settlement efforts did not matter anyway, the agriculture officer noted at the end of his October report, as the refugees were sure to return to Rwanda after their rations were cut, particularly in light of their communications with other refugees in Burundi who planned to attack Rwanda.[48]

So it was that at the end of the first tripartite agreement, and after two years in Muyenzi, the refugees had not become self-sufficient and continued to display an extreme reluctance toward farming. The UNHCR and the LRCS had failed to "solve" the refugee "problem," thus endangering their reputations and institutional interests at the national and international levels. And, despite the widely held idea that the refugees would voluntarily repatriate, there was evidence to the contrary.[49] Indeed, with the increases in refugee raids into Rwanda during 1964, particularly from Burundi and Uganda, the number of refugees fleeing Rwanda only increased. Nevertheless, the LRCS departed Ngara in June 1964, leaving behind rations for only one month. In early July the regional agriculture officer visited Muyenzi and noted that the LRCS's estimate that each refugee family had cultivated between 2 and 2.5 acres of land was overly optimistic, as the refugees "could not possibly have grown enough in March–June to provide food until the next harvest in February."[50] He estimated that rations would have to be increased by October, with some of the more recently settled villages requiring full rations once again.

The Tanganyikan Christian Refugee Service in Muyenzi, 1964–1969

The TCRS was born in late 1963 and began operating in Tanzania in January 1964.[51] It was the first of many refugee agencies created by the World Service division of the Lutheran World Federation (WS-LWF) over the next fifty years.[52] In 1963 Bishop Begnt Sundkler, head of the Evangelical Lutheran Church of Northwest Tanganyika, sent a letter to Bruno Muetzelfeldt, director of the WS-LWF in Geneva, citing the pressing need for humanitarian assistance to Rwandan refugees in Ngara district.[53]

Sundkler's timing was good. The WS-LWF had only recently received a report detailing the need for development in Africa, as well as the plight of refugees throughout the continent. The report noted, tellingly, that the early 1960s would be a crucial period in the transformation of Africans' religious beliefs: half the African population would "be in a religious vacuum," providing the Christian Church with a "missionary opportunity as never before in the history of Africa."[54] Indeed, Sundkler's letter had mentioned the actions of the Catholic Church—a competitor in the ongoing struggle for converts in the region.[55] The TCRS thus encapsulated the commingling of institutional self-interest and humanitarian sensibilities so often at the center of aid activities.

On receipt of Sundkler's letter, Muetzelfeldt sent two LWF representatives to Ngara to report on Muyenzi. High-level discussions between the WS-LWF and UNHCR were then initiated, as both the UNHCR and the Tanzanian government were interested in finding a voluntary implementing agency to replace the LRCS in Muyenzi. From the start, TCRS officials understood the agency's responsibility in Tanzania as one of integrating refugees in local communities. The leadership was explicit that the "TCRS not be institutionalized" and that its goal was to assist "not only new settlers but the whole district" and "the Government . . . in its integration policy, which must be in [the] best interests of the new settlers, the local district and the nation as a whole."[56] In this sense, the TCRS was similar to many nongovernmental organizations (NGOS) and development agencies with ties to Scandinavian countries, which tended to favor Nyerere's vision of African socialism and supported the Tanzanian government and its leader.[57] It was also a different approach from that of the UNHCR, whose mandate does not include the needs of local communities, a fact that would eventually lead to heightened tensions between the two agencies.[58] Additionally, the TCRS was set up not as a spiritual ministry but as an agency involved in material relief, although tensions between religious and material services would plague the organization.[59] In Tanzania, the TCRS took over management of the Muyenzi refugee settlements, as well as those in Karagwe district. It would remain the UNHCR's primary operational partner in Tanzania until 1994.

The problems at Muyenzi, however, did not cease with the change in management. Throughout the fall of 1964, there were reports of malnutrition and famine at Muyenzi. An estimated 10 percent of the Muyenzi population left the area, looking for food among friends and relatives.[60] Despite this, the TCRS, UNHCR, and local government officials believed the refugees "were still slightly over protected as far as food is concerned," compared with the rest of Ngara district.[61] The food shortage led to supplemental rations for a limited period because, in the words of a UNHCR officer, "if on every occasion when the settlers do not receive completely what they feel to be their requirements, someone leaps in and provides all that they ask, any efforts made to develop this group of people as permanent settlers are a complete waste of time."[62] This analysis of events, which, in the words of

106 · CHAPTER 5

one UNHCR official, was based on "our feeling that the general situation of the refugees has been . . . exaggerated," was roundly criticized by David Zarembka, an American teacher in the Muyenzi schools who claimed that the incidence of malnutrition was very high.[63] Disparate claims as to the veracity of refugee complaints are common throughout the archives and endemic to refugee aid in general, illustrating the distrust officials on the ground and in Geneva harbored toward the refugees.

Food distribution continued, at a rate of five pounds of cornmeal or bulgur wheat per person, well into 1965.[64] However, due to a lack of transportation, "those refugees who needed it most did not receive food in sufficient quantities." Other issues included the destruction of refugees' crops by vermin (wild pigs and deer), such that "whole villages have expressed the desire to be moved to other areas of Tanzania because of this demoralizing factor."[65] Nevertheless, the refugees increased their agricultural activities, planting beans, maize, cassava, soya beans, sweet potatoes, and banana shoots donated by the local community.[66] Additionally, the refugees worked with local groups to hunt the animals that threatened their crops.[67] The TCRS also funded several water supply projects at Muyenzi. Despite these improvements, the "number of refugees requesting rations continue[d] to grow" in late 1965, with reports of malnutrition increasing.[68] Meanwhile, the government made plans to resettle two thousand refugees, perceived as troublemakers who were "not willing to settle," in another region. Although this move never occurred, the plan led to rumors of forced removal from Muyenzi.[69] The 1966 census revealed nine hundred fewer inhabitants in Muyenzi than the previous year.[70] Refugees, particularly men, left the settlements for months at a time, moving throughout WLR and the wider Great Lakes region. And although cultivation increased during 1966, refugees still showed no interest in "building good permanent houses."[71]

Adding to these problems were ongoing allegations of refugee violence. In January 1965 there was "unrest" in Muyenzi following an attack on local Arabs by people "speaking the refugees' language."[72] After this incident, two hundred refugees left Muyenzi for Burundi but later asked to return. There were also rumors that the refugees planned "to attack the mission for money and the police station for more arms," fears that led the police to double their strength in Busubi and to deploy the Tanganyika Rifles to the area.[73] Isaac Laiser, the TCRS field officer in Muyenzi, requested a gun and a night watchman due to safety concerns.[74]

There were also continued allegations of refugee military training in Ngara.[75] In the summer of 1966 Rwandans from Muyenzi participated in a raid into

Rwanda from bases allegedly in Ngara district.[76] A year later, Rwandan refugees at Muyenzi were arrested for "subversive activity against Rwanda" and sent to prisons outside the district.[77]

Nevertheless, by the close of 1967, there was "much evidence of consolidation in" Muyenzi, with only "supplementary assistance" provided by the international community for health, agricultural development, and community development projects.[78] Despite these improvements, "a host of economic and political problems" continued to plague the refugees in the Muyenzi settlement.[79]

Host Views

Ngarans came to recognize Rwandans as refugees largely due to their centralization in segregated camps and settlements.[80] Some locals benefited from the presence of the refugees, trading local produce for donated goods and working on internationally funded refugee development projects.[81] Conversely, others grew angry at the aid given to refugees, particularly as local councils were themselves in "great financial difficulties."[82] Many Ngarans resented the international aid that provided refugees with free schools, rations, and clean water.[83] Ngarans blamed the refugees for thieving, harboring violent individuals, and even attacking local people.[84] Rwandans' association with violence, laziness, and privilege contrasted starkly with local notions of progress and peace.[85]

Ngaran perceptions are perhaps best accessed through the language people used to describe Rwandans in the district. Charles Gasarasi, a former refugee in Muyenzi camp, noted that Rwandans were first described as *watoro*, meaning "those who flee justice."[86] According to Gasarasi, it was only later that the word *wakimbizi* was institutionalized in reference to Rwandans in Ngara, meaning "those who run." Throughout their first years in Ngara, government officers referred to Rwandans almost interchangeably as immigrants, Banyaruanda tribesmen, settlers, and refugees. Over time, the local people came to call the Rwandans *wakimbizi* as opposed to *wageni* (guests), given that they had fled a struggle, were unable to return to the place where they belonged, and were housed in controlled camps and settlements.[87]

Ideologies of decolonization were becoming central to identity during the late 1950s and early 1960s in Ngara, and it was partly through different notions of the meaning of independence that divisions sprang up between the refugees and those who had lived in Ngara before the refugees' arrival. Rwanda was a space of increasingly violent struggles for power. For many who fled

Rwanda, liberation often meant the reclamation of power in Rwanda. After Rwandan independence in 1962, this reclamation increasingly took the shape of a military conquest of a sovereign African state. As Van der Meeren notes, refugees in 1959 did not see themselves "as a privileged aristocracy . . . but as victims of colonial policy in the struggle for political power."[88]

It is likely that this notion of liberation sat uncomfortably with the notion of independence, which was becoming increasingly attractive to Ngarans. Following *Mwalimu* Nyerere, liberation for many in Ngara district was based on notions of equality, self-help, and progress. The other, ostensibly Rwandan version of liberation was based on the violent overthrow of one ethnicity by another, on the rule of a small elite. Their fight was over what kind of nation would emerge in Rwanda and who would lead it. Some Rwandan refugees therefore fought a war against African leaders, not colonizers.[89] As such, they represented the vanguard of a new kind of war in sub-Saharan Africa, one in which refugees fought against African rulers. This must have been unsettling for a population in the throes of becoming Tanzanian, who took pride in their values of equality and self-help.

Interviewing Ngarans about the 1960s refugee influx comes with its own unique challenges, not the least of which are the tricks of memory that caused some to conflate the 1960s crisis with that of the 1990s. Nevertheless, for many people who lived in Busubi and Bugufi, it was clear that the refugees represented a privileged minority, a situation that was made more obvious by their consolidation in internationally funded and controlled refugee camps. While refugees and locals alike suffered from malnutrition, Western humanitarians transported rations only to the refugees. Likewise, the presence of two tractors dedicated to refugee settlement presented a visible reminder of the refugees' exceptionality—particularly as the entire WLR had only six tractors to share among four districts. Furthermore, the region suffered from a severe lack of staff, which led to the curtailment of development work in Ngara—exacerbated when agriculture and land planning staff concentrated almost exclusively on refugee projects. There were scarce planting seeds in the region and few spare parts to be found in the country by 1964. The optimism of independence had not translated into material life improvements, and cash-crop schemes suffered due to failures and broken promises from a government struggling with the exigencies of decolonization. Indeed, many farmers could have benefited from the aid given to the refugees, but agencies refused to have their donations used by local people. Ngarans themselves remembered that refugees received more aid than local people and that they exacerbated food shortages in the district.[90]

Understandably, most people I interviewed did not want to admit to feelings of hostility toward the refugees, instead lauding the Tanzanian ideal of hospitality. Yet an undercurrent of resentment existed in many narratives. Some individuals said there were no problems with the refugees who had come to Ngara in need of help, and local communities often donated banana shoots to Muyenzi (which were sometimes planted upside down). Others remembered "many losses" to the refugee community.[91] Many people were quick to point out that the refugees stole cattle throughout the district, and the "natives suffered."[92] And it is here that we reach a crucial juncture in the history of identity in Ngara district—with the word *native*. Whereas before migrants from Burundi and Rwanda who traveled through and settled in the district became Tanzanian with independence, these migrants of decolonization, these *wakimbizi*, were never truly integrated into the district. They remained Other, those who do not belong to the land, and in this time and place, they remained outside the nation-state. For some, this otherness existed in the laziness of the refugees, who had been given so much and yet still demanded more—a laziness inimical to the values of Tanzanian citizenship. For some Ngarans, the otherness consisted of a tendency toward criminality, whether this took the form of local theft or military incursions to Rwanda. For most people, this otherness existed in the refugee camps, spaces of privilege and yet difference. In between life as Rwandan and Tanzanian citizens, they would not be "permanently settled," as the UNHCR and state had so hoped to achieve.

Conclusion

For the UNHCR, the problems of the Muyenzi tripartite contract would be solved not by recognizing the political nature and vulnerabilities of refugee groups but rather by replacing the voluntary implementing agency with one more amenable to the national government. And so it was that the TCRS came to be a mainstay and bellwether of the politics of refugee aid in Tanzania. Tellingly, in attempting to evaluate the ambiguous reports of famine in Muyenzi in 1964, the UNHCR chargé de mission in Dar es Salaam wrote to his superior, "Who is exaggerating or who is being deceived?" A handwritten note on the bottom of the page replied, "Always the same question."[93] Over the next fifty years of operation, UNHCR officials would continue to grapple with the different versions of events that reached them from the central and local governments in Tanzania, refugee groups, TCRS officials, and other sources. The fear of deception would continue to plague UNHCR operations in Tanzania and throughout the world for decades to come.

For the UNHCR and TCRS, the case of Muyenzi represented what not to do in future dealings with refugee settlements in Tanzania.[94] Moving forward, both organizations would attempt to retain firmer control over refugee movements and refugee labor. Following their experiences in Muyenzi, TCRS and UNHCR officials noted that their future efforts would "not have to be more successful to compare favourably" to their work at Muyenzi.[95] Conflicts among local, national, and international officials would also continue in the decades to come, as local officers would frequently balk at aid plans that privileged refugees and international expertise over local concerns. Indeed, tension between local and national staff at Muyenzi convinced the central government that it needed to exert more control over refugees, local officials, and expatriate aid workers.

While the encamped Rwandan population in Ngara would eventually stabilize if not necessarily settle in the district, they remained *wakimbizi* as local people associated more closely with the socialist values of the Tanzanian state. In many ways, this was a "thin" version of citizenship, one that expressed political belonging to the Tanzanian state despite the inability to either successfully make claims or secure rights from that state.[96] Yet it became increasingly attractive to a population who sought peaceful independence and resented the aid given to the seemingly violent refugees in their midst. In this way, Ngarans increasingly identified with the ideology of a national political community, while simultaneously engaging in illegal trade (discussed in chapter 7). Though Ngarans continued to fit uneasily within the new nation-state system, they gravitated toward the discursive strength of centralized leaders—as evidenced by the return of migrants during the early 1960s to help develop the district (see chapter 3).

In Muyenzi, the Rwandan community's resistance to settlement and development was itself anchored in the chaotic politics of decolonization and identity. Certainly not all Rwandans in Muyenzi were interested in violently overthrowing the new Rwandan state and seizing its bureaucratic apparatus. However, the majority defied governmental and international orders to settle in Muyenzi during their first years in Tanzania, albeit for different reasons. While some refugees sought a violent overthrow of the Rwandan government, others wanted to settle in Tanzania, and still others took advantage of what they could from aid agencies, as the example of multiple registrations reveals.

During the early 1960s in Ngara district, then, nation-building efforts coincided with a broader project of global governance that endeavored to create and maintain a world of sovereign nation-states. Through decolonization, Ngarans began to see themselves as part of an idea called Tanzania, an amalgamation of 120 different groups within a territory that previously had connoted poverty and alienness. Rwandans shared cultural and familial links with Ngarans. They shared similar languages and, in many cases, migratory routes and work experiences in the Uganda protectorate. Linguistic and cultural linkages facilitated communication and economic activities, as well as sympathy. And yet, while the physical borders between Ngara, Rwanda, and Burundi remained porous, the violent context of decolonization in Rwanda combined with national and international refugee policies to create a space between Ngarans and those "across the line."[97]

6. CONFLICTING SOVEREIGNTIES

COMPETITION AT MWESI REFUGEE

SETTLEMENT, 1963–1970

During the spring of 1970, more than one hundred Rwandan refugees held at Dabalo settlement, in central Tanzania, went on hunger strike.[1] The strike was staged to protest the refugees' continued confinement in the settlement; the UNHCR's refusal to relocate the refugees to Congo, their first country of asylum; and the issuance of state-mandated refugee permits, which they refused to sign. The protest was emblematic of a spirit of noncooperation at the Mwesi Highlands Refugee Settlement, one that threatened the agricultural viability of the settlement scheme and thus the development of the refugees and the region in accordance with state and internationally formulated plans.[2] In response to the strike and to the refugees' perceived recalcitrance, UNHCR representatives advised the Tanzanian government to sentence the refugees to forced labor, believing that if they were compelled to work, the refugees would cease their stubborn resistance.

The history of the Mwesi refugee settlement represents a formative moment in the history of nation-state creation and refugee aid and regulation in Africa and in the world. At a time when leaders and policymakers were negotiating the contours of African nation-states, the political future of refugees became the subject of debate and conflict. A fundamental tension existed over which peoples and organizations would decide the place of Rwandan refugees in the new world of nation-states. Multiple agencies and actors claimed sovereignty over this group, including the Tanzanian state as it negotiated its own definition of citizenship, the UNHCR as it promoted its institutional interests, and the refugees as they sought political autonomy. Each of these multiple categories of actors had its own agenda, allegiances, and politics and, ultimately, its own ideas about how the refugee population in Mwesi should be treated and why.

Rwandan refugees in Mwesi, like those at Muyenzi, came to inhabit multiple and often conflicting domains of sovereignty. Those vying for political power and control in Mwesi included the Tanzanian government, the UNHCR, and the refugees themselves. So far, this book has explored the history of Ngara district in analyzing the formation of political identities over time and the influences of different actors and organizations on those political imaginaries. This chapter deviates, in that it explores the politics around the Mwesi Rwandan refugee settlement, located south of Ngara in Mpanda district. In so doing, it reveals the self-interested, tumultuous, and ambiguous nature of refugee aid in Tanzania—and in the decolonizing world more generally—during the 1960s, when nation-state building and UNHCR programs in sub-Saharan Africa both experienced rapid growth.

The three thousand refugees who eventually came to inhabit the Mwesi Highlands had left Rwanda for the Kivu province of Congo (currently the Democratic Republic of the Congo) in the late 1950s and early 1960s. The UNHCR then airlifted these refugees to the Mwesi Highlands—a refugee settlement the Tanzanian state and UNHCR had originally built to resettle ten thousand Rwandan refugees living in Burundi. The UNHCR undertook the considerable expense of airlifting these three thousand refugees to Mwesi for reasons that had less to do with humanitarian concerns about the sixty thousand Rwandan refugees in Kivu and more to do with maintaining the agency's image in the shifting international arena of humanitarian aid. Faced with the embarrassment of advertising, funding, and building a settlement for ten thousand refugees who then refused to move to Tanzania, the organization took advantage of the refugee crisis in Congo to populate Mwesi with a different group of Rwandan refugees.

By all accounts, the Mwesi settlement failed to achieve its objectives of refugee containment and development. Governmental and international notions of the refugees' political future as Tanzanian residents and citizens

114 · CHAPTER 6

conflicted with the refugees' images of their political future. For the Tanzanian state, refugee agency—manifested by the population's refusal to accede to evolving Tanzanian laws—was construed as a threat to Tanzanian sovereignty over its lands and its populations. This was particularly the case as refugees refused to abide by the newly enacted 1965 Refugee (Control) Act, a piece of legislation meant to increase state control over refugee settlements in light of the difficulties posed by Rwandan refugees in Muyenzi.[3] Anger over refugee aid was then heightened in Mpanda as local officials became frustrated with international agencies that privileged refugee aid over and above the well-being of the local population.

For UNHCR officials, in spite of their avowedly apolitical mission, a major tension became the content of the state's refugee laws, which legal representatives tried and failed to alter—thereby revealing the UNHCR's own political ambitions. Paradoxically, UNHCR representatives' understanding of their mission as apolitical blinded them to the very political actions of refugee leaders and groups. Thus, for UNHCR officials, refugee agency and claim making could only be interpreted as stemming from the actions and manipulations of an irrational and stubborn refugee elite, a conclusion that dovetailed remarkably well with colonial interpretations of African agency and belied officials' own observations of the political climate at Mwesi. These officials were incapable of grasping the political logic that underpinned refugee agency at Mwesi, despite their detailed knowledge of the contentious politics occurring within the settlement. As a result, UNHCR representatives encouraged the Tanzanian state to sentence noncompliant refugees to hard labor, revealing the inhumane measures the agency was willing to advocate to solve refugee issues in Africa. This chapter examines the contradictions at the heart of the UNHCR's mission, both as a nonpolitical agency and as a humanitarian organization.

Refugee Sovereignties

Competition over sovereignty in Mwesi entailed conflicting visions of how refugees should be treated, what kind of rights refugees could claim, and whether refugee groups should have a voice in determining their political future. For refugee leaders, the answer was clear: Rwandan refugees should determine their own political status, regardless of the wishes of the asylum state or the aid organizations involved. This expression of political agency conflicted dramatically with state and international plans for the refugee community. Refugee actions, and state and international reactions, shaped the events that unfolded at Mwesi and in Tanzania, impacting state and international thinking on the place and purpose of refugees and refugee aid for decades to come.

The history of Mwesi thus brings into focus the power of refugee political imaginaries.[4] The political circumstances that lead to refugee exile are not addressed in the formula of transnational refugee aid. Rather, international aid intended to confine, neutralize, and settle refugees may inadvertently delay, dislocate, and even intensify the political ambitions of refugee leaders and populations. Refugees bring with them the social, economic, and political contexts of their prior lives and subjectivities. As such, not all refugees want to settle in host nations, and many retain political ambitions that are altered or even solidified by their experiences in exile. If, in the abstract, refugee populations challenge the notion of an interlocking, static world of sovereign nation-states, their political ambitions can also present a very real threat to the governments involved (both sending and receiving).[5] It is for this reason that state leaders seek to neutralize the refugee "problem" by resettling such figures within the framework of sovereign nation-states.

The political aspirations of Rwandan refugees exacerbated conflicts over authority and legislation at Mwesi. Nationalist movements during the process of decolonization and beyond involved struggles against imperial powers and conflicts "between contenders of different visions for the nation."[6] Rwandan refugees often remained loyal to an imagined vision of nation (a Tutsi-governed Rwanda) that existed in opposition to the political reality of the Rwandan state under Hutu rule. Within the refugee community itself there also existed contending visions of the idealized Rwandan nation, images that provoked contentious in-group politics. The power struggles among those who sought to define and defend their vision of nationalism extended to the space of Mwesi and impacted all the national and international organizations involved. However, UNHCR representatives' insistence on separating their humanitarian mission from the realm of politics led to an intractable and ideological impasse among all the actors involved. Representatives' failure to consult refugees about settlement plans and individual and group aspirations led to institutional interests taking priority over the UNHCR's protection mandate. These priorities then led to conflicts with Tanzanian government officials who refused to acquiesce to the agency's legal mandate.

Because refugees are "anomalous," those who wish to govern refugee populations must create "conditions in which they do not upset the conventional, predictable and normal."[7] But what happens when the "conventional, predictable and normal" are also in a state of flux? The process of Tanzanian

116 · CHAPTER 6

state making (or nation building) was long and is, in many ways, ongoing. The first ten years of the state's existence were marked by policy fluctuations and the increasing power of the central state and bureaucracy. In increments throughout the 1960s, central state governors increased their power and authority over the territory through a series of laws, including the creation of a one-party state and an increasingly coercive bureaucracy.[8] Simultaneously, the state's relations with international powers "changed abruptly" after the 1964 union of mainland Tanganyika with Zanzibar, and diplomatic tensions following British failure to enact tougher measures against non-African colonial regimes in southern Africa.[9]

While Tanzanian statesmen understood international aid as necessary for the country's progression to Nyerere's ideal of self-sufficiency, they also viewed aid with suspicion. Such aid could very well threaten the new autonomy of the country, both politically and economically. By the late 1960s, the state increasingly turned to authoritarian policies in an attempt to retain control over its population and resources.[10] As the government tried to navigate the terrain of independence, it often came into conflict with the international community and with the UNHCR. This conflict was manifested in UNHCR officials' objections to the 1965 Refugee (Control) Act, which vastly increased the government's power over all aspects of refugee settlement and administration, to the detriment of UNHCR control. Refugees at Mwesi, through their active and passive demonstrations of noncompliance and, specifically, their refusal to accept and sign the refugee permits mandated by the 1965 act, brought tensions between the state and the UNHCR to new heights while undermining the authority of both. The "humanitarian arena" of Mwesi then became a space where state, transnational, and refugee actors negotiated and contested "the [everday] micro-physics of power."[11]

Mwesi Conceived

Mwesi was supposed to be a big project for the TCRS and UNHCR—"big business" even. The original tripartite agreement signed in May 1964 by the Tanzanian government, UNHCR, and TCRS outlined plans for the resettlement of ten thousand Rwandan refugees from Burundi to Mwesi. This would be the first time the UNHCR transferred refugees to a second asylum nation. The project was named for Armond Kuijpers, the Belgian member of the UNHCR executive committee who had died during the May session at which the project was approved. The agency was scaling up its activities.

The idea was for the UNHCR, through funding from UN nation-states, to pay for and organize the movement of the Rwandan refugees 250 miles from Burundi to Mwesi. The TCRS, through donations from its international and largely Christian partners, would provide operational support and oversight for the settlement, in consultation with the UNHCR and in collaboration with local government officials and the central government. The Tanzanian state would provide the land and oversight necessary for the refugees' development as settler-farmers. The agreement carefully laid out each organization's discrete responsibilities. The signatories imagined that by meeting the refugees' "basic vital needs" in the areas of transportation, health care, and agricultural supervision, they would become self-supporting within two years.[12] The refugees would then remain in Mwesi and contribute to the overall development of the region and the country. Refugee desires, as a group and as individuals, were not included in the agreement.

The initial project was as carefully conceived, perhaps even as necessary, as it was to become an embarrassment to the state and aid organizations concerned. The situation for Rwandan refugees in Burundi was certainly unstable. There had been threats of violence against Rwandan Tutsi, and the new Burundian government asked the UNHCR to transfer ten thousand of the more than fifty thousand Rwandan refugees in the country. Burundi, so the argument went, lacked the arable land to settle the Rwandans, whose leaders attacked the Rwandan state and involved themselves in the nascent and tumultuous politics of the Burundian government. The Armond Kuijpers project provided a peaceful solution that ostensibly benefited all involved: the refugees would receive access to a safe environment and aid through which they could become self-reliant; the Tanzanian government would receive international funding and labor power with which to develop an isolated area of the country; and the UNHCR and TCRS would receive increased media coverage and donations, bolstering their global reputations in the new world of international humanitarian aid.

From the start, the resettlement scheme was plagued by problems, none larger than the Rwandan refugees' lack of interest in moving from Burundi to Tanzania.[13] In the summer and fall of 1964, Rwandan leaders in Burundi repeatedly refused to travel to Tanzania.[14] When it finally became apparent that Mwesi was not going to be utilized for the Rwandan refugees in Burundi, UNHCR and TCRS officials scrambled to avert a public relations nightmare. At stake was the two new agencies' reputations among their donor constituencies. The Tanzanian government, LWF/TCRS, and UNHCR had started work on the expensive, ambitious, and highly publicized Mwesi

118 · CHAPTER 6

settlement in the spring of 1964. They would find themselves in a "serious predicament" if the investment of hundreds of thousands of dollars in the settlement was not utilized in ways deemed appropriate by those who had donated the funds.[15] Eventually, UNHCR officials found a solution that fit within their conscribed mandate and did not challenge the modus operandi of refugee aid at the time. Mwesi then became home to three thousand Rwandan refugees who had previously sought refuge in the Kivu province of Congo.

Aid and Its Constituents: The Aid Spectacle

To whom does humanitarian aid belong, and whose interests does it, can it, serve? When the first director of the TCRS, George Farquharson, arrived in Dar es Salaam in March 1964, the UNHCR director of operations told him, "You're in business brother—big business."[16] But what sort of "business" was it to be? Mwesi, as the first UNHCR refugee settlement in a second asylum country, held great publicity value for the UNHCR and LWF. To meet the perceived demand for UNHCR services, agency officials appealed to UN member states to approve its budget.[17] In the case of the UNHCR, funding is funneled through its executive committee, which collectively debates and approves the UNHCR's annual budget. The approval of the executive committee is crucial to the continuance and expansion of UNHCR programs. And, as with donors, approval is based on the appearance of success.

Similarly, the TCRS, through its parent organization the LWF, depended on outside resources to fulfill its budgetary needs. The resettlement of ten thousand Rwandan refugees from Burundi to Tanzania required the approval of myriad groups and people. In this case, the enormity of the undertaking required almost unprecedented publicity efforts. In May 1964 the executive committee approved a budget of $309,000 for the transfer of ten thousand Rwandan refugees from Burundi to Mwesi.[18] The tripartite agreement signed by the UNHCR, LWF, and Tanzanian government stated that the LWF would contribute $100,000 for the construction of a school, roads, and other essential infrastructure.

When Jorgen Norredam, the first TCRS program officer, arrived in Mwesi in the spring of 1964, he had a monumental task ahead of him. The Mwesi Highlands existed in a virtual absence of infrastructure and state personnel. Situated seventy miles from Mpanda town in Tabora region, the area was far from administrative centers and nearly unknown territory. The location was ideal in the context of Nyerere's nation-building plans, which were predicated on populating and developing the state's vast unoccupied territories. The Mwesi Highlands fit the leadership's definition of remote and depopulated areas—a perfect example of a place that, through villagization, self-help, and hard work, could be made into a self-sufficient, cash-crop-producing area.

However, many Rwandan refugees in Burundi did not share this view of Mwesi as a potential developmental paradise. As early as June 1964, LWF correspondence began to hint at the refugees' reluctance to move to Mwesi. By July, aid workers in Burundi estimated that refugee resettlement had only a 50 percent chance of occurring.[19] By late September, it was clear to TCRS officials that the refugee leaders in Burundi (considered representative of the refugee population as a whole) would not relocate.[20]

Despite these early delays and warnings, articles in Lutheran magazines praised the LWF's efforts to save the Rwandan "Watusi" in Burundi. An August 1964 headline in *Viewpoint* read: "Watusi Tribe Will Dance Again," with a corresponding article that heroized the LWF and erroneously reported that the "actual transfer [of Rwandan refugees] began in June" and would be completed in September.[21] When LWF officials acknowledged that the movement had not actually begun, they reported that the delay was due to "extensive flooding." The *Viewpoint* article posited that the postponement was actually a boon to the project, as it gave the organization more time to prepare Mwesi for the refugees' arrival.[22]

Despite the confidence projected to outside audiences, within the UNHCR and LWF/TCRS there was great confusion and anxiety about why the refugees refused to leave Burundi. Perhaps the most useful theory was that refugee leaders were unwilling to have the population divided, separated, and moved "so far from their native land."[23] Additionally, rebellions in neighboring Congo during the summer and fall of 1964 may have motivated Burundian officials to keep the refugees where they were, in the "hope that the general instability in Central Africa will make it possible for Watutsies [*sic*] to stage another invasion of Rwanda."[24] Given the tension among the Burundian, Congolese, and Rwandan governments, such an invasion—if successful—would have benefited the political interests of the Burundian nation-state. This theory bears merit, based on the Burundians' explanation to the UNHCR regarding the failed movement of four hundred refugees on September 1, 1964. Word that the Burundian government had canceled this resettlement reached UNHCR officials only one day prior to the (re)scheduled move, with the government claiming it had called off the operation "because of new political developments in Central Africa." A representative of the

120 · CHAPTER 6

UNHCR, Gilbert Jaeger, then traveled to the region to examine the situation "and to take all measures to carry through the original plan."[25] From the start of the operation, then, regional politics affected what was an essentially a political act: the resettlement of Rwandan refugees.

In spite of these escalating warnings, work continued in Mwesi. The government and the TCRS employed Kikuyu and local settlers to build roads in the isolated area, as well as grass reception huts for the refugees.[26] An airstrip was completed. By the end of August, work crews had finished the construction of huts to receive the first thousand refugees. Due to delays in US approval of food aid, Norredam received permission from Geneva and the Tanzanian government to buy maize and oil locally—despite the obvious and continued absence of any refugees in Mwesi.[27]

Simultaneously, the UNHCR's office of public affairs negotiated access for American news teams to record and report on the refugee movement from Burundi to Mwesi. Both WS-LWF director Bruno Muetzelfeldt and TCRS director George Farquharson cautioned that the presence of news crews might disrupt the refugees' "trek." However, their concerns were voiced in terms of the TCRS's international reputation in the event of program failure, to which the National Lutheran Council's executive secretary of public relations replied: "I am not too much worried about the way the LWF would come off even if full success in the project were not realized. In other words, the fact that a valiant attempt to minister is being made in the face of tremendous difficulties would in itself put the LWF in a very favorable light. As a matter of fact, it might have more favorable impact than a neat success story all tied up in pink ribbons."[28] And yet, by September 25, the movement had been postponed at least three times. As a result, in late September the UNHCR delegate to Tanzania met with Tanzanian Minister of State Sijaona to discuss the problem and to raise the question of the government's attitude toward a possible resettlement of "Rwanda settlers in Kivu."[29]

Around the same time, the Congolese government began hinting at plans to expel the sixty thousand Rwandan refugees residing in Kivu province (both inside and outside of UNHCR camps).[30] Many observers, including one LWF representative, expressed skepticism about this plan, noting that the Congolese government had neither the political will nor the manpower to enforce such legislation even if it had been enacted.[31] Nevertheless, during the late summer and fall of 1964, UNHCR representatives increasingly called attention to the "precarious position" of Rwandan refugees living in Congo.[32]

There can be no doubt about the instability and violence that threatened Rwandans living in Kivu.[33] There was acute conflict in the area, and many

Rwandan refugees were caught up in the violence related to Congolese state formation and the Mulelist rebellions in the east.[34] Furthermore, in both Kivu and Burundi, UNHCR officials believed that the governments had "not taken active steps in resettlement" and that the refugees were not permitted to live above subsistence levels.[35]

What remains questionable is the UNHCR's hastily prepared and expensive plan to airlift three thousand Rwandans in Congo to Mwesi. The UNHCR representative in Goma, Pierre Coat, noted at the start of the airlift that "the present movement, bearing as it does on 3,000 people . . . can at best relieve some of the most acute local tensions and that the only thing to do for the majority" was to have them remain and work where they are.[36] The utility of the airlift as a settlement and pacifying tool for Rwandans in Congo was therefore much in question.

The expensive and unprecedented airlift was, reportedly, based on the "immediate need" for movement of the refugees.[37] Yet LWF correspondence indicated a different kind of urgency—one based on the reputation and organizational survival of the transnational agencies involved. In November 1964 the director of WS-LWF wrote:

> I have, of course, no delusion that the UNHCR went to this considerable expenditure of an airlift primarily for the purpose of getting LWF/ WS out of the embarrassing situation of having the Mwesi Settlement prepared without the original plan. . . . They had their own interests to preserve and their own faces to save, as the UNHCR is at least as implicated in this undertaking as we are. On the other hand, the fact remains that their readiness to institute an airlift from the Kivu Province despite the heavy financial implications for them has helped us out of a somewhat difficult public relations situation vis a vis our donors.[38]

And yet the resources of Mwesi might have been directed toward other purposes. The first TCRS director noted that "a reassignment of the project to meet very urgent needs among indigenous Tanzanians" would be possible and would boost the TCRS's image in the new nation by supporting the "National Building Villagisation ambition."[39] The proposal to use Mwesi for the benefit of Tanzanians echoed an earlier letter in which Muetzelfeldt suggested that it be utilized for Tanzanian development.[40] The area commissioner of Mpanda, Mr. Sungeru, had also requested that Mwesi be made available to 150 to 250 local families interested in relocating to the area. However, in response to this request, the deputy high commissioner wrote that "the actual settlement of Tanzanian citizens does not fall within the competence of my office," thereby ending the discussion of using Mwesi to benefit Tanzanians.[41]

The TCRS had also offered to make Mwesi available to Mozambican refugees in Tanzania, but the vast distance between their location in the country's extreme southeast and Mwesi (a thousand-mile journey) made this an unlikely scenario.[42] What seems in hindsight to be an even more unlikely scenario is what actually came to pass. During the fall of 1964 and spring of 1965, the UNHCR, in collaboration with the Congolese and Tanganyikan governments, airlifted three thousand Rwandan refugees from Goma in Kivu to Tabora in Tanzania. From there, local government officials, UNHCR field officers, and TCRS personnel transported the refugees by railroad to Mpanda town and then via trucks on the final leg of the journey to the Mwesi settlement. This movement was as difficult as it became contentious.

The Airlift and the Authentic Refugee

When the first 250 refugees arrived at the Tabora airport from Congo, the Tanzanian regional commissioner (RC) who met them was aghast at their appearance. To the RC, as well as TCRS staff, the first refugees from Congo looked "more like tourists than refugees." As a result, the RC "was furious. He tore through their luggage, cross examined them and claimed they were not refugees at all."[43] The commissioner then attempted to stop their transport to Mwesi, and when this proved impossible, he attempted to forbid them to stay the night at Mpanda.

The RC's belief that these were not *real* refugees underscores the central question of the time and one that continues to this day. Who determines refugee status, and why is this status a marker of *authentic* relief? By virtue of their appearance and language, the commissioner deemed the Rwandans undeserving of the many services provided to them. Such remarks highlight the tension between those who determine refugee status and provide refugees with aid and those who receive and/or host refugee populations—a tension on prominent display in Tabora between the UNHCR representatives and local government officials.

The RC's shock at the first refugee group's appearance stemmed from their apparent wealth—which he assumed made them either criminals or missionaries.[44] It is, of course, far from clear whether the refugees' economic status put them in less danger in Congo than other refugees; however, the procedure by which refugees in Kivu were selected for the airlift is opaque. It is also telling that the last groups of refugees sent to Mwesi from Kivu in

Conflicting Sovereignties · 123

1965 were in "very poor" health.[45] Paradoxically, when these last refugees were airlifted to Tabora in May 1965, the situation in Kivu had largely stabilized, although the food situation remained critical.[46]

Tensions between UNHCR and TCRS personnel were also exacerbated by the situation at Mwesi. When Norredam arrived in Mwesi, he expected to make the settlement ready for ten thousand refugees arriving imminently from Burundi. By the fall of 1964, he and his staff were faced with inexorable delays and uncertainty, leading to poor morale.[47] Additionally, throughout the first years of the settlement, TCRS and UNHCR authorities were plagued by continuous and "obvious . . . problems" among the international staff, as each attempted to blame delays and budget shortfalls on the other.[48]

The airlift itself suffered from unexpected delays due to heavy rainfall in Mwesi and, most important, the intense regional and global politics of the time. Regional officials in Tabora continued to resist the refugee settlement, causing one TCRS administrator to write in late November 1964, "It is impossible for me to make even an educated guess as to the future settlement of Mwesi."[49] The year 1964–1965 was one of upheaval and conflict in both regional and international politics. The April 1964 union of mainland Tanganyika with Zanzibar heralded the beginning of a new, more aggressive policy by the Tanzanian state. No longer content to passively accept Western aid—particularly British aid following Britain's refusal to accede to the OAU's demands regarding Rhodesia—the Cold War was heating up on the continent.[50] In January 1965 the Tanzanian government expelled two US officials from Tanzania, casting uncertainty over the continuation of US food aid. That same month, the Cuban pilot who flew the chartered Transair planes from Goma to Tabora was arrested in Tanzania, likely because officials suspected he was an agent of the Congolese authorities.[51] As a result of these issues, the Tanzanian government halted the airlift indefinitely in December 1964.[52]

The ongoing delays following the transport of the first thousand Rwandans from Goma to Mwesi affected the reputations of both international agencies involved. Bernard Confer, executive secretary of Lutheran World Relief, who was responsible for ascertaining funding and personnel for the settlement, wrote to WS-LWF in early February 1965, "I can foresee trying to explain why the refugees are not moving and not sounding plausible in the process!"[53] While Transair attempted to find another pilot, the Tanzanian and Congolese governments entered into negotiations regarding the airlift's resumption. In the meantime, conflict abounded between the UNHCR representatives at Tabora and TCRS staff.

124 · CHAPTER 6

It was this "very shaky ship" that Brian Neldner, the new director of TCRS, took control of in December 1964.[54] In the Mwesi settlement, Neldner experienced his first crisis. There was the ongoing issue with the Americans, a "difficult administrator in Tabora," and an expatriate staff riven by internal divides and accusations "of insulting local staff." The Tanzanian government was changing by the time Neldner arrived, and British civil servants were being replaced by Tanzanians. Moreover, Norredam and his staff had been unprepared for the 1964 rains, and the grass huts built for the refugees could not keep the storms out.[55] By December 1964, the Mpanda-Mwesi road was well over budget and still incomplete.[56] And, as the opening paragraphs of this section attest, local government officials were not pleased with the presence of, or provision of aid to, Rwandan refugees.

In Tabora, it was clear that local leaders resented the aid given to the Rwandan refugees, particularly because these authorities had unsuccessfully lobbied the UNHCR to make Mwesi's facilities available to the Tanzanian population in light of Mpanda's "progressively deteriorating economic situation."[57] The RC continued to hinder expatriate operations throughout the duration of the airlift.[58] He went so far as to confiscate expatriate passports, and at one point he kicked two UNHCR officials out of his office—apparently because he perceived them as "the typical colonialist civil servant."[59]

The commissioner's correlation of expatriate UNHCR and TCRS workers with colonial officials reveals the power dynamics underlying the refugee scheme. Many officials in the national and local government compared expatriate aid workers to members of the British colonial regime. Indeed, although the original settlement officer at Mwesi, Mannington Allushula, had an excellent working relationship with TCRS staff, TCRS officials noted that Allushula was "thought to be smarting under a social complex [that discriminated] over [and] against the expatriates."[60] The TCRS's reputation was also undermined by the fact that it employed few Tanzanians.

To the TCRS's credit, its representatives attempted to understand local and particularly national sentiments and to fit their programs into existing state policies. This was particularly the case at the upper echelons of the agency. Muetzelfeldt made it clear that the TCRS existed and operated within the context of the government's authority and that national priorities and cultural context took precedence over international ambitions. Muetzelfeldt was therefore careful to ensure "that no misunderstanding arises in government circles as to TCRS interfering in matters which are government policy and decisions."[61] Neldner also took pains to respect national laws and

Conflicting Sovereignties · 125

authority, relying on Cassius Njunde, a Tanzanian TCRS employee, to inculcate incoming expatriate staff in the Tanzanian milieu.[62]

However, the reality of aid "on the ground" was different from the atmosphere envisioned at the top. Based on the field correspondence of the expatriates who resided in Tabora and Mwesi in the 1960s, it becomes easier to understand why Tanzanians perceived refugee aid as similar to colonialism—that is, aid bestowed by white patrons who often underestimated the intelligence, the potential, and occasionally the humanity of the locals. On the ground in Mwesi, Norredam epitomized this view, at least in his correspondence with the TCRS and LWF. For example, in October 1964 Norredam wrote in his official field diary that he had put the "black boys"—referring to the Kikuyu workers from Katama—to work under his wife's direction. He went on to note that "if you give your orders with a smile, you can get a lot of activity out of Africans for a while—provided this is not unduly prolonged."[63] This condescending attitude would likely not have been lost on local workers and officials.

Indeed, in February 1965 the regional commissioner requested that three TCRS staff members vacate the settlement, leaving it seriously understaffed. In response, Muetzelfeldt noted that "something of this kind . . . was already expected . . . since the end of January the passports and identity papers of all ex-patriates (Africans and non-Africans alike) had been scrutinized more than once."[64] This increased attention to papers, a tool of bureaucratic control, reflected an increase in statism occurring throughout Tanzania; it also reflected a growing friction between local and international officials.[65]

It was not just the attitude of expatriates and the apparent wealth of the refugees that rankled local authorities. In 1964 Tanzanian officials estimated that throughout the country there was only one doctor for every twenty-five thousand people.[66] The fact that the TCRS had hired an expatriate doctor for the three thousand refugees at Mwesi and provided the settlement with a state-of-the-art medical clinic was an affront to many local officials. As a result, when refugees could not be adequately treated at Mwesi and needed to be sent to Tanzanian hospitals, officials at Tabora and Mpanda often refused transportation.[67]

Worse still, the first refugees to arrive at Mwesi were "town" people who were not interested in farming.[68] As a result, government and TCRS staff had a difficult time convincing them to engage in self-help agricultural activities. In addition to local officials' perceptions that the refugees received preferential access to development materials and a high turnover among TCRS staff, the first years of the settlement were marked by tensions between and among settlers and the various officials who planned their future at Mwesi.[69]

126 · CHAPTER 6

Despite these difficulties, by 1967, less than three years after the first refugees arrived at Mwesi, they had achieved food subsistence, allowing TCRS staff to phase out food rations.[70] Relations between settlement and district leaders had also improved, and the new area commissioner invited the TCRS to represent Mwesi on the Mpanda district development committee.[71] It seemed that the Mwesi settlement was well on its way to becoming self-sufficient not only in terms of food but also with regard to community services and agricultural development broadly conceived. However, the UNHCR's efforts to decrease funding to Mwesi during this time led to conflicts with the TCRS. Additionally, the government and UNHCR continued to refuse refugees' requests to introduce cattle to the settlement.[72] Various institutional and refugee interests thus continued to diverge during this early phase of the Mwesi settlement.

The Refugee (Control) Act

The UNHCR representative for Tanzania, G. de Bosch Kemper, was taken by surprise when the draft of the Refugee (Control) Act first came to his attention in November 1965. The legislation's drafters took as their model the British Alien Control Act, enacted during World War II to protect the mandate's resources from enemy agents.[73] The idea of protecting Tanzania from potentially subversive refugee populations was prominent throughout the act's articles and tone, which, according to legal experts at the UNHCR, violated both the spirit and the letter of the 1951 Refugee Convention to which Tanzania was a signatory. In this sense, the act was a precursor to the 1969 Organization of African Unity (OAU) Refugee Convention, which both expanded the definition of refugees—in particular to accommodate those fleeing minority-rule governments—and simultaneously prohibited any "subversive" acts against any OAU member nation.[74] For the Tanzanian government, Rwandan refugees' attacks against the Rwandan state presented a danger to an independent OAU state that needed to be controlled and contained—in the process, contravening some of its obligations under the 1951 Refugee Convention.[75] As UNHCR officials in East Africa and Geneva grew increasingly concerned about the ramifications of the act, they sent numerous revisions to Tanzanian officials.

The struggle over the Refugee (Control) Act and subsequent events related to its application to Rwandan refugees reveals the basic contradiction of the UNHCR during this time. As a nonpolitical agency, the UNHCR was not involved in political decisions. However, particularly during the

1960s, the agency was involved first and foremost in the legal protection of refugees and secondarily in their material aid. The very existence of the UNHCR's legal division and legal officers implied its intent to influence the juridical canon of sovereign nation-states concerning the issues most relevant to state sovereignty: control over borders and the treatment of noncitizens.

To UNHCR officers, the entire premise of the 1965 act contradicted the 1951 convention, which states "that refugees not be treated indiscriminately as subject to special legislation even when circumstances require such legislation." The UNHCR had additional concerns about the greater authority given to Tanzanian officials without a "provision to bar abuse of power."[76] The UNHCR legal division proposed changes to the legislation throughout the fall of 1964, all of which were rejected by the Tanzanian legislature.[77] In response, the UNHCR representative to Tanzania was asked to convey "the disquiet of this Office at the conjunction of necessary refugee control measures and quite distinct security measures in one Act to the discrimination of refugees from other aliens. In future in order to achieve our cooperation it would be much preferable if this Office could be associated with or consulted on such legislation which concerns refugees at an earlier stage."[78] The idea that "control measures" for refugees should be distinct from "security measures" necessitated by "other aliens" reveals the paradox of the UNHCR's depoliticized approach to refugees—as does the suggestion (and implicit threat) that if the Tanzanian government wanted to ensure the UNHCR's continued "cooperation," it should consult the UNHCR before creating national laws. Unlike earlier events in Muyenzi, this time, the central government did not acquiesce to UNHCR demands.

The 1965 Refugee (Control) Act enabled unprecedented governmental control over refugee camps and settlements in Tanzania. It also led to the decree that all refugees had to accept, sign, and carry a state identity document in the form of a refugee permit.[79] More than half the three thousand refugees at Mwesi, in addition to two thousand refugees at Muyenzi, refused to sign or accept the permit.

Apolitical Agency and Political Refugees

The permit issue began at Mwesi in June 1967. By early February 1968, two-thirds of the refugees at Mwesi "had categorically refused to accept Refugee Permits for various reasons, none of which logically make any sense."[80] The original misunderstanding, according to the UNHCR, occurred when the settlement commandant apparently led the refugee leadership to believe that the permits were optional. Additionally, perhaps due to language differences, many refugees believed that if they signed the permit they would lose any claim to Rwandan citizenship.[81]

The UNHCR representative for Tanzania visited Mwesi on February 11, 1968, to explain that accepting the permit did not preclude repatriation and that the refugees had to obey Tanzanian law or "face the consequences of legal measures."[82] This was the same message relayed by R. M. Kawawa, the second vice president, in November 1967. Both the regional and area commissioners and the settlement staff blamed the refugees' refusal to adopt the permits on "the influence of certain local 'leaders,'" sixty-three of whom were jailed under the Preventative Detention Act.[83]

In January 1968 the Tanzanian government arrested more than seventy refugees and sentenced them to one month's imprisonment in Mpanda, where they were nevertheless held until April. Seventy-two refugees were then sent to Uyui, the state central prison in Tabora. Government officials from the second vice president's office, as well as the senior prison superintendent, frequently visited the imprisoned refugees to explain why they had been detained and to try to persuade "them to adhere to the law of the country," with little success.[84]

From the beginning, UNHCR officers framed the problem of refugee permits in terms of actively seeking a "solution which is acceptable to the Government, without thereby giving the refugees the feeling that they have won a victory which may induce other refugees simply to follow suit."[85] This became more difficult in November 1968, when the government "decided to get rid" of the uncooperative Rwandans at Tabora and asked the UNHCR to repatriate them "elsewhere as soon as possible."[86]

The government's request stemmed from Kawawa's visit to Mwesi and Tabora and the refugees' persistent refusal to sign the permits. The UNHCR's director of operations, Thomas Jamieson, noted that in light of this continued resistance, "some face-saving device" was needed. Jamieson suggested a "compromise solution" that involved having the refugees accept a letter, which would not require a signature, instead of the refugee permit, but this was rejected.[87] In March 1970 the new settlement commandant at Mwesi began legal action against those who refused to sign.[88] Despite the government's tacit agreement to "defer any new action in the hope that time would solve the problem," Kawawa stated, "if necessary the Government would declare all the refugees as prohibited immigrants, since they are illegally in the country."[89]

Conflicting Sovereignties · 129

Refugees at Mwesi escalated the stakes of the permit issue by extending the legal confrontation into agricultural development, thus compromising the entire settlement.[90] The UNHCR representatives were therefore faced with a large group of refugees "determined to force the government's hand, being convinced that international help" would be forthcoming.[91] Simultaneously, they were confronted with the "icy inflexibility of the Government" in insisting that the refugees sign the permits.[92] In response to these events, and to the refugees' continued "de-escalating [of] their co-operation," the UNHCR branch office determined that "under no circumstances should any further assistance be granted to these refugees," despite the likelihood of an "acute shortage of food"—a practice opposed by the TCRS director.[93] The UNHCR legal officer for East Africa also suggested that the government subject refugee leaders to forced labor to exert "a certain influence on the attitude of these Rwandese," and Kawawa's office agreed to approach the attorney general on the matter.[94] The UNHCR's suggestion that the refugees be subjected to "hard labor" was certainly ironic, given that the legal division had previously protested the Refugee (Control) Act on the grounds that it violated the refugees' human rights.[95]

By March 1968, the agricultural impasse at Mwesi had not changed. Refugees refused to plant seeds, and TCRS personnel were forced to curtail community development, health, and education programs because "the people who have not signed the documents voluntarily refrain from participation."[96] As punishment, food rations and medical services were cut for two weeks, a situation that Neldner noted was against the "humanitarian principles" of the TCRS, which started to distribute food in contradiction of UNHCR orders.[97]

In the meantime, UNHCR representatives searched for the "crux of the problem" and "the real motive for the [refugees'] refusal," as "the presently available explanations are hardly creditable."[98] Based on the archival evidence, however, it seems that UNHCR representatives were well aware of the crux of the problem, which was inherently political and went beyond the influence of individual leaders to involve issues of power in the refugee community. In February 1969 the UNHCR representative for Tanzania wrote about the political parties (tellingly referred to as "groups") whose "competitive feelings . . . are still dominating the otherwise dull lives of the refugees, particularly those of the older generation, who closely watch each other's movements for leadership in the settlement."[99] According to de Bosch Kemper, 35 percent of the adults at Mwesi, primarily those from the Rwandan middle class who were "cooperative" and accepted the permits,

130 · CHAPTER 6

belonged to RADER (Rassemblement Démocratique Rwandais). In contrast, 55 percent of adults belonged to UNAR (Union Nationale Rwandaise) and objected to the permits "mainly because RADER is in favour of the document." The remaining 10 percent of adults changed their opinion based on "mood or benefit expectations." In a rare moment of clarity, de Bosch Kemper went on to note that "the introduction of the Refugee Permit has given the two major groups an unique possibility to . . . use it as a platform in their internal fight for leadership and drive for power." Despite this articulation of blatant political maneuvering, de Bosch Kemper created an image of a recalcitrant refugee population that, failing to understand the original settlement commandant's explanation of the permits in Kiswahili, refused to accept the truth and "rectify their obvious mistake!"[100]

De Bosch Kemper's letter provides rare insight into the refugee community and the divisions and political maneuverings that dominated refugee life. Refugees brought to Mwesi not only loyalties based on politics but also socio-economic and generational divisions based on their lives in Rwanda. Here we have a picture of a complex society, with individuals and groups debating their lives in exile and planning their autonomous future through an oppositional politics that, in this instance, revolved around the refugee permit.

As for the Rwandan refugees still detained in Tabora prison in late April 1969, the refugees stated that because they had "been brought into Tanzania by the High Commissioner against their will . . . they should be returned to the Congo by the High Commissioner."[101] According to the UNHCR representative, the refugees believed that because "five refugees have died in prison since their admission there, . . . they are fated to die in Tanzania whereas in the Congo they at least have a chance of survival. . . . It seems impossible to make them see reason on this subject especially in view of the strength they seem to have gained in the motto 'living and dying together.'" Tellingly, the official went on to posit that although there were different political affiliations among the refugees at Mwesi (RADER and UNAR), the "political element bears no particular weight on the existing problem."[102] It is difficult to imagine how UNHCR officials reconciled these visions of the refugees as both political subjects and apolitical actors.[103]

In addition to visits from government officials and the prison superintendent to try to educate the prisoners about the law, the UNHCR representative spent ten hours with the refugees explaining that the government required every foreigner in Tanzania to have an identification card and that the refugee permits had nothing to do with citizenship. He also told them that even if the Congolese government would accept them back, neither the Tanzanian

Conflicting Sovereignties · 131

government nor the UNHCR would pay for such a move "after all the financial assistance and effort" put into the refugees' resettlement in Mwesi.[104] The refugees vowed to continue their noncooperation and said that if they could not return to Congo, they would prefer to move to either Uganda or Burundi rather than remain in Tanzania.

After a March 1969 visit to the Mwesi refugees, 1,030 of whom had signed the permits out of a population of 3,144 (540 were exempt because they were younger than ten years of age), UNHCR representative R. C. Kohaut noted that the refugees believed the UNHCR "should return them to the country from which they were 'abducted.'" Kohaut found it strange that, after learning that other countries required refugee permits, "they expressed their willingness to comply with this regulation—*somewhere else!*" Kohaut went on to comment that the non-permit-holding refugees had leaders other than those in detention, but after those initial arrests, they "do not come out in the open." Kohaut concluded by suggesting that a "change of environment including supervised manual labor might have the required effect," but such measures were likely to fail due to the refugees' "stubbornness."[105]

By the end of April 1970, there was still no end in sight. Nils Gussing, the new UNHCR representative for Tanzania, noted that "only time" could solve the problem.[106] But Kawawa's decision to begin legal proceedings against non–permit holders at Mwesi meant that time was up.[107] A frustrated Gussing lamented the government's actions, which had "only open[ed] the wounds again."[108] Gussing wrote of his meeting with refugees at the Dabalo settlement (where some of the imprisoned refugees had been moved), "My discussion with this Group was if possible more frustrating and discouraging than my talk with the refugees in the prison. The same stubbornness and the same arguments."[109] By the close of 1970, the majority of the Rwandan refugees at Dabalo had gone on a hunger strike, protesting their confinement and demanding that the UNHCR return them to Congo.

Faced with an intractable government and an illogical refugee group that had taken noncooperation to a new level with the 1970 hunger strike, the UNHCR continued to view the refugees as stubborn and irrational. Despite the political overtones of this process and the ongoing communication between UNHCR officials and political representatives of various Rwandan groups in exile, the agency's apolitical mission colored its representatives' perceptions, such that the permit issue was transformed from a political conflict into a psychological one. If only the refugees could be forced to adopt the right mindset and see reason, UNHCR officials argued, permits would cease to be a problem. For the UNHCR, the dilemma at Mwesi centered on

132 · CHAPTER 6

the need for refugees to acquire the correct mentality. The lack of expatriate understanding of their motivations led to their frustration, an emotion that permeates the archival material. These refugees, for whom so much had been done, seemed ungrateful and maddeningly to an agency trying to adhere to a budget, irrational.

Conclusion: Documents of Sovereignty

In his discussion of state bureaucratic power, James Scott describes a process by which, in attempting to make populations "legible," state officials map their citizenries in defined categories—pigeonholes that enable state interventions and, simultaneously, exclude a "whole world lying 'outside the brackets'" of a simplified and technical frame of reference.[110] Similarly, in describing development discourse, James Ferguson writes that beneficiary populations become "constructed as a certain type of problem to be solved," one that is amenable to technical and replicable interventions.[111] What both analyses have in common is the view that politics operates by concealing the power dynamics inherent to both state and transnational projects, a concealment enacted through bureaucratic procedure. This is a politics made possible through the attempted simplification and subsequent categorization of localized lived experiences. But how can we understand a localized politics of a population in exile?

In one respect, UNHCR representatives in Tanzania have already done this for us, although, due to their "narrow bureaucratic vision" of the refugee population, they seemed unable to understand the ramifications of their observations. In attempting to find the crux of the refugee problem, representatives of the UNHCR, the government, and the TCRS continually came into contact with the localized politics of the refugee camp. Here, factors stemming from the refugees' lives prior to flight became paramount, such as group membership and affiliations with political parties, as well as education and wealth.

Many refugees at Mwesi attempted to subvert the state's imposed technologies of categorization and control inherent in the 1965 legislation by refusing to accept the mandated refugee permit. Perhaps members of the refugee population grasped, in a way that UNHCR officials could not, the undertones of political power and control inherent in the permit. Even if they did not see themselves as participating in an oppositional politics, it is clear that Tanzanian and UNHCR officials grasped the political challenge of refugee noncompliance, as their shared concern about allowing the refugees the appearance

Conflicting Sovereignties · 133

of a "win" (a feat that might become contagious among other refugee populations) makes clear.

Therefore, instead of being "frustrating," "stubborn," and "illogical," the refugees' refusal to sign the permit might have been an indication that they understood its potential utility all too well. The permit was the next step in a bureaucratic order of control that, "in creating an official status," ingrained "the asymmetrical relationship between power and powerlessness."[112] Rwandan refugees, and their leaders in particular, remained engaged in a politics of "'imagined decolonization' or fantasy of what their postcolonial state should be."[113] As people intent on determining their own destinies, the refugees found restrictions on their lives grating. This is not to suggest that all the noncooperating refugees at Mwesi and Muyenzi thought of their resistance as a method of political activism, or to valorize their noncooperation. Rather, their noncooperation signified that "pre-flight moral standards and social constraints" remained important to the population at Mwesi.[114] And like all populations, a desire existed to maintain some control over individual and group decision making, control that was actively constrained by the expatriate and state officials in their midst.[115]

In this light, the refusal to sign refugee permits becomes a claims-making project—one that utilized the few resources available within the layered and unequal sovereignties that sought to govern them: the choice not to sign the government document. Along with noncompliance in agricultural development, this was a concrete challenge to state and transnational authority—and one of the only paths available, given the asymmetrical powers involved. Both Tanzania and the UN were intent on maintaining the system of sovereign nation-states in Central Africa. This program was based on solidifying a new status quo based not on justice or human rights but on stability. In refugee contexts, "the sovereign rights of individual states, constituted or not, have paramountcy over the individual rights of exiles."[116] This statement becomes more prescient in light of continued UNHCR funding of the Rwandan state despite ongoing human rights violations, including actions that led to the creation of Rwandan refugees. Certainly, the refugees at Mwesi did not have much reason to trust either the UNHCR or the Tanzanian state with their political futures.

The struggle for control in Mwesi is clarified by the fact that the decision to reject the refugee permit corresponded to an exclusion from the settlement's state- and UNHCR-sanctioned "official" political life. Non–permit holders did not take part in Refugee Council elections, which made this council useless to the government, the TCRS, and the UNHCR. Likewise, the detainees'

134 · CHAPTER 6

insistence that they had been "abducted" by the UNHCR, which was therefore obligated to return them to Congo, illustrates a claim to mobility—and to political choice. In Congo—or indeed, in Burundi or Uganda—state and UNHCR representatives were either unwilling or unable to control refugee actions because they lacked the political control and stability of the Tanzanian state, such as it was.

Mwesi was constantly and embarrassingly over budget, from the first days of road building through the permit crisis. It was difficult for UNHCR and TCRS officers to explain to their donors why a project planned for ten thousand refugees was insufficient to maintain the three thousand who actually arrived. The constituency of donors was not easily appeased, and even more than Muyenzi, Mwesi retained the stain of failure.[117] Indeed, by the 1980s, almost all the Rwandan refugees had moved elsewhere, and both the state and the UNHCR were unable to track their locations.[118]

In the years and decades to come, the conflicting and unequal sovereignties so prominently on display at Mwesi would come to haunt refugee settlements in Tanzania. However, before that happened, Nyerere and the state would embark on their most ambitious development plan yet—one that saw the state become more involved in the lives of Tanzanians than ever before. *Ujamaa* would bring many changes to Tanzania, including the use of coercion to force citizens' compliance with state policies. What would not change, however, were local efforts to retain autonomy in the face of powerful interference.

Conflicting Sovereignties · 135

PART III
THE MAKING OF CITIZENS

7. OF "NATURAL" CITIZENS AND "NATURAL" ILLEGALITY

UJAMAA, MAGENDO, AND NATURALIZATION

IN NGARA DISTRICT, 1970–1984

Marco Bautbula leaned back in his chair and laughed when I asked about *ujamaa* in Ngara district. "Some researchers got degrees on that policy," he said, smiling.[1] It is not quite a reproof, but I think I know what he meant. Historical attention to Tanzania's *ujamaa* policies during the late 1960s and 1970s have often dwarfed other inquiries.[2] I nodded my understanding to Marco, explaining that my work explores Ngara's history—how a border space became a national place and what role migrants (refugees, expatriates, and citizens) played in that process. Surely, *ujamaa* must have played a role in that evolution.

This chapter elucidates the contradictory meanings of citizenship in Ngara during the 1970s and early 1980s. There is a substantial and growing scholarship on *ujamaa*, encompassing everything from rural resistance to heavy-handed state programs to the internal dynamics and discourses of state and party leaders.[3] What historians have yet to thoroughly explore, however, is how the failure of these policies, both perceived and actual, affected rural identity politics during and since the 1970s. Located at the margins of an increasingly centralized bureaucracy, Ngarans engaged in practices that both undermined and consolidated state ideologies of nationhood and citizenship. Ngarans thus simultaneously resisted the edicts of local bureaucrats and adhered to the moral ideologies of self-reliance and nation building at the heart of national *ujamaa* policies.

The discourse of 1970s state politicians is apparent in the ways Ngarans speak of *ujamaa*. Those who lived through villagization and the failed naturalization of Rwandan refugees frequently echo the words and tropes used by state politicians to describe the motivations for villagization and citizenship ideologies. While some Ngarans acceded to, and others resented, forced villagization in their district, almost all recognized that illegal trade with Rwanda and Burundi was central to their livelihoods. It is clear that such trade increased during *ujamaa* and the subsequent time of *hamna* (nothing), when shortages of goods and markets plagued the district and the country. However, Ngarans speak about such trade with a nonchalance that indicates its banality and its ever-present existence as a time-honored strategy of survival. This trade was conducted not out of greed but out of necessity and tradition, which is clear when compared with the selfish traders (*wahujume*) whose actions were perceived as threatening to the new nation. Illicit trade did not exist to counter Nyerere's nation-building strategies but rather speaks to the irrelevance of borders as material boundaries in Ngaran imaginations. And yet, notions of a Tanzanian identity opposed to that of refugees continued to gain traction, even as Ngarans utilized the knowledge and trading skills of Rwandan refugees to further their own endeavors.

It is difficult to tease out the place of Rwandan refugees within the *ujamaa* villages that became emblematic of citizenship in Ngara. In many ways, the Rwandan refugee camps were forerunners of *ujamaa* villages, as they emphasized equality of land, cooperation, labor, and technical expertise, with which both the UNHCR and the Tanzanian state hoped to constitute new communities. Indeed, the area of the central Muyenzi refugee camp itself became an *ujamaa* village for Ngarans during the 1970s. However, it seems that refugees who had lived in internationally funded camps did not become integrated into *ujamaa* villages, indicating the extent to which separation and transnational funding distanced these groups from the people who were meant to build the new Tanzanian nation.

While remaining geographically focused on Ngara and, to a lesser extent, West Lake Region, my examination of Ngaran nationalism includes the leaders who promulgated citizenship ideals from the nation's economic and political center in Dar es Salaam. Although such ideals rarely translated into effective implementation programs, particularly during the acute economic crises of the late 1970s, state discourse around the nation and the proper conduct of citizens had a lasting impact on how Ngarans imagined their communities.[4]

The 1970s and 1980s were a time of movement for Ngarans—movement to state-planned *ujamaa* villages and less coercive forms of migration linked to illicit trade—as they negotiated new state policies designed to define a new citizenry. At the central state level, the definition of a proper Tanzanian citizen was increasingly linked to ideals of African socialism, familyhood, agricultural cooperation, self-reliance, and equality.[5] However, few Tanzanians became socialists; most remained "uncaptured" by abstract state policies that offered little in the way of concrete economic progress.[6] The majority of Ngarans negotiated an economic existence that combined individual subsistence farming, communal agriculture, and illegal transnational trade—strategies that blended new state policies with older, time-proven circulations of materials and people.

State policies also vastly expanded, in theory, who could be included as members within the Tanzanian citizenry. In 1980 the Tanzanian state ostensibly granted citizenship to the "old" caseload of Rwandan refugees. Fraught with bureaucratic inefficiency and corruption, this program illuminates not only contradictions in Tanzanian refugee policies during the 1970s and 1980s but also a deep paradox in official ideas about citizenship.

International and national attempts to naturalize the Rwandan refugees of the 1960s, and to weed out the unwanted from the legally sanctioned, were premised on an ideal vision of the useful Tanzanian citizen. This state vision, however, was as distant from refugee realities as it was from Tanzanians. To be eligible for citizenship, refugees had to have entered the country between 1962 and 1964, and their applications had to be screened by local officials before being sent to immigration headquarters for approval. This left the future of the thousands of Rwandan refugees who had entered Tanzania in the late 1960s, 1970s, and early 1980s in question. While naturalization was therefore in some respects a salve on the Rwandan refugee "problem," it was also part of an uneven process of inscribing individuals within a national community, within an accepted order of sovereign nation-states. The process of legibility then worked in reverse as low-level government officials obscured the process of citizen making by withholding the tools of citizenship: identity papers. The naturalization program displayed the hollowness

Of "Natural" Citizens and "Natural" Illegality · 141

of prescribed "nationality" as an identity linked to stable membership in the world of nation-states, and it reveals the inefficiencies and corruption that *ujamaa* policies eventually bred in Tanzania.

Ujamaa: The View from Above

In 1967 President Julius Nyerere presented Tanzania and the world with the Arusha Declaration, a document committed "to the principles of self-reliance and socialism."[7] This paper detailed the themes that would be the basis for citizenship and development—a framework that joined traditional African rural communities with modern, "expert" approaches to agricultural development. Specifically, Nyerere detailed the motives and creative processes that would establish *ujamaa* villages as self-governed, cooperative, and equal rural societies devoted to the work of agricultural and national development.[8] Such villages were to be populated by hardworking volunteers who understood the benefits of a "new way of life" because, according to Nyerere, the "people themselves must decide whether and when they are prepared to make this movement."[9]

The programs and villages discursively known as *ujamaa* refer to two separate government resettlement schemes. In Nyerere's writings from 1967–1968, the values of voluntarism, democratic decision making, and grassroots participation and control emerged as the primary aspects of *ujamaa vijijini* (*ujamaa* in the villages).[10] By 1973, however, it was clear to the administration that the people did not understand the importance of villagization, as few opted to move to the new *ujamaa* villages. With the failure of voluntarism during the 1960s and early 1970s, the state increasingly used force to accelerate its version of national development, often disregarding specific local topographies and time-tested agricultural practices in the process. Ironically, then, initial state policies aimed at administrative decentralization and democratization led to a centralized and interventionist state, one that gave local party and government officials unprecedented power and led to corruption at all levels of the bureaucracy.

If, during the 1960s, poverty was a "villain" to be fought with voluntary rural participation and local knowledge, by the mid-1970s, the weapons had become forced compliance, bureaucratic control, and adherence to technical, replicable techniques.[11] Attention to local conditions and knowledge was lost during this transition, particularly as Nyerere's insistence on rapid results pressured regional and district commissioners to create and populate villages quickly.[12] Administrators often became obsessed with appearances,

142 · CHAPTER 7

reflected not only in statistics but also in the villages' modern appearance.[13] Communal life was to be strictly ordered along the lines of community farming and adult education. Model villages and farms were created and often used to "show off" the success of local officials' work to visiting higher-ups.[14] Local officials used such villages to conceal villagers' cultivation problems and, often, their apathy.

According to many, *ujamaa* led to a ten-year period of *hamna* during the late 1970s and 1980s, when one needed government permits to acquire any goods or foreign exchange.[15] By the late 1970s and 1980s, if an official found a person with "even $1 US," he was accused of economic sabotage.[16] For many scholars of Tanzania, responsibility for the disasters during and after the *ujamaa* period lay with the government bureaucrats charged with implementing state policies.[17] These bureaucrats cared more about appearances than the productive potential of the land or the welfare of the villagers. The timing of village planting, decided by government and party officials, was frequently wrong, leading to poor harvests. When the harvests were good, the village secretary or chairperson often swindled villagers out of their fair share of the earnings.[18] Later, the permit system bred corruption. For some, the fact that Tanzanians did not revolt against these coercive, failed policies is a testament to their "good hearts"—their ability to put up with a lot if it meant keeping the peace.[19] As this chapter argues, it was also due to their ability to maneuver inside and outside state policies and laws.

Ujamaa: The View from Ngara

In Ngara, I interviewed several people who had been low-level government or village officials during the forced villagization of the mid-1970s. Their perceptions of how *ujamaa* policy unfolded in Ngara tended to valorize the government's programs. For example, according to a former village leader, Ngarans were eager to move to *ujamaa* villages and were never forced to do so. Ngarans liked living in *ujamaa* villages and did not return to their former homes.[20] Most people, however, have a more complicated understanding of what *ujamaa* policies meant.

In Ngara, *ujamaa* took the form of voluntary and forced movements to preplanned village sites. Most frequently, government officials moved people from the district's lowlands to highland ridges close to the few roads, regardless of the land's fertility or proximity to water sources.[21] Most Ngarans I interviewed spoke of *ujamaa* in words that echoed those of Nyerere—indicating a strong penetration of government rhetoric in Ngaran imaginations. Crispin

Of "Natural" Citizens and "Natural" Illegality · 143

Ubuzutwe, a retired teacher and hospital worker, answered my questions about the meaning of *ujamaa* in words that mirrored those of many other respondents. After chuckling—a response that may indicate both nostalgia for the Nyerere era and the foolhardiness of villagization—Ubuzutwe stated that *ujamaa* meant that one was dependent on oneself while simultaneously working with others on farms, that "we are all relatives."[22] This simultaneous emphasis on self-reliance (*kujitegemea*) and cooperation reflected a contradiction inherent in the rhetoric of *ujamaa*, but this did not seem to bother any of my interviewees. To the Ngarans I interviewed, *ujamaa* evoked notions of sharing everything from *pombe* (beer) to agricultural work in communal villages. The idea of *ujamaa* remains attractive to many Ngarans, even though they acknowledge its impracticality, given the current atmosphere of political corruption and greed.

Administrators implemented compulsory villagization unevenly in Ngara district. Some individuals and families in Ngara were eager to move to the new government villages. As a young boy living among the scattered homes and farms in Keza ward, Peter Kato remembered the excitement of moving to a village that was closer to government provisions—to the road, the dispensary, and the school.[23] In contrast, Simon Ndyaderi remembered that government officials burned people's homes in Keza, forcing members of the community into a consolidated village along the Busubi highlands. Ndyaderi's father was forced to move to this new village, which had poor soil. According to Ndyaderi, by 1979, people had moved out of these government villages, realizing there could "be no development there."[24] Many returned to their former homes and farms, while others built homes in new locations in the Keza lowlands—areas with excellent soil for banana farming.

Father Lazarus, a priest working at the Rulenge mission in Busubi for more than forty years, described a different version of the same event. For Lazarus, Nyerere was "almost mad about *ujamaa*," a system that "never worked properly." At the beginning of villagization, some people secretly moved back to their own homes, to avoid the ire of local officials. After a few years, movement from the state villages became more frequent.[25] Even during their stay in *ujamaa* villages, however, people tended to move back and forth from the new villages to their old houses and farms.[26]

The reasons people left the state villages, often in defiance of the law, varied.[27] For wealthy farmers, who had been loath to leave their big farms in the first place, the motivation was a desire to either return to their own farms or move to other areas. Men with multiple wives tended to have one wife stay on their original *shamba*, while a second wife moved to and worked in the new villages, thus maximizing crop production as well as their families' economic security—an insurance policy against the potential failure of the new villages.[28]

Illegal migration from *ujamaa* villages likely stemmed from the state's disregard of villagers' intelligence, hopes, and frustrations. Officials measured the success of regional villagization by the number and population of new villages, rather than local experiences and perceptions.[29] Many people noted that government promises of rations and infrastructure, such as schools and electricity, went unfulfilled in the new villages.[30] Local traditions and culture also played a part, as people missed their former farms, "where they had their own culture, where their family and graves are."[31] The desire to live near family and ancestral homes and graves was an important reason why many people were reluctant to move to new villages in the first place and why they returned to their former villages thereafter.[32]

For a minority of the people I interviewed, *ujamaa* was a successful program. According to them, people were not forced into *ujamaa* villages, and only those who were greedy or lazy returned to their former villages.[33] For this minority, *ujamaa* never ended—a fact evidenced by the continuing presence of *ujamaa* villages.[34] It cannot be disputed that many *ujamaa* villages in Ngara—places such as Keza, Muyenzi, Ntobeye, and Shanga, among others—have remained viable communities where people live close together near roads and services, although they no longer farm communally.[35]

Magendo and *Uhujume*: Morality and Illegal Trade

Ujamaa villagers were tasked with the production of cash crops for export. In Ngara, these cash crops included bananas, coffee, and beans.[36] However, as in the rest of the country, crop marketing increasingly became the domain of centralized parastatals, such that producers' share of crop sales dropped from 66 percent in 1970 to 42 percent in 1980.[37] Throughout Tanzania, this led to an increase in domestic food production, to the detriment of cash-crop production and export. By 1981, the output of commercial agriculture and cash-crop exports dropped to half their 1970s level.[38] Recurring droughts during the 1970s and 1980s, in addition to the oil-price shocks of the 1970s, worsened the state's precarious economic position.[39] These problems were compounded by the 1978–1979 border war with Uganda, which cost an estimated $500 million and increased the government's deficit.[40] Rampant inflation during the 1970s also undermined the official economy, as did "port congestion, transport difficulties . . . industrial slow down due to lack of petrol, water and particularly spare parts, inadequate storage facilities for food ... [and] corruption at all levels."[41]

There had always been shortages in Ngara district, particularly of items that were not manufactured locally, such as salt, petrol, clothing, and luxury goods such as Primus beer, bicycles, sheet metal, and liquor.[42] During the 1970s, these shortages increased in Ngara and in the nation due to a variety of factors. Trade deficits and inflation, as well as state price controls, all resulted in acute shortages.[43]

Additionally, state closures of privately owned shops began during Operation *Maduka* in February 1976, leading to commodity shortages throughout the nation. Responding to public pressure, Nyerere eventually slowed the pace of the market closures, hoping to ensure that for each shop closed a "viable village shop" was established in *ujamaa* villages.[44] Such shops acquired goods from government-run Regional Trading Corporation (RTC) stores. By removing private traders, the government was attempting to excise exploitative middlemen from commodity exchanges, thereby replacing "the market mechanism with bureaucratic controls."[45] However, individuals with connections to the state generally received preferential access to such rationed and controlled goods, to the detriment of the wider population.[46] Those without such connections waited in long lines outside communal and government shops, often to find that the supply of essential items ran out well before the last customer had been served.[47] Given the government's "legal monopoly" over marketing and crop distribution, as well as control over the production and importation of finished goods, illicit trading increased throughout the country.[48]

In Ngara, illicit trade became an essential strategy of economic sustainability and survival. Without fail, every person I spoke with well remembered (*nakumbuka sana*) the years of hardship and shortages that marked the mid-1970s to the 1980s. Many attributed these shortages to the 1979 border war with Idi Amin and Nyerere's declaration that the population had to "tighten their belts" to fund the war and deal with the economic depression that followed.[49] A few linked these shortages to *ujamaa* policies and the agricultural disruptions caused by rapid villagization.[50]

In each of my interviews, I asked people about local trading patterns, often specifically referring to cross-border trade with Rwanda and Burundi. Usually, my informants replied negatively, stating that no trade had occurred with Rwanda and Burundi (particularly during the postcolonial period). It was only when I asked specifically whether there had been *magendo* (informal trade) during a certain time that people nonchalantly remarked on what

146 · CHAPTER 7

they considered a common, if illegal, activity. The exchange often went something like this:

> "Was there trade with Rwanda and Burundi during that time [*ujamaa*]?"
>
> "No."
>
> "Was there *magendo*?"
>
> "Oh yes, of course, it is always there. People use the *panya* (mouse) routes."[51]

This exchange was typically followed by a description of the types of goods Ngarans (usually men) traded across the borders of Rwanda and Burundi.

Particularly in Busubi, people frequently sold bananas (*ndizi*) in Burundi and, to a lesser extent, in Rwanda in exchange for beer. As one former teacher recollected, *magendo* through *panya* routes was necessary because people could not sell what they grew "even to buy coffee" in Tanzania.[52] In some cases, I heard stories about Rwandans bringing minerals and cattle to Ngara in exchange for crops such as beans, while Burundians were more likely to bring only cattle in exchange for local crops.[53] Ngarans also frequently entered Rwanda and Burundi at night to procure goods such as sugar, salt, clothing, and soap.[54]

Ngarans also linked increases in *magendo* activity with the presence of Rwandan refugees, who shared their considerable business acumen with local farmers and traders.[55] Some Rwandan refugees engaged in a far-reaching form of *magendo*, buying cows and crops from as far away as Sukumaland to sell in Rwanda and Burundi.[56] People in Ngara, and particularly in Busubi, continually remarked that Rwandans were excellent businessmen—"born traders," even—and that they taught local people new skills in business and animal husbandry.[57] According to a former teacher, "Rwandan refugees had much experience in illegal trade, [and they] taught locals" to go to Rwanda to obtain milk to sell in Ngara, as well as clothes and other goods—a practice that increased during the 1980s.[58] Rwandan refugees' interactions with Ngarans centered around small village markets and the churches that both groups attended.

We can think about *magendo*, and about *panya* routes, in a variety of ways. Certainly the practice seems to fit James Scott's definition of the "weapons of the weak," or the ordinary forms of resistance marginalized people engage in.[59] From another vantage point, the illegal circulation of people—and goods—seems to validate Goran Hydén's notion of an uncaptured peasantry, of people continuing to subsist on a mixture of barter, subsistence farming, and money.[60] In reality, however, *magendo* was both more complex and, in some ways, simpler.

Magendo not only represented resistance to state authority but also complemented state efforts and allowed state policies to continue (for a time), as it enabled people to sustain themselves and their families without completely breaking away from failing state programs. *Magendo* therefore constituted a "safety valve for the state," a strategy that allowed people to live economically outside of state laws while remaining politically loyal to the state.[61] Popular use of illicit trade was both a conscious survival technique and an unconscious affirmation of, and simultaneous resistance to, heavy-handed state policies.

Recent scholarship tends to subsume a variety of actions under the label of "resistance," often as part of an effort to resuscitate the agency of the economically and politically marginalized.[62] Illicit trade, variously referred to as the "second economy," the "informal economy," and the "parallel economy," has become a favorite topic of scholars studying state-society interactions in Africa.[63] However, local opinions about illegal trade should also be taken seriously.[64]

When Ngarans speak of *magendo*, they do so with a sense of history and purpose that belies attempts to valorize such trade through the lens of resistance. For Ngarans, *panya* routes were nothing new. Many people remarked that it was natural for Ngarans to trade with their "neighbors" across borders. The paths to Burundi and Rwanda were well worn by centuries of trade and migration. Selling materials in Burundi and Rwanda, whether food, livestock, or other commodities, did not necessarily constitute a conscious act of state resistance or even an unconscious one. Rather, such trade was a method by which people circumvented scarcity, created and expanded their opportunities, and fed their families as generations before had done. In this peripheral district, the state does not exist as such at the border, although its bothersome and corrupt emissaries occasionally do, as evidenced by the confiscation of goods by district police.[65] Such officials are not always associated with the state either, particularly with the distant central state. While Ngarans recognize that such functionaries are employed by the state, they often perceive these individuals as acting on their own impetus. Similarly, Ngarans know that *magendo* is illegal, but few care about this designation. The illegality of *magendo* is almost irrelevant to Ngarans, or perhaps it is no more than a nuisance that occasionally impedes time-tested economic strategies of sustainability and survival. To call such trade "resistance" gives

148 · CHAPTER 7

magendo a meaning that few in Ngara would agree with. *Magendo* was, and remains, a part of life in Ngara, irrespective of colonial or state actors.[66]

Scott and others have been careful to point out that they do not intend to valorize the resistance strategies of the poor.[67] Nevertheless, Western scholars' romanticization of subaltern subjects and frequent vilification of non-Western states and statesmen may lead to a disconcertingly replicable and uncomplicated view of the motivations of the world's poor. My argument here is that for the majority of Ngarans, *magendo* was not, nor was it meant to be, a threat to state power and certainly not to the state's legitimating ideals of socialism. Instead, *magendo* represented a time-honored strategy of economic security, one that did not threaten the development of the population. Indeed, Ngarans use a different word to describe illegal economic accumulation that they perceived as threatening to both local and national communities: the antinationalist, corrupt, and greedy forms of exchange practiced by the *wahujume*.

When I spoke with Ngarans about life during the late 1970s and 1980s, about the failure of *ujamaa* and the hardship that followed, they brought up the notion of greed. In a context where having money and employees was seen as inimical to the development of the country, the presence of rich men who would not adhere to the national ethic of self-reliance, community, and equality continually threw a wrench into the workings of *ujamaa*.[68] These men were referred to as *wahujume*, individuals opposed to the ideals of citizenship percolating through Ngara. The *wahujume* often engaged in illicit transnational trade, but on a larger scale than most Ngarans and in a way that was detrimental to the aims and livelihood of the community and the nation. Most frequently, Ngarans described *wahujume* as hoarders, people who bought vast amounts of sugar and other rare goods to keep market prices high.[69]

When I asked Ngarans what *uhujume* (sabotage) was and how it affected people's lives, one name continually came up: Edward Sokoine.[70] Prime Minister Sokoine was a central figure in the national fight against economic saboteurs, and the invocation of his name indicates a high degree of official discursive penetration and accommodation in Ngara. Since the late 1960s, the government had arrested and fined a number of businesspeople accused of fraud and other economic crimes. Almost all these individuals were of nonindigenous origin and typically of Asian descent.[71] According to Ron Aminzade, despite government assertions that economic saboteurs come in all colors, "because mainly Asians were accused, tried, and convicted of tax evasion, smuggling, and illegally hoarding scarce goods . . . most Africans attributed the commodity shortages and high prices they experienced to Asian profiteers."[72] In Ngara, popular opinion added Arab businessmen to this list, as the district had a minority of wealthy Omani traders.[73] At the national level, the prosecution of economic saboteurs reached new heights under the leadership of Prime Minister Sokoine.

For many Ngarans, Sokoine remains a tragic, if heroic, figure in the history of Tanzania.[74] He publicly chastised government and party leaders who engaged in illegal trade or bribery. In 1983 he led a highly publicized campaign to round up saboteurs involved in hoarding goods and foreign currency. Although this crackdown impacted predominantly small businessmen, leaving the more powerful African officials involved in commodities marketing unscathed, the publicity surrounding the confiscation of expensive luxury goods had a significant effect on Tanzanians who had experienced acute economic hardships.[75] When Sokoine died in a mysterious car crash in 1984, many Ngarans blamed his death on a conspiracy involving wealthy businessmen and corrupt officials.[76]

Uhujume therefore connoted something different from illegal or illicit trade. Almost all Ngarans participated to some extent in informal economies. However, *magendo* existed within what Aili Mari Tripp has called the "moral code" under which informal economies operate.[77] For Ngarans, breaking state laws was accepted and was often perceived as a necessity with a neutral, if not positive, connotation. In contrast, the word *uhujume* represented a spectrum of economic activity that was popularly perceived as morally abhorrent because it harmed society and even the nation.

Citizenship Considered

Understanding the meaning of *ujamaa* and *uhujume* in Ngaran lives requires an appreciation of what it meant to be a Tanzanian citizen during this time and to whom that label applied. This task is not clear-cut or easy, as "the ideology of African socialism that informed the Tanzanian nationalist project . . . was simultaneously inclusive, universalistic, and state-centered, as well as exclusive, particularistic, and culture-centered."[78] To understand what these contradictions meant to lived experiences and national ideologies in Ngara requires attending to changing state policies regarding refugees and *ujamaa*, in addition to the haphazard and irregular implementation of these policies.

For Nyerere, *ujamaa* was about building a new nation, complete with a citizenry devoted to cooperation and equality as "the whole rural society must be built on the basis of the equality of all Tanzanian citizens and their common obligations and common rights."[79] But who was to be included in this citizenry? The answer was often ambiguous.[80] Certainly citizenship was not based on race, as Nyerere made clear to the population.[81] According to Nyerere, the Arusha Declaration did "not talk about racial groups or nationalities" but about socialists and capitalists.[82] Nyerere was also a Pan-Africanist who vocally and materially advocated for African liberation movements, noting that as long as "colonialism and racialism" exist in "this continent none of us can really be free to live in peace and dignity."[83] And yet, by necessity, Nyerere was also practical in his thinking about African solidarity. After the failure of East African federation and the difficulties in achieving East African cooperation following independence, Nyerere addressed the leaders of Uganda, Kenya, and Tanzania by commenting, "Ultimately we are not in fact 'East Africa' leaders, but leaders of states in East Africa; and regional loyalty has sometimes to come second to our national responsibilities."[84]

One way to answer the question of who was considered a Tanzanian citizen is to examine who was involved in nation building or, in other words, villagization. As Nyerere wrote in September 1967, "Most important of all, any increase in the amount of wealth we produce under this system [*ujamaa*] would be 'ours'; it would not belong to one or two individuals, but to all those whose work has produced it."[85] Thus, one avenue to understanding citizenship is to analyze who worked to produce the wealth of the nation—that is, who performed the agricultural work in government villages.[86] Specifically, did Rwandan refugees live in state villages and participate in *ujamaa* as conceived by the central state? Did they want to? Which populations were involved in this most Tanzanian of policies, and why? My questions resulted in contradictory answers from Ngarans. Most respondents agreed that the refugees were not allowed to live in *ujamaa* villages, which were meant only for citizens.[87] However, a vocal minority stated that "of course" refugees were part of villagization.[88] It seems certain that refugees engaged in trade with local people and frequently attended the same churches, but it is less clear whether they moved, or were forced to move, to *ujamaa* villages or attended schools or training therein.

I was interviewing Roland Ndurande, an elderly farmer, outside a run-down shop in the center of Muyenzi village when a revealing argument broke out.[89] When I asked Ndurande whether Rwandan refugees had been included in the *ujamaa* village that became Muyenzi, he replied that they had. Justice Numyogoro, who was standing a few feet away listening to our conversation, angrily intervened, and an argument ensued in which the two

Of "Natural" Citizens and "Natural" Illegality · 151

men hurled Kiswahili, Kisubi, and English words at each other. As other people, mostly men, joined in, my research assistant had trouble following the discussion.[90] The argument ended with a tenuous agreement among the gathered men: Those Rwandans who had entered Ngara in small groups during 1959–1960 were incorporated into *ujamaa* villages. Those who came with the larger influx of people during and after 1961 did not take part in villagization. Reading between the lines, I discerned that only those refugees who never became part of UNHCR settlements, those who arrived sporadically and in small groups and were able to settle without international assistance, became part of the *ujamaa* project. The majority of the refugees who had at some point lived in internationally aided settlements and who had arrived primarily after 1961 in larger, more visible groups were not permitted entrance to the nation-building work of *ujamaa*.[91]

Refugee Citizens? Naturalization—the View from Above

In October and December 1980 celebrations took place in the Mwesi, Muyenzi, and Kimuli/Nkwenda Rwandan refugee settlements, replete with official visits, proclamations, and speeches. The refugees were informed that, thanks to the generosity of the Tanzanian government, they were eligible to become Tanzanian citizens. The archives speak of much refugee joy and fanfare.[92] Meanwhile, UNHCR publications declared that the Rwandan refugee problem in Tanzania had been solved: official statistics noted that during 1980, thirty-seven thousand Rwandan refugees in Tanzania had been naturalized and were no longer refugees but Tanzanian citizens.[93] The idea that the Rwandan refugee problem had been even partially solved by naturalization would, of course, prove to be a delusion on the part of the Tanzanian government and the international community.[94] Accordingly, by 1984, UNHCR officials were despondent: only 3,340 refugees had received citizenship amid allegations of corruption, inefficiency, and recalcitrance.[95]

As we have seen, at this time, national definitions of citizenship focused on the qualities that created "good" Tanzanian citizens among those who already were or might become citizens. National policies toward Rwandan refugees mimicked these tropes, wavering between acceptance and naturalization of "good" refugees and rejection of troublesome, illegal, or "bad" refugees. Increasingly during the 1970s, the government linked the moral qualities of proper citizens to sedentarization (in *ujamaa* villages), hard work, and self-reliance.[96] The movements of Rwandan refugees—like other itinerant groups in Tanzania—provoked the ire of government officials. Plans to naturalize some, but not all, Rwandans illuminate the dilemmas the state faced in defining and implementing plans for citizens, development, and nation building. It also revealed deepening tension between the UNHCR and the Tanzanian state.

In October 1984 a UNHCR representative noted that "the Banyarwanda refugee question was one of the gravest in Africa, and is potentially explosive."[97] The need for a "permanent solution" to the Rwandan refugee problem was therefore urgent. Not only was it impossible to contain, or even monitor, Rwandan refugees throughout the region, but the ongoing political meetings of refugees—including in Tanzania—threatened the political stability of the Great Lakes region.[98] Unlike other refugee groups in Africa, the Rwandan refugee situation was becoming permanent. The Rwandan government claimed the country, which had one of the highest population densities in the world, was full. Rwanda's population density issue was so dire that Rwandan and Tanzanian officials discussed the possible resettlement of one million Rwandans in Tanzania in 1979 and 1980.[99] Clearly, then, repatriation was not a viable option. With violence against Rwandan refugees increasing in countries such as Uganda, the idea of naturalization in Tanzania must have seemed like the only solution for UNHCR officials.[100] Naturalization would also prove that resettlement—the UNHCR's preferred "durable solution" for refugee groups in Africa—could be successful, providing a public relations boon for the agency.[101]

The language used by government and international refugee officials to refer to these events evokes their misunderstanding of the potency of "citizenship" in refugee political imaginations, which often continued to revolve around ideologies linking political identity with an imagined home in Rwanda and a future homecoming. Officials wrote in 1980 that the refugees had been "naturalized," as if in becoming Tanzanian citizens the refugees had re-entered the proper order of nation-states, the "natural" order. What does it mean to change one's nationality, to receive the offer of citizenship and the documents espousing one's new place within the transnational order of sovereign nation-states? Can it mean forgetting, or laying aside, the injustices (whether real or perceived) experienced by the refugee as an individual and as a group? Some refugees advocated for naturalization, and others eagerly anticipated receiving their citizenship papers, but for some, the idea of becoming Tanzanian was unthinkable.[102]

The Tanzanian government's decision to offer Rwandan refugees naturalization was likely motived by a desire to appease donor nations, the United Nations, and the UNHCR and by the perception that, through citizenship,

Of "Natural" Citizens and "Natural" Illegality · 153

"a bone of contention between the two governments" would be removed.[103] Nyerere also used the naturalization of "the 36,000 Rwandese" in Tanzania to showcase his country's "generous and humanitarian policy" toward all refugees.[104] However, in determining that only the "older" refugees were eligible for citizenship, the state left out the thousands of Rwandans who had entered Tanzania during the late 1960s through the 1980s.[105] Such classifications represented the government's continued anxiety about uncontrolled refugee movements, as later arrivals were particularly difficult to keep track of.[106]

Complicating the issue was officials' inability to distinguish between "old" and "new" Rwandan refugees.[107] Determining which refugees had entered the country at what time was almost impossible for state officials. This problem was compounded by the fact that settlement commandants and other local officials often traded in official documents, such as refugee permits, for financial gain. This trade increased with passage of the Tanzania Immigration Act of 1973, which declared that all aliens had to register and receive permits from the government. As a result, all nonregistered refugees were illegal aliens in danger of repatriation or detention, making refugee permits a "precious commodity" in refugee camps.[108]

The language used by local government officials also evoked their lingering frustration and anger with the refugees. At the Muyenzi ceremony on December 13, 1980, the Kagera regional commissioner, Ndugu P. N. Kafanabo, said of (and to) the gathered refugees, "So far, there are brutals, among them. These brother[s] were well informed that the expense for registering as citizens was being met by the United Nations High Commissioner for Refugees. . . . It was however strange to learn that this group of brutals went round saying that it is the government which was forcing them to be naturalized."[109] The commissioner also stated that while the settlement would now "be ordinary villages," those who decided not to become naturalized would be transferred to other refugee settlements. Noting that the applications of such "brutal refugees" were still being considered and that officials were "looking carefully on their behavior and character they have to improve," the commissioner indicated the extent to which "good" characteristics had become a prerequisite for citizenship. The commissioner went on to state that "lazy, jobless, and unlawful traders will not be tolerated," emphasizing the behavioral traits that qualified one for Tanzanian citizenship. The commissioner then distributed certificates of citizenship to some of the refugees, saying that the settlement commandant would issue the rest after the applications had been processed.[110]

The language used by Kafanabo is similar to the words some Ngarans used to describe which Rwandans received citizenship. According to Jacob Kanani, the refugees "who became citizens were the ones with good habits" who had not committed crimes.[111] Additionally, some Ngarans noted that the UNHCR had attempted to "buy" citizenship for the refugees.[112] In the case of Tanzanian citizenship, governmental rhetoric since independence had emphasized the moral, developmental, and communal character of citizenship. As Emma Hunter has shown, the Arusha Declaration was in part a rejection of the parasitic behavior of those who did not work for the greater good of the nation. Metaphors about citizenship thus became a way for the state and the people to talk about "proper economic and social behavior," as well as to describe a socialist "moral vision within which to debate a just ordering of society."[113] However, like the government's haphazard and ambiguous approach to *wahujume*, the granting of citizenship to Rwandans was far from the idealized rhetoric of state or social justice.

The failed naturalization program reveals much about life in Ngara district, and in Tanzania in general, during the early 1980s. Bureaucratic inefficiency and corruption were rife, as was the power of a well-connected few. Much like Ngarans, refugees were migrants during this period. In many ways, they lived outside the confines of the state—in "very remote areas" that were difficult for the state to reach.[114] When they did interact with state representatives, it was often through local officials whose power and authority had increased along with the state's decentralization policies. The claim that Rwandan refugees should not become citizens because of their involvement in smuggling matched party and government politics that vilified smugglers and, to a lesser extent, foreigners as economic saboteurs. However, such claims also silenced the myriad ways citizens engaged in these activities and benefited from the business acumen of Rwandans. Additionally, the UNHCR's 1984 decision to fund and spearhead a separate program for naturalization reflected expatriate officials' distrust of and disdain for government officials whose reports left "many questions unanswered."[115] UNHCR officials also bemoaned the government's lack of progress and noted the need for "good [international] control" over the naturalization process, particularly as local officials blocked applications "with no good reason."[116]

The urgency behind the UNHCR representative's request for funds with which to implement naturalization procedures also reflected changes in the Tanzanian government's approach to refugees. Government officials were increasingly frustrated with refugees' seeming "ungratefulness."[117] This disdain for refugee populations increased partly because, "with the declining standards of services available to Tanzanians, refugee-settlements benefiting from international assistance and implemented according to theoretical Government policies have tended to increase the disparity between the standards of living of refugees and nationals."[118] Comments on UNHCR funding for refugees' naturalization applications mirrored local feelings of resentment about refugees receiving aid from international groups while local Tanzanians experienced the devastating effects of economic depression. Such feelings were then put into action as the vast majority of Rwandan refugees, including those who had eagerly applied for citizenship, never received it.

Conclusion: *Ujamaa*, Naturalization, and Citizenship

The 1970s and 1980s were a time of movement for Ngarans, many of whom were forced to relocate to new state villages against their will. Others moved voluntarily, and some returned to their former homes and villages after the perceived failure of state policies. Migration also took the form of increased illegal cross-border trade in Burundi and Rwanda, a trade often influenced by Ngaran dealings with refugee businessmen and traders. During these decades, Ngarans adhered to the ideology of their new state while simultaneously transgressing the laws and borders that marked Tanzanian sovereignty.[119]

The ideology of citizenship promulgated by the nation's leaders during this time continues to be attractive to Ngarans, who remember Nyerere with nostalgia and fondness. To be a citizen in Tanzania was to work hard, cooperate with one's neighbors, and be peaceful. To be Ngaran was to be a citizen, albeit one who engaged in *magendo* trade and cross-border circulation. Rwandan refugees sat uneasily within this matrix of moral citizenship and material reality. Those who had not been "self-settled" but rather lived within the UNHCR's sphere of governance continued to be outsiders, even as aid from international refugee agencies waned. The mark of difference between camp refugees and Ngarans thus continued during *ujamaa*, setting refugees apart from the nation-building exercise that, in an earlier iteration, Tanzanian leaders had planned for them.

Citizenship, as Ivor Chipken reminds us, is a single term with "three distinct qualities: a constitutional *status*, a moral-ethical *disposition* and a political *identity*."[120] The 1970s was a time of molding the proper citizen in Tanzania, as haphazard as it turned out to be. At the close of the decade and into the 1980s, the conversation would turn into a debate about whether

156 · CHAPTER 7

Rwandan refugees possessed the moral qualities necessary to become Tanzanian citizens. At the local level, state officials agreed: they did not.

By the mid-1980s, the time of *ujamaa* had passed in Tanzania.[121] The National Economic Survival Programme of 1981–1982, implemented to address economic stagnation through "self-imposed austerity measures . . . designed to stave off acceptance of IMF/World Bank policy prescriptions," did not have the intended effect.[122] In July 1986, faced with aid cuts from many Nordic countries and threats of reduced Western aid, Tanzania entered into a three-year structural adjustment program with the International Monetary Fund (IMF); a second program was implemented in 1989.[123] Trade liberalization led to the opening of small businesses throughout the country, while currency devaluations led to less local purchasing power.[124] Faced with structural adjustment, endemic corruption, and the failure of *ujamaa* villages, Nyerere stepped down—effectively closing the door on African socialism and on Tanzania's refugee policy. With new president Ali Hassan Mwinyi came new ideas about who deserved to enter Tanzania and why.

The policies of the *ujamaa* era continued the process whereby Ngarans saw themselves as part of the Tanzanian nation-state, just as those policies led to increased reliance on older, nonstate means of economic accumulation and survival. This type of citizenship was flexible, adjusting to national discourses filtered through local needs, traditions, and moralities.[125] Just as few Ngarans became socialists, few Rwandans become Tanzanians. However, even if every Rwandan in Tanzania had legally become a Tanzanian, the festering hope, belief, and planning for a collective homecoming probably would have proved stronger than the new identity papers.[126] When such plans manifested in 1990, they would contribute to one of the largest refugee crises the global community has ever experienced. The "problem" of Rwandan refugees in Ngara and the region was far from solved.

Of "Natural" Citizens and "Natural" Illegality · 157

8. COMPETITION AND BACKSTABBING

THE INTERNATIONAL RESPONSE TO THE RWANDAN

REFUGEE CRISIS, 1994–1996

We were standing just below the crest of hill K9 when Joseph Rwagaba told me about "African gear." It was one of our first days in Ngara district, and the car's brakes had almost failed, sending up billowing clouds of smoke as we attempted to descend K9—the nearly deserted hilltop that, for two years in the mid-1990s, had been home to more than twenty international aid agencies. There was nothing to do but wait for the brakes to cool down and continue on to Ngara town—over the steep slopes of the hills that mark this part of the Great Lakes region. According to Joseph, "African gear" was a strategy used by Tanzanian drivers, who were employed by numerous refugee agencies during the Rwandan "refugee emergency" in Ngara, to generate a profit off their cargo—a type of creative theft. The drivers of large lorries would turn off their engines at the top of a steep slope, enabling them to descend without using any petrol. Such petrol then found its way into local markets and grain mills, becoming "liquid gold."[1] "African gear" was a favorite method of theft in Ngara during the Rwandan refugee emergency, an event that began in April 1994 and, in many respects, has continued ever since.

For the international community, the emergency began on April 28–29, 1994. Over that twenty-four-hour period, an estimated 200,000 Rwandan refugees crossed the Rusumo border into Ngara district. For Rwandans, the emergency started much earlier, even before April 6, 1994, the day the plane carrying the Rwandan and Burundian presidents was shot down over Kigali. Ngarans were well aware of the crisis occurring across the border prior to the rapid descent of the international humanitarian community on their "sleepy" town and district, replete with helicopters, media personnel, satellite phones, and hundreds of millions of dollars. For many Ngarans, the crisis began in the early 1990s. For others, it began when the first bodies appeared in the Kagera River, before hundreds of dead women, men, and infants were caught in the catchment area below Rusumo Falls. And of course, for many Rwandans and Ngarans, the crisis began in the 1960s, when refugees first crossed the boundaries of the new nation-states, fleeing the violence of decolonization and, for some, planning their eventual return.

The Rwandan genocide and refugee crisis represented a new dispensation in humanitarian aid, just as the 1960s had represented a new paradigm in refugee relief. The world's powers had largely stood by and watched as the country's orderly and terrifying massacres unfolded. It was only when the international media reported on the more accessible tragedy of the millions of Rwandan refugees in Ngara and in North and South Kivu, Zaire, that the great powers sprang to action, spending an estimated $1.29 billion to care for Rwanda's refugees in the second half of 1994 alone.[2] The refugee crisis involved media and humanitarian actors in novel ways. It also represented a new post–Cold War dispensation of the global community in Ngara. The only permanent solution the international community could agree on was swift refugee repatriation, an essentially political solution that would eventually take place in the complete absence of political commitment by either the world powers or the humanitarians.[3] The crisis also reflected a new era of refugee relief, one marked by organizational competition for visibility, in-fighting to distribute blame and credit, and retreat from local commitments. The TCRS's perceived failures and successes during this time, as well as the agency's struggle to help host communities affected by the refugee crisis, eventually led to an intractable rift with the behemoth the UNHCR had become.[4]

The experience of the TCRS, as an agency and as individuals, during the two and a half years between the refugees' arrival en masse in Ngara and their forceful repatriation by the Tanzanian state is indicative of changes within both the international arena of humanitarian aid and the district of Ngara. According to the sectoral approach to humanitarian emergencies adopted by the UNHCR, each aid agency had specific duties to perform under the UNHCR's general oversight.[5] In theory, UNHCR officials were supposed to conduct an orchestra of humanitarian aid. To be successful, the relief effort required cooperation at every level: between agencies and the Tanzanian government (both local and central), among the various NGOs, between each NGO and the UNHCR, and, perhaps most important, among the various funding agencies and their constituents. Precise planning, collaboration, and obedience to the chain of command were required for the aid operation to proceed smoothly. Tensions among aid agencies quickly surfaced, however, as the various organizations jostled for media attention and funding. The "business" of refugee aid was on full display in Ngara in 1994, as agencies competed to be responsible for the most "visible" sectoral needs, such as camp management, and assigned blame for the inevitable problems they encountered.

This chapter reveals the evolution of a new dispensation of humanitarian aid to refugees, in Ngara district and globally, by examining the dueling priorities of the aid endeavor from the perspectives of TCRS personnel. Through their writings and words, TCRS employees engaged with the complex ethical issues of humanitarian aid, including how to address the needs of the host community while caring for hundreds of thousands of refugees, some of whom had taken part in the violence that was still unfolding in Rwanda. In so doing, they frequently conflicted with UNHCR policies that privileged refugee needs over those of the host community and expatriate safety over that of local workers. Moreover, as UNHCR officials continued to treat the refugee crisis as a short-term "emergency" situation that would be solved through voluntary repatriation, TCRS officials struggled to plan and carry out their sectoral responsibilities, including the provision of fuel and water. Mistakes were made by all sides, which was likely inevitable, given the rapidly expanding logistical task of aiding more than 500,000 refugees in overcrowded refugee camps in this remote area of Tanzania.

Background to the Emergency: The Rwandan Genocide

When does a refugee emergency begin? At what point are the forces of slaughter and flight set in motion, and by whom?[6] In 1990 the Rwandan Patriotic Front (RPF), an army composed of Rwandan refugees, invaded northern Rwanda from Uganda. The refugees of the 1960s, led by their children, were going home.[7] The group was made up of both Tutsi refugees and a smaller number of Hutu exiles, many of whom had received military training when they helped Yoweri Museveni gain control in neighboring Uganda. Despite all the talk and all the money spent on naturalizing Rwandan refugees in Tanzania, many young men—sons of the 1960s refugees—left Ngara to join the rebel army.[8] Other Rwandans in Ngara sent money and food to aid the military effort. The refugee army demanded that the Rwandan government grant all refugees who had left Rwanda the right to return. It also demanded a substantial change in the Rwandan government, including multiparty elections and power sharing between Hutu and Tutsi.[9] During the next four years, the struggle over power in Rwanda took place within the nation-state and within a transnational arena of peacemaking and democratization. At international peace talks held in Arusha, Tanzania, Rwandan president Juvénal Habyarimana delayed signing the peace deal while promising to reform the country's politics.[10]

Within Rwanda, the battle for power raged between moderate groups, who sought reform, and increasingly hard-line Hutu groups, whose leaders were desperate to maintain their power base. This was a time of democratization in Africa, as the end of the Cold War made it unnecessary for Western leaders to support their dictatorial allies on the continent. International funds were therefore increasingly tied to "good governance" initiatives, most visibly multiparty elections, which threatened the political and economic power of both the dictators and their elite allies. Following the economic decline of the 1980s and disastrous structural adjustment programs, such elites resorted to scapegoating to offset blame for economic hardship and to close down democratic openings that threatened their status.[11] In response to the civil war and the threat of power sharing, hard-line Hutu in Rwanda created new political parties to oppose power sharing and to villainize Tutsi and moderate Hutu.[12] The infamous Radio-Télévision Libre des Milles Collines (RTLM) broadcast increasingly virulent diatribes against the Tutsi, warning Rwandans of a return to an imagined history of Hutu servitude under evil Tutsi masters should the RPF and the Arusha Accords prevail.[13] Hutu political parties then formed militias, composed largely of the country's underemployed young men.

Displacement was another feature of the lead-up to genocide, as internally displaced persons (IDPs) fled the fighting in the north, exacerbating land and food scarcity issues further south.[14] They grouped in makeshift camps around the capital, Kigali, and were primed to join the militias that promised them victory against the Tutsi "cockroaches" (*inyenzi*) who (as they were repeatedly told) threatened to exterminate them and take their lives and livelihoods. In Kigali, these internal refugees were joined by refugees from the vicious ethnic power struggles in Burundi, many of whom fled the attempted Tutsi military coup in late 1993, which took the life of the first democratically elected (and Hutu) president. Rundi stories of Tutsi atrocities were then used as propaganda in Hutu extremists' narratives of Tutsi rapists and killers.[15] On the radio, RTLM broadcast the message that the majority Hutu population had to kill the Tutsi or be killed by them.[16] Extremist leaders, many from the president's own party, thought the president was bowing too low to Tutsi and international pressure.[17] Then, on April 6, 1994, President Habyarimana's plane was shot down over Kigali as he returned from signing the latest peace agreement.[18] The extremists responded by killing anyone who might oppose them, particularly moderate Hutu and all Tutsi. Lists of opponents had been prepared over the previous months, and orders to kill them were sent from the leadership to each commune and village. The killings began and swept through the country; any local leader who did not enthusiastically participate in the massacres was replaced and/or murdered. By the end of April, tens of thousands had been killed. Many bodies were thrown into the Kagera River, sending the Tutsi dead "back" to their colonially inspired origins in Ethiopia.[19]

As soon as the killings began, the RPF restarted its offensive. The international community watched as the country massacred itself. As the rebels moved first south and east, taking control of the territory closest to Karagwe and Ngara districts, civilians, politicians, and militiamen fled from their path, fearing both the violence of the war and the wrath of reprisal killings. At first, as David Ntahura remembered, Tutsi fled into Tanzania.[20] Then, on April 28, the Rwandan military opened the Rusumo Bridge, which links eastern Rwanda with Ngara. In twenty-four hours, one of the largest refugee exoduses ever recorded took place. An estimated 150,000 people, including many who had planned, enacted, witnessed, and suffered the genocide, fled into Rusumo town.[21]

The international community sprang into action, as the humanitarian needs of the refugees in Tanzania became a rallying cry around the world. By the end of the emergency in December 1996, more than $180 million had been spent on refugee aid in Ngara by more than twenty international agencies.[22] The reaction was spurred by the reporting of the international media, which saw the refugee crisis as an opportunity to "obtain a dramatic and visually powerful story of the Rwanda tragedy," which had been difficult to cover due to its complexity and the security concerns prevailing in Rwanda.[23] The refugee influx into Ngara provided the international media with a story

162 · CHAPTER 8

that was more easily accessible than the genocide that continued to unfold within an unstable, violent, and chaotic Rwanda. The media presence was also heightened by the fact that many journalists had just been in South Africa, covering that nation's first multiracial general elections.[24]

Refugee Aid in Western Tanzania, 1990–April 1994

The refugee crisis, though not entirely unexpected, took place at a time when refugee aid activities in Tanzania were in fact winding down. To comprehend the haphazard yet vigorous international response to the Rwandan refugee emergency, it is necessary to examine the climate of refugee aid in Tanzania, in Ngara, and in all of the global South prior to the Rwandan influx. In the early 1990s, TCRS staff expected that the coming years would bring a scaling down of their activities in the country, as international funding for refugees in Tanzania had dramatically decreased. Additionally, UNHCR officials had declared 1992 a "year of repatriation" and, ironically, aimed to help 55,000 Rwandan refugees return to Rwanda following the Arusha peace negotiations—out of an estimated 590,000 Rwandan refugees abroad.[25]

In 1990 Bernhard Staub, director of the TCRS, wrote about the possibility of refugees from the civil war in Rwanda entering Tanzania: "with all the problems one hears on the news about the Ruandese situation, one thing is clear here in Tanzania, it is not affecting us." With the Kagera River forming "an effective demarcation between the two countries," and with the Tanzanian government closing the border, the TCRS and UNHCR were expecting "about max 100 refugees in total" from Rwanda in 1990. Officials of the two agencies thought the Burigi settlement could accommodate this small number of refugees, even though it suffered from a lack of funds.[26]

During the 1970s and 1980s, the TCRS increasingly moved away from refugee aid and toward development work in Tanzania. This policy change was likely due in part to increased tensions between UNHCR and TCRS officials caused by alterations in the UNHCR's accounting practices. Beginning in the mid-1970s, donor governments placed "growing pressure" on the UNHCR "to monitor, inspect and supervise the implementation of the projects it supports" and to guarantee "effective monitoring."[27] Such donor demands were part of a growing "culture of accountability" in aid organizations in general, one that put a premium on agencies' ability to justify funding through the achievement of quantitative results.[28] This led to a spiraling increase in administrative costs for the TCRS, whose officials felt that "poorly informed"

Competition and Backstabbing · 163

UNHCR staff members were "more actively involved in planning and visiting settlements," to the detriment of refugee care.[29] This was compounded by a feeling of "competitiveness" on the part of UNHCR staff and the TCRS's continued understanding that its "basic relationship" in Tanzania was with the host government rather than the UNHCR.[30] Thus, by the early 1980s, the relationship between the UNHCR and its primary implementing agency in Tanzania had frayed, leading to tensions between the two staffs and, likely, a desire to decrease coordination on major projects. Issues of accountability and staff relations would continue to hinder the relationship between the two agencies into the 1990s, eventually leading to an intractable rift during and after the Rwandan refugee crisis.[31]

Another reason for the TCRS's move into development-related activities was the perception that the number of refugees in Tanzania was decreasing, as well as the perceived success of the TCRS's self-sustaining Burundian refugee camp at Mishamo, which had become a model for the integrated development-refugee paradigm. The TCRS thus began funding self-settled refugee integration projects, including one to develop refugee and host communities in Kibondo and a water development project at Singida.[32] In 1992, ironically, it "looked as if TCRS was in the process of scaling down" activities in Tanzania, a process that was severely disrupted by the "unexpected upheavals in Burundi and Rwanda."[33]

The forthcoming crises and the problems with voluntary repatriation were nevertheless on display in Tanzania in the months prior to April 1994. The Burundian refugee population in Tanzania constituted the largest group of refugees in the country since the early 1970s, as Hutu fled the Tutsi government's genocide that began in 1972.[34] However, by 1992, the prospects for repatriation seemed good. That year, the Burundian people elected a new government led by Hutu president Melchior Ndadaye, who promised peace and development. In the wake of these unprecedented elections, many Rundi refugees expressed an eagerness to repatriate. Tripartite agreements among the UNHCR, the Tanzanian government, and the Burundian government were signed, and a massive repatriation project was set in motion. With this largest refugee caseload in Tanzania on its way to being resolved, the TCRS began to finance other, non-refugee-related projects in Tanzania—including a famine relief project in the Northern Diocese.

Indeed, by August 1992, the UNHCR and the Burundian government had facilitated the repatriation of 5,474 refugees, with plans to help repatriate an additional 92,000.[35] The Burundian government, however, lacked the land and the material capacity to (re)absorb this enormous number of refugees,

164 · CHAPTER 8

leading to a dramatic slowdown in the repatriation process. In early October the repatriation of Burundian refugees was suspended, which did not surprise the TCRS, as it was well aware of the land availability issue. As a result, TCRS director Staub "still" felt that "the real solution" to the problem of Burundian refugees in Tanzania was "naturalization."[36]

Then, on October 21, 1993, an attempted coup by the predominantly Tutsi military killed the new Burundian president, and Rundi refugees once again began arriving in western Tanzania. Massacres of Hutu by the Tutsi army and massacres of Tutsi by Hutu militias occurred in the Burundian countryside, and hundreds of thousands of new refugees fled into neighboring Tanzania. As the UNHCR's implementing agency, the TCRS was involved in Ngara during the first six months of the operation, after which the Red Cross and Caritas took over in Ngara and the TCRS focused on the larger concentrations of refugees in Kibondo and Kigoma districts.[37]

By late November, there were more than 250,000 new Rundi refugees in Tanzania, including 50,000 in Ngara district; new arrivals were estimated at 300 (mainly women and children) per day.[38] By January, the number of refugees in Tanzania was downgraded, with an estimated 20,000 in Ngara district and 113,500 in the country's Kasulu, Kibondo, and Kigoma districts.[39] Many of these refugees repatriated due to a lack of aid in Tanzania, as the international community was unable to fund the refugee camps.[40] Many would later return to Tanzania when the "relative calm" of October 1994 was shattered by escalating violence in subsequent months and years, revealing the cyclical nature of refugee flows in the region and the elusiveness of repatriation as a "durable solution."[41]

Throughout the Burundian crisis in late 1993 and early 1994, a major problem continued to be a lack of funding. "Constraints are being felt with funding from UNHCR," Staub wrote, and "TCRS is not getting funds fast enough from UNHCR to do all the necessary local purchase."[42] Significantly, in light of the massive funding response to the Rwandan crisis only five months later, the TCRS was unable to secure UNHCR funding for water development and sanitation in the Burundian refugee camps. In addition, an inadequate number of trucks for the transport section plagued the program.[43] The lack of international donations to the Rundi refugee crisis meant that the transnational refugee community was able to supply only 20 percent of the necessary food, with the "goodwill of the Tanzanian communities" helping to provide the rest.[44] In Ngara district, the hungry refugees often stole food from local homes and farms.[45] As the civil war in Burundi dragged on for years, refugees continued to cross into Tanzania,

Competition and Backstabbing · 165

albeit without the international media attention that catalyzed the Rwandan refugee emergency. Eventually, many Rundi refugees would be included in the mixed Rwandan-Burundian camps in Ngara.[46]

Desperate Images and the Chaotic Business of Refugee Aid

It was only on April 28, 1994, when hundreds of thousands of Rwandans crossed the Rusumo Bridge accompanied by international journalists and photographers, that funding flooded into the aid sector in northwestern Tanzania. Remembering those early days of the relief program in Ngara, Tony Waters remarked that it "felt like being drunk."[47] Wobbly from travel and overwhelmed by the number of refugees and the "swirl of activity," Waters arrived in Ngara on May 2, 1994. Like many members of the TCRS team in Ngara, Waters had previously worked for the agency in Tanzania. He spent 1984–1987 at the Kasulo Burundian refugee settlement in Kibondo district and then served as a project officer in the Kigoma resettlement project. In April 1994 the TCRS hired Waters to work in Kibondo with Burundian refugees. Just as he arrived in Tanzania, however, Rwandans began streaming across the border, so Waters was sent to Ngara district instead. As the refugees flooded into the district, first across the Rusumo Bridge; then, when the bridge was closed, across all the borders of the district and beyond (especially from the north),Waters became the TCRS program logistics officer and later a senior program officer.[48]

Those first few weeks at the end of April and into May were chaotic for the UNHCR and its implementing agencies. Maureen Connolly, who headed the UNHCR emergency response team in Ngara, along with S. Wilson of the International Federation of Red Cross Societies, had done some "minor planning" in the area prior to the April 28–29 influx and determined that the area around what became the Benaco camp was ripe for refugee settlement.[49] Reporting on the situation in Ngara on May 4, Admasu Simeso, the TCRS emergency program coordinator, noted that Benaco was "the biggest gathering of people, in desperate situation, I have ever seen in one place."[50] In the same letter, Simeso reported that the refugees were living in circumstances of extreme overcrowding, and regional and district authorities were reluctant to provide more land. He concluded, "there is no way in which the people can be kept there for a long time." He estimated that there were more than 200,000 people in the camp, at least a quarter of whom had brought cattle, goats, and other livestock with them, causing concerns about sanitation. At this early

166 · CHAPTER 8

date, Simeso already had a fair grasp of some of the issues that would plague the operation for the next two and a half years:

> I just could not help but to think, of all those eyes staring at me how many of them were really innocent eyes. My normal understanding of refugees being a victim of persecution, running away for his/her life to a place of safety, these ones I thought, were probably a strange mixture of all sorts of people. While I still believe that the majority of them were innocent, on the other hand I had to ask myself as how many of those were really clean? How many of those people had participated in the violence, killed someone and slipped over the border along with the innocent victims? It may be that nobody will ever find out about the whole episode, as who killed who and as who committed the atrocities? But to us they are all refugees.[51]

At the Rusumo Bridge, Simeso witnessed women carrying loads on their heads and babies on their backs and questioned "why the innocent ones have to suffer always for the action of the very few." Stopping at the bridge, Simeso joined a crowd of Tanzanians watching dead bodies float down the river in what was "the most troublesome scene I ever came across. The people told us that it has been like that, day and night, for the last 3 weeks."[52] Three weeks then of bodies flowing past Ngaran villages near the Kagera, polluting the water, and forcing the residents to witness the material effects of the Rwandan atrocities.[53]

As an agency involved in refugee aid and development work in Tanzania for thirty-years, the TCRS was well placed to understand the effects of the refugee situation on Ngaran lives. Therefore, unlike the international agencies that flooded the district with expatriate workers, the TCRS was the only agency "with very few international people," a situation that would prove problematic in its dealings with the UNHCR.[54]

The Rwandan Refugee Crisis

By early May, the UNHCR's emergency response team, headed by Connelly, was "over worked and overwhelmed."[55] Logistics was a "nightmare," and the TCRS was asked to help coordinate the feeding and sheltering of an estimated 200,000 refugees.[56] In the "marathon meetings" that took place among aid agencies, "the situation [was] very confused," and the UNHCR had problems deciding which agency should do what.[57] "The gap in communication even among UNHCR staff" led to initial confusion and disorder, particularly as the UNHCR initiated the new sectoral program.[58] Nevertheless, twelve days into the emergency, the international community already had 120 trucks to transport the food and nonfood items flown into Mwanza, and vaccinations against measles had begun.[59] By May 21, Staub wrote, "Many people coming to help have only been in Benaco for a day or two and one is already counted a veteran if you have been there for two weeks!" Staub went on to note, "It is quite amazing to see the resources that have been mobilized . . . this is especially so when one understands that 8 months ago the same number of Burundi refugees crossed ovar [sic] to Tanzania and we were struggling just to get enough food for the refugees."[60]

Simeso's May report also commented on the "business" of the refugee crisis, particularly the myriad media personnel who had descended on the area. "The place was crowded by a large number of international reporters, U.N. and other relief agencies roaming around. The sleepy little village of Ngara is overwhelmed with more Muzungus than the locals, seen every where with the most sophisticated high-tech communication system connected to North America and Europe via satellite." Reflecting on the situation, Simeso wrote, "It is amazing . . . how much we are captivated by the power of the media and always follow it wherever it takes us. It is also interesting to observe the very interdependence and mutual existence between the victims of disaster, man-made or otherwise, and the media. For the refugees it is the only way that their case could be known to the outside world and they get some assistance. For the media it is a business, actually a big business."[61] It was also "big business" for the refugee agencies and expatriates. By 1996, there were more than twenty different international agencies operating in Ngara district. Most of these agencies, like the UNHCR, focused on the priorities emanating from Geneva, headquarters of most of the international humanitarian NGOs and the UN. Bureaucrats in Geneva were similarly focused on the views of their major donors, people who were influenced by media reports from the region. In the spring and summer of 1994, the media had descended not only on the Rwandan refugee crisis in Ngara but also on the crisis unfolding across the western borders of Rwanda in Goma, Zaire. Just as Rwandans had fled across their country's eastern border to Tanzania, they fled in ever greater numbers into Zaire—a country with even less infrastructure and weaker control of its border region.[62]

Goma, the capital of North Kivu, Zaire, made headlines around the world due to the poor living conditions of the half a million Rwandan refugees who took shelter there in the spring and summer of 1994. Early on, an

168 · CHAPTER 8

outbreak of cholera led the international media to demand increased international aid to Rwandan refugees in Zaire. The Kivu health and transport infrastructure had been stretched beyond its limits by the influx, and international humanitarian agencies descended on the border town.[63] Over in Benaco, agencies feared a similar cholera disaster (and subsequent media attention), prompting quick action to create and maintain healthy sanitary conditions in the Ngara and Karagwe camps.[64]

The agreed-on solution to the refugee crisis, one shared by the Tanzanian government, the international community, and aid agencies, was a quick repatriation of the refugees. Despite the issues that plagued the Burundian repatriation project and the long history of failed Rwandan refugee repatriation, the UNHCR and the Tanzanian government treated the refugees in Ngara as a temporary problem to be solved by voluntary repatriation.[65] Yet, as of October 10, 1994, it was estimated that twelve hundred Rwandans were arriving in Ngara every day, with three hundred to five hundred entering Karagwe.[66] These numbers were actually a reduction from the peak in July, when an estimated five thousand refugees entered the district each day. During July, TCRS lorries "removed up to 4,000 refugees per day from the over-crowded villages along the border," a removal made urgent by "the total lack of sanitation, water, or feeding facilities at these sites."[67] By late September 1994, Benaco camp, built to hold 70,000, housed 241,013 refugees living in conditions of extreme overcrowding.[68] By October, the whole area of Benaco was "devoid of trees and vegetation," and efforts to stop the deforestation were "frustrated by the lack of water resources available."[69] By May 1995, the "whole area, within [a] 10–14 kms radius of the camp" had "been completely cleared."[70]

Refugees continued to enter Tanzania from the west and south. By the end of March 1995, government sources estimated that 100,000 Rwandans who had been living in refugee camps in northern Burundi, in addition to 40,000 Burundians, had fled into northwestern Tanzania.[71] In view of the "gravity of the situation," including the depletion of UNHCR stocks, local environmental destruction, and "deterioration of [the] security situation between the refugee camps and the villagers," the Tanzanian government took the novel step of closing the border with Burundi to all refugees.[72] This decision was likely politically motivated in part, as "clearing up the corruption problem in Tanzania . . . and ridding Tanzania of these refugees" were the main themes of the country's first multiparty presidential elections in 1995.[73] By the end of 1995, an estimated 500,000 Rwandan and Burundian refugees were present in Tanzania, while fewer than 4,000 Rwandans had been repatriated.[74]

Prior to the closing of the border, refugees who entered Ngara from Burundi had been moved via TCRS trucks to a camp set up in Keza, near the old Muyenzi settlements. From there, many were moved to Kitali Hills refugee camp, right over Ngara's border with Biharamulo. In Busubi subdistrict, people still remembered the Rwandans and Burundians who fled to the area during the early 1990s. Thomas Barondo recalled that the refugees first stayed in Keza; they were then moved to a transport camp and later to Kitale Hills.[75] He said refuges numbered 400,000 and were a mix of Warundi and Wanyarwanda.[76] According to Barondo, refugees stole from wealthy locals, murdered four people, and burned people's homes if they did not open their doors (particularly after the locals put trees outside their doors to deter robberies). The village leaders in Keza met with camp leaders to try to stop refugees from leaving the camp, but control was difficult to attain. At night, Barondo remembered refugees engaging in military training in the forest far from the camp.[77]

Of Fuel and Water

From the early months of the operation, the TCRS had been engaged in the logistical requirements of caring for more than 200,000 refugees in an area of Tanzania far from serviceable roads or other reliable infrastructure.[78] Eventually, this meant that the TCRS, with its fleet of trucks and drivers, was responsible for transporting, storing, and distributing fuel for the entire refugee program in Ngara, including to the myriad humanitarian agencies.[79] The TCRS logistics section of the Ngara program comprised three interrelated sectors: transportation, workshop construction, and fuel provisioning.[80] By November 1994, the TCRS was distributing six thousand liters of fuel per day, with the amount "rapidly rising towards 10,000 liters a day."[81] Every agency working with the UNHCR, including the UNHCR itself, relied on the TCRS for their daily fuel needs. The pressure on the agency was great. If the fuel supply ran out, the pumps that provided the refugees with water would fail, and if food delivery to the "overcongested" camps, "where tempers flare easily," was interrupted, it might have resulted in "disaster."[82] By May 1996, the TCRS operated ninety trucks, and by August, the agency had transported more than five million liters of diesel fuel.[83]

A major problem with trucking fuel to the camps in Ngara was loss due to "the rampant theft of fuel by a large percentage of the drivers."[84] In both Mwanza and Dar es Salaam, TCRS officials purchased fuel on behalf of the UNHCR, and when it arrived in Ngara, a logistics officer assigned fuel to

170 · CHAPTER 8

each agency.[85] The trip for a lorry with fifty thousand liters of fuel from Dar es Salaam to Ngara took seven days in the dry season and fifteen in the rainy season (from Mwanza, it took two to five days), giving truck drivers plenty of time to siphon fuel.[86] Officials attempted to curb losses by dyeing the fuel prior to embarkation. It was hoped that the easy identification of stolen fuel would prevent theft if the perpetrators believed they would be reported to the police. However, once the drivers "recovered from their initial scare," they resumed stealing, and petrol became a "medium of exchange at the grinding mills throughout the area."[87] In February 1995 the TCRS estimated that 500,000 liters of fuel would be lost or stolen, at a value of 160 million shillings, or $300,000.[88]

Theft was just one of many problems the agency experienced in attempting to support humanitarian efforts in Ngara. Five different companies manufactured the trucks used by the agency, which made the ordering of spare parts and vehicle maintenance a "nightmare."[89] The TCRS was also responsible for building, staffing, and maintaining workshops to service the program's vehicles, but workshop construction was continually delayed. In November 1994 repair and maintenance of the "ever growing fleet" took place wherever possible—including "in the mud where mechanics perform small miracles to keep the fleet moving."[90]

By January 1995, the fleet, which was also involved in transporting refugees from border villages to temporary camps, was in crisis. Due to high turnover in personnel, poor working conditions, rampant theft, and rapidly increasing needs, the TCRS found itself unable to meet the fuel requirements of the refugee program.[91] The result was that in January 1995 the UNHCR began to ration fuel.[92] Personnel from the UNHCR and other NGOs heaped blame on the TCRS, a situation that continued even after it fixed the situation. Compounding tensions were the alleged "bureaucratic delays" in sending promised UNHCR funds to the TCRS, forcing the latter to prefinance its operations.[93] Rumors swirled that "only 60% of UNHCR commitment" had been assured, even though the TCRS and other NGOs were required to continue operating as usual, albeit with some proposed cutbacks.[94]

Another issue between the UNHCR and TCRS was supplying water to refugees in Ngara, as well as financing the operation. These problems indicate larger failures of responsibility for and management of an "emergency" refugee situation that lasted more than two years.[95] Oxfam was the first partner agency involved in providing water to refugees in Ngara. In this capacity, and in collaboration with Médecins Sans Frontières [MSF] and UNICEF, it drilled new boreholes around Benaco, and by July 1994, the average water consumption in Benaco was 12.3 liters per person per day.[96] However, because Oxfam worked only in emergency operations, the TCRS "reluctantly" took over the Oxfam water treatment plant in July.[97] In September 1994 Staub wrote to the UNHCR "that OXFAM was handing over water too soon."[98] Nevertheless, the TCRS took over the water department—a responsibility it retained until the following summer. Presciently, in January 1995 a TCRS official noted that "it is impossible for TCRS to absorb all activities that others leave behind and we must be careful that we are not to be blamed for future collapses."[99]

One of the issues with water in Ngara was whether more permanent boreholes should be drilled or the initial system of tankage and purification should be continued—a question that became more serious when the lake next to Benaco began to dry up.[100] By January and February 1995, there were "severe water shortages," and "new water schemes were proposed under great pressure."[101] Pumping and tanking of water from K9 lake began, and by March, a TCRS drilling team had found new water sources near Benaco, "where others before had claimed there was no water present."[102] A water engineer hired by the TCRS, Fridtjov Ruden, drilled for water around the various camps in Ngara, as well as drilling boreholes for local communities. The idea of providing water to local communities was not popular in the UNHCR or even in TCRS's water department. On the issue of water, the political nature of the refugee operation became clear, as some TCRS employees were seen as adhering too close to the UNHCR's priorities.

In this respect, Ted Jones, head of the water department in Ngara, made it clear that "the water 'belongs to the Rwandans'"; he did not want any Tanzanians or even TCRS administration personnel in the water office.[103] In addition, Jones thought Ruden's proposals for finding water, which went against those of other hydrologists in Ngara, were a "waste of time." The TCRS's interim emergency coordinator attributed Jones's position to the perception of "a threat to Ted's kingdom and the possibility, however remote, of [Ruden's] success makes him terrifically angry."[104] The success of the drilling teams throughout Kagera region thus occurred "under very difficult circumstances and in a highly competitive environment, with different political agendas."[105] By April, the water service was "still in the emergency phase since we have never provided enough water to the refugees and currently we are still at the 10 liters per person and in many cases even lower than that."[106] The result was that in July 1995 the TCRS handed back the majority of water service functions to Oxfam, although the agency continued to explore and dig wells in the Kitali Hills and Keza refugee settlements.

172 · CHAPTER 8

Part of the water problem was that as the refugee population rose by 194 percent between July 1994 and June 1995, water production increased by only 109 percent, the result of borehole deterioration and depletion of local water sources.[107] Another issue was a delay in equipping boreholes drilled in early 1995 due to the use of standard rather than emergency procurement procedures.[108] The UNHCR blamed these issues on TCRS's poor "technical and managerial suitability."[109] Additionally, the UNHCR severely criticized TCRS's handling of fuel transport and workshop building during early 1995, and the TCRS responded by streamlining operations and consolidating the program.

By the end of 1995, it seemed that many of the TCRS's shortcomings had been addressed.[110] However, new problems arose that had to do with reputation and funding.[111] Shortfalls in the UNHCR's budget for the Great Lakes region meant drastic cuts in funding for Ngara in 1996. Additionally, the UNHCR had difficulty repaying the $3 million the TCRS had prefinanced out of its 1995 budget. As a result, the TCRS threatened to halt all activities in Ngara unless a formal letter of intent was signed by February 12, 1996 (it was eventually signed on February 8).[112] Although TCRS officials believed the UNHCR's financial duress was real, the tension between the two agencies stemmed from the UNHCR's scapegoating of the TCRS within the international community. Thus, Staub noted, "TCRS is ready to accept responsibility where there is a clear case, however it is difficult to accept to be a kind of scrape [sic] goat when it is convenient to UNHCR to pass on the blame and responsibility."[113]

Problems continued into 1996 as the European Community Humanitarian Organization (ECHO), which, together with the US government, funded 50 percent of the UNHCR's budget, refused to have any of its UNHCR funding distributed to the TCRS. Some in the TCRS attributed this to ECHO's "desire for visibility and for ownership of the 'sexy' components of the UNHCR programme."[114] Other TCRS officials believed the UNHCR had submitted poor TCRS performance reports to ECHO to cover up its own difficulties during 1995. Still others believed the strain in Ngara came from the fact that "UNHCR feels that TCRS is too big and that TCRS also expresses its own opinion. UNHCR clearly does not like any NGO having its own opinion and basically UNHCR always wants to be in charge and boss everybody around."[115]

By the fall of 1996, relations between UNHCR Ngara and TCRS Ngara were at a breaking point. In October the UNHCR confirmed its decision to discontinue TCRS camp management of Chabalissa II in Karagwe district. The UNHCR had initially asked the TCRS to take over Chabalissa II camp management in September 1994, when Caritas management of the overcrowded Chabalissa I was "a mess."[116] By all accounts, TCRS's work in Chabalissa II was exemplary, even in light of the central transport activities "pushed and expanded" on it by the UNHCR.[117] And yet, two years later, the UNHCR decided to hand over camp management to Caritas. The TCRS appealed the decision, to no avail. Although the UNHCR hoped the TCRS would continue its other sectoral responsibilities in Karagwe, such as transport and fuel provisioning, the TCRS announced that it would pull out of Karagwe completely. "The reasoning behind our decision," Jaap Aantjes wrote, "is, that we cannot accept to be pushed by UNHCR in another Ngara style project, with fuel and logistics only, this time in Karagwe. We have decided to make a firm policy statement," declaring TCRS's wish to care for "people first and machines later."[118] Simeso put the situation more bluntly, noting that TCRS's logistical duties placed it "not in [a] forefront position with the refugees to be able to attract publicity," yet it was responsible for "by far the most difficult and complicated" aspect of relief.[119] The TCRS expressed, however, its wish to continue its involvement in refugee host assistance in Ngara and Karagwe, a program that would receive little support from the international community.

Conclusion

This chapter has presented some of the logistical challenges faced by the international community during the Rwandan refugee crisis, as well as how the crisis and the international response to it transformed refugee aid. Never before had the international community responded so quickly, and with so much money and media attention, to a refugee crisis. The business of refugee aid expanded, and donors became preoccupied with the most visible and "sexy" aspects of humanitarian aid. In response, the UNHCR initiated its sectoral approach to refugee care, an approach that continues to be used today. This led implementing agencies to compete for more attractive sectors of operation, such as food distribution and camp management, to the detriment of the less visible yet essential sectors of the aid program. The UNHCR's insistence that program planning remain in the "emergency" phase then hindered agencies' ability to properly plan and administer much-needed aid to the growing refugee population.

It was perhaps inevitable that the response to the refugee crisis would encounter grave logistical and political problems. As one TCRS employee put it, "The project became too big too fast . . . [and] nobody knew" just how large the response, in terms of trucks, water, firewood, and of course money, would become.[120] What was novel about this "emergency" was the speed with which it occurred and the competition for visibility among the aid organizations, as well as their quick assigning of blame. The vast amount of media attention and funding initially available pushed the humanitarian response into a maelstrom of visibility politics and in-fighting, as well as confrontations over which populations deserved aid. All the aid agencies in Ngara worked under difficult conditions; however, as we will see, many were indifferent to the effects their operations had on local Tanzanian lives and livelihoods.

The next chapter explores the challenges and opportunities the refugee crisis presented to the people living in Ngara district—a population of around 190,000 living among half a million refugees in one of the poorest districts of Tanzania.[121] Some of these issues, such as the deforestation around Benaco, have already been mentioned. We have also seen the rapidly diminishing water reserves in the district and the engineer's remark that the "water belongs to the refugees." Such notions had a significant impact on the populations living around Benaco and other Rwandan refugee camps. A few agencies, the TCRS included, attempted to assist the local population. However, as the refugee population continued to grow and international attention waned, funding dried up.

Competition and Backstabbing · 175

9. OF *GÉNOCIDAIRES* AND HUMANITARIANS

THE RWANDAN REFUGEE EMERGENCY

IN NGARA DISTRICT

What was continually left out of UNHCR and implementing partner plans for the refugee crisis was the situation of the local, or host, communities. As early as one month into the refugee emergency, Admasu Simeso noted that, "as usual," local agencies and "ordinary" people did not get any "visibility" from the international community, despite the fact that "local communities ... get the burden of influx by receiving the refugees and sharing ... their meager resources, before the international help arrives." Correctly predicting the future, Simeso continued, "Long after the international[s] have gone back or shifted to new center[s] of attention, the local communities are the ones who will be left with the scars ... the already poor local communities are the ones who end up losing the most" as they receive no international funds or even recognition.[1]

From the start of the refugee crisis in Ngara, UNHCR officials approached program planning with the understanding that the refugee emergency was temporary. The solution to the crisis—what would qualify as a successful end to the refugee emergency—was for the refugees to voluntarily repatriate to

Rwanda. As the possibility for repatriation became increasingly remote over the months and years that followed, UNHCR officials nevertheless continued their activities in Ngara under "emergency" program planning. As early as November 1994, TCRS staff members had noted the difficulty of taking over tasks designed for an "emergency phase" while realities on the ground led gradually "towards a semi-permanent situation" that was unsustainable due to the lack of resources in Ngara district.[2] The largest issue identified by TCRS officials was that the "actual political decision on the future of the Rwandan refugees" had not been made, leading to difficulties in deciding how to alleviate problems such as overcrowding and inadequate water supplies.[3] When the Tanzanian government eventually made that decision in December 1996, ordering all refugees to return to Rwanda, it did so without the input of the humanitarian community and despite the *non-refoulement* clause of the Refugee Convention.[4] Just a few months later, almost all the relief agencies left Ngara—departing almost as quickly as they had arrived and taking almost all their materials with them—to the shock and dismay of Ngaran residents.[5] As one former aid worker recalled, they even took the water pipes.[6]

For the two years the Rwandan refugees lived in Ngara, they and those who aided them fundamentally altered the landscape of the district and of Ngaran lives. The refugee complex in Ngara, which included both refugees and expatriate aid workers, created a space of contradictory violence in the district—a violence that was simultaneously disruptive and productive. Ngarans experienced the material and psychological harms of dislocation and physical violence associated with the refugee camps. Many Ngarans also took advantage of novel economic opportunities created by the transnational refugee complex and the refugee population.

Looking only at the existing scholarship on Ngara, it would be understandable to think the district did not exist until April 1994. Certainly, the majority of observers then and since have understood the district only in terms of those two years of refugee hosting, reducing the Basubi and Bahangaza people to winners and losers in the refugee-humanitarian drama. The end of the twentieth century saw a comparative deluge of scholarly attention to the humanitarian response to the refugee crisis in Ngara, most of which was aimed at understanding the failings and benefits of the "refugee regime" in the district.[7] Common questions include: Who benefited and who was harmed by the transnational response? What did the agencies do wrong, and what could they have done better? The authors generally attempt to understand the response in terms of wider refugee policies, with little attention to what was contingent about the people, the personalities, and the events involved. Scholars such as Beth Whitaker have added new complexity to our understanding of refugee crises by attending to the effects on host communities and, most importantly, by disaggregating the notion of the host community to understand how variables such as location, economic standing, gender, and age affect local populations' experiences as hosts.[8] This chapter builds on such work to understand the contradictory ways the refugee crisis (meaning the actions of both refugees and of humanitarians) affected the everyday lives of Ngarans. I utilize interviews with local residents and aid personnel, in addition to archival holdings, to demonstrate the effects of the refugee crisis. These effects include the physical effects of the refugee-aid complex in Ngara district and how the evolution of this presence influenced local ideas about identity, nationalism, and morality—changes that built on the longer history of refugee hosting and aid in Ngara.

For Ngarans, the refugee emergency became a pivotal factor in how people viewed themselves and their neighbors. The material effects of the emergency included the destruction of ecological resources and the loss of physical and material security for those who came into contact with refugees. These effects solidified Ngaran perceptions of self and community, perceptions that centered on an oppositional understanding of the national character of Tanzanians and Rwandans. The process of ideological nationalism, begun during decolonization and furthered by the presence of Rwandan (and, to a lesser extent, Burundian) refugees in the district, was thereby consolidated during the mid-1990s. Perceptions of identity in Ngara have, since 1994, revolved around a popular saying: "If you catch ten thieves in Ngara, seven will be Rwandan, two Burundian, and maybe one Tanzanian." I heard this often during my research in Ngara, and it has become a lens for understanding how the people who were formerly members of the Bugufi and Busubi chiefdoms became both Ngaran and Tanzanian. The effects of the refugee emergency continue in Ngara—both the scars left on people's bodies and the landscape and the perceptions of self and those who live "across the line" of nationality and its constituent "other."[9]

"The Whole Country Was Coming"

For many Ngarans, the Rwandan emergency began well before the influx of expatriate personnel to the district in 1994. For David Ntahura, the Rwandan emergency began in 1992, when "some people came running" from Rwanda into Tanzania.[10] To Ntahura and many others, the first people who

178 · CHAPTER 9

crossed into Ngara could not be described as refugees because they were not helped by international aid organizations, nor were they sequestered in refugee camps. Rather, such people were better understood as individuals and families who were able to care for themselves with the help of family and friends who already lived in the district. Absent the aid of international and national actors, these people more closely resembled the immigrants who had traveled through and settled in Ngara during the 1940s and 1950s, as well as the small groups who had arrived during the 1970s—although these individuals were more closely associated with the Rwandan state than their predecessors.

Ntahura remembered the people who followed in 1994 very differently. In April, after the presidential plane crash, first Tutsi and then Hutu began arriving in increasing numbers in Rusumo town.[11] They slept on the road, and local people gave them food and shared what little they could. After three days, Ntahura recalled, the problem of food acquisition for local residents and refugees alike became acute, as prices for basic foodstuffs skyrocketed. It was only after the refugees moved to the transnationally funded camp at Benaco about two weeks later, however, that real problems began for Ntahura and his neighbors. Refugees killed animals in neighboring forests, they killed people in the camp, and men with guns and other weapons hijacked cars traveling on the local roads. According to Ntahura, ten or more refugee men would stop a car, two armed with guns and the others with pangas and hammers. Ntahura himself was accosted twice, when hijackers robbed him and beat his friend "very badly."[12] Other residents and local aid workers described similar incidents. The refugees' attacks were sometimes arbitrary or motivated by the victims' perceived wealth, but they were often based on the perceived ethnic affiliations of the potential victims, such as those who, due to their height, long nose, or slim bearing, looked Tutsi. One aid worker remembered that buses were often stopped, and the passengers were targeted based on their appearance. His own daughter was forced to flee into the woods to escape one such attack.[13]

On the heels of the refugees came the aid agencies. Some people in Rusumo procured employment as drivers with the international agencies or as food distributors in the ever-expanding refugee camps. Others were employed by the transnationally funded body retrieval program on the Kagera River. Ntahura clearly remembered the enormous influx of people into Ngara. In addition to refugees and *wazungu* expatriates, Tanzanians from all over the country arrived in Ngara to take advantage of the business opportunities in the burgeoning refugee camp markets and with the international agencies that scrambled to provide the refugees with shelter, food, health care, and community services. Ntahura recalled that in 1995 and 1996 food prices started to decrease as refugees received more and more goods from the international community—goods they often sold to local people. As a result, many local farmers lost their incomes, unable to compete with the low prices of internationally donated commodities. When the Rwandan refugees suddenly left Ngara in late 1996, all the aid agencies left with them.

A government officer in Rusumo related a similar narrative. I asked him when he first knew about the war in Rwanda, and he responded that the war started in 1991.[14] That was the year he crossed the border into Rwanda to sell some fish and was captured by Rwandan soldiers. He lifted his shirt to show me the scars from that incident, the physical reminders of a machete blow and an emergency that defied geography and time. According to this man, "If you go there with a big nose, they think you are Tutsi"; they "don't care about passports."[15] The refugees began to arrive, according to this government officer, in April 1994—first Tutsi and then, one week later, Hutu. First they stayed at Kahaza, a small reception camp set up by the UNHCR. At the start, the refugees were few, so the locals were able to provide food and shelter to the people streaming across the Rusumo Bridge. That stopped when they saw "that the whole country was coming."[16] Some refugees arrived with cattle and goats; others had pangas, hoes, and even guns. The refugees knew they would not be allowed to bring their weapons into the UNHCR camps, so they left their guns in the forests around the villages. Later, villagers collected whatever weapons they could find and took them to the police station.

Soon, according to the government officer, serious problems began. The price of food went up astronomically, and many people went hungry.[17] The refugees robbed local people. If they went into a house, they took everything.[18] They destroyed local water sources, forests, properties, and crops. Women from inside and outside the refugee camps showed up at internationally funded clinics to report that they had been raped by refugees.[19] All across the district, at entry points and along transit routes, people placed barriers made of tree trunks across their doors, hoping to deter theft and violence.

K9: Security for *Wazungu*

In contrast to the chaos experienced in other parts of the district, the early days of the Benaco camp were surprisingly calm and orderly. Despite rapid overcrowding, everything from food distribution to camp settlement seemed to be well organized.[20] This situation reflected the power of the refugee elite—

180 · CHAPTER 9

those leaders who retained the ability to manipulate the Rwandan population in the refugee camps.[21] However, despite the appearance of calm among the refugee population in the early months of the emergency, tension and insecurity could quickly mount, as events in October 1994 attested. That month, the Tanzanian police arrested a refugee leader in Benaco, leading to "a massive protest demonstration towards the police station," and the Tanzanian militia had to be called in "to keep the crowd under control and protect the police."[22] As a result, the TCRS evacuated staff living next to the camp.

The problem of camp security, although not as acute as in Zaire, continued throughout the refugees' stay in Ngara.[23] The situation was exacerbated when international agencies used existing commune leaders to oversee food distribution, which gave the political elite (many of whom had planned and orchestrated the genocide in Rwanda) the power to determine rations. The ability to control the population's access to food heightened the elites' power in the camps, as well as their ability to benefit from the sale of donated food in the growing camp markets.[24]

From the start of the emergency, the international community in Ngara was aware that the refugee population included elite political leaders. Their trucks, cars, and motorcycles crowded the parking lots next to Benaco.[25] Efforts to separate these refugee leaders, who were not legally protected by the 1951 Refugee Convention, the 1967 Protocol, or the OAU Refugee Convention due to their participation in crimes against humanity, quickly led to disaster. Most famous was the Gatete incident, which occurred in mid-June 1994. The Tanzanian police, with UNHCR support, attempted to arrest Gatete, the former burgomaster of Murambi, who had allegedly led massacres against Tutsi. This led to riots in Benaco involving thousands of refugees and caused the international agencies to temporarily withdraw from the camp.[26] Simultaneously, the use of former political leaders as food distributors and in other positions of authority in Benaco provided a measure of control over the camp, as those who provoked unrest or riots would then offer to help restrain the population. The aid agencies, "having no ready alternative . . . would agree and hence treat them as camp leaders."[27]

The insecurity of the camp prompted the removal of international staff and agency headquarters to K9, the isolated outpost at the top of a large hill located nine kilometers from the main road. However, Tanzanian aid workers did not initially move to this new headquarters, which was built for expatriate staff.[28] In contrast to the majority of aid agencies that "built their camps and workshops out in the bush (nowhere) at K9," the TCRS "fought a battle" to locate its workshop, offices, fuel station, staff quarters, and

Of *Génocidaires* and Humanitarians · 181

warehouses in Ngara town, where its resources and infrastructure could eventually be handed over to local churches and the district government.[29] When this decision was later criticized by a UNHCR logistics officer, a senior TCRS official explained, "At the time it was defended by stating the advantages of the infrastructures benefitting the local council and it not being wasted on top of a muddy hill called K9, the closeness to banking and other infrastructures and the presence of UNHCR itself in Ngara." Furthermore, he noted, "The presence of a large contingent of local Tanzanian staff within TCRS was not welcome at the time in K9, that we perceived to [be] more of a Mzungu type set-up."[30] Colin Pryce, the UNHCR logistics officer, had chastised the TCRS in early 1995 for the extraordinary decision to move its operational base from Benaco to Ngara. This was seen as inconvenient, as it led to extra fuel consumption and wear and tear on vehicles, and by moving to Ngara rather than to K9, "TCRS successfully alienated itself from the rest of the Team."[31]

This March 1995 exchange between TCRS and UNHCR officials indicates larger problems with the refugee settlement scheme, the most blatant being the prioritization of the expatriate staff's safety over that of Tanzanian staff and local residents. This is apparent in the reference to Tanzanians not being welcome at K9, which was seen as the preserve of *mzungu* who had to be protected from the dangers of the refugee camp. The expatriates' disdain for Tanzanian workers is evident throughout the archives. Later in the program, when the UNHCR found itself short of funds for the Great Lakes region refugee emergency, its officials would encourage partner NGOs to hire local workers (who could be paid less, due to differential pay scales for locals and expatriates). However, during the first year or so of the operation, Tanzanians were thought to be untrustworthy and incompetent. Indeed, when Tanzanian staff members were eventually moved to K9, they generally lived in segregated areas, across the road from the expatriate and largely white relief workers.[32]

In contrast, and due in part to the organization's decades of operational experience in Tanzania, the TCRS employed a large number of Tanzanians. At the start of the emergency, many Tanzanian and expatriate employees (who were often from other African countries) were shifted to Ngara from TCRS programs elsewhere.[33] At the end of April 1995, almost one year from the start of the emergency, Bernhard Staub noted that although the TCRS needed more senior managers, "where we tend to disagree with UNHCR is that there should be expatriates every where." He went on to posit that "UNHCR still has the feeling that the number of expatriates is all important."[34]

182 · CHAPTER 9

At the same time, the TCRS's Tanzanian staff members were seldom treated on an equal footing with expatriates. Tanzanian administrative staff complained that they were "on the very edge of the decision-making" and felt "left out of most of the TCRS work done in Ngara." Two permanent Tanzanian staff members recalled "numerous instances when they were not welcomed by section heads to different parts of the program."[35] Even TCRS's emergency coordinator concurred, noting in November 1994 that the local staff, many of whom continued to live in tents, "need to be more involved in the decision making process, consulted more in areas of their competence and not constantly be confronted with the results of decision made by expatriate staff."[36] Nevertheless, the differential treatment of local staff continued to be an issue.

Part of this differential treatment likely stemmed from the lower salaries paid to Tanzanian staff. Aid organizations almost always pay local staff members less than their expatriate staff, an issue the TCRS was well aware of in Ngara. The emergency coordinator reported in 1994 that "the local economy in Ngara is completely out of control and prices of basic commodities are sky rocketing," thus "seriously affect[ing] the purchasing power of the local staff."[37] Charles Franzen, the TCRS interim emergency coordinator in Ngara in February 1995, was sympathetic to this problem. Describing the performance of Tanzanian employee Everready Nkya, he wrote, "It amazes me to see the amount of work he does . . . while those with 20 times the pay achieve 10% of the results." However, Franzen was able to distinguish among national staff, praising Nkya while deriding the drivers who stole "countless liters of fuel every day."[38]

In contrast, UNHCR officials took a more singular approach to all Tanzanian employees, writing, "One serious problem is to expect national staff to discipline other national staff, when it is well known about the social problems this creates amongst national staff."[39] It remains unclear why UNHCR personnel believed that expatriate staff were more efficient at disciplining other expatriate workers and Tanzanian employees.

The culture of humanitarian aid organizations was biased against Tanzanian employees at a basic level. Tanzanian staff were not afforded the same security measures as expatriates, indicating a basic discrepancy between the human rights rhetoric of aid agencies and their discriminatory policies on the ground. Such discrimination was evident in the unequal salaries between expatriate and local staff. But perhaps most gratingly, local staff members' ideas and strengths were occluded by an international humanitarian regime that privileged expatriate "expert" knowledge over local knowledge.

Of *Génocidaires* and Humanitarians · 183

This logic extended into the host community as well, where the legal refugee remained the "authentic" object of relief, to the detriment of the needs of locals.[40]

Host Communities

It was no secret to the international community present in Ngara that local people suffered due to the refugees' presence. The UNHCR's decision to move its base to K9, along with almost all other NGOs operating in Ngara, was predicated on the insecurity of the refugee camps. In addition to being "victims of robbery, violence, and abuse while at the same time experiencing high prices, diminished water resources, depleted availability of firewood and destroyed crops," the local population lost many highly trained educators, doctors, and mechanics to "the higher paying NGOs."[41] According to one expatriate, Tanzanians in Ngara described the refugees by saying, "Even the wood is cut for them."[42]

In none of the camps was "there enough control by the UNHCR or the Tanzanian authorities to prevent refugees from walking into (or out of) the camps and simply settling down."[43] Tanzanians who worked for international agencies were sometimes attacked by refugees while performing their duties. One man who worked for CARE and Norwegian People's Aid (NPA) during the crisis showed me his own knife wounds when I asked about problems with the refugee community. He was attacked one day on his way home from work in Benaco and explained that people were afraid to sleep in their own homes. The refugees took his bicycle and everything he carried.[44]

The perception of refugee gain at the expense of the local community was widespread. One resident who lived close to Benaco remembered that the "local people called [them]selves refugees within [their] own country," and Tanzanians became "beggars to refugees."[45] Refugees boasted to Tanzanians, "We are the UN you have no power." This rang true to many Ngarans, as the refugees were given "everything" for free, including good hospitals, education, food, and water, while Ngarans often suffered.[46] Local Ngarans therefore competed with refugees "for land, water, fire-wood and space."[47] Although some local people were able to take advantage of refugee dispensaries, they were not allowed to attend refugee schools.[48]

The issue of water was particularly acute, as local sources were depleted by and even diverted to the refugee camps. As noted earlier, the TCRS's own water manager saw water resources as "belonging" to the Rwandans, no matter where the water came from. Almost everyone I interviewed remem-

184 · CHAPTER 9

bered local water resources being diverted to the refugees, and some of the local people living around Benaco and Kasulu bought water from the refugees, albeit at lower prices than usual. Most people agreed that, at the very least, the relief agencies should have left the water pipes when they departed.

Theft was an ongoing issue for community members, even those living some distance from the refugee camps.[49] As refugees continued to enter the district all along Tanzania's border with Burundi during 1995 and 1996, they stripped the area bare of livestock and infrastructure; they even destroyed border villages' primary schools, where the refugees often slept. In Rulenge, people remembered that although the UNHCR improved some infrastructure in the area of Benaco, the refugees en route to camps used desks, chairs, shutters, and doors they stole from local dwellings and schools for firewood—basic necessities that were not compensated.[50]

In addition to deforestation, depletion of water resources, and theft and insecurity, local communities suffered from the health effects of living in proximity to a large refugee population. As the cost of living rose, so did HIV rates in local communities.[51] The prevalence of sexually transmitted infections and other diseases, such as dysentery, increased while local health staff were recruited away from government jobs to higher-paying work with relief agencies.[52] In particular, HIV became a problem in the district, as many local (and refugee) women reported being raped by refugees.[53]

As refugees cut down trees for firewood, local people had to walk farther to obtain their own fuel for cooking. Simultaneously, the cost of meat, salt, soap, and kerosene skyrocketed by an estimated 100 to 400 percent.[54] The toll was hardest on schoolteachers and civil servants who remained on government payrolls and were thus forced to make do with existing salary structures that failed to keep up with the rising cost of living. Women in particular were affected by these developments, as it was generally men who took "control of petty trade activities" when they became profitable.[55]

Food prices varied throughout the refugee presence. The refugees were supplied with food from the World Food Programme (WFP), without regard to cultural preferences. In many cases, the only cereal distributed to the refugees was unmilled maize—a grain that was unfamiliar to the refugees and difficult for them to cook.[56] As a result, refugees frequently sold their maize rations in refugee markets, leading to a decrease in the price of maize throughout the area.[57] Huge markets sprang up in the refugee camps, particularly in Benaco, where thousands of Tanzanians traveled to take part in the exchange of food and other materials donated by the international community. In contrast to maize, the price of cooking bananas, a favorite food

Of *Génocidaires* and Humanitarians · 185

in both Ngara and Rwanda, increased. Prices were also affected by the timing and quality of food distributions. Beans, another favorite of both communities, were distributed by the WFP after being shipped into the country. The result was a decrease in bean prices, which hurt many local farmers. This situation might have been avoided if the international agencies had purchased beans locally.[58] In general, food security near the camps decreased as refugees stole food and as they (and their cattle) traveled through the area destroying banana and cassava crops and leading to the "real possibility of famine in the area."[59]

Simultaneously, many Ngarans benefited from the refugee emergency. Aid agencies hired many locals to work at the refugee camps. Although these jobs were temporary, they allowed some individuals and families to save money and pursue educational opportunities that would have been impossible otherwise.[60] Tanzanians from all over the country flocked to Benaco to take part in refugee markets, and by 1996, Ngara was home to the second largest city in Tanzania. Ngarans also created their own opportunities from the crisis, including stealing fuel from aid agencies' trucks and convoys. Additionally, some local people hired refugees for farm and domestic labor.[61] However, because the refugees were willing to work for lower wages than Ngarans, many Ngarans lost their seasonal work to refugees.[62]

When I asked about the impact of the Rwandan refugee crisis on local communities, the answers often varied based on proximity to refugee camps. In Mugoma, close to the Rwandan border but farther from Benaco than many other villages, some people remembered no problems with the refugees, although the price of food went up.[63] In Shanga village, people gave refugees shelter and food; they even closed the primary schools for about a month to allow the refugees to shelter there.[64] Bernard Kadene did not remember the refugees as violent, but his neighbor Samwel Rwanzi recalled that even though the local people gave the refugees food, the refugees stole from them.[65] Edward Teadi explained the issue of refugee theft in Mugoma this way: "If a man is hungry he has to steal." The refugees "broke in our houses and stole bananas" before the UNHCR and the government took them to the camps.[66] Closer to Benaco, in the village of Kumnazi, people remembered that UNHCR-funded pipes diverted their local water sources to the refugee camps.[67] Many people left villages close to Benaco to avoid the security threats posed by refugees.[68] Some people recalled that Tanzanians occasionally collaborated with refugees to steal from wealthy Ngarans.[69] Others emphasized that those with long noses who looked Tutsi were singled out for violence.[70]

186 · CHAPTER 9

Conditions continued to deteriorate throughout 1996 as more Rwandans entered the district from Burundi, leading to a worsening of the security situation. For a time, more than nineteen thousand refugees were held at Keza.[71] Around Keza, residents remembered refugees attacking local homes and participating in military training outside the camp.[72] In 1996 TCRS staff noted a "serious imbalance" in the living conditions of the local Tanzanian population and the refugees, whose "water, food, education, social services, firewood, [and] medical attention" were all "up to international standards."[73] In spite of the refugees' better living standards, the security situation continued to deteriorate for Ngarans during 1996, as "attacks on Tanzanian villagers" increased when international funding began to dry up.[74]

One undeniable benefit of the refugee crisis continues to be the infrastructure built by the international community in Ngara, such as the tarmac road connecting Ngara town to the main road from Mwanza to Rwanda, as well as the creation of the first radio station in Ngara district. Radio Kwizera, begun in 1995, was funded by the UNHCR and operated through the Jesuit Refugee Service. The station was created to transmit information to the more than 400,000 refugees living in the district.[75] Broadcasts sent peaceful messages to the refugees and informed them about decisions made by leaders in Rwanda, Tanzania, and the UNHCR—particularly regarding the security situation in Rwanda and safe opportunities for repatriation.[76] The station broadcast in Kiswahili and Kirundi, as these languages were most intelligible to both Tanzanians and refugees. Today, the radio station still operates in Ngara, which, due to its peripheral location, had difficulty receiving broadcasts over Radio Tanzania.[77] Radio reports concentrate on environmental and human rights issues, as well as sports, politics, and other news of interest to Ngarans. Many in Ngara see the radio as a lasting benefit from the refugee crisis, as it keeps them informed about what is happening in the district and the country, in addition to educating the community about issues such as women's rights and family planning.[78]

Refoulement and Humanitarian Flight

On December 6, 1996, the government of Tanzania released a statement that all Rwandan refugees had to return to Rwanda by the end of the month: "Message to all Rwandese refugees in Tanzania from the Government of the United Republic of Tanzania and the office of the High Commissioner for Refugees. . . . The Government of the republic of Tanzania has decided that all Rwandan refugees can now return to their country in safety. . . .

the Government of the Republic of Tanzania has decided that all Rwandan refugees in Tanzania are expected to return home by 31 December 1996."[79] Although the announcement took many aid agencies by surprise, it seems that the refugees had been expecting the decision. By December 9, they had already started moving eastward. According to TCRS employees, a "massive intimidation campaign" was occurring in the camps in Karagwe, where "intimidators" warned that the Tanzanian military would surround the camps and force the population to walk back to Rwanda through swamps. Meanwhile, the situation in Ngara was "very tense and our staff have been advised not to travel into the camps. Small groups are meeting everywhere . . . and the atmosphere is hostile."[80] Almost immediately, the vast majority of the Rwandan refugee community vacated the refugee camps and took to the bush, willing "to [go] anywhere else but back home."[81] By December 13, TCRS officials reported that "the Great Benaco area is empty now"; all refugees had started moving east, following what appeared to be directives from refugee leaders in Benaco.[82] Lazarus Mezza, a TCRS official, wrote on December 13 that he had seen "thousands" of refugees walking in any direction but Benaco.[83] The Tanzanian government responded by burning some of the refugee shelters and bringing in the military to direct the refugees to Rwanda. The repatriation then became the exclusive purview of the Tanzanian army, causing many of the UNHCR's implementing partners to call the situation "inhuman."[84]

By December 16, there were reports of refugees waiting in lines ten to fifteen miles long to cross from Rusumo into Rwanda.[85] Neither the UNHCR nor other agencies were allowed near the camps or the lines.[86] Not all the refugees went back to Rwanda, however. Many fled into the bush, where some continued to hijack vehicles and steal from local communities. In later years, the new RPF-led Rwandan government would claim that dangerous Rwandan refugees continued to reside in Tanzania, some of whom allegedly took part in raids against the new government as well as the repatriated refugees.[87]

Observers at the time and since then have noted that the majority of the refugee population was "held hostage" by their political leaders, who feared repatriation due to their crimes and attempted to use their position in exile to continue their war against the RPF and the Tutsi.[88] Although some intimidation undoubtedly took place, it cannot be denied that conditions in Rwanda justified refugees' fears about returning. The lack of repatriation was due in part to a lack of political will by the UN and world leaders who were unable "to come up with a united approach in solving the problem in

Rwanda, with regards to normalizing the situation there so that the refugees may go back."[89] The possibly dire repercussions of repatriation were illustrated by the Kibeho incident, in which thousands of internally displaced Rwandans were killed in southwestern Rwanda when the RPF attempted to close the camp.[90] In addition, the inefficient judiciary operating in Rwanda led to hundreds of thousands of prisoners languishing in overcrowded jails.[91]

For Ngarans, one of the most disappointing aspects of the refugee emergency was the quick disappearance of the aid agencies following the forced repatriation. Employees were suddenly without the jobs they had relied on.[92] Agencies took much of the infrastructure they had built with them. Although locals compiled lists of their losses and gave them to UNHCR officials, there was little compensation for destroyed land and stolen food.[93] While the UNHCR and WFP tents remained, and they were put to good use in Ngaran markets, for the most part locals were astonished by how quickly the international agencies left the area.

From the beginning of the refugee emergency, and based on decades of work in refugee resettlement in Tanzania, Bernhard Staub of the TCRS included an assessment of "the development needs of the refugee impacted area" in the list of activities he sent to the UNHCR as possible TCRS projects.[94] Although such activities were not included in TCRS's or any other agency's sectors of UNHCR programming, TCRS personnel began to mobilize funds for a project in the refugee-impacted areas.[95] In July 1995, in an effort "to see how our programs can promote the smooth provision of assistance to the refugees in the context of the massive effects that the influx continues to have on the local community," the TCRS began work to alleviate the plight of host communities in Ngara.[96] These early projects included the construction of a police post at Kasulu (funded by the UNHCR) and local infrastructural rehabilitation. The agency then sought outside funding to build wells for local communities, plant trees to replace those cut down by refugees and aid agencies, and rehabilitate some of the district roads that had been destroyed.[97] Unfortunately, due to a lack of funding and UNHCR support, many of these programs were delayed for several years, and others were never begun.[98]

Additionally, once the UNHCR left the major camps, all TCRS project materials funded by the UNHCR had to be returned as well. Thus, because "practically everything we built/possessed for refugee operation had been out of UNHCR funding . . . it was all handed over to them," and in 1997, the TCRS was forced to start "from scratch."[99] Nevertheless, TCRS officials attempted to continue their project in refugee-impacted areas, surveying thirty-four villages and planning a program to rehabilitate the district's environmental, water, sanitation, and infrastructural resources in collaboration with community and church leaders. The program continued to suffer from a lack of financing, so much so that TCRS emergency coordinator Jaap Aantjes sent an urgent email: "We will loose [*sic*] all credibility with community and leaders in Tanzania if we fail to do something for the Tanzanian population . . . PLEASE HELP in SECURING FUNDS!"[100] By 1998, the program was on hold.[101] A few years later, the LWF "localized" TCRS, which then became a Tanzanian-operated agency.

Conclusion

The Rwandan refugee emergency is remembered vividly by aid workers, host communities, and (surely) refugees. There is no doubt that many Ngarans benefited from the emergency, particularly those who were young and educated and therefore well placed to obtain well-paying jobs in international agencies. Yet these jobs vanished with little to no warning with the precipitous departure of aid agencies after the massive refugee repatriation at the end of 1996. A few agencies in addition to the TCRS remained in Ngara to help the local communities and repair some of the damaged landscape.[102] In addition, RODESO, a Tanzanian NGO that focuses on environmental sustainability, was born out of the crisis and continues to operate in Ngara and Benaco.

When people in Ngara town heard that I was going to conduct interviews in Kasulo-Benaco, they wrinkled their noses. "Be careful," I was repeatedly warned. "Benaco is home to thieves, there is no morality there." The scars of the refugee crisis extend past the ecology and the environment then, to pollute the very essence of what was once a small village that became one of the largest towns in Tanzania—for a time.

The Rwandan refugee crisis entrenched the notions of identity and community that began during decolonization. Never before had the lines between refugee and host, between Rwandan and Tanzanian, been so clearly demarcated. Never before (or since) had the district seen so much money funneled to those who qualified as refugees. As Lazarus Mezza, the Tanzanian coordinator of TCRS activities in Ngara, wrote of the government's decision to forcefully repatriate the refugees: "Who qualifies to be a Refugee? Who was barn [*sic*] to be a Refugee?—who has the right to be not a Refugee?"[103]

While Ngaran lives had changed in the thirty years since Rwandan refugees first entered their district, in some ways they had stayed the same. True,

190 · CHAPTER 9

there were more schools and roads, but there was nothing that people would really call "development." Schooling is a privilege. So is health, a varied diet, and clean water. The late 1980s and early 1990s were certainly not easy for Ngarans. Some had new opportunities, but most had farmwork and family. The arrival of half a million Rwandans and perhaps the greatest and most expensive refugee assistance program the world has ever seen changed many Ngaran lives. For those who lived closest to the border and the refugee camps, these changes were more violent and more permanent.

Should the humanitarians have let the refugees starve? Would it have been possible for the aid agencies, the international community, to weed out the *génocidaires*? If they could have, should they have done so?

There is only a moral gray area when we speak of the humanitarian response to the Rwandan emergency in Ngara. There were no right answers. Obviously, some aspects of the response should have been different, and surely an effort at prevention and robust peacekeeping within Rwanda would have alleviated the search for durable solutions in Ngara.[104] But, faced with hundreds of thousands of men, women, and children, with little time for planning and even less for moral contemplation, the international system of refugee relief sprang into action. The relief agencies arrived in force by May 2, 1994, stayed for more than two years, and largely vacated the area shortly after the forced refugee repatriation of late December 1996.[105] There are certainly lessons to be learned from the international response to the genocide and refugee crisis that followed. Ngarans teach us that all people matter, not just those labeled refugees. Security and water matter, as do fuel and land—the very things refugee populations need and threaten in host areas. At the same time, Ngarans can teach us something about compassion and generosity, about creative theft, and, most pertinent to this study, about how a people living on a border become part of a nation.

CONCLUSION

THE BUSINESS OF NATIONALISM
AND HUMANITARIAN AID

In May 1994 Admasu Simeso, an aid worker with the TCRS, stood on the Ngaran side of the Rusumo Bridge and watched as crowds of people crossed from Rwanda into Ngara. He realized that many of these refugees had likely taken part in the Rwandan genocide. Simeso wrote to his headquarters, expressing his frustration that civilians and murderers were mixed together. But, he noted, "To us they are all refugees and need assistance regardless of what they had gone through or what they had done."[1] It is telling that Simeso was unequivocal in his conclusion that "they are all refugees" who "need assistance," a statement that seems self-evident but gets to the heart of the logic of humanitarian assistance and the ambiguities of this reasoning and the paradoxes of its effects. What is it about the label *refugee* that imbued it, at this time and place, with such importance that even genocide could be set aside? And what does it mean for those who are not labeled refugee? How has this moral vision of the humanitarian been constituted, and why?

Throughout the years examined by this book, the definition of the UNHCR's mandate evolved, the aid regime grew, and definitions and redefinitions of *refugees*, or "'authentic' candidates" for relief, went in and out of vogue.[2] However, this definition rarely included Ngarans, just as it rarely led to the protection of human rights.

It is perhaps not surprising that the business of refugee aid, the need for agencies to attract funding and media attention, determines the actions of humanitarians. It is also not surprising that in creating a distinct category of beneficiaries, refugee agencies contribute to contentious identity politics in the places where they operate. Such differences become even clearer in the case of food insecurity, where both host communities and refugee groups would benefit from humanitarian aid. Particularly in border regions, where populations share histories of migration and cultural connections, international interventions contribute to a sense of difference between aid recipients and those left out of the aid agenda. The politics of difference is only enhanced by the attempt to secure those labeled refugees in carefully delineated and restricted camp settings.

Resentment toward Rwandan refugees in Ngara was heightened by a sense that these refugees—or at least those in transnationally funded camps—often resisted the aid given to them. For refugees, as both individuals and groups, this resistance was often part of a claims-making project to secure autonomy from the multiple groups that were trying to control their lives and restrict their movements. However, refugees never constituted a homogeneous group, despite their classification as such by the UNHCR, the TCRS, and even the Tanzanian state. The inability to understand the various economic, political, and social divisions among refugees contributed to an aid perspective that viewed refugee actions as illogical and lazy, rather than the product of negotiations among the refugee populations as well as with the organizational representatives they encountered. It also reflected an ongoing colonial mentality among aid workers, who viewed African refugees as qualitatively different from European refugees.[3] The endurance of such ethnocentric and racist biases within the humanitarian arena are well on display today, as European states and citizenries welcome Ukrainian refugees while closing their borders to African refugees and others from the global South.

The conflicts over refugee aid and protection in Ngara reveal the competing and uneven sovereignties that contour the world of nation-states heralded by decolonization and the creation of the United Nations. Just as more powerful states influence the economic and political agendas of the less powerful through organizations such as the International Monetary Fund and the World Trade Organization, membership in a transnational refugee community configures negotiations on national legislation and the

194 · Conclusion

treatment of citizens and noncitizens alike. The Tanzanian state both welcomed and resisted transnational aid over time as it struggled to defend its own sovereignty internally and within the international arena. As local and national actors, refugees, and international officials all attempted to control the lives and futures of refugee groups, they contested the authority of the nation-state and the international refugee regime. They also became entangled with local ideas of citizenship and nation building.

Examining the history of refugees and refugee aid during and after decolonization reveals insights into the ongoing processes by which colonized peoples become national citizens and the stumbling blocks in this transition. The production of different nationalities in Ngara occurred at the interstice of decolonization and the ascendancy of an international regime created to operationalize the borders of new nations and the populations therein. Rwandans did not enter Ngara as refugees. Rather, they became *wakimbizi*— "people on the run"—over time as local perceptions evolved alongside national and international categories of the citizen and the nation-state.

Ngaran relationships to the nation-state, and to those who do not belong in that space, reveal both the "limits of political community" and the negotiations over "who is included [in] and excluded [from]" that community.[4] Notions of citizenship did not correspond to a simplistic obedience to and acceptance of national laws; rather, they were based on the ethical perceptions of individual and group actions within both national and regional spaces. Thus, even as local practices elided state laws by relying on regional economic circulations, they also served as a "safety valve" for the nation-state, allowing Ngarans to use traditional strategies to ensure their standards of living and survival without formally contesting the legitimacy of the state.[5] For Ngarans, like so many others who exist in the physical and ideological borderlands of the nation-state system, citizenship and sovereignty are related to "bundle[s] of claims, images and assertions of authority" that exist and evolve at several levels simultaneously.[6] Ngarans could therefore reject the blatantly incompetent and often corrupt actions of government officials while simultaneously embracing, over time, the image of a benevolent and peaceful center.

Refugees in Tanzania: "Illegals" in Ngara

In 2002 UN agencies estimated that twenty-five thousand Rwandan refugees remained in refugee camps in Ngara district.[7] During September of that year, Rwanda, Tanzania, and the UNHCR reached an agreement to repatriate the remaining Rwandans by 2003. Many refugees in Tanzania then migrated to Uganda to avoid forced deportation.[8] In 2007 humanitarian agencies estimated that the Tanzanian government had deported sixty thousand people "who speak the Kinyarwanda language" to Rwanda.[9] Tanzanian authorities noted that "those deported were illegal immigrants, some of whom have lived in Tanzania since the early 1960s." The commissioner for Kagera region, Enos Mfuru, stated that the deportees had self-settled in Tanzanian villages and therefore did not have "refugee status."[10]

During my interviews in Ngara, I frequently heard about Tanzanian authorities searching for "illegals" in villages and towns and forcing them across international borders. During the late summer of 2013, people were once again forced across the lines that divide Tanzania and Rwanda, lines drawn by European bureaucrats during the age of imperialism. Friends in Ngara told of Tanzanian soldiers herding Rwandans, many of whom had lived in the district for decades or longer, across the Rwandan border. The UN humanitarian news agency reported that Tanzania had forcibly expelled fifteen thousand Burundian and seven thousand Rwandan "nationals," many of whom "had lived in Tanzania for several decades."[11] In July 2013, Tanzanian president Jakaya Kikwete ordered the "35,000 irregular migrants from Rwanda, Burundi and Uganda to leave the country by 11 August."[12] Those who remained were reportedly rounded up at markets and in their homes with little notice and deported. Rwandan government officials estimated that by September 13, 2013, between seven thousand and eight thousand Rwandans, "mainly women and children," had been deported from Kagera region's districts of Biharamulo, Ngara, Muleba, and Karagwe. Most of these people wound up in "transit camps" in Rwanda. Humanitarian aid agencies then warned of a looming humanitarian crisis.[13]

Tellingly, not all those deported were "illegal" immigrants. According to Simon Siro, a spokesperson for the Tanzanian police force, about four hundred people "had been erroneously identified as illegal immigrants," necessitating a screening process to prove the citizenship of suspected "illegal migrants."[14] It was thus difficult even for Tanzanian authorities to discern the citizenship of those residing in the region and district, revealing how uneasily Ngarans, as well as "illegal migrants" and their histories, sit within the nation-state framework.[15]

In Tanzanian newspaper accounts of these events, historical understandings of the long history of migration in the area were deployed for political purposes. These historical narratives, expressed in national media sources, represent traces of the past in the present—the selective use of historical

196 · Conclusion

facts to justify current political agendas. In response to the Rwandan press's allegation that Tanzania's former first lady, Salma Kikwete, is related to former Rwandan president Habyarimana, a businessman in Dar es Salaam asked if Mama Salma "looks Rwandan."[16] Dr. Benson Bana, a political scientist at the University of Dar es Salaam, noted: "In the recent past Kagera and other regions along the border have been in a crisis with so many bandits entering from abroad turning our citizens into slaves, so what does one expect President Kikwete to do in such a situation?"[17] The Rwandan press then cited historian Gerard Prunier in making political claims against Kikwete.[18]

Time will tell how this particular forced migration turns out. Many of those deported may have returned to Ngara through *panya* routes across the border. The deportations in 2013 came as tension increased between Tanzanian president Kikwete and Rwandan president Kagame over Rwanda's actions in the Democratic Republic of the Congo (DRC). Simultaneously, the World Bank approved more than $300 million in funding for the Regional Rusumo Falls Hydroelectric Project, which aims to provide low-cost energy to Rwanda, Burundi, and Tanzania and increase regional integration and cooperation. World Bank reports make no mention of the political turmoil in the region, noting only that the project will "pave the way for more dynamic regional cooperation, peace and stability."[19] The World Bank expects to resettle an estimated 166 households in Ngara.[20] Some external agencies estimate that thirty thousand to forty thousand people living in Rwanda and Ngara will be affected.[21] It is unclear how much cooperation among the three states can be expected, as each government seeks to ensure its own sovereign rights. The World Bank might do well to take into account the long history of migration and identity formation in Ngara district, the legacy of which will no doubt inform how local people perceive, access, and distribute the work of this latest development project.

The revamped East African Community (EAC) has also seen Benaco and Rusumo become hubs for trucks crossing the borders of Rwanda, while Rwanda has become a center of securitization for goods and of people.[22] As the fortunes of Rwanda have increased under the leadership of Paul Kagame, so has fortification of the border. The Rwandan side of the Rusumo crossing now has banks, as well as digital fingerprinting devices and the police to use them. The border crossing itself has been enlarged, with barbed wire fences on either side. Security has thus been heightened at this particular node between Tanzania and Rwanda.

The Tanzanian government has also attempted, with limited success, to control its border with Burundi. By October 2017, more than 234,110

Burundians had entered Tanzania, fleeing the violence following the contentious 2015 elections.[23] Many of these refugees first entered Ngara district and were then transferred to camps in Kigoma region. In 2018 voluntary repatriation efforts began, with Tanzanian president Magufuli encouraging refugees to return to a "stable" Burundi.[24] It is still unclear how "voluntary" these efforts have been, and the political context in Burundi remains unstable.

This new refugee influx is in addition to the "old caseload" of Burundian refugees who fled to Tanzania in 1972. In 2014 Tanzania announced that it would grant citizenship to these "old caseload" refugees, most of whom lived in Tabora and Katavi regions and were self-reliant. However, by 2017, after meeting with Burundian president Pierre Nkurunziza in Ngara town, President Magufuli suspended the program.[25] Like the naturalization of Rwandan refugees in the 1980s, the granting of citizenship to Burundians has been bureaucratically cumbersome and shot through with tension between the UNHCR and the Tanzanian government.[26] Transnational plans for regional development and integration will thus likely conflict with ongoing conflicts and the increasing solidification of national boundaries in the area.

Return to Ngara

It is perhaps understandable that scholars from disciplines such as anthropology and political science, as well as aid practitioners, focus narrowly on the implications of the 1994 Rwandan refugee emergency in Ngara. Ngara town is visibly marked by the vestiges of Rwandan refugees and the humanitarian organizations that accompanied them during the two long years of the Rwandan refugee emergency. A long aluminum-sheeted building looms over the town's wood and concrete structures, dominating Ngara's main street. Once used by the UNHCR to house refugees in transit, the building now serves as a local marriage hall. Women at Ngara's daily market buy and sell vegetables, fish, fruit, and, when they can afford it, meat under voluminous tents with "UNHCR," "WFP," and "Concern" logos plastered across their sides. Refugee agencies built the tarmac road that links Ngara town with the main road from the Tanzanian interior to the Rwandan border. Abandoned buildings, constructed and left behind by these same organizations, hulk on top of the road's midpoint: K9. One such building now serves as an all-girls secondary school.

Ngarans were marked by the 1994 encounter with refugees and humanitarians. Some carry physical scars of violence; others suffer the emotional effects of dislocation.[27] Some Ngarans exhibit signs of wealth gained through

198 · Conclusion

the refugee and aid encounter, such as degrees earned with the money paid by aid agencies or businesses begun during the emergency. The houses that were once confined to the inner ridge of the high escarpment where Ngara town sits now overflow the ridge, reaching partway down the steep slope. Thanks to the EAC, new banks have opened, and more cars can be seen on the tarmac road through town.

As for the old caseload of Rwandans in Ngara, beginning as early as August 1994, following the RPF's victory in Rwanda, many began to leave the district. This was in addition to the many second-generation refugees who had joined the RPF during the late 1980s and early 1990s. By the time I arrived in the district in the spring of 2012, almost all those who had arrived in Ngara during the 1960s had departed for Rwanda. In Muyenzi, people remember lines of thousands of cattle setting out for the border, headed for an imagined "home."[28] Of course, not every Rwandan refugee from the old caseload left, and some had Tanzanian spouses who stayed behind, so they would come back and visit occasionally. Nevertheless, the overwhelming majority of the 1960s refugees left Ngara. Their departure signals the potency of the desire to return "home" and the longevity of memories of what the Rwandan state should have been.

Ngarans' reaction to the departure of many of their neighbors and friends was mixed. Only a few of the people I interviewed in places such as Muyenzi and Keza expressed anger or disappointment. Those who felt a "loss" tended to brighten at the realization that those who went back to Rwanda left behind cleared, fertilized land. In Busubi, many farmers took advantage of the opportunity to expand their *shamba*. And yet, for some commentators, the voluntary repatriation of these refugees after more than thirty years in Ngara caused an increasing wariness toward refugees who seemed ungrateful for the decades of Tanzanian generosity and hospitality.[29]

When Ngarans talk about Rwandans today, they most often express anger over illegal cattle grazing or thievery. Due to Rwanda's growing population and limited space, the government has restricted the number of cattle a person may own and the type of grazing practices permitted. The result has been an influx of Rwandan cattle to Ngara. Although Rwandans occasionally bring their own cows to graze in the district, they more commonly hire a local Ngaran, or a Rwandan residing in Ngara, to graze their cattle. Particularly in Bugufi, people complain about the crops destroyed by cattle and cattle keepers. I was told that if Ngaran farmers complain to the cattle owners or grazers, they are beaten or even murdered. Rwandans, Ngarans say, are dangerous.

There are also Rwandans in Ngara district and elsewhere in the region who evaded the forced repatriation in 1996. It is said that many are still hiding in the forest preserves, and for a long time, cars along the Rusumo-Ngara and Karagwe-Ngara roads were hijacked at gunpoint. Others who managed to escape the government's reach live peacefully in local communities.

The Production of Refugees, Citizens, and Humanitarians

In Ngara district, the process of identity formation and nation building remains entwined with the processes by which Banyaruanda migrants became Rwandan refugees and Bahangaza and Basubi became Tanzanians. Over the past half century in Ngara, novel forms of refugee aid collided with nascent and evolving state laws, as well as with actual migrant and host populations, each affecting the operations of the other. This analysis probes deeper than the actions and reactions of political elites to uncover the international, national, and local processes that consolidated the primacy of the nation-state in global politics during and after decolonization.[30]

The idea that relations between states can be premised on a genuine moral community grounded in the protection of human rights, as opposed to power and interest, has led to debate among theoreticians of international relations, humanitarian aid, and human rights. Scholars have analyzed the necessity of a humanitarian rights framework that engages politics as well as individual minds, the need for legal charters of protection and accountability that operate on a grassroots level, and proposals for a "rights-based humanitarianism."[31] This literature generally calls for an increase in protection and guarantees by humanitarian agencies, while ignoring the institutional interests and constraints of individual aid agencies. In the absence of any clear demarcation of responsibilities within the international community (for both states and aid agencies), relief agencies have inconsistently called for the protection of human rights based on their own "willingness to be accountable."[32] Moreover, humanitarian agencies have invoked a human rights discourse to legitimize interventions and to discredit those who obstruct and criticize their actions.[33] Humanitarian ideals are thus secondary to humanitarian aid, such that the role of human rights in aid policy and practice is predicated on institutional strategic interests, as well as local contexts.[34]

From the start, the UNHCR was involved in more than just the aid and protection of refugees. Despite its claims of political neutrality, the organization represented the interests of its funders, the great powers of the Cold War era. Its officials involved themselves in the legal domains of host states

200 · Conclusion

and made distinctions between potential beneficiaries of refugee aid—distinctions based on internationally reified definitions of citizenship. As the decades passed, the mission of the UNHCR remained largely unchanged. However, over time, the application of aid to refugees became increasingly mired in the business of humanitarianism. By the 1990s, this business included competition among refugee agencies for media visibility and funding, a competition that led to the unequal promotion of rights in Ngara district, to the detriment of many Ngarans.

It is perhaps too easy to judge those who worked for the aid agencies that created and maintained the Rwandan refugee camps and settlements examined in this book.[35] With the benefit of hindsight and more than fifty years of refugee interventions in Africa, as well as dedicated scholarship on aid programs, it is difficult to imagine the lived experience of the actors involved in the creation of the international refugee regime in Tanzania. The 1960s marked the first days of international aid to refugees in sub-Saharan Africa. For all involved, it was uncharted territory. Looking back on those early days of aid in Tanzania, Brian Neldner, former director of the TCRS, remarked that the agency had not had time to make mistakes or to learn from them.[36] Ngara would provide one of the first such opportunities.

Similarly, during the 1990s the aid community was confronted with a massive human crisis whose complexity baffled and overwhelmed aid workers. In the rapidly evolving situation, aid workers had to balance institutional directives with attempts to alleviate the devastation that threatened to engulf a heterogeneous refugee population. They did so largely without being able to speak the local languages and in the glare of the international media. They undoubtedly saved many lives. They also engaged with people who had committed genocide, with a leadership that demanded its own political sovereignty and was willing to use violence to achieve it.

A former US government official once asked me, rather angrily, what I thought would have happened in Ngara had the UNHCR not stepped in during the 1990s Rwandan refugee crisis. He was referring to the assumption that Rwandan refugees, in particular those who had committed genocide, would have engaged in violence in Ngara had international agencies not provided for their basic needs. I had just presented a paper on how the humanitarian response affected Ngaran lives, and the question he asked is an important one. I have long grappled with the ethical dilemmas of this work. As refugee crises proliferate around the world, the answer cannot be to stop aiding those who flee across and within borders in search of safety, in search of life. However, such aid can be more attentive to the aspirations of both refugees and hosts—to the needs of these people as they understand them.[37] Recognition of the importance of refugee agency has burgeoned in the humanitarian community, but with dwindling resources to confront the largest human displacement since World War II, it is unclear how such policies will evolve. Instead of asking what would have happened in Ngara in the mid-1990s without the actions of humanitarian agencies, I think it is more useful to ask how aid agencies have affected local understandings of citizenship and sovereignty both during and after decolonization.

I have argued that refugees, as a discursive and bureaucratic category, became constitutive in the ongoing process of creating and maintaining the nation-state, of determining what type of nation colonial territories would become and for whom. The evolution of the business of refugee aid affected the contours of nation building in Ngara. Located at the margins of an increasingly centralized bureaucracy, Ngarans engaged in practices that both undermined and consolidated central-state ideologies of nationhood and citizenship. Most Ngarans negotiated an economic existence that straddled individual subsistence farming, communal agriculture, and illegal transnational trade—strategies that navigated new state policies by deploying older, time-proven circulations of materials and people.

Frederick Cooper reminds us that "to talk about citizenship is to talk about the relationship of units of belonging to units of power."[38] In the case of Ngara, refugees arrived just as those units of power were being negotiated at the local, national, and international levels. Self-settled refugees were frequently able to exist within the gaps of the nation-state, at least for a while. Neither citizen nor refugee, they were emblematic of the "gradations of gray" inherent in regional relationships and circulations that exist alongside national identities.[39] Simultaneously, however, aiding and securing those Rwandan refugees who became encamped reinforced an Ngaran sense of belonging that has congealed over time—one that is linked to Tanzanian citizenship against a refugee "other."

For Ngarans prior to decolonization, identity, like the movement of people and goods, tended to be rooted in the culture and geography of the Great Lakes region. However, during and after decolonization, what *Tanzania* meant to people in Ngara began to change. State Afro-socialist policies, as well as transnational discourses around the newly categorized figure of the refugee, combined to influence the evolving local adoption of a Tanzanian identity in Ngara. As Rwandans in Ngara were increasingly segregated and made the subjects of exclusionary national and transnational aid projects—aid the refugees frequently rejected and subverted—Ngarans began to see themselves as part of the Tanzanian nation. This process has been as uneasy as it is ongoing.

"Every year in April, the rains come." The line is from a movie about the Rwandan genocide, *Sometimes in April*.[40] In one of the opening scenes of the movie, we see an old colonial map of Africa. The camera then gets closer and closer, zeroing in on the center of the continent, on the boundary lines of the Great Lakes region, on a map that is both a colonial relic and a current reality. The history of the movement of people blurs the lines on the map. In one version of Great Lakes history we see waves of migration, the tides of human entry and egress. What happens if we place migration at the center of history? In so doing, the clean borders and corresponding nationalities they represent become unsettled. To zoom in on the history of the map is to reveal the layered porousness of categories such as citizen and refugee, legal and illegal, local and foreign. As international agencies and the state attempted to separate, settle, and assist Rwandan refugees they worked to solidify the lines of the map. In their everyday lives, Ngarans and Rwandans at once consolidated and belied such lines of difference.

NOTES

INTRODUCTION

1   The epigraph to this chapter is from Lazarus Mezza, "Repatriation," Tanganyikan Christian Refugee Service Ngara Project, December 13, 1996, Tanzania 1996, DWS, Y.1, LWF.

2   As opposed to those who were "self-settled" and did not receive international aid in refugee camps.

3   I am not suggesting a lack of differentiation between those who lived in the area that would be called Ruanda-Urundi and those who lived in Tanganyika during the precolonial period; rather, I argue that, like many areas surrounding the current states of Rwanda and Burundi, the relationship between Bugufi and Busubi and these centralized and expansionist states was in flux and contested. Newbury, "Precolonial Burundi and Rwanda"; Des Forges, *Defeat Is the Only Bad News.*

4   On the idea of borders as "theatres of opportunity," see Nugent and Asiwaju, "Introduction," 11.

5   Nugent and Asiwaju, "Introduction," 10.

6   Geschiere, *Perils of Belonging*, 171–73. New research has added to our understanding of nationalism during decolonization, including Moskowitz, *Seeing Like a Citizen*; Lal, *African Socialism.*

7   Geschiere, *Perils of Belonging*, 26.

8   Cooper, "Possibility and Constraint."

9   Quoted in Kibraeb, "Revisiting the Debate," 386. See also Malkki, "National Geographic."

10 Kelly and Kaplan elucidate a post–World War II nation-state system "made obligatory globally . . . as a tool not only for the expression of national will but as a means to radically limit national aspirations." Kelly and Kaplan, "'My Ambition,'" 134.

11 Glynn notes that although the definition of *refugee* has constantly evolved, international refugee law remains tethered to the 1951 Refugee Convention. Glynn, "Genesis and Development," 135.

12 Chaulia, "Politics of Refugee Hosting," 150.

13 Defining the "rightful" inhabitants of a nation-state is a continual process, as evidenced by ongoing competing claims and subsequent violence and displacement in countries such as Cameroon, Myanmar, and countless others. The politics of

asylum in the global North attests to the power of exclusion as part of continual nation building.

14 For some African leaders this was not always so, particularly during the early years of decolonization. See Cooper, "Possibility and Constraint"; Iliffe, "Breaking the Chain," 192.

15 Kapil quoted in Khadiagala, "Boundaries in East Africa," 268.

16 Khadiagala, "Boundaries in East Africa," 266.

17 Tague, *Displaced Mozambicans*, 6.

18 Marfleet, "Explorations in a Foreign Land"; Kushner, *Remembering Refugees*, 6; Panikos and Virdee, "Preface."

19 Happily, refugee history is emerging as a subdiscipline in historical scholarship. See Banko et al., "What Is Refugee History?"; Terretta and Janzen, "Historical Perspectives." On exiled southern African liberation movements and nationalism, see, for example, Williams, *Exile History*.

20 Kushner, *Remembering Refugees*, 1.

21 Packard, *Chiefship and Cosmology*; Newbury, *Kings and Clans*; Schoenbrun, *Green Place*; Chrétien, *Great Lakes*.

22 The scholarship on African frontiers and borders is vast. For an introduction, see Kopytoff, *African Frontier*.

23 Arendt, *Origins of Totalitarianism*; Malkki, *Purity and Exile*. For a review of recent scholarship that examines African refugee history, see Williams, "African Refugee History."

24 As the limiting nature of the word *refugee* becomes more apparent, particularly in terms of legal rubrics of protection, the term *refugee studies* is gradually giving way to *forced migration studies*. Chatty and Marfleet, "Conceptual Problems," 2.

25 Marfleet, "Making States," 18; Chatty and Marfleet, "Conceptual Problems"; Panikos and Virdee, "Preface." Exceptions include institutional histories (Glynn, "Genesis and Development"; Salvatici, "'Help the People'") and legal histories (Chaulia, "Politics of Refugee Hosting"; Mendel, "Refugee Law"; Kamanga, "(Tanzania) Refugees Act").

26 Black, "Fifty Years"; Turton, "Conceptualizing Forced Migration."

27 Marfleet, "Making States," 15.

28 Alix-Garcia and Saah, "Effect of Refugee Inflows;" Whitaker, "Refugees in Western Tanzania"; Landau, "Beyond the Losers"; Rutinwa, "Tanzanian Government's Response."

29 Scholarship on South Asian nation-state formation has explored the role of displacement. See, for example, Panikos and Virdee, "Preface"; Zamindar, *Long Partition*. For scholarship on refugees and nationalism, see Soguk, *States and Strangers*; Gatrell, *Making of the Modern Refugee*. Other scholars have explored the history of refugees within Great Lakes regional politics. See Jackson, "Sons of Which Soil?"; Pottier, *Re-imagining Rwanda*; Sommers, *Fear in Bongoland*; Malkki, *Purity and Exile*; Daley, "Politics of the Refugee Crisis;" Lemarchand, *Rwanda and Burundi*.

30 Marfleet, "Refugees and History," 140.

206 · Notes to Introduction

31 Marfleet, "Refugees and History," 140.

32 Mbembe and Randall, "At the Edge of the World," 270.

33 State territorialization refers to the naturalization of identity among people, place, and nation. Malkki, "National Geographic," 26.

34 Malkki, "Refugees and Exile," 503.

35 One notable exception is Peterson, *Ethnic Patriotism and the East African Revival.*

36 Scholars of the Great Lakes region tend to overlook this part of northwestern Tanzania, with Francophone scholars examining Rwanda and Burundi and Anglophone scholars concentrating on Buganda and Bunyoro in southern Uganda and Buhaya in northern Tanzania. Archival evidence on Ngara was particularly difficult to find in the Tanzanian National Archives.

37 Newbury, "'Rwakayihura' Famine."

38 See, for example, Adelman and Suhrke, "International Response to Conflict and Genocide: Study 2"; Borton et al., "International Response to Conflict and Genocide: Study 3"; Rutinwa, "Tanzanian Government's Response"; Whitaker, "Refugees in Western Tanzania"; Landau "Beyond the Losers."

39 On the influence of colonial migration control on contemporary policies, see Mongia, *Indian Migration.*

40 The UNHCR's statute states that "the work of the High Commssioner shall be of an entirely non-political character." Statute of the Office of the United Nations High Commissioner for Refugees, chapter 1.2, https://www.unhcr.org/4d944e589 .pdf.

41 As Sheehan asserts, sovereignty may be easy to define, but to understand it, "we have to examine the relationship between the abstract and the concrete . . . between sovereignty as a way of thinking and sovereignty as a way of acting." Sheehan, "Problem of Sovereignty," 1.

42 Sheehan, "Problem of Sovereignty," 3. These claims "made by those seeking or wielding power" are "about the superiority and autonomy of their authority. State making, therefore, is the ongoing process of making, unmaking, and revising sovereign claims." Sheehan, "Problem of Sovereignty," 3. On the "ongoing negotiation [of sovereignty] in the internal and external contexts of the state," see Bjerk, *Building a Peaceful Nation*, 16.

43 Anderson, *Imagined Communities.*

44 Metin Çorabatir quoted in Shawn Carrié and Asman Al-Omar, "'It's Not Legal': UN Stands by as Turkey Deports Vulnerable Syrians," *Guardian*, August 23, 2019, https://www.theguardian.com/global-development/2019/aug/23/its-not-legal-un -stands-by-as-turkey-deports-vulnerable-syrians.

45 Mongia posits the colonial origins of migration control by revealing how the need to regulate free labor, in particular Indian migration within the British Empire, led to the evolution of "what is now a truism, that (nation-) states must exercise a monopoly over migration practices." Mongia, *Indian Migration*, 21.

46 Fassin, *Humanitarian Reason*, 141, 135. I argue that the "humanitarian government" and "mobiliz[ation] of compassion rather than justice" that Fassin analyzes

Notes to Introduction · 207

in late twentieth-century western Europe have a longer lineage in former colonies. Fassin, *Humanitarian Reason*, 7–8.

47 Thus, Anghie shows how the mandate system and the League of Nations began the task of "creating sovereignty" by devising "the technologies of management and control that have become entrenched" in international institutions, thereby forming a kind of sovereignty in the third world that is "completely consistent with economic subordination." Anghie, "Evolution of International Law," 747.

48 Loescher, *Beyond Charity*, 76. Lui posits that, after World War II, the "first world" framed refugees in the "third world" as inherently different from refugees in Europe. Refugees in places like Africa were thought to be victims of underdevelopment ("the 'discovery' of the displacement-development nexus as a way of explaining and resolving the refugee problem in post-colonial Africa"); they were therefore in need of development to solve the problem of their "refugee-ness." Lui, "International Government," 118, 128.

49 "Attitude of the High Commissioner in New Refugee Situations," March 29, 1963, SA/529, box 15, fonds 11, series 1, UNHCR.

50 Turner suggests that Burundian refugees in Lukole camp, Tanzania, saw themselves as citizens of the UNHCR, although he is careful to point out the similarities, rather than the equation, of UNHCR citizenship to national citizenship. Turner, "Under the Gaze," 235. For the international refugee regimes' production of statecraft, see Soguk, *States and Strangers*, 206.

51 Instead, human rights and justice claims "are advanced not to some global cosmopolis but against a certain state which is the 'contractual guardian' of its citizens." Lui, "International Government," 120. Therefore, as Agamben notes, the refugee signals a "radical crisis," as the "sacred and inalienable rights of man show themselves to lack every protection and reality at the moment in which they can no longer take the form of rights belonging to citizens of a state." Agamben, *Homo Sacer*, 126. Recent work has sought to move UN policies toward a framework of "sovereignty as responsibility," such that nation-states would have the right and responsibility to interfere when states fail to protect their citizens. This formulation is thought to redress one of the most fundamental paradoxes of the UNHCR, which deals with the effects, not the causes, of refugee flight. See Etzioni, "Sovereignty as Responsibility." On the need for a "rights-based humanitarianism," see Harrell-Bond, "Can Humanitarian Work."

52 On the United Nations' limited original mandate, see Mazower, *No Enchanted Palace*. Anghie suggests that international law itself, and sovereignty in particular, have always been used to promote the interests of imperialism by sanctioning European or Western control over the non-Western world. Anghie, "Evolution of International Law."

53 Soguk refers to the international regime's intimate involvement "in the active production and stabilization of what counts as the territorial being of the modern citizen, the very ground of the sovereign state—the citizen-man." By breaking the natural hierarchy of citizen-nation-man, the refugee reveals that there

is indeed an "outside" beyond the fiction of an interlocking world of sovereign nation-states. Soguk, *States and Strangers*, 21; Agamben, *Homo Sacer*.

54 Lui, "International Government," 121.

55 As Lui suggests, by ordering the "relations between states and between populations of citizens and non-citizens," the international refugee regime "play[s] a crucial role in sustaining the order of territorial states." Lui, "International Government," 117.

56 Bakewell refers to this as the "arena" of the refugee camp, populated by "social actors with competing interests and strategies." Bakewell, "Uncovering Local Perspectives," 103–4. See also Hilhorst and Jansen, "Humanitarian Space," 1137.

57 Barnett, *Empire of Humanity*, 222–23.

58 Polzer and Hammond, "Invisible Displacement."

59 Marriage, *Challenging Aid in Africa*; Terry, *Condemned to Repeat?*

60 Scholars are beginning to (re)think of the League of Nations as a successful international regime (rather than an abject failure), particularly in terms of its ability to cloak empires' economic exploitation as humanitarianism during the early twentieth century. Anghie, "Colonialism and the Birth"; Pedersen, *Guardians*.

61 Scalettaris, "Refugee Studies," 40.

62 Hyndman, *Managing Displacement*; Ferguson, *Anti-Politics Machine*; Li, *Will to Improve*; Barnett, *Empire of Humanity*.

63 Mosse, *Cultivating Development*, 3; Cooper and Packard, *International Development and the Social Sciences*.

64 Edelman and Haugerud, "Introduction," 5. Notable exceptions include Mosse, *Cultivating Development*; and Rich, *Protestant Missionaries*.

65 Malkki, "National Geographic."

66 Malkki has taken up this challenge by examining the motivations and experiences of humanitarian actors. Malkki, *Need to Help*.

67 The historical archive necessarily privileges state and organizational voices due to the plethora of records in institutional archives. It is more difficult to trace the actions and perceptions of individual refugees—particularly without the help of oral interviews. Nevertheless, archival information, reports, and interviews with aid personnel and host communities shed light on the divisions and contexts that led to refugee choices.

68 This is particularly true in the early life of an organization, prior to the establishment of organizational "rituals, values, codes of conduct, and standard operating procedures." Walkup, "Policy Dysfunction," 47.

69 Ferguson and Gupta warn of the dangers of naturalizing the "vertical" hierarchy of state and international bureaucracies. Ferguson and Gupta, "Spatializing States."

70 About refugee workers in Kenya, Verdirame notes, "what happens on the ground is much more the result of individuals' decisions and personalities than of the application of standards and procedures." Quoted in Harrell-Bond, "Can Humanitarian Work," 68.

71 Additional interviews took place in 2015.

Notes to Introduction · 209

72 I have altered the names of many of my informants to preserve their anonymity.

73 I am grateful to Rose Jaji for pointing out that this practice might impede future researchers who are unable to pay for interviews.

1. TRACING A BOUNDARY

1 Van Den Berg, chief of the cartographic mission, Kivu, represented the Belgian section of the joint commission, and A. H. White, provincial commissioner of Bukoba, led the British section. "Demarcation of the Interterritorial Boundary between Tanganyika and Belgian Congo on the Kagera River," 10, 56, Ethnological and Anthropological Notes, Bukoba District, file 19784, TNA.

2 Mr. Laws, a British staff surveyor, noted that due to malaria, it was better to "employ local labour as possible in spite of the very poor capacity for work of the local tribe, the Wanyambo." It is unclear whether Bahangaza porters were employed in the area further south or whether Laws knew the difference between members of the chiefdoms, as they shared similar languages and cultures. "Report on the Proposed Rectification of a Part of the Anglo-Belgian Boundary," by Mr. Laws, staff surveyor, from Director of Surveys to Chief Secretary, Dar es Salaam, November 4, 1930, 102, Foreign Countries: Boundaries between Tanganyika and Ruanda Urundi, 1928–1947, Ethnological and Anthropological Notes, Bukoba District, file 12736, TNA.

3 "Report on the Proposed Rectification of a Part of the Anglo-Belgian Boundary," by Mr. Laws, staff surveyor, from Director of Surveys to Chief Secretary, Dar es Salaam.

4 Herbst, "Creation and Maintenance of National Boundaries"; Lefebvre, "We Have Tailored Africa."

5 Recent work has highlighted the "interactivity of space-making" in colonial Africa, which often included the influence of local elites and intermediaries. Castryck, "Introduction." See also MacArthur, *Cartography and the Political Imagination*; Lefebvre, *Frontières de Sable*.

6 For a description of the "combination of imperialist policies, personal ambitions, and simply unusual coincidences" that created "the new borders in the area west of Lake Victoria," particularly between German East Africa and the British protectorate of Uganda, see Hydén, *Political Development*, 93.

7 During the German era, a "travel certificate" allowed caravans to trade in people, ostensibly disguised as trade in goods, from Tabora in southwestern Tanganyika to Rwanda. It is possible that such trade went through Ngara district. See Bukoba station officer's letter to the Governor, March 17, 1902, in Chrétien, "Slave Trade," 217. It is likely that the salt trade from Kigoma to Ruanda-Urundi passed through present-day Ngara district. Interview with Simwanka Urias Ntamarangelo, Muhangaza, May 25, 2012. There was also a thriving trade in cattle and ivory throughout the area during the precolonial and early colonial periods.

8 Government Notice No. 58 of 1947 separated the Ngara division of Biharamulo district into Ngara district, effective April 1, 1947. The Ngara division had already been administered separately as "for all routine matters; the Sub-accountancy and Native Treasury" were already separate. Letter from Assistant District Officer, Ngara, to Provincial Commissioner, Lake Province, February 26, 1947, 34/R-5/9, 1, TNA-Mwanza.

9 The Union of South Africa acquired South West Africa.

10 Recent violence in Cameroon is related to the arbitrary borders created by the League of Nations. For an introduction, see Konings and Nyamnjoh, "The Anglophone Problem."

11 Great Britain received the official mandate for the Tanganyika Territory in July 1922.

12 Anghie, "Colonialism and the Birth," 515.

13 Anghie, "Colonialism and the Birth," 518.

14 Interview with Daniel Izabaro, Rusumo, July 12, 2012.

15 Interview with Bernard Simi, Ntobeye, July 25, 2012.

16 For an early examination of the historical significance of the Bacwezi and the Kitara complex, see Kiwanuka, "The Empire of Bunyoro Kitara."

17 For example, scholars disagree on what is known about identity in Rwanda and when. Vansina begins his discussion on identity and the Rwandan court in the seventeenth century. Vansina, *Antecedents to Modern Rwanda*, 38. Yet, according to Chrétien, there can be no factual precision regarding events in the region prior to the eighteenth century, and Pottier observes that historians know little about how people perceived identity in Rwanda prior to the 1860s. Chrétien, *Great Lakes*, 13; Pottier, *Re-imagining Rwanda*, 13. See also Newbury, "Precolonial Burundi and Rwanda"; Newbury and Newbury, "Bringing the Peasants Back."

18 See Sanders, "Hamitic Hypothesis."

19 This refers generally to the areas of present-day Rwanda, Burundi, and western Tanzania.

20 Around 1 percent of the population of Ruanda-Urundi was designated "Twa," referring to the original "pygmy" inhabitants of the area.

21 See, for example, Vidal, "Alexis Kagame."

22 Occasionally, respondents in Ngara emphasized that Rwandan chiefs originated from Ethiopia, indicating the extent of the integration of the Hamitic hypothesis in the region.

23 Newbury posits that Rwabugiri attacked Busubi, although his main conquests were in areas to the west. Newbury, "Precolonial Burundi and Rwanda," 308.

24 See Newbury, "Preface," 2011.

25 Newbury, "Precolonial Burundi and Rwanda," 265. Chrétien notes that Rundi king Ntare Rugamba conquered Bugufi in the first half of the nineteenth century but administered the area through existing "local chiefs." Chrétien, *Great Lakes*, 163.

26 The 1891 rinderpest epidemic had "contradictory effects" in the region. Some areas experienced decimation due to cattle loss (such as the Karagwe areas north

Notes to Chapter 1 · 211

of Ngara), whereas others (such as Rwanda and Burundi) consolidated surviving cattle in the hands of elites, thereby increasing the power of those associated with the monarchy. Chrétien, *Great Lakes*, 221.

27 There is also evidence of increasing encroachment by slave traders in the region during the 1890s, with routes from Gisaka to Bukoba and perhaps into Ngara as well. Chrétien, "Slave Trade."

28 On flight from the expanding Rwandan kingdom east, see Newbury, "'Rwakayihura' Famine," 274.

29 Schoenbrun argues that "intensive" banana farming existed by AD 1400 or 1500, with bananas originally introduced between AD 500 and 1000. Schoenbrun, "Cattle Herds," 52.

30 Petition from Christopher Rusage, Ngara, July 12, 1949, to Permanent Representative of British at the UN, CO 691/201/4, NA.

31 Interview with Daniel Runzanga, Ntobeye, July 25, 2012. According to Newbury, long-haired cattle were present in Rwanda no later than 1100 CE. Newbury, "Precolonial Burundi and Rwanda," 268–69.

32 Interview with Mary Justin Bamenya, Mugoma, July 12, 2012; interview with John Karsurahaba Mtamziheza, Muyenzi, June 11, 2012. On the evolution of clientship in Rwanda, see Newbury, *Cohesion of Oppression*.

33 Hans Cory, "Bugufi Land Report, Ngara 1944," August 22, 1944, 18, Hans Cory 61, UDSM.

34 For "social health" in the Great Lakes region, see Schoenbrun, *Green Place*; Packard, *Chiefship and Cosmology*.

35 While the states of Burundi and Rwanda are often conflated, it is crucial to note the important influence that regional and clan affiliations had on politics as well as ethnicity. In Burundi, for example, the herding elite were divided into at least three categories, with the *Baganwa*, or monarchical class, having power over Hima and Tutsi pastoralists. Belgian rule would diminish the role of clans in politics to some extent, although both regional and clan affiliations continued to impact the trajectories of these countries.

36 In 1910 representatives from Germany, Belgium, and Great Britain agreed on the boundaries of the Belgian Congo, the British protectorate of Uganda, and German Tanganyika, which were codified by the 1911 International Delimitation Commission. However, due to a lack of manpower, there was little the colonists could do to alter the loyalties of people in the area, who generally maintained their allegiance to the Rwandan central state or others, as they saw fit. Des Forges, *Defeat Is the Only Bad News*, 118–19. On the complex negotiations between Great Britain and Germany over the boundary between Uganda and German East Africa, see Médard and Kidari, "The Kagera River."

37 The brutal suppression of the Maji revolt along the Swahili coast required a large expenditure of German resources and manpower.

38 According to Cory, like experiences under German rule in Ruanda-Urundi, Ngarans "came later and less intensively in contact with Europeans." Cory, "Bugufi Land Report, Ngara 1944," 14.

39 The "good African" quote in the subheading is from Cameron, *My Tanganyika Service*, 92.

40 The Covenant of the League of Nations, Office of the Historian, US Department of State, https://history.state.gov/historicaldocuments/frus1919Parisv13/ch10subch1. Article 22 required annual reports on mandatory territories and gave the league control over alterations in the mandates' terms. The Covenant of the League of Nations was included in the Treaty of Versailles and entered into force on January 10, 1920. The League Council approved the texts for the "B" mandates in July 1922. Pedersen, *Guardians*, 55.

41 One need only examine the Belgian Congo's colonial record to realize how far European states would go to reap profits from their colonies.

42 While "A" mandates were viewed as having local "nationalities," the "B" and "C" mandates' "inhabitants remained minors, defined more by incapacity than by nationality. European perceptions of civilization were therefore tied to (lack of) nationality and so sovereignty." Pedersen, *Guardians*, 72.

43 As Anghie notes, the principles of economic development and self-determination for mandate colonies became popular at "precisely the time when their [colonies'] economic value and their significance for the metropolis were becoming increasingly evident." There thus existed a "fundamental tension" within the mandate system "which simultaneously had to promote the self-government of the mandate territory on the one hand, and economic integration of the mandate territory into the metropole's economy, on the other." Anghie, "Colonialism and the Birth," 563. Additionally, while discursively adhering to the idea of development, many development plans were rejected or never started—revealing British ambivalence toward actual development in Tanganyika. On the distance between the rhetoric of development plans and reality, see Weiskopf, "Living in 'Cold Storage,'" 10.

44 Thus the Belgian administration of Ruanda-Urundi used the existence of famine as an excuse to impose draconian policies to correct Rwandans' "laziness" and avoid future famines. Newbury, "'Rwakayihura' Famine"; Pedersen, *Guardians*, 245–52.

45 Anghie, "Colonialism and the Birth," 589.

46 Callahan, *Sacred Trust*, 25.

47 Callahan, *Sacred Trust*, 43. On literate Tanganyikans' contributions to a new "globalization of concepts," see Hunter, "'Our Common Humanity,'" 283.

48 Pedersen, *Guardians*, 4.

49 Charles Strachey, who drafted the Tanganyika Territory laws, was "conscious of Britain's accountability to the League and routinely reminded his colleagues of the shifting culture of colonialism in the early postwar period." Callahan, *Mandates and Empire*, 79.

50 As MacArthur argues, the colonial "obsession with territorial ordering" and mapmaking "made possible the possession of distant territories, bringing 'light' to dark, unknown places and peoples." MacArthur, *Cartography and the Political Imagination*, 16–17.

Notes to Chapter 1 · 213

51 Bukoba District Book, "Ethnological and Anthropological Notes," 1–2, file 925, TNA.

52 Bukoba District Book, "Ethnological and Anthropological Notes."

53 After the Supreme Allied Council gave Great Britain the mandate for German East Africa in May 1919, Belgium protested, claiming entitlement to part of the territory due to its participation in the African battles of World War I and its occupation of part of German East Africa. From Visiting Mission of the Trusteeship Council to E.A., August 27, 1948, "Subject: U.N.O. Petitions-Tanganyika Bahaya Union, Nairobi," K.1.265.36953/11 U.N.O. Petitions-Tanganyika Bahaya Union-Nairobi, 1948–1949, TNA.

54 Early on, the British "made clear their intentions to replace all the Rwandan notables in Gisaka with descendants of the original aristocracy of the Gisaka. They even considered restoring the old kingdom itself." Des Forges, *Defeat Is the Only Bad News*, 178. These remarks indicate that the British Colonial Office was well aware of the complicated history and local loyalties in Gisaka.

55 During its second session in August 1922, the PMC identified the partition of Rwanda as "the most important individual question" concerning the "B" mandates. Commissioners thought the alleged unification of Rwanda would enhance the League of Nations' reputation and powers of international supervision, as well as repair the tarnished image of European colonialism, by "placing the alleged priorities of colonized people above those of the metropole." Callahan, *Mandates and Empire*, 85–86.

56 Des Forges, *Defeat Is the Only Bad News*, 26.

57 Callahan, *Mandates and Empire*, 85–86. On the Belgian and Rwandan court's claims to Gisaka, see Newbury and Newbury, "Bringing the Peasants Back," 848–50.

58 Callahan, *Mandates and Empire*, 85.

59 Callahan, *Mandates and Empire*, 88.

60 "Foreign Countries: Boundaries between Tanganyika and Ruanda Urundi," Foreign Office, S.W.1., March 21, 1930, 62, Ethnological and Anthropological Notes, Bukoba District, file 12736, TNA.

61 Callahan, *Sacred Trust*, 43.

62 The British had previously used this technique to demarcate territory in their Kenyan colony. On local attempts to subvert these mapping practices in western Kenya, see MacArthur, *Cartography and the Political*, 62.

63 The two powers also questioned whether they required the PMC's consent to alter the 1924 boundary to "safeguard the reciprocal rights of the inhabitants of both territories." Letter from the Foreign Office to His Excellency the Right Honourable Earl Granville in Brussels, May 12, 1930, 74, Ethnological and Anthropological Notes, Bukoba District, file 12736, TNA.

64 Letter from Acting Controller of Mines to Chief Secretary, Dar es Salaam, "Tanganyika-Congo Boundary," file 12736, TNA. There are an additional twenty-six references to mining, tin, and the international boundary in this file alone. For indications of alluvial deposits of cassiterite in the valleys and swamps on both sides of the river, see letter from Secretary of State (Mayers, Chief Secretary

214 · Notes to Chapter 1

to the Government) to Director of Surveys, Commissioner of Mines, May 28, 1931, Ethnological and Anthropological Notes, Bukoba District, file 19784, TNA.

65 Callahan, *Sacred Trust*, 45.

66 Article II Treaty Concerning a Modification of the Boundary between Tanganyika Territory and Ruanda-Urundi, Ethnological and Anthropological Notes, Bukoba District, file 19784, TNA.

67 This was not the only instance of border demarcation after World War I, or what Anderson and O'Dowd refer to as the "great wave of border creation" in the defeated European territories. Anderson and O'Dowd, "Imperialism and Nationalism," 946.

68 On April 18, 1946, the League of Nations formally ended the mandate system and transferred all assets to the United Nations. Callahan, *Sacred Trust*, 192.

69 Callahan, *Sacred Trust*, 192–93.

70 Thus discrediting colonial rule based on race. Cooper, *Decolonization*, 173.

71 Pedersen, *Guardians*, 399. On the mandates as a system "in motion," see Pedersen, *Guardians*, 406.

72 Callahan, *Sacred Trust*, 180.

73 TC Resolution 25, March 1949, Petitions to Trusteeship Council, Petition from Mwambutsa, Chief of Urundi (part II) 1948–49, CO 691/201/4, NA.

74 "The Bugufi Petition," July 25, 1948, Petitions to Trusteeship Council, Petition from Mwambutsa, Chief of Urundi (part II) 1948–49, CO 691/201/4, NA.

75 TC 4th Session Petition from Mwambutsa, Brief for the UK Representative, CO 691/201/4 Petitions to Trusteeship Council from Mwambutsa, Chief of Urundi (part II) 1948–49, NA.

76 "Bugufi Petition."

77 Letter from E. G. Rowe, Provincial Commissioner Lake Province, to Secretary Dar es Salaam, September 8, 1949, CO 691/201/8, NA.

78 See, for example, petition from Christopher Rusage, Ngara, July 12, 1949, CO 691/201/4 Petitions to Trusteeship Council Petition from Mwambutsa, Chief of Urundi (part II) 1948–49, NA.

79 Appendix B, copy of Balamba letter to the editor of the *Times*, Petitions to Trusteeship Council, Petition from Mwambutsa, Chief of Urundi (part II) 1948–49, CO 691/201/4, NA.

80 Extract from UNTC record of 6th Session, February 9, 1950, Petitions to Trusteeship Council, Petition from Mwambutsa, Chief of Urundi, CO 691/209, NA.

81 The Belgian colonial state allowed the Rwandan court to appoint chiefs to rule the various regions, many of which had been autonomous. These chiefs were given unprecedented power over local populations, including control of corvée labor. In places like Gisaka, local elites often fled eastward into Tanganyika to escape the control of these foreigners. Newbury, "'Rwakayihura' Famine," 274.

82 The following is necessarily a brief history of ethnicity and Belgian rule in Ruanda-Urundi. See Newbury, *Cohesion of Oppression*; Newbury and Newbury, "Bringing the Peasants Back"; Longman, *Christianity and Genocide*; Linden and Linden, *Church and Revolution*.

Notes to Chapter 1 · 215

83 For the influence of the "White Fathers" in this process, see Linden and Linden, *Church and Revolution*.

84 Newbury takes a "processual approach to ethnicity" that attends to changing regional, socioeconomic, and political factors. Newbury, *Cohesion of Oppression*, 14.

85 Mamdani, *When Victims Become Killers*, 34.

86 The Belgians also imposed compulsory cultivation of famine crops. Corvée labor included the construction of roads, marsh drainage, terracing, and projects on chiefs' lands.

87 On the promulgation and evolution of British colonial policies of indirect rule, see Lugard, *Dual Mandate*; Falola and Heaton, *A History of Nigeria*.

88 Thus, in Ngara, governance adhered to regional "tribal" designations of Hangaza and Subi, not Tutsi or Hutu. On the distortions of customary rule that became the "language of force" and "decentralized despotism," see Mamdani, *Citizen and Subject*, 22–24. For a critique of Mamdani and the limits, alterations, and contradictions of indirect rule, see Cooper, "Review: Mahmood Mamdani." In Ngara, the state's criticism of the native authorities in the 1940s corresponded to changing notions of development during late-stage colonialism.

89 MacArthur, *Cartography and the Political*, 34.

90 As colonial sociologist Hans Cory noted, when crossing from Belgian Ruanda-Urundi into British Ngara, "everyone should feel after a few miles, perhaps only intuitively, the difference in the policy of two Governments towards their natives." Cory, "Bugufi Land Report, Ngara 1944," 29, 61. The border therefore had a very real sociological impact on those who lived and died by those ethnic turns of phrase in the twentieth century. Colonial officials used the terms Tusi, Tutsi, Batutsi, Hutu, Bahutu, Hamite, and others to describe the population in Ngara; however, over time, the salience of these terms changed. See, for example, Hans Cory, "Report on Busubi. Survey of the Busubi Utwaliates. Ngara, 1944," 168, UDSM. Nevertheless, Ngarans still refer to people with many cattle, particularly when referencing the colonial or precolonial periods, as Tutsi.

2. CANALIZATION AND CONTROL

1 As MacArthur notes, these new administrative districts were "more than mere lines on a page." In terms of geography, "colonial mapping practices worked to transform previously relational geographies of exchange and community into top-down, scientific, and measurable demarcations." MacArthur, *Cartography and the Political Imagination*, 53.

2 Colonial officials attempted to recruit Ngarans to work on sisal plantations, as well as mining enterprises, to the east.

3 The movement of colonized bodies outside prescribed circulations thus represented a threat not only to settler colonies in the global North but also to colonized territories themselves. As Mongia posits, early forms of interterrito-

rial movement within the British Empire (specifically, the regulation of Indian laborers—a system first based on the regulation of "free" labor and then on the exclusion of "colonized" bodies) evolved into current migration controls, including the nation-state's association with control over borders and the technology of the passport. Mongia, *Indian Migration*. The role Africans played in influencing new forms of migrant control and statism during the colonial period requires further study.

4 Malkki, "Refugees and Exile," 516.

5 Mbembe and Randall refer to this as the "imaginaries and autochthonous practices of space" that exist and change based on "sociocultural solidarities" and commerce, among other factors. Mbembe and Randall, "At the Edge," 262.

6 Ngarans thus engaged in a form of "countermapping" that relied less on new "geographic imaginations" than on the expansion of previous practices of livelihood maintenance in the region. MacArthur, *Cartography and the Political Imagination*, 34, 8.

7 The German administration introduced taxation in 1904. In Bugufi in 1926, "pressure was brought to bear on the 'watoli' or landowning Bahutu and Batusi to pay taxes. Prior to this most transactions were conducted on a barter system and tribute was payable with banana beer, cattle, and/or labor." About this time (1926), "the new system of administration . . . was forced on these people, and they were obliged to pay their taxes in cash. Naturally there was very little ready cash available." Labour Department, Mwanza, "A Report on Migrant Labour Entering Uganda," September 26, 1949, 9, 541/11/1, 460, TNA.

8 I use the term *monetization* to indicate the process by which diverse economic activities were transformed under colonially imposed economies. Specifically, in this part of the Great Lakes region, various forms of wages and "cash" existed during the precolonial era, including the exchange and pasturage of cattle and likely the circulation of fiber bracelets (*butega*). Under colonial rule, these forms of remuneration were largely converted to colonially mandated currencies. On *butega*, see Newbury, *Land Beyond*, 71–72.

9 In 1953 Tim Mayhew, the district commissioner of Ngara, wrote that "even" for a Hutu, bride wealth was several hundred shillings, and this was "one of the basic reasons" young men traveled to Uganda for work. Tim Mayhew, District Commissioner, Ngara, to Senior Provincial Commissioner, Lake Province, "Hangaza Law and Custom by H. Cory," August 18, 1953, Hangaza Law and Custom, Hans Cory, 99, UDSM.

Based on colonial edicts, chiefly tribute and service theoretically ended in 1927, but it "continued unabated at first and only began gradually to fade away on the opening of an administrative station. . . . Tribute and service to village Headmen . . . partook of no such diminution." Fees and tribute were then converted to shillings "painfully earned by the lengthy journey to Uganda." "Memorandum on the Draft Bugufi (Ngara District) Land Rules, 1951," Ngara (District) Bugufi (Ngara District) Land Rules, 1951–1955, Hans Cory, 353, UDSM.

10 Miller, "Tanzania: Documentation," 195–96. See also "Obituary: Hans Cory."

11 The period in which Cory wrote corresponds to the post–World War II "second occupation" of Africa by the British, when new forms of aggressive "development" became crucial to British policy. Low and Lonsdale, "Introduction," 12–16.

West Lake Province (WLP) included the four districts of Bukoba, Karagwe, Ngara, and Biharamulo. After independence, the province was renamed West Lake Region (WLR) and in 1978 Kagera Region.

12 [Illegible] to the Provincial Commissioner, Lake Province, "Mr. Cory's Bugufi Land Report," August 14, 1944, Bugufi Land Report, Ngara, Hans Cory, 61, UDSM.

13 For example, Hans Cory, "Bugufi Land Report, Ngara 1941," 23, Hans Cory, 61, UDSM.

14 "Memorandum on Draft Bugufi (Ngara District) Land Rules, 1951."

15 Reflecting on Cory's land report, a colonial official noted that "the whole purpose of getting Mr. Cory to do the work in this instance was to right something that was wrong, to make some alteration in native custom." [Illegible] to Provincial Commissioner, Lake Province, Mwanza, "Mr. Cory's Bugufi Land Report," August 14, 1944. Thus, before beginning his work in Ngara, Cory would have understood the district, its people, and their customs as problems in need of correction.

16 As the district commissioner noted in 1949, there was more work of "every kind" in Bugufi than in Busubi. C. B. Gordon, District Commissioner, Ngara, to Provincial Commissioner, Lake Province, December 13, 1949, 4, R-5/9, 34, TNA-Mwanza.

17 Hans Cory, "Bugufi Land Report, Ngara 1944," August 22, 1944, Hans Cory, 61, UDSM.

18 Hans Cory, "Report on Busubi, Survey of the Busubi Utwaliates, Ngara 1944," 1, Hans Cory, 168, UDSM.

19 Hans Cory, "Introduction, Ngara," August 22, 1944, 15, Bugufi Land Report, Ngara 1944, Hans Cory, 61, UDSM.

20 Cory, "Introduction, Ngara," 15.

21 District Commissioner to Provincial Commissioner, Lake Province, February 13, 1947, R-5/0, 34, TNA-Mwanza. On contemporary colonial notions of feudalism in neighboring Rwanda, see Maquet, *Premise of Inequality*. For an early critique of the use of the word "feudal" to describe African societies, see Goody, "Feudalism in Africa?"

22 On the salience of the *abatungwa* (ritualists) to the political health of the community, see Cory, "Bugufi Land Report, Ngara 1944," 10. Cory also noted that "the rules of land tenure are generations old and even the victims of its shortcoming consider their fate as justified by tradition." Cory, "Bugufi Land Report, Ngara 1944," 27. Cory made no reference to the increase in elite power afforded by British rule through native administrations, which created colonial servants out of traditional leaders, often altering the meaning and practices of *tradition* in the process. Moore, *Social Facts and Fabrications*.

23 Cory, "Bugufi Land Report, Ngara 1944," 10. Similarly, while Cory noted that "the habit of obeying any demands on their [Bahangaza] services, is so deeply rooted

in these people," he also observed that the Bahangaza frequently refused colonial edicts, suggesting that their obedience may have been more contoured than was acknowledged. Cory, "Bugufi Land Report, Ngara 1944," 13.

24 Hans Cory, "Bugufi, Survey of the Utwaliates of Bugufi," Ngara 1944, 3, Hans Cory, 62, UDSM.

25 Accordingly, in Busubi, "the Bahutu show neither the submissive attitude nor the dullness caused by continuous serfdom which everyone notices in Bugufi." Cory, "Report on Busubi, Survey of Busubi Utwaliates," 2.

26 Cory, "Report on Busubi, Survey of Busubi Utwaliates," 1. According to Chrétien, "The small kingdom of Bushubi, threatened by Rwandan expansion, attributed its foundation sometimes to Karagwe and sometimes to Burundi." Chrétien, *Great Lakes*, 117.

27 Cory, "Report on Busubi, Survey of Busubi Utwaliates," 13.

28 Cory, "Bugufi Land Report, Ngara 1944," 14.

29 Thus: "We have to consider the mentality of the Bahutu, who in many ways are impragnated [*sic*] with submissive ideas. . . . I have heard several times that the Bahutu do not resent the payment of ngorole, tribute and service to the people who are traditionally entitled to ask for it, but they feel it as an increased burden to have the same duties now to the people set over them by the Government." Cory, "Bugufi Land Report, Ngara 1944," 23. Cory believed the "serf" attitude had been intensified by Barundi immigrant settlers, who "bring with them an atmosphere of serfdom." Cory, "Bugufi Land Report, Ngara 1944," 15.

30 Cory, "Bugufi, Survey of Utwaliates of Bugufi," 15.

31 In reality, in 1949 the Labour Department estimated that labor migration to Uganda brought "back to Bugufi a million shillings a year, worth more than the entire coffee crop." Labour Department, Mwanza, "A Report on Migrant Labour Entering Uganda," September 26, 1949, 11, 541/11/1, 460, TNA.

32 Thus, "the greater part of the population sits undisturbed on their holdings since receiving them," although there was a possibility they could be deprived of their land. Labour Department, Mwanza, "Report on Migrant Labour Entering Uganda."

33 Cory, "Report on Busubi, Survey of Busubi Utwaliates," 12.

34 Coffee and communal cultivation were both despised by local people: "Coffee is so unpopular [in Bugufi] that most heirs refuse to inherit coffee trees and a voluntary heir has to be found." Hans Cory, "Hangaza Law and Custom," n.d., Hans Cory, 98, UDSM. See also chapter 3.

35 During Cory's time in Ngara, David Balamba II was chief of Bugufi, and Protas Nsoro was chief of Busubi. Balamba succeeded his father, Kinyamazinge, who "was considered not fit to rule." Balamba ruled through regents until 1943, when he officially became chief. Cory, "Bugufi, Survey of Utwaliates of Bugufi," 1; Cory, "Hangaza Law and Custom," 2–3.

36 This was true of respondents from both Bugufi and Busubi. For example, interview with Ivan Mbonamasabo, Muruvyagira, June 13, 2012; interview with Victoria Kajugusi, Kanyinya, June 28, 2012.

Notes to Chapter 2 · 219

37 For example: The "chief owned all the cattle, all those who kept cattle were tutsi under the chief." Interview with Stafodi Rumisi, Ntobeye, July 25, 2012. "All cows were called chief's ornament, it was not ok, like thieving." Interview with Bernard Kadene, Shanga, July 9, 2012.

38 Those who remembered only the good attributes of Balamba II and Nsoro tended to come from upper-class families, many of whom worked directly under the chiefs.

39 These perceptions included the erroneous belief that chiefs were not involved in collecting taxes. Interview with Adrian Mudende, Rulenge, July 11, 2012; interview with Ephraim Mitabaro, Rusumo, July 12, 2012; interview with Joseph Mwijage, Keza, July 17, 2012.

40 There were few people who remembered chiefs and subchiefs collecting taxes for the district commissioner. Interview with Nasan Nkurikie, Shanga, July 9, 2012; interview with John Kasurahaba Mtamniheza, Muyenzi, June 11, 2012; interview with Peter Kato, Keza, June 17, 2012; interview with Peter Banzi, Ntobeye, July 25, 2012.

41 Interview with Deus Rwanzo, Kumnazi, August 4, 2012.

42 In the heading for this section, "the color of money" is from Cameron, *My Tanganyika Service*, 158–60: "Away in the west of Biharamulo there is a distant Chiefdom on the borders of the Belgian Mandated Territory of Ruanda-Urundi . . . the people of this Chiefdom . . . were ill-nourished and practically never saw the colour of money except when some of the young men walked hundreds of miles to Uganda to work as labourers." What Cory referred to as the "Uganda Complex" began in 1924 and, two decades later, included at least two-thirds of Ngara's male population, "including youngsters." Cory, "Bugufi Land Report, Ngara 1944," 12.

43 "Memorandum on Draft Bugufi (Ngara District) Land Rules, 1951."

44 Commentary by District Commissioner, Ngara-Lake Province, Ngara (District) Bugufi (Ngara District) Land Rules, 1951–1955, Hans Cory, 353, UDSM. The 1948 census showed that 30 percent of the male population of Ngara was absent. "Memorandum on Draft Bugufi (Ngara District) Land Rules, 1951," 2.

45 In January 1944 famine conditions in Uganda led to a four-month ban on all immigrants from Ruanda-Urundi, both those traveling directly to the protectorate and those traveling through Tanganyika. "Memorandum on Proposed Discussion on Immigrant Labour from Ruanda-Urundi," n.d., 3, 541/17, 460, TNA.

46 People often told me that there was "no money in Tanzania" (interviews with Venance B. Munyaru, Mbuba, July 19, 2012; Stafodi Rumisi; Peter Banzi; Ernest Nkurikie, Shanga, July 9, 2012; Jacob Butabiya, Kanyinya, July 19, 2012), that there was "more development there [in Uganda] than Tanzania" (interview with Bernard Kadene), that to work in Tanzania was to be seen as a "low person" (interview with Samwel Rwanzi, Shanga, July 9, 2012), and that people were "not paid in Tanzania" and were forced to "work as slaves" (interview with Joseph Bwizi, Shanga, June 20, 2012.).

47 Interview with Mary Justin Bamenya, Mugoma, July 12, 2012.

48 Interview with Eliazari Ruzige, Chivu, June 14, 2012.

49 Respondents noted that in Buganda, "the culture resembles here [Ngara], not like other parts of Tanzania." Even in terms of food, Buganda was more attractive because Ngarans do not enjoy eating *ugali*—a staple in other parts of Tanzania. Interview with Rachel Celestine, Rulenge, June 28, 2012.

50 Interview with A. Nzuri, Rulenge, June 25, 2012.

51 "Even to get 100 shillings was like a gift . . . when [I] worked [in Uganda I] received 15 to 20 shillings a day, [this money] was needed to buy cows, a cow was 20 shillings, a goat 8 shillings, [they] had much more value than now." Interview with Samwel Rwanzi.

52 These crops included bananas and sweet potatoes. Interview with Mary Christopha. Muyenzi, June 18, 2012.

53 Interview with Samwel Rwanzi. It is likely that avoiding taxes motivated other men as well, who might have been unwilling to admit such illegal activity, especially to a *mzungu* interviewer.

54 Interview with Peter Kato, Keza, June 17, 2012.

55 One man went to Uganda because "there were not many wazungu" there and because Africans in Uganda "got money early." Interview with Simon Ndyaderi, Keza, July 17, 2012. See also Richards et al., *Economic Development*, 4–5. De Haas reveals that the highest percentage of labor migrants from Ruanda-Urundi between 1930 and 1950 originated from areas neighboring Ngara. De Haas, "Moving Beyond Colonial Control?," 394, Fig. 5.

56 One former migrant commented that women did not work in Uganda "as a rule," although they occasionally accompanied their husbands to Uganda and generally stayed for at least a few years. Interview with Samson Sankwale, Ntobeye, June 21, 2012.

57 Interview with Edwardi Teadi, Mugoma, July 12, 2012.

58 Interview with Celestine Kaheri, Kanyinya, June 28, 2012. The "permanent loss" of men to Uganda in 1946 and 1947 reportedly exceeded six hundred. "Memorandum on Draft Bugufi (Ngara District) Land Rules, 1951," 2.

59 Interview with A. Nzuri; interview with Peter Banzi. According to a Belgian official, "the motive power behind this emigration results from a particular mental outlook which attributes a certain prestige to the fact of having made a journey or stay abroad." "Minutes of a Meeting Held at Kisenyi on the 24th and 25th November, 1948, to Discuss the Employment of Runda-Urundi Labour in Tanganyika and Uganda," 11–12, 541/11/1, 560, TNA. Similarly, the Tanganyika Labour Department noted that men in northwestern Tanganyika often went to Uganda without "good reasons," and upon their return, they "have proved themselves men and earned eligibility for marriage from both the moral and financial aspects." Labour Department, Mwanza, "Report on Migrant Labour Entering Uganda."

60 Interview with Euphrasia Vitahs, Munweje, June 27, 2012; interview with Rachel Celestine; interview with Peter Banzi; interview with Venance B. Munyaru.

61 Interview with Ivan Mbonamasabo.

62 Interview with Mary Christopha.

63 Interview with Sylvia Rwabani, Muyenzi, June 18, 2012. Another respondent reported that mothers-in-law helped when husbands went to work in Uganda. Interview with Maria Andrew, Muyenzi, July 18, 2012.

64 Writing in August 1953, Cory posited that many migrants had to borrow money for their journey, which had to be paid back at 100 percent interest. Cory, "Hangaza Law and Custom."

65 Compare with Peterson, *Ethnic Patriotism*, chap. 5.

66 Born in a village in Bugufi, interviewee Edwardi Teadi recalled that it was "easy" for Rwandans and Burundians to work in Ngara. Interview with Edwardi Teadi.

67 For example, interview with Celestine Kaheri. Indeed, many respondents did not distinguish between migrants from Ruanda-Urundi and those from Biharamulo, the neighboring district to the east in the Tanganyika Territory.

68 Interview with Edwardi Teadi; interview with Crispin Ubuzutwe, Mugoma, July 12, 2012; interview with Mary Justin Bamenya; interview with Joseph Mwi-jage. Very few respondents replied that no Rwandans or Burundians lived in Ngara prior to independence. Interview with Adrian Mudende.

69 Most respondents indicated that Banyarwanda, Barundi, and Ngarans worked on different farms and lived in different camps. For example, interview with Joseph Bwizi.

70 In particular, the migration of Rwandan workers had been of concern to British authorities in Uganda from the 1920s. Richards et al., *Economic Development*, 29–32. Authorities were also concerned about the migration of juveniles to Uganda. "Extract from the Annual Report from the Labour Officer Mwanza for the Year Ending 1955," 541/21, 460, TNA; interview with A. Nzuri; interview with Peter Banzi.

71 "Memorandum on Proposed Discussion on Immigrant Labour from Ruanda-Urundi," 2. British officials often called labor migrants from Ruanda-Urundi "Congolese," referring to Belgium's large colony to the west to which the mandate of Ruanda-Urundi was administratively linked. Similarly, the term *Warundi* was often used to signify all natives of Ruanda-Urundi. "Note of Discussions Held in the Office of the Labour Commissioner Tanganyika at Dar es Salaam on Thursday the 27th of March 1947," 541/17, 460, TNA.

72 In 1943 "detailed recommendations for the construction of a series of camps at intervals of a day's march along the two convergent routes from Tanganyika and Ruanda-Urundi" were made, but work was held up by the war. A. I. Richards, "Note on the Summary of Report on Tribal Admixture in Buganda," April 1952, CO 927/164/7, NA.

73 "Extract from 'Agreed Conclusion of the Anglo-Belgian Colonial Discus-sions, Held at the Colonial Office, London, 26th to 28th June, 1946,'" June 28, 1946, 541/17, 460, TNA. Bilateral conversations between officials in Uganda and Ruanda-Urundi had taken place previously. From the perspective of Tangan-yikan companies, the issue was that residents of Ngara and Biharamulo preferred to work in Uganda, rather than on the sisal plantations and mines in Tanganyika. "Extract from the Minutes of the 18th Meeting of the Labour Board Held at

222 · Notes to Chapter 2

Headquarters Department of Labour, Dar-es-Salaam on Monday, 24th October, 1955," 541/13/V, 460, TNA.

74 G. St. J. Orde-Browne, "Report on Labour Conditions in East Africa," 1, 541/17, 460, TNA. There was a long history of colonial encampment schemes for diseases such as sleeping sickness in Tanganyika. See, for example, Webel, "Ziba Politics."

75 In Uganda, Rwandans were reportedly viewed as dirty, savage people. Richards et al., *Economic Development*, 161.

76 The labor commissioner in Kampala remarked on the desire of the Ruanda-Urundi government to settle "a million people permanently . . . in fact he asked me point blank what Uganda's reaction would be to an offer of 200,000 Banyaruanda settlers." The Ugandan commissioner declined, citing the protectorate's own issues. "Extract from Letter Dated 25th April, 1944, from Labour Commissioner, Kampala, to Chief Secretary, Entebbe," 541/17, 460, TNA.

77 Orde-Browne, "Report on Labour Conditions in East Africa."

78 "Memorandum on Ruanda-Urundi Labour," n.d., 541/11/1, 460, TNA.

79 Orde-Browne, "Report on Labour Conditions in East Africa."

80 Labour Department, Mwanza, "Report on Migrant Labour Entering Uganda."

81 Letter from Acting Labour Commissioner, "Major Orde Browne's Proposal for the Establishing of Conditioning Camps for Immigrant Labour," December 23, 1946, 541/17, 460, TNA.

82 Jennings, "Building Better People," 95.

83 "An Excerpt from a Letter No. 8/29 Dated the 19th July 1945, by the Labour Officer, Masaka, Addressed to the Labour Commissioner, Kampala," 541/17, 460, TNA.

84 Secretariat, Uganda, to the Chief Secretary to the Government, Tanganyika Territory, Dar es Salaam, "Ruanda-Urundi Immigrant Labour Route and Camps," August 30, 1945, 541/17, 460, TNA.

85 M. J. B. Molohan, Labour Commissioner, to the Honourable Member for Social Service, Dar es Salaam, June 16, 1950, 2, 541/17, 460, TNA. Ugandan labor officials agreed, at least in theory, with the proposal to build "conditioning" camps in the Biharamulo and Ngara areas. M. J. B. Molohan, Acting Labour Commissioner, to Labour Commissioner, August 30, 1945, 541/17, 460, TNA.

86 Governor of Uganda to Secretary of State for Colonies, December 14, 1943, CO 536/213/4, NA.

87 See, for example, J. M. Caldwell, Senior Medical Officer (Labour), to Director of Medical Services, Entebbe, Labour Commissioner, Kampala, "Re: The Barundi and Banyaruanda Immigration Routes in Tanganyika," October 15, 1951, 541/11/1, 460, TNA. The Ugandan and Tanganyikan governments built holding camps at the Kyaka ferry in Bukoba district (from December 1953 to September 1954), but the ability to monitor these camps and the circulation of labor migrants remained suspect throughout the colonial period. The cost of the conditioning camp system and the low productivity of many laborers from Ruanda-Urundi led some officials to conclude that Orde-Browne's recommendations were "not practical." "Memorandum on Proposed Discussion on Immigrant

Notes to Chapter 2 · 223

Labour from Ruanda-Urundi"; "Note of Discussions Held in the Office of the Labour Commissioner Tanganyika at Dar es Salaam on Thursday the 27th of March 1947."

88 This was in addition to labor camps at Merema Hill, as well as other "experimental" camps. The large, expensive camp at Kyaka ferry was, by 1954, "little used" by migrants. Labour Commissioner, Kampala, to Labour Commissioner, Dar es Salaam, September 28, 1954, 541/21, 460, TNA.

89 L. R. Ray, Assistant Labour Officer, "Report on the Tour of Immigrant Labour Routes in Tanganyika and Southwestern Uganda," n.d., 541/11, 460, TNA.

90 Although some Rwandan Tutsi did migrate to Uganda for work, the majority of migrants were Hutu. As lorry transport increased, the number of migrants who stopped and worked in Ngara for short periods decreased. The interviews contained many contradictions regarding the presence of people from Rwanda and Burundi in Ngara during the late colonial era. Some people remembered only Rundi migrants passing through Ngara district, including Robert Ruphuzi, who drove a bus on the Rulenge-Bukoba route carrying migrant laborers to the Ugandan border. Interview with Robert Ruphuzi, Rulenge, June 25, 2012. Others recalled traveling with migrants from both Rwanda and Burundi to Kyaka ferry in Bukoba, including another bus driver who drove the Ngara-Bukoba route. Interview with John Karserahuba Mtamriheza, Muyenzi, June 11, 2012. One man who recalled traveling to Uganda with Rwandans insisted that no Rwandans or Burundians lived in Ngara during the colonial period, leading to questions about people's memories as well as the identification of territories prior to independence. Interview with Jacob Butabiya; interview with Adrian Mudende. It is clear that people born in Ruanda-Urundi did live in Ngara district prior to independence. Interviews with Charles Gasarasi, Butare, July 3, 2012; Crispin Ubuzutwe; Edwardi Teadi; Mary Justin Bamenya; Joseph Mwijage.

91 Ray, "Report on the Tour of Immigrant Labour Routes in Tanganyika and Southwestern Uganda."

92 For example, speaking about the need to recruit "Warundi" for work in the Tanganyika Territory, the deputy labor commissioner noted that "this Government will require all the labour it can get" for projects such as the groundnut scheme and the expanding gold, lead, diamond, and tin industries (all enterprises owned and managed by Europeans), and he suggested the need for "early and active" propaganda. R. C. Jerrad, Deputy Labour Commissioner, to [illegible], n.d., 541/17, 2, 460, TNA; "Minutes of a Meeting Held at Kisenyi on the 24th and 25th November, 1948."

93 Acting Labour Commissioner to Labour Commissioner, Kampala, August 9, 1945, 541/17, 460, TNA.

94 SILABU apparently employed "press ganging" to recruit Banyarwanda and Barundi migrants. As a result, Rundi migrants carried spears on the trip north to Uganda. "Note on Discussion on Various Subjects with Ruanda Urundi Authorities," November 11, 1949, 541/11, 460, TNA.

95 Letter from Acting Labour Commissioner, December 23, 1946, 541/17, 460, TNA.

224 · Notes to Chapter 2

96　"Extract from Annual Report from the Labour Officer Mwanza for the Year 1955," October 12, 1955, 541/13/v, 460, TNA. "In spite of being so backward these Africans are still essential individualists who dislike being tied down to specified tasks especially at a forced pace." Moreover, all migrants were deeply suspicious of any attempts to recruit them, particularly after rumors of "press-ganging" by recruiters. "Note on Discussions on Various Subjects with Ruanda Urundi Authorities." November 21, 1949, 541/11/1, 460, TNA.

97　The reference here is to Biharamulo district. K. J. Sanders, Labour Commissioner, to Senior Provincial Commissioner, Lake Province, "Recruiting in Biharamulo District," March 24, 1955, 541/13/v, 4460, TNA.

98　Hans Cory to Ngara District Commissioner, Tim Mayhew, October 26, 1953, "Bugufi (Ngara District) Land Rules, 1951–1955," 353, UDSM.

99　Newbury, "'Rwakayihura' Famine," 272, 277.

100　Newbury, "'Rwakayihura' Famine," 281.

101　Ray, "Report on the Tour of Immigrant Labour Routes in Tanganyika and Southwestern Uganda." With a dearth of administrators in the area, it is difficult to judge how accurate these numbers are, or the exact origins of newcomers as colonizers tended to refer to people from Ruanda-Urundi as "Warundi" (see note 75 above). Migrants from Ruanda-Urundi continued to enter Ngara, despite the British having "forbidden" such migration. Cory, "Bugufi Land Report, Ngara 1944," 15. The colonial government attempted to direct much of this migration toward the depopulated area around the Busubi chief's home in Keza.

3. DEVELOPMENTAL DISAPPOINTMENT

1　This paragraph is based on interviews conducted with elders throughout Ngara district. Examples were provided in interviews with Cyprien Rwatametage, Kanyinya, June 28, 2012; John Karsurahaba, Muyenzi, June 11, 2012; Gahinyuza Ntole, Ntobeye, June 21, 2012; and Bernard Simi, Ntobeye, July 25, 2012.

2　Interview with Samwel Rwanzi, Shanga, June 20, 2012.

3　Interview with Peter Banzi, Runzenzi-Ntobeye, July 25, 2012. Mary Bamenya explained that her two brothers migrated to Buganda as laborers and never returned to live in Ngara. Interview with Mary Justin Bamenya, Mugoma, July 12, 2012. In contrast, Mutahaba suggests that migration continued to plague the newly elected District Council in Ngara. However, this may be related to the council's inability to travel and collect taxes, which was blamed on Ngarans paying taxes in Uganda or Bukoba. Mutahaba, "Decentralized Administration," 148–51. Both explanations are likely accurate.

4　On nostalgia in Tanzanian historiography, see Fair, "Drive-In Socialism," 1079 n.9. See also Fouéré, "Julius Nyerere."

5　See Leys, *The Rise and Fall*; Edelman and Haugerud, "Introduction," 16.

6　Coulson, "Agricultural Policies," 79.

7　Schneider, "Colonial Legacies," 109.

Notes to Chapter 3 · 225

8 Ngarans were not the only people to take advantage of their proximity to borders. As Paul Nugent observes, West Africans were quick to see the "advantages to living in proximity to an international frontier." Paul Nugent, "Arbitrary Lines," 59. See also Roitman, *Fiscal Disobediance*.

9 This "new discourse" was formulated during the mid and late 1930s and implemented during the mid-1940s. Jennings, "Building Better People," 95.

10 Jennings, "Building Better People," 99.

11 Jennings, "Building Better People," 107.

12 To the colonial state, *traditional* included resource-poor, subsistence economies. In contrast, *capitalism* represented modernity, as evidenced by thriving cash crops and wage employment. Burton and Jennings, "Introduction," 4.

13 Escobar, *Encountering Development*; Ferguson, *Anti-Politics Machine*.

14 In this sense, Roosevelt and Truman did not necessarily anticipate a swift end of colonialism but hoped that colonially inspired development campaigns would foster democratic self-rule over time. Louis, "United Kingdom," 10.

15 Louis, "The United Kingdom," 8; Kelly and Kaplan, "'My Ambition Is Much Higher.'"

16 Weitzberg, *We Do Not Have Borders*, 71.

17 Cooper, *Decolonization and African Society*.

18 Low and Lonsdale, "Introduction," 12–16.

19 The original amount of £17.8 million was revised in 1950 to slightly more than £24 million. Stephens, *Political Transformation*, 79.

20 The majority of funds for development, however, was concentrated in certain regions, such as the controversial groundnut scheme. See also the issue of European settlement as exemplified in the Meru land case. Coulson, "Agricultural Policies," 75.

21 Iliffe, *Modern History*, 456; Coulson, "Agricultural Policies," 74.

22 Even where cash crops flourished, subsistence agricultural did as well, leading many to question how far capitalism had really penetrated. Iliffe, *Modern History*, 459; Hydén, *Political Development*.

23 Jennings, "'Very Real War,'" 75; Coulson, "Agricultural Policies," 78.

24 On passive and active resistance, see Coulson, "Agricultural Policies," 77.

25 According to Iliffe "the desire to end labour migration led officials in Bugufi to enforce coffee cultivation so strongly that many Hangaza long believed that the government owned their coffee trees." Iliffe, *Modern History*, 289.

26 Agricultural Officer, West Lake Division, to Assistant Director of Agriculture, Lake Province, April 3, 1958, A/3/1, 217, TNA. See also "Minutes of the West Lake Sub-Provincial Team, 27.9.58," 2, WL/C.5/6, 64, TNA.

27 Iliffe, *Modern History*, 45.

28 Hindering the establishment of coffee as a cash crop was the government's vacillation about the type of coffee that should be grown in the district. The first coffee trials in Ngara began with the 1925 planting of six Robusta coffee plants. However, six years later, the Robusta "was uprooted as unproductive," and the colonial government decided to grow only Arabica in Ngara. Agricultural Officer,

West Lake Division, to Secretary, Bugufi Coffee Cooperative Union, Ngara, December 17, [1959?], A/3/1, 217, TNA.

29 Hans Cory, "Bugufi Land Report, Ngara 1941," 22, Hans Cory, 61, UDSM.

30 District Commissioner, Ngara-Lake Province, "Commentary," Bugufi (Ngara District) Land Rules, 1951–1955, Hans Cory, 353, UDSM.

31 "Memorandum on the Draft Bugufi (Ngara District) Land Rules, 1951," 11, Bugufi (Ngara District) Land Rules, 1951–1955, Hans Cory, 353, UDSM.

32 "Memorandum on the Draft Bugufi (Ngara District) Land Rules, 1951," 2.

33 The district commissioner noted that Ngarans distrusted colonial resettlement schemes, fearing that the unoccupied land would be used for European settlement. R. J. Hopkins, District Commissioner, Ngara, to Senior Provincial Commissioner, Lake Province, "The Bugufi (Ngara District) Land Rules 1954," February 6, 1954, Bugufi (Ngara District) Land Rules, 1951–1955, Hans Cory, 353, UDSM.

34 Hans Cory, "Bugufi Land Report, Ngara 1944," 22, Hans Cory, 61, UDSM.

35 Cory wrote that "primitive people" could not understand the intricacies of coffee cultivation and that, without European supervision, native agricultural instructors became "tyrannical and arbitrary." Cory, "Bugufi Land Report, Ngara 1944," 23.

36 Cory, "Bugufi Land Report, Ngara 1944," 23.

37 "District Commissioner Ngara's Comments on Mr. Cory's Comments on Proposed Amendments to the Bugufi Land Rules," Bugufi (Ngara District) Land Rules 1951–1955, Hans Cory, 353, UDSM.

38 According to the WLP agriculture officer, the coffee crop (presumably for the district) amounted to 9,000–10,000 tons per annum. "Minutes of a Meeting of the West Lake Provincial Team held to Meet Members of the World Bank Mission to Tanganyika Held . . . 7/7/59," 4, WL/C.5/6, 64, TNA.

39 In the 1950s the Agriculture Department supported the growth of local cooperatives to control the marketing of the territory's crops. These societies were protected by compulsory marketing orders, which made it illegal for unapproved agents to purchase specified crops. Coulson, "Agricultural Policies," 83–84.

40 Jennings, "'Very Real War,'" 77.

41 Eckert, "Useful Instruments," 108.

42 McCallum, Agricultural Officer WLD, to Secretary Bugufi Coffee Cooperative Society, Ngara, June 20, 1957, A/3/1, 217, TNA; Agricultural Officer, WLD, to Director of Agriculture, April 24, 1957, A/3/1, 217, TNA.

43 District Commissioner, Ngara, to Agricultural Officer, West Lake, June 3, 1958, A/3/1, 217, TNA.

44 McCallum, Agricultural Officer, WLD, to Secretary, Bugufi Coffee Cooperative Society, Ngara, June 20, 1957.

45 Murray Lunan, Assistant Director of Agriculture, Lake Province, to Agricultural Officer, West Lake et al., "Coffee-Policy Ngara," December 4, 1957, A/3/1, 217, TNA.

46 Later research revealed that intercropping coffee with bananas is beneficial. See van Asten et al., "Agronomic and Economic Benefits."

Notes to Chapter 3 · 227

47 For the poor quality of Ngaran roads, see "Minutes of the West Lake Regional Development committee . . . 29/6/64," FA/D.10/6, 600, TNA. Additionally, a cooperative officer commented on the "inadequate" rest facilities in Ngara. "Minutes of a Meeting of the West Lake Provincial Team . . . on 27/6/60," 6, C.5/23, 527, TNA.

48 D. K. Healey, District Commissioner, Ngara, to Provincial Commissioner, West Lake Province, July 29, 1959, A/3/A, 217, TNA.

49 Smuggling continued through independence; from 1960 to 1963, 800,000 shillings were lost to smuggling. "Minutes of the Special West Lake Regional Development Held on 22nd July, 1963 . . . ," 6, FA/D.10/6, 600, TNA.

50 "Minutes of a Meeting of the West Lake Provincial Team Held . . . 26/8/60," WL.C.5/6, 64, TNA.

51 Stephens, *Political Transformation*, 123.

52 The African Association (AA) became the TAA after the August 1948 split with branches in Zanzibar. Iliffe, *Modern History*, 433.

53 Iliffe, *Modern History*, 432.

54 For the role of the Lake Province branch of the Tanganyika African Government Servants Association (TAGSA), as well as politicization in Sukumaland and the northeast, see Iliffe, *Modern History*, chap. 15. In 1977 TANU merged with the Afro-Shirazi Party (ASP) of Zanzibar to form Chama Cha Mapinduzi (CCM).

55 Stephens, *Political Transformation*, 141. GA Resolutions 1064 and 1065 (1957) requested independence target dates. Stephens, *Political Transformation*, 147. Nyerere thought a period of ten to twelve years would be sufficient. Chidzero, *Tanganyika and International Trusteeship*, 171.

56 Iliffe, *Modern History*, chap. 16.

57 For the motivations behind this decision, see Iliffe, "Breaking the Chain."

58 Iliffe, *Modern History*, 563.

59 Quoted in Iliffe, "Breaking the Chain," 185.

60 See Turnbull to Gorell Barnes, January 13, 1959, in Iliffe, "Breaking the Chain," 190.

61 Indeed, by 1965, the administrative secretary of WLR wrote to the region's area commissioners to inquire why TANU cell formation had not yet been completed, as "almost all regions in the country have already done this." T. Mweri, Administrative Secretary, WLR, to Area Commissioners Bukoba, Biharamulo, Ngara, and Karagwe, n.d., 3/2, 71, TNA.

62 Indeed, there was little to no mention of the TANU Youth League (TYL) in interviews, and Mutahaba notes that TANU "was a low key organization" in Ngara during the 1960s. Mutahaba, "Decentralized Administration," 265.

63 In Ngara, TANU had undertaken a "rather weak but commendable start" to organize voluntary teachers to work with the social development officer, but budget cuts likely impaired the program. "Social Development Report for 1960," 3/2, 71, TNA. On the removal of social development staff from WLP, see "Meeting of the Provincial Team Held on 24th March 1961," 4, 64, WL/C.5/6, TNA.

64 Hydén notes that Edward Barongo, a former police officer and TANU member and politician, "was the single most important person in the work of extending

228 · Notes to Chapter 3

TANU throughout Buhaya and the other areas of the province, Biharamulo and Ngara." Hydén, *Political Development*, 127. In 1957 Bukoba became the provincial center for TANU's activities. That same year, Nyerere made his first official visit to Bukoba as TANU chairman; he also visited Nyakahanga-Bugene, where around ten thousand people gathered to hear him speak. There are few data on the location and economic status of TANU membership during the late 1950s, but most scholars agree that after 1957, most new recruits were in the countryside. Between December 1957 and July 1958, TANU membership increased from 175,000 to 300,000, and the number of branches rose from 48 to 134. TANU probably tapped into potential sources of support by utilizing existing agricultural marketing cooperatives. Hydén, *Political Development*, 128, 143.

65   Pratt, *Critical Phase*, 96.

66   Pratt, *Critical Phase*, 97. This included the creation of a Westminster-style parliament.

67   The 1964 army mutiny was in part a response to low wages and the slow pace of Africanization. Bjerk, *Building a Peaceful Nation*, 132–54.

68   According to administrative secretary G. P. Allsebrook, two of the seven factors "desirable for an acceptable development scheme" were "the attraction of overseas capital . . . [and] if possible [a] definite proposal for external financial assistance." "Minutes of the Regional Team Meeting Held on 12th March, 1962 . . . ," 2, 3/2, 71, TNA.

69   Pratt, *Critical Phase*, 103.

70   Helleiner, "Trade, Aid and Nation Building," 68.

71   Nyang'oro, "Challenge of Development," 30.

72   Nyerere was slow to Africanize the civil service in part because he recognized the importance of Western expertise and experience. Bjerk, *Building a Peaceful Nation*, 81, 200.

73   Rweyemamu, "Overview of Nation-Building," 7.

74   Jennings, "'Very Real War,'" 75.

75   Political Ngara (W. A. Haldane D.C.) to Landmines Dar es Salaam, 12/1/49, 7, File P.5, Station Ngara, TNA. The election of traditional elites is compatible with Emma Hunter's observation that local debates over nationalism frequently blend new ideologies with older institutions that "should be adapted to fit the modern age." Hunter, *Political Thought*, 176.

76   "Famine" itself is, of course, a politically charged term as it indicates a collapse of political accountability and so legitimacy. The new government advocated that "each tax payer should grow at least one acre" each of sorghum and cassava to avoid famine. Regional Commissioner, West Lake Region, to Permanent Secretary, Dar es Salaam, "Ngara District Development Plan," September 3, 1962, P.1/2, 197, TNA. In interviews, Ngarans usually did not remember an acute famine during this time but noted the constant threat of famine in the area. The colonial and post-colonial governments themselves seemed confused as to whether famine existed in Ngara. See, for example, "Minutes of a Meeting of the Provincial Team Held on 28th January 1961," 2, C.5/23, 527, TNA.

77   This comment stemmed from the fact that local people often asked staff from the Ministry of Agriculture for help improving their water supply, requests that were ignored by the relevant area commissioners. "Minutes of the West Lake Regional Development Commission," May 7, 1963, 7, FA/D/6, 600, TNA.

78   Mutahaba, "Local Autonomy," 523.

79   As evidenced by the "power of the word 'education'" in the district, which led the Ngara Council to abolish school fees and expand education, despite governmental warnings. E. M. Martin, Provincial Commissioner, "West Lake Province Annual Report—1960," p.5, Station Ngara, TNA.

80   See Ivaska, "Of Students."

81   Interview with Joseph Barogo, Kanyinya, June 28, 2012.

82   District Commissioner, Ngara, to Provincial Commissioner, West Lake Province, April 2, 1947, R-59, 34, TNA-Mwanza.

83   This number does not include auxiliaries, such as women and children, involved in tobacco cultivation. "Crop Figures for Four Years as per District-Cross," June 15, 1964, C/Tob/Fic, box 25, 19, TNA-Mwanza.

84   During the first two years of independence, the number of societies grew from 877 to 1,533. Coulson, "Agricultural Policies," 85. In 1961 the central government created the Cooperative Union of Tanganyika to organize and support the expansion of local cooperative societies. Eckert, "Useful Instruments," 113.

85   Coulson, "Agricultural Policies," 86.

86   Coulson, "Agricultural Policies," 86.

87   Administrative Secretary, Kigoma Region, to Director, Agricultural Extension, Ministry of Agriculture, May 29, 1963, 9, C/Tob/Fic, box 25, 19, TNA-Mwanza.

88   Administrative Secretary, Kigoma Region, to Director, Agricultural Extension, Ministry of Agriculture, May 29, 1963, 9; emphasis in original.

89   Field Officer Grade II, Kibondo, to Regional Agricultural Officer, Bukoba, "Tobacco Marketing Ngara," November 1, 1963, 9, C/Tob/Fic, box 25, 19, TNA-Mwanza. The field officer wrote, "admittedly the situation is grim for many growers," but their "suffering" should not be "exaggerated."

90   The Tanganyikan government had arranged for Ugandan buyers to purchase around 800,000 pounds of tobacco annually from Kibondo, Ngara, and Biharamulo. General Manager, Bukoba Cooperative Union Ltd., to Manager, Kampala, "Fire-Cured Tobacco Marketing, Kibondo, Ngara, Biharamulo Districts Tanzania," May 17, 1965, 9, C/Tob/Fic, box 25, 19, TNA-Mwanza; M. Macatta, Marketing Officer II, Ministry of Commerce and Cooperatives, and I. S. Mkwawa, Executive Officer, TTB, "Report on Fire-Cured Tobacco, a Visit to Kigoma, Kibondo, and Biharamulo Areas," March 7, 1966, 9, C/Tob/Fic, box 25, 19, TNA-Mwanza.

91   Macatta and Mkwawa, "Report on Fire-Cured Tobacco."

92   I. S. Mkwawa, Executive Officer, TTB, to RAO Kigoma et al., "Fire-Cured Tobacco in the Nyamirembe Area i.e. Kibondo, Kasulu, Biharamulo and Ngara Districts," October 21, 1966, 9, C/Tob/Fic, box 25, 19, TNA-Mwanza. In part, this new drive may have been to justify expenditures to recondition a leaf redrying facility at

230 · Notes to Chapter 3

Nyarumbugu; however, the efficacy of increasing tobacco production without a local drying facility remains in doubt.

93 Macatta and Mkwawa, "Report on Fire-Cured Tobacco."

94 According to the OIC of the Ngara Agriculture Office, "the first schedules which we arranged with Kigoma buyers were totally unfollowed, then these buyers popped in Ngara unexpectedly [and] . . . they did not even follow the second program so that only 87 lbs of tobacco . . . were collected from the nearby villages (Rulenge Trading centre)." Officer in Charge, District Agricultural Office, Ngara, to Regional Agricultural Officer, WLR, January 24, 1967, 9, C/Tob/Fic, box 25, 19, TNA-Mwanza. The regional agricultural officer noted that "Farmers should have been advised in December or January that the Board would not buy the crop." K. J. Rwisa, Regional Agricultural Officer, to the Executive Officer, Tanganyika Tobacco Board, June 28, 1967, C/Tob/Fic, box 25, 19, TNA-Mwanza.

95 Officer in Charge, District Agricultural Office, Ngara, to Regional Agricultural Officer, WLR, "Tobacco Marketing," August 31, 1967, 9, C/Tob/Fic, box 25, 19, TNA-Mwanza.

96 In September 1967, TTB agreed to commence tobacco marketing in Ngara and Biharamulo districts, only to cancel these arrangements in early October. Field Officer, I, Regional Agricultural Officer, Tabora Region, to Executive Officer, TTB, August 18, 1967, 9, C/Tob/Fic, box 25, 19, TNA-Mwanza; I. S. Mkwawa, Executive Officer, TTB, to Principal Secretary, Ministry of Agriculture and Cooperatives, October 2, 1967, 9, C/Tob/Fic, box 25, 19, TNA-Mwanza. The executive director wrote that this cancellation was due to the fact that most of the tobacco had already been sold.

97 Regarding smuggling: the "1966 estimates do not allow for possible smuggling of tobacco. In some areas like Ngara . . . most tobacco was either used locally or sold over the borders." Faustine N. Mabula, Kigoma Region Cooperative Union Limited, to Executive Officer, Tanganyika Tobacco Board, "Report and Account 1966 for Fire-Cured Tobacco," December 16, 1966, 9, C/Tob/Fic, box 25, 19, TNA-Mwanza.

98 Coffee and tobacco prices in Rwanda, Burundi, and Uganda were higher than in Tanzania. Officer in Charge, District Agricultural Office, Ngara, to Regional Agricultural Officer, WLR, "Tobacco Marketing," August 31, 1967. On illicit trading of Ngaran tobacco, see C. Y. Mpupua, Regional Agricultural Officer, West Lake Region, to Katibu wa Mkoa, Bukoba, "Tubako-Ngara/Biharamulo," February 8, 1967; Officer in Charge, District Agricultural Office, Ngara, to the Regional Agricultural Officer, WLR, August 31, 1967.

99 Regional Agricultural Officer, Kigoma Region, to Officer in Charge, District Agricultural Office, Kibondo, "Fire Cured Tobacco," August 5, 1967, 9, C/Tob/Fic, box 25, 19, TNA-Mwanza.

100 I. S. Mkwawa, Executive Officer, Tanganyika Tobacco Board, to Director of Agriculture, "Tobacco Marketing," August 31, 1967, 9, C/Tob/Fic, box 25, 19, TNA-Mwanza.

101 Regional Agricultural Officer, WLR, to Officers in Charge, District Agricultural Officers, Biharamulo, Ngara, April 3, 1968, 9, C/Tob/Fic, box 25, 19, TNA-Mwanza.

102 Regional Agricultural Officer, WLR, to Director of Agriculture, Ministry of Agriculture and Cooperatives, "Nyamirembe Fire Cured Tobacco," April 3, 1968, C/Tob/Fic, box 25, 19, TNA-Mwanza.

103 Regional Agricultural Officer, WLR, to Director of Agriculture and Cooperatives, "Nyamimrembe Fire Cured Tobacco," April 3, 1968, 9.

104 For an example of the peripheral status of Ngara district within West Lake Region, see the reduction of tractor units for Ngara in favor of additional tractors for Bukoba in "Minutes of the West Lake Regional Development Committee Held on 30th August 1963," 3, FA/D.10/6, 600, TNA.

105 "Minutes of West Lake Regional Development Commission Held on 30th December 1963."

106 "Minutes of the West Lake Regional Development Committee Held on 30th December 1963."

107 The presence of such courts indicates that Ngarans did not view the government as an available, or perhaps an appropriate, mediator of local justice. "Minutes of a Meeting of the Provincial Team Held on 9 December 1960," C.5/12, 527, TNA.

108 Even with little access to radio or newspapers, Ngarans likely engaged in small-group, vernacular discussions of government pronouncements made at the district level, such as those Emma Hunter analyzes in Mwanza. Hunter, *Political Thought*, 29 n. 96, 156. National slogans such as "independence and work" (*uhuru na kazi*) were therefore likely common in the district.

109 On similar problems with postcolonial development programs and subsequent smuggling of crops, see Giblin, *History of the Excluded*, 259.

4. DEVELOPMENTAL REFUGEES

1 Burundi has a high population density, and the influx of tens of thousands of Rwandans taxed the land's capacity and threated the chaotic politics of decolonization in the state. Lemarchand, *Rwanda and Burundi*.

2 In 1960 WLP became independent from Lake Province, becoming WLR in 1962.

3 Marfleet, "Refugees and History," 140.

4 The need for Hutu leadership was most notably expressed in the 1957 publication "Notes on the Social Problem of Racial Indigenous in Rwanda," also known as the "Bahutu Manifesto."

5 Chrétien, *Great Lakes*, 299.

6 For the role of the Catholic Church in decolonization and changes in Belgian politics after World War II, see Linden and Linden, *Church and Revolution*.

7 Estimates of the number of Rwandan refugees vary. Watson includes 150,000 camp refugees and perhaps another 100,000 self-settled refugees by 1964. Watson, "Exile from Rwanda," 5.

8 Watson estimates that from March 1961 until July 1966 there were ten "major" *inyenzi* attacks. Watson, "Exile from Rwanda," 5.

9 Prunier, *Rwanda Crisis*, 14.

10 Pro-Hutu governments deployed the term *inyenzi* as a propaganda and scapegoating device to justify violence against Tutsi and bolster loyalty to the regime during the 1973 coup and events leading up to and during the 1994 genocide. Tanzanian and UNHCR officials also used the term to refer to the raids and to Tutsi leaders in exile.

11 Stockwell's Diary, 7712/40/8, 1977-12-40, NAM.

12 For example, Stockwell's Diary, June 17, 1962.

13 Just as the Congo crisis "shaped European and American reactions" to events surrounding the 1964 union with Zanzibar, it would affect British anxieties around potential territorial alterations and instability in East Africa. Bjerk, *Building a Peaceful Nation*, 9. Fear of communist influence in the Congo motivated Western intervention and reactions to the secession attempts and civil war(s) that followed the Belgian Congo's independence—as well as the assassination of Patrice Lumumba, the first prime minister of the Republic of Congo. See Nzongola-Ntalaja, *Congo from Leopold to Kabila*, 121–40.

14 Nyerere floated the idea of federation in January 1961. Bjerk, *Building a Peaceful Nation*, 195. The British were somewhat ambiguous, if anxious, about the possibility of federation, as some "outside" the "Soviet Bloc" hoped "to see this troublesome territory [Ruanda-Urundi] linked to a more stable neighbor." K. C. Thom, September 7, 1961, FCO, 141/17926, NA. On the possibility of federation, see Bjerk, *Building a Peaceful Nation*, 195–96; Russell, "Punctuated Places," 138–41. On the need for stable postcolonial states that would "preserve their economic and political ties with the West," see Louis and Robinson, "Empire Preserv'd," 157–58.

15 In Uganda, the British feared Rwandan refugees would be "potential 'spoilers'" of a "smooth transition" to home rule. Long, "Rwanda's First Refugees," 213.

16 Interrogation teams were planned for phase II of the operation. Ministry of Home Affairs, Dar es Salaam, "Operation Instruction No. 1 Operation 'Book In,'" August 17, 1961, FCO, 141/17926, NA.

17 D. C. Hill, Chairman—Planning Committee Operation "Book In," Ministry of Home Affairs, Dar es Salaam, "Operation Instruction No. 1 Operation 'Book In,'" 2.

18 Refugees from Ruanda-Urundi with "cross-border ethnic loyalties" thus "threatened the notional integrity of colonial boundaries." Bjerk, *Building a Peaceful Nation*, 196. The field force units were to assist the military and provide "escorts and guards as required for the control of refugees." Members of the Special Branch were to send daily situation reports on the number and "race" of the refugees. Hill, "Book In," Ministry of Home Affairs, Dar es Salaam, "Operation Instruction No. 1 Operation 'Book In,'" 2.

19 Echoing Cooper, MacArthur notes that African borders are "the product of decolonization not colonization," as there was a "moment during decolonization when the imagining of alternative nations was not just possible but prevalent." MacArthur, *Cartography and the Political Imagination*, 194. New political elites at the Organization of African Unity transitioned from disparaging colonial borders to embracing them after secession attempts in places like Katanga and Kenya. MacArthur, *Cartography and the Political Imagination*, 222. More work

is needed to understand the role former colonizers played in hardening these boundaries; the presence of Operation Book In attests to British preoccupation with border control during decolonization. On British troops' role in pacifying the 1964 East African mutinies, see Parsons, *1964 Army Mutinies.*

20 On "reliable reports" of ANC training, see Cypher from Uganda (Sir F. Crawford) to S. of S., April 1, 1961, CO 822/2491, NA. Regarding possible perceptions of communism in the ANC, see Nzongola-Ntalaja, *Congo from Leopold to Kabila*, 88, 116.

21 The Belgian government refused responsibility for Rwandan refugees in part because it blamed the exodus on UN policies, specifically Resolution 1605, which called for a united Ruanda-Urundi state. G. M. Warr, British Embassy—Brussels, to T. M. Wilford, FO, London, January 30, 1962, CO 822/2492, NA.

22 H. S. H. Stanley, British High Commission, Dar es Salaam, to K. Eastl, Esq., Commonwealth Relations Office, March 30, 1962, CO 822/2492, NA.

23 Governor's Deputy, Uganda, to Rt. Hon. Iain Macleod, Secretary of State, October 24, 1960, CO 822/2492, NA.

24 On UNHCR officials referring to Tutsi as "Nilotes," see "Brief for Mr. Ghosh of FAO," April 11, 1963, 15/SA, 259, fonds 11, series 1, UNHCR.

25 Stockwell's Diary, June 30, 1962. Similarly, Uganda officials noted in 1962 that Rwandan Hutu and Tutsi arrived in "equal numbers." Long, *Rwanda's First Refugees*, 218.

26 Stockwell's Diary, June 30, 1962.

27 Stockwell's Diary, June 30, 1962.

28 Letter from Tanganyika (Sir R. G. Turnbull) to Sec. of State for the Colonies, October 26, 1961, CO 822/2451, NA.

29 Telegram from Sir R. G. Turnbull to S. of S., October 26, 1961, CO 822/2491, NA.

30 Stockwell's Diary, June 23, 1962. A letter from Muyenzi camp in March 1963 alleged that two-thirds of the camp's inhabitants were "wahutu and watwa." [Unknown sender], "Muyenzi Refugees Camp, Muyenzi" to Regional Commissioner, West Lake Region, March 25, 1963, 7712/40/8, 1977-12-40, NAM.

31 Lal notes that the Nyerere administration originally referred to refugees as *wageni wakazi*, or "resident guests," thus marrying the terms *guests* and *workers* in Kiswahili. Lal, *African Socialism*, 125.

32 Large numbers of Mozambican refugees entered Tanzania in 1964. On disputes over how to label these populations, see Tague, *Displaced Mozambicans*, 122. On contradictory Tanzanian views on Mozambican refugees, see Lal, *African Socialism*, 125.

33 Bjerk, *Building a Peaceful Nation*, 196.

34 Eckert, "Useful Instruments"; Schneider, "Colonial Legacies," 67.

35 For aid agencies, "legibility" entails defining the beneficiary population— generally through acts of quantitative management, such as counting people, and qualitative assessments, including a general "needs analysis." Hilhorst and Jansen, "Humanitarian Space," 1134.

36 On the relationship between refugee aid and development in the "third world," see Malkki, "Refugees and Exile," 505–7.

37 Scholars have argued that, as Tutsi, many of the refugees were pastoralists and unused to farming. Daley, "From the Kipande," 23. Although this was certainly true

234 · Notes to Chapter 4

of the refugee elite, and although Rwandan Tutsi did have "slightly more access to cattle than Hutu," many Tutsi were also agriculturalists. Newbury and Newbury, "Bringing the Peasants," 867. Nevertheless, as cattle represented wealth and success, the absence of a cattle scheme in the settlements likely frustrated many refugees.

38 For an overview, see Gatrell, *Making of the Modern Refugee*, chap. 3.

39 Malkki, "National Geographic"; Salvatici, "'Help the People.'"

40 The Geneva Convention Relating to the Status of Refugees defines a refugee as someone who, "as a result of events occurring before 1 January 1951 and owing to well-founded fear of being persecuted for reasons of race, religion, nationality, membership of a particular social group or political opinion, is outside the country of his nationality." Article 1, Convention Relating to the Status of Refugees, UNHCR, https://www.unhcr.org/en-us/3b66c2aa10.

41 The UNHCR statute was adopted in 1950. The agency was originally envisioned as a temporary, nonoperational organization with a three-year mandate. The United States did not sign the convention, or any other treaties regarding refugees, until 1968. Loescher, *Beyond Charity*.

42 Loescher, *Beyond Charity*, 60. On European refugees being "too important" to leave to the UN, see Loescher, "UNHCR," 35.

43 These agencies encouraged eastern Europeans to "vote with their feet" (discredit communism by fleeing to Western countries). Thus, of the 233,436 refugees admitted to the United States between 1956 and 1968, "all but 925 were from communist countries." Loescher, *Beyond Charity*, 59.

44 Loescher, *Beyond Charity*, 68; Gatrell, *Making of the Modern Refugee*, 117. This was in addition to perceived success in the 1953 West Berlin refugee crisis.

45 Gatrell, *Making of the Modern Refugee*, 87–88. Through careful diplomacy, High Commissioner Auguste Lindt gained the cooperation of some Soviet republics as well. Loescher, *Beyond Charity*, 71.

46 The problem was that these refugees fled conditions that had clearly occurred after 1951 and outside Europe, putting them beyond the purview of the high commissioner. Not only that, but the anticolonial violence was aimed at France, a US ally in the Cold War.

47 The strategic importance of Africa is bolstered by its position as a producer of strategic raw materials.

48 The UNHCR's executive committee enabled it to use its "good offices" to protect refugees until the 1967 Protocol, which extended protection activities beyond the constraints of the 1951 Convention. On the struggle between "universalists" and "Europeanists" in the creation of the 1951 Refugee Convention, see Glynn, "Genesis and Development," 135.

49 For a contrasting view that highlights the UNHCR's "independent agenda," see Loescher, "UNHCR," 34.

50 The attention of the great powers was particularly drawn to the "disaster" in the Congo. See Gibbs, "The United Nations." Such interests were, of course, deeply entwined with competition for resources and loyalty in the region.

51 An estimated twelve thousand refugees were first grouped at Muyenzi in 1961. Following the government's October 1961 request, a UNHCR representative investigated the situation and ordered the UNHCR chargé de mission in East Africa to assist the Tanzanian government. Cable from Temnomoroff, Bukavu to Jamieson, Hicomref, Geneva, received May 9, 1963, 15/SA, fonds 1, series 2, UNHCR.

52 The Red Cross did not formally begin archival documentation until 1994. As a result, many reports and memoranda between headquarters and Tanzania, as well as within the Tanzania office itself, have been lost.

53 "3rd Session of the Disaster Relief Advisory Committee, Resettlement of Refugees: Defining a New League Policy," Geneva, September 17–19, 1964, Congo Circulaires & Communiqués, Rapports, 22/1/2, A1022, box 3, IFRC.

54 On student protests in 1966 and 1968, see Roberts, *Revolutionary State-Making*, 82, chap. 5.

55 For regional and national planners, Ngara district represented one such underpopulated area. According to the 1957 census, Ngara's population density was 92.9 persons per square mile; however, most of this population was concentrated in northern Bugufi. "West Lake Province, Annual Report—1960 by E. M. Martin, Esq., Provincial Commissioner," 3, Bukoba District Book, TNA.

56 Refugee settlements were in many respects pilot projects of later *ujamaa* villagization. Turner, "Under the Gaze," 232; Tague, *Displaced Mozambicans*, 161.

57 For example, according to Van der Meeren, the government attempted to make the refugees self-sufficient by dispersing them among Bukoba coffee farmers to replace traditional Hutu labor migrants. This resulted in "disastrous failure." Van der Meeren, "Three Decades," 259.

58 Such issues were compounded by the "parlous state of the Ngara treasury." "Minutes of a Meeting of the West Lake Provincial Team . . . 27/6/60," 3–4, C.5/23, 527, TNA.

59 K. B. A. Dobson, District Officer, Ngara, to Provincial Commissioner, Lake Province, Mwanza, March 20, 1944, 64/668, TNA.

60 "Minutes of the Provincial Team Meeting Held on 31 July 1961," WL/C.5/6, 64, TNA.

61 Criteria included the ability to attract international funding and the settlement of at least twenty families. "Minutes of the Regional Team Meeting held on 12th March 1962," 3/2, 71, TNA; "Minutes of the West Lake Regional Development Committee held on 4th March 1963," 3/2, 71, TNA.

62 "Minutes of the Provincial Team Meeting Held on 7th November, 1961," WL/C.5/6, 64, TNA. Most of those present at the meeting would have been nationally appointed rather than locally elected figures. In contrast, the district councils were locally elected and limited to TANU members in 1965. Mutahaba, "Decentralized Administration," 29, 38.

63 "Minutes of the Provincial Team Meeting Held on 7th November, 1961."

64 "Minutes of the Provincial Team Meeting Held on 7th November, 1961."

65 "Minutes of the Provincial Team Meeting Held on 7th November, 1961."

66 In December 1961 local officials agreed "that the only practicable method" of refugee settlement was "by absorption." "Record of the Meeting of the National Resources Committee on 28 December 1961," WL.A/3/10, box 65, 19, TNA-Mwanza.

236 · Notes to Chapter 4

67 Regional Extension Officer, West Lake Region, to Director of Development, Ministry of Agriculture, October 15, 1962, G/35, 290, TNA.

68 LRCS officials estimated that there were 10,600 refugees in the Muyenzi area by October 1963. Letter from Agriculture (W.D. and I.D.), Bukoba, to Agriculture, Dar es Salaam, October 11, 1963, G/35, 290, TNA.

69 "Development Plan Ngara District," January 6, 1962, LG.48/0127, 208, TNA.

70 "Minutes of the West Lake Development Committee Held on 29th September, 1963," 6, FA/D.10/6, 600, TNA.

71 Letter from G. P. Allsebrook, December 12, 1962, G/35, 290, TNA.

72 District Commissioner, Biharamulo, to Provincial Commissioner, WLP, December 29, 1961, A.4/2 v.I, 529, TNA.

73 "Minutes of a Meeting of the West Lake Provincial Team Held on . . . 27.9.60," 2, WL/C.5/6, 64, TNA; W. Z. Talawa, District Commissioner, Biharamulo, to Provincial Commissioner, WLP, December 29, 1961, A.4/2 v.I, 529, TNA; E. B. M. Barungo, M.P. Busubi, WLP, to All Citizens from Ruanda and Urundi, December 27, 1961, A.4/2 v.I, 529, TNA.

74 D. A. Mwakosya, Regional Extension Officer, WLR, to Director of Extension Division, Dar es Salaam, "Refugees-Ruanda/Urundi," September 18, 1962, WL.R4/16E, 71, TNA.

75 Senior Labour Officer, Mwanza, to Province, "Ruanda Refugees," October 30, 1961, A.4/2 v.I, 529, TNA.

76 Province, Bukoba, to Admin. B'mulo, October 27, 1961, A.4/2 v.I, 529, TNA.

77 In 1953 the Catholic ecclesiastical hierarchy divided the area of West Lake into two dioceses: Bukoba and Rulenge. Sundkler, *Bara Bukoba*, 40.

78 The government initially intended to move refugees from the Muyenzi camp to a settlement further from the Ruanda-Urundi border. A. G. Administrative Secretary, for Regional Commissioner, WLR, to District Commissioner, Biharamulo, July 26, 1962, A.4/2 v.I, 529, TNA. Areas that received refugees outside of the increasingly formal camp and settlement system were given some aid from the central government and international agencies. In 1962 the provincial commissioner usually authorized the purchase of rations and seeds by either the district commissioner or the *Mwami* of a specific *gombolola* (subcounty).

79 In March 1962 all refugees at the Nyakanyasi camp had to make a choice: either settle in Missenye without rations or move to camps in Karagwe. A total of 977 refugees remained in Missenye, working on local *shamba*. "Report on Nyakanyasi Refugees Settlement in Missenyi," April 14, 1962, WL.A.4/10, box 67, 19, TNA-Mwanza. The government relocated refugees deemed more amenable to settlement to Karagwe district (mostly those from the Gisaka area of Rwanda). Van der Meeren, "Three Decades," 260.

80 Telegram from Makarua, DSM, to Police Ngara for Campcom, February 22, 1963, A.4/I/III, 527, TNA.

81 G. P. Allsebrook, Administrative Secretary, WLR, to All Area Commissioners, Biharamulo, Bukoba, Karagwe & Ngara, July 19, 1963, A.4/2 v.I, 529, TNA.

82 D. A. Mwakosya, Regional Extension Officer, WLR, to Director of Extension Division, Dar es Salaam, "Refugees-Ruanda/Urundi," September 18, 1962, G/35, 290, TNA.

83 Mwakosya to Director of Extension Division, "Refugees-Ruanda/Urundi."

84 Refugees who were "not properly absorbed" in other regions were often transferred to Muyenzi, such as the twelve hundred sent from Bukoba to Muyenzi in 1962. "Minutes of the West Lake Regional Development Committee Held on 29 November 1962," 3/2, 71, TNA.

85 Tributary, Bukoba, to Water, Dar es Salaam, "Water Supplies for Refugees Ngara District," November 21, 1961, G/35, 290, TNA.

86 The regional extension officer for WLR posited that the refugees' lack of cultivation was due to the seemingly indefinite provision of free food, the possibility of returning to Rwanda, and the lack of agricultural implements. Mwakosya to Director of Extension Division, "Refugees-Ruanda/Urundi."

87 Tributary, Bukoba, to Water, Dar es Salaam, "Refugee Camp—Muyenzi Water Supplies," November 9, 1962, G/35, 290, TNA. While the directors of the agricultural extension offices were likely appointed nationally, much of the staff would have been local to the region and district. Mutahaba, "Decentralized Administration," 152.

88 On the lack of paper and ledger books, see Tanganyika Police Message Form, "For Regcom from Campcom," November 8, 1962, WL.R4/16E, 71, TNA. On petrol shortages, see "Mr. Julius Paul's Letter of 11 November 1963," translation by L. R. Ruhinda, G/35, 290, TNA.

89 The goal was for the refugees to eventually grow food crops such as maize, sorghum, beans, cassava, bananas, and sweet potatoes, in addition to cash crops such as tobacco and groundnuts. The high cost of transport made the success of cash crops questionable from the start.

90 Regional Extension Officer, West Lake Region, to Regional Commissioner, "Refugee Resettlement, Ngara District," January 21, 1963, G/35, 290, TNA.

91 Over seven months beginning in October 1962, approximately eighty square miles around the Rulenge area were reconnoitered. D. W. Edwards, Officer in Charge, West Lake Region, "Notes on Water Supplies—Refugee Settlement Areas," n.d., G/35, 290, TNA.

92 "All refugee labor" was unpaid. Telegram from administrative secretary, West Lake Region, G.P Allsebrook, 18/1/63, G/35, 290, TNA.

93 Tributary, Bukoba, to Water, Dar es Salaam, August 25, 1962, G/35, 290, TNA.

94 Edwards, "Notes on Water Supplies—Refugee Settlement Areas." Edwards suggested that if the international community insisted on donating to refugee settlements, the funds should be used to benefit "local settlers" as well.

95 "Financial Request from G. P. Allsebrook," February 29, 1964, Film Projects . . . 1964, Tanzania, Director, General by Countries, W.S., I.2, LWF.

96 For example, "Mr. Julius Paul's Letter of 11 November 1963."

97 C. J. H. Rogers, Acting Officer, Land Planning, to Director, Development Division, Ministry of Agriculture, "Resettlement Rulenge—Final Report and Summary," August 26. 1965, T/LAN/ST/NU, box 62, 532, 19, TNA-Mwanza.

238 · Notes to Chapter 4

98 G. B. R. Nyombi, Field Officer, Agriculture, "Report on Refugee Settlement Scheme," March 25, 1963, T/LAN/ST/NU, box 62, 532, 19, TNA-Mwanza.

99 According to Gasarasi, the withdrawal of food rations and other relief services led to "fake compliance" by the refugees, who would plant dead tree trunks or cut off the roots of seedlings. Gasarasi, "Mass Naturalization," 91.

100 Tanganyika Police Message from CampCom, July 12, 1962, WL.R4/16E, 71, TNA. Both archival and oral sources contain accusations of refugee thievery and violence.

101 "Refugees 1959–1960," November 30, 1961, 58, A/4994, fonds 1, series 2, UNHCR.

102 This paragraph is based primarily on an interview with Charles Gasarasi, a former Rwandan refugee in Muyenzi settlement, and the letters and articles written by Rachel Yeld (later Rachel Van der Meeren), an Oxfam employee who worked with Rwandan refugees in Ngara and Karagwe districts (1961–1964).

103 Gasarasi, "Mass Naturalization," 95.

104 Van der Meeren, "Three Decades," 257. There were also interpersonal rivalries over positions of power within the refugee community. Leadership positions entailed the potential for both material gain, with greater access to rations and decision making, and political power in the eventuality of military or political success against the Rwandan regime. Gasarasi, "Mass Naturalization," 90. See also the petition to the TC, signed by Rwandan pro-monarchists in Kenya, Uganda, Tanganyika, Burundi, and Rwanda. "Petition from the Abanyarwand M'Abarundi Abadahemuka," October 23, 1961, T/PET.3/L.33, fonds 1, series 1, UNHCR.

105 Van der Meeren, "Three Decades," 259.

106 Daley, "From the Kipande," 23.

107 Interview with Charles Gasarasi, Butare, July 3, 2012.

108 Gasarasi alleges intimidation and threats in this process. Interview with Charles Gasarasi.

109 Gasarasi, "Mass Naturalization," 90.

110 For example, although the government spent substantial money ($12,600) to provide the refugees with tools and seeds in 1961, they arrived too late for the planting season. "Africa Survey," sent by Eugene Ries to Bruno Muetzelfeldt, August 15, 1962, Africa General, May 1–Dec. 31 1962, W.S., I.2, LWF. The government nevertheless blamed the lack of self-sufficiency on the refugees.

111 In 1962 the UNHCR estimated there were thirty-five thousand Rwandan refugees in Tanganyika. Long, "Rwanda's First Refugees," 217.

112 Thus, as Long shows for Uganda, in Tanzania the British likely "above all feared" that a mass refugee influx would "disrupt stability." Long, "Rwanda's First Refugees," 215.

113 On Rwandan refugees' links to "communist China," see Loescher, The UNHCR and World Politics, 127.

114 Sheehan, "Problem of Sovereignty," 3.

5. CITIZENS AND REFUGEES

1 Rachel Yeld to Mr. Kirkley, Administrative Secretary (WLR), April 26, 1963, Joint Service Program, Tanzania 1963, Director, General by Countries, W.S., I.2, LWF.

2 The new country of Tanganyika became Tanzania following the 1964 merger with Zanzibar. For simplicity, I use *Tanzania* throughout this chapter.

3 Although many people said their lives did not materially change after independence, they applauded the demise of chieftainships, which were often seen as unequal and exploitative institutions. Interview with Peter Kato, Keza, June 17, 2012. Others posited that with the end of chiefly power, social equality between Hutu and Tutsi became more of a reality. Interview with Bernard Simi, Nyakahira, July 25, 2012. Nevertheless, almost all those interviewed posited that Bugufi chief Balamba II and Busubi chief Nsoro were "good chiefs."

4 The incomplete nature of nation-state formation in Tanzania is exemplified by the fact that unification with Zanzibar did not occur until 1964. In many ways, the process of nation-state formation remains unfinished, as recent antigovernment protests in Zanzibar make clear. For continuities in the late colonial and early postcolonial administrations, see Burton and Jennings, "Introduction." On shifting Tanzanian nationalist discourses in the early independence period, see Brennan, "Blood Enemies."

5 Such slogans as *uhuru na kazi* (freedom and work) would have been repeated at local meetings—their meanings translated into local languages.

6 The situation in Ngara during the 1960s affirms that Tanzania, as a nation, "was a symbolic construct, dependent less on policies than on the constant communication and popular acceptance" of the discursive ideology of central actors. Bjerk, *Building a Peaceful Nation*, 204.

7 Telegram from Police Ngara, Agric. Ngara to Provcom Bka. for Regional Agricultural Officer, n.d., T/LAN/ST/NU, box 62, 532, 19, TNA-Mwanza.

8 "Safari Report from Gabriel Kiami, Tech. Asst. Gd. IV," n.d., G/35, 290, TNA.

9 On use of the term *troublemakers*, see Agriculture, W.D. and I.D., Bukoba, to Agriculture, Dar es Salaam, June 5, 1963, G/35, 290, TNA.

10 On the critical food situation in Muyenzi in January 1962, see A.D.S. Head, Biharamulo, to Provincer, Bukoba, January 7, 1962, A.4/2, v. I, 529, TNA. On inadequate clothing, see A. W. Mtawali to Camp Commandant, Muyenzi, August 13, 1962, WL.R4/16E, 71, TNA.

11 Telegram from Provincial Commissioner, WLP, to Admin., Biharamulo, January 10, 1962, A.4/2, v. I, 529, TNA.

12 In January 1963, for example, 155 families who refused to move to Kanyinya were deprived of rations. Campcom to Police, Biharamulo, January 31, 1963, A.4/2, v. I, 529, TNA. *Mwami* Kigeri V himself toured the area and expressed his disapproval of the proposed settlement sites. Others objected to the lack of consultation with the refugees over their dispersal. Van der Meeren, "Three Decades," 260–61.

13 R. J. Grant, Settlement Officer, O.I/C Refugees, to Administrative Secretary, Office of the Regional Commissioner, Bukoba, September 4, 1962, WL.R4/16E, 71, TNA.

240 · Notes to Chapter 5

14 "Minutes of a Meeting of the District Development Committee Held at Ngara on 27/6/62 . . . ," 3, P4/1, V, box 21, 23, TNA-Mwanza.

15 Rachel Yeld to Mr. Kirkley, April 26, 1963.

16 The administrative secretary, Mr. Allsbrook, took issue with this version of events, declaring that Yeld was "too emotional" and too critical of the Tanganyikan government. According to Bishop Sundkler, Yeld had "complained to authorities in Usumbura, and this seems to have caused quite some embarrassment to the Tanganyika government." Bishop Sundkler to Bruno Muetzelfeldt, June 30, 1963, Tanganyika 1963, Director, General by Countries, W.S., I.2, LWF.

17 G. B. R. Nyombi, Field Officer, Agriculture, "Fortnightly Report on Refugee Settlement Scheme," n.d., T/LAN/ST/NU, box 62, 532, 19, TNA-Mwanza.

18 G. Nyombi (F.O. Muyenzi Camp), to Regional Agricultural Officer, WLR, "Fortnightly Report," May 7, 1963, T/LAN/ST/NU, box 62, 532, 19, TNA-Mwanza.

19 Field Officer, Muyenzi, to Regional Agricultural Officer, WLR, "Monthly Report on Refugees Settlement Scheme—Muyenzi," July 1, 1963, T/LAN/ST/NU, box 62, 532, 19, TNA-Mwanza.

20 G. Nyombi, "Fortnightly Report on Refugees Settlement Scheme," May 21, 1963, T/LAN/ST/NU, box 62, 532, 19, TNA-Mwanza.

21 Nyombi to Regional Agricultural Officer, WLR, "Fortnightly Report," May 7, 1963.

22 By the time of Tanganyika's official request for the "general administration of Rwanda refugees in Tanganyika," the UNHCR had already contributed $86,500 for seeds, tools, transport, and other basic requirements. The UNHCR's initial contribution to the first tripartite agreement was $140,000, with the LRCS supplying $28,800 for administrative expenses. Warren A. Pinegar, Director Deputy, UNHCR, to Henrik Beer, Secretary General, League of Red Cross Societies, November 8, 1963, Congo Divers, Office due Haut Commissaire pour les Réfugiés, 22/1/2, box 3, A1022, IFRC.

23 The US surplus food program supplied most of the donated food for refugees in Ngara. However, as the director of the Catholic Relief Service (CRS) pointed out, "it would be cheaper to buy local foods" in Tanzania than to transport donated food inland from Dar es Salaam. Quoted in Brian W. Neldner and Joseph Thompson, "Tanganyika Refugee Survey," September 1963, 3, Reports, Tanzania 1964, Director, General by Countries, W.S., I.2, LWF.

24 Ernst Rohner, League Delegate, "Refugees from Rwanda in Tanganyika: Report on Survey Mission to West Lake Province and Dar es Salaam, 11–25 June 1963," 2, Congo Délégués Eâ2, 22/1/2, box 3, A1022, IFRC.

25 This was further described as a "climate of distrust and reciprocal discontent." Eric Fischer, Permanent Delegate of the Office of Emergencies, "Reinstallation of Tutsi Refugees in Tanganyika Muenzi [sic] Center; Mission Report, January/July 1964," 2, trans. Lauren Kretz, Refugees Africa, box 19737, IFRC.

26 The LRCS aided the initial reception camps in Tanzania in 1962. The British Red Cross also sent two medical officers, Dr. Jean Gemmel and Dr. Freda Bonner, to work in the camps for eight months each.

Notes to Chapter 5 · 241

27 "3rd Session of the Disaster Relief Advisory Committee, Resettlement of Refugees: Defining a New League Policy," Geneva, September 17–19, 1964, Congo Circulaires & Communiqués, Rapports, 22/1/2, box 3, A1022, IFRC.

28 The report's comments refer to Muyenzi specifically, as well as to all LRCS projects for Rwandan refugees.

29 "3rd Session of the Disaster Relief Advisory Committee."

30 Such qualities included "practical experience and preferably previous knowledge of the country, ethnic considerations and customs." "3rd Session of the Disaster Relief Advisory Committee." Conversely, today's refugee "expert" is generally perceived as someone with the technical prowess to replicate aid inputs, regardless of local context—thus not the kind of personnel called for here. The LRCS's evaluation of work at Muyenzi differs markedly from other archival sources. For example, prior to the LRCS's departure in 1964, "satisfactory progress" had taken place in refugee settlement. Additionally, a 1964 LRCS report noted that "considerable progress towards self-reliance" had occurred and "by the beginning of July 1964 agriculture had been placed on a sound basis." The emphasis in these reports is on the work of the league's delegate, Mr. Fischer, who is personally credited with the success achieved in Muyenzi. "Muyenzi—A Stride Towards Success," n.d., Tanzania, Reports, box 16529, IFRC.

31 Henrik Beer, Secrétaire Général, to P. Stanissis, Délégué en chef de la Ligue des Sociétés de la Croix-Rouge, February 13, 1964, Congo-délégués . . . 1965/1964, 22/1/2, A1023, IFRC; Fischer, "Reinstallation of Tutsi Refugees," 2.

32 The report also claims that politicians in Ngara were particularly troubled by the Tutsi "intelligence and ambition [which] are feared and fearsome." Fischer, "Reinstallation of Tutsi Refugees," 2. Although this report claims the businessmen were Basubi, secondary literature indicates that the Basubi welcomed Rwandan Tutsi. Daley, "From the Kipande," 22.

33 Fischer, "Reinstallation of Tutsi Refugees," 2.

34 This occurred despite the central government's apparent resolve to permanently settle the refugees. It is possible that confusion over lines of command allowed local officials the leeway to make their own policy (in 1963 there were three separate ministers in the Tanganyikan government tasked with refugee responsibility). For the alleged "serious difficulties" caused by dividing families and "people who were naturally inclined to work together" into various settlements, see "Annex 1," 6, Refugees from Rwanda 1963, Refugees Africa, box 19737, IFRC.

35 Officer in Charge, Agricultural Office, Ngara, to Regional Agricultural Officer, WLR, "Monthly Report on Rwandan Refugees Resettlement Scheme—September 1963," September 27, 1963, T/LAN/ST/NU, box 62, 532, 19, TNA-Mwanza.

36 "Annex 1," 6.

37 Officer in Charge, Agricultural Office, Ngara, to Regional Agricultural Officer, WLR, "Monthly Report on Rwandan Refugees Resettlement Scheme—September 1963." Emphasis in original.

38 Letter to Regional Agricultural Officer, WLR, "Monthly Report on Rwandan Refugees Resettlement Scheme, October 1963," October 28, 1963, T/LAN/ST/NU, box 62, 532, 19, TNA-Mwanza.

39 R. K. Makao, Administrative Secretary, WLR, to Permanent Secretary, V.P. Office, Dar es Salaam, "Refugees Ngara," January 17, 1964, T/LAN/ST/NU, box 62, 532, 19, TNA-Mwanza.

40 Officer in Charge, Agricultural Office, Ngara, to Regional Agricultural Officer, WLR, November 29, 1963, T/LAN/ST/NU, box 62, 532, 19, TNA-Mwanza.

41 J. M. Ainley to Regional Water Engineer, "Refugee Water Supplies Ngara District," August 19, 1964, T/LAN/ST/NU, box, 62, 532, 19, TNA-Mwanza. See, for example, the November 1963 report alleging that, against the agriculture officer's advice, refugees were moved to Mbuba IV and Kumunazi I, which could not absorb the additional population. Officer in Charge, Agricultural Office, Ngara, to Regional Agricultural Officer, WLR, "Monthly Report on Rwandan Refugees Resettlement Scheme—November 1963," November 29, 1963, T/LAN/ST/NU, box, 62, 532, 19, TNA-Mwanza.

42 Officer in Charge, Agricultural Office, Ngara, to Regional Agricultural Officer, WLR, "Monthly Report on Rwandan Refugees Resettlement Scheme—September 1963."

43 Officer in Charge, Agricultural Office, Ngara, to Regional Agricultural Officer, WLR, "Monthly Report on Rwandan Refugees Resettlement Scheme December 1963," December 30, 1963, T/LAN/ST/NU, box, 62, 532, 19, TNA-Mwanza.

44 Director, Agricultural Extension Division, Ministry of Agriculture, Dar es Salaam, to Regional Agricultural Officer, WLR, September 30, 1963, T/LAN/ST/NU, box 62, 532, 19, TNA-Mwanza.

45 Knud Dahl, R.C. Delegate, to Jim Ainley, December 22, 1963, T/LAN/ST/NU, box, 62, 532, 19, TNA-Mwanza.

46 Officer in Charge, Agricultural Office, Ngara, to Regional Agricultural Officer, WLR, "Monthly Report on Rwandan Refugees Settlement Scheme—January 1964," January 30, 1964, T/LAN/ST/NU, box 62, 532, 19, TNA-Mwanza. By January 1964, the only settlements with cultivated land, producing 2.5 bags of beans harvested per family, were Kanyinya IIA and Kanyinya IIB. In other settlements, the refugees claimed the soil was "too hard to til." Officer in Charge, Agricultural Office, Ngara, to Regional Agricultural Officer, WLR, "Monthly Report on Rwandan Refugees Settlement Scheme—January 1964."

47 Officer in Charge, Agricultural Office, Ngara, to Regional Agricultural Officer, WLR, "Monthly Report on Rwandan Refugees Resettlement Scheme, December 1963."

48 J. M. Ainley, Regional Agricultural Officer, WLR, to Director, Agricultural Extension Division, Dar es Salaam, "Rwanda Refugees—Ngara District, Dated 30th September 1963," October 9, 1963, T/LAN/ST/NU, box 62, 532, 19, TNA-Mwanza.

49 Violence against Tutsi in Rwanda actually increased during this time. For example, a handwritten note at the end of a December 1963 report noted, "Around

140 people are reported shot dead by the Rwandan Govt. at Rusumo-border with Tanganyika." Officer in Charge, Agricultural Office, Ngara, to Regional Agricultural Officer, WLR, "Monthly Report on Rwandan Refugees Resettlement Scheme, December 1963."

50 Regional Agricultural Officer, WLR, to Administrative Secretary, WLR, "Refugees, Ngara District," July 4, 1964, T/LAN/ST/NU, box 62, 532, 19, TNA-Mwanza. Additional factors included poor rainfall.

51 Bruno Muetzelfeldt to Dr. F. J. Homann-Herimberg, UNHCR, December 18, 1963, Program Proposals, Tanzania 1963, Director, Correspondence by Countries, W.S., I.2, LWF.

52 The TCRS was operated by WS-LWF "in Consultation with the Christian Council of Tanganyika [CCT] and on behalf of the World Council of Churches [WCC]." Bruno Muetzelfeldt to Richard Mutembei, ELCT-Northwest Diocese, December 18, 1963, General Correspondence and Program Proposals, Tanzania 1963, Director, General Correspondence, W.S., I.2, LWF.

53 Specifically, Sundkler noted that "the Roman Catholics have insisted on dominating the scene" of refugee assistance in WLR. Rev. Bengt Sundkler, Bishop in Bukoba, to Dr. Bruno Muetzelfeldt, June 13, 1963, Joint Service Programme . . . , Tanzania 1964, Director, General by Countries, W.S., I.2, LWF.

54 "Africa Survey," 7, sent by Eugene Ries to Bruno Muetzelfeldt, August 15, 1962, Africa-General 1955–1969, Director, General by Countries, W.S., I.2, LWF.

55 Sundkler to Muetzelfeldt, June 13, 1963.

56 "Lutheran World Federation, Tanganyika Christian Refugee Service, June/August, Fiscal Year 1964," 3, Reports, Tanzania 1964, Director, General by Countries, W.S., I.2, LWF. See also George Farquharson to Bruno Muetzelfeldt, "Re: Monthly Activity Reports," September 8, 1964, Reports, Tanzania 1964, Director, General by Countries, W.S., I.2, LWF.

57 While the LWF encompassed Lutheran churches and officials worldwide, many donor churches and personnel came from Scandinavian countries. On links between Scandinavian countries and development programs and support for Nyerere's government during the socialist period, see Jennings, *Surrogates of the State*.

58 It is unclear why zonal development programs, set up by the UNHCR in Congo and Burundi for Rwandan refugees and hosts, were not created in Tanzania.

59 Bernie Confer to Bruno Muetzelfeldt, July 23, 1964, CCT . . . , Tanzania 1964, Director, General by Countries, W.S., I.2, LWF. Tensions also existed among the TCRS, the CCT, and the Catholic Church, all of which jockeyed for primacy in the refugee camps, particularly around education and school building.

60 George Farquharson, the TCRS director in Dar es Salaam, noted that local people made "similar journeys" due to a "general shortage of food in the district." The refugees reportedly traveled to Burundi, Karagwe, and Uganda. George Farquharson to Bruno Muetzelfeldt, November 23, 1964, Muyenzi Settlement, Tanzania 1964, Director, General by Countries, W.S., I.2, LWF.

61 G. de Bosch Kemper, Chargé de Mission, Dar es Salaam, to J. Cuenod, Regional Representative, Bujumbura, "Situation at Muyenzi," December 19, 1964, 15/TAN/RWA, box 260, fonds 11, series 1, UNHCR.

62 De Bosch Kemper, "Situation at Muyenzi," December 19, 1964. This is an early example of aid workers' fears of "dependency syndrome."

63 Regarding increasing aid, the UNHCR did not want the refugees to feel that they would automatically get "pennies from heaven." O. R. Nottidge to T. Jamieson, Director of Operations, UNHCR, "Assistance in Muyenzi," January 4, 1964, 15/TAN/RWA, box 260, fonds 11, series 1, UNHCR; interview with David Zarembka, Skype, November 2, 2012.

64 I. E. Laiser, TCRS Field Officer, Muyenzi, to Programme Director, TCRS, "Monthly Report—October, 1965," October 31, 1965, Muyenzi (New Ambulance) . . . , Tanzania 1965, Director, General by Countries, W.S., I.2, LWF.

65 Report from Representative for Tanzania, UNHCR, to Mr. O. Gobius, UNHCR Headquarters, Geneva, "Muyenzi Settlement," September 24, 1965, 15/TAN/RWA, box 260, fonds 11, series 1, UNHCR.

66 Laiser noted that the refugees' increased productivity was due to his strategy of having the refugee leaders plant model *shamba*. Interview with Isaac Laiser, Arusha, March 16, 2012.

67 Report from Representative for Tanzania, UNHCR, to Mr. O. Gobius, UNHCR Headquarters, Geneva, "Muyenzi Settlement," September 24, 1965. Fifteen refugee men also formed a small cooperative for marketing vegetable products in Bukoba. David Johnson to Eugene Ries, Secretary for Relief and Resettlement, LWF, October 27, 1965, Muyenzi (New Ambulance) . . . , Tanzania 1965, Director, General by Countries, W.S., I.2, LWF.

68 Johnson to Ries, October 27, 1965.

69 Gilbert Jaeger to Representative, UNHCR Branch Office in Dar es Salaam, "Muyenzi and Mwesi," September 22, 1965, 15/TAN/RWA, box 260, fonds 11, series 1, UNHCR.

70 Kohaut, Dar es Salaam, to Hicomref Geneva, July 1, 1966, 15/TAN/RWA, box 260, fonds 11, series 1, UNHCR.

71 Report by I. E. Laiser, Officer I/C, Muyenzi Settlement, to Regional Commissioner, West Lake Region, January 9, 1966, T/LAN/ST/NU, 532, box 62, 19, TNA-Mwanza.

72 Brian Neldner, Director TCRS, to Bruno Muetzelfeldt, January 27, 1965, Muyenzi (New Ambulance) . . . , Tanzania 1965, Director, General by Countries, W.S., I.2, LWF.

73 Neldner to Muetzelfeldt, January 27, 1965.

74 Neldner to Muetzelfeldt, January 27, 1965. Laiser denied fearing for his safety while at Muyenzi. Interview with Isaac Laiser.

75 Cable from Hordijk, Bujumbura, to Hicomref, Geneva, June 27, 1966, 15/TAN/RWA, box 260, fonds 11, series 1, UNHCR.

76 Cable from Hordijk, Bujumbura to Hicomref, Geneva, June 27, 1966.

77 These arrests were made under the 1965 Refugee (Control) Act (see chapter 6). Representative for Tanzania to UNHCR Headquarters, Geneva, "Muyenzi-Detained Refugees," November 16, 1967, file 2, part I, 6/1/TAN, fonds 11, series 1, UNHCR.

Notes to Chapter 5 · 245

78 "TCRS Report, July–December 1967," 10, Tanzania 1967, vol. I, Director, General by Country, W.S., I.2, LWF.

79 H. F. Miller, Secretary for Relief and Service, to Kodwo E. Ankrah, Refugee Secretary, AACC, Nairobi, "Re: Report on Pastoral Care for Refugees," May 2, 1967, Tanzania 1967, vol. I, Director, General by Country, W.S., I.2, LWF.

80 Many Ngarans noted that *wakimbizi*, by definition, live in camps and receive aid from *wazungu*. For example, interview with Celestine Kaheri, Kanyinya, June 28, 2012.

81 Adams, "Safari Report on Surveys in Ngara District September 16 to 21," G/35/67, TNA; interview with Claudian Kabogie, Muyenzi, July 11, 2012.

82 So much so that "only just over 50%" of taxes had been collected and "it was doubtful" if the district would have a "working balance for 1964." "Minutes of the West Lake Regional Development Committee," December 30, 1963, 4, FA/D.10/6, 600, TNA.

83 Interview with David Natori, Rulenge, July 27, 2012; interview with David Zarembka.

84 "Note for the File, Tanzania," February 3, 1965, 15-TAN.RWA, box 260, fonds 11, series 1, UNHCR.

85 For Tanzanian nationalist ideologies that vilified lazy and later foreign "parasites," as well as violations of "the national work ethic" as a "form of exploitation," see Brennan, "Blood Enemies," 403. On the various meanings of self-reliance in Tanzania, see Lal, "Self-Reliance."

86 Gasarasi noted that this word was used mainly by settlement commandants and government personnel. Interview with Charles Gasarasi, Butare, July 3, 2012.

87 This section is based on interviews conducted in Ngara, and particularly in Busubi, during 2012.

88 Van der Meeren, "Three Decades," 256.

89 Tanzania's "open door" refugee policy at this time was particularly oriented to those refugees who were deemed "freedom fighters"—that is, groups and individuals who fled and fought in wars of decolonization against white minority rule. The Tanzanian government understood these refugees to be African "liberators" and therefore ideologically essential to notions of Pan-Africanism. The different policies applied to freedom fighters from southern Africa versus Rwandan refugees rankled many of the latter, who viewed themselves as freedom fighters. Interview with Charles Gasarasi; Representative for Tanzania, to Mr. O. R. Nottidge, UNHCR legal division, Geneva, "Tanzania Refusal of Return Visas," August 16, 1965, 6/1/TAN, folder I, box 167, fonds 11, series 1, UNHCR.

90 For example, interview with A. Nzuri, Rulenge, June 25, 2012.

91 For example, interview with Augustine Urias, Ngara, May 25, 2012.

92 Interview David Natori.

93 G. de Bosch Kemper, UNHCR Chargé de Mission, Dar es Salaam, to UNHCR Regional Representative, Bujumbura, "Conditions at Muyenzi," December 15, 1964, 15/TAN/RWA, 260, fonds 11, series 1, UNHCR.

94 "Everyone is anxious to be assured that the lessons learned in Muyenzi will not be wasted." Letter from George Farquharson, August 25, 1964, Tanzania 1964,

246 · Notes to Chapter 5

Personnel, Director, General by Countries, W.S., I.2, LWF. Perhaps because of this tension with the government, in 1967 the TCRS made a donation to a development scheme in Second Vice President Wambura's home district. Bruno Muetzelfeldt to R. S. Wambura, M.P., 2nd Vice-President's Office, March 16, 1967, Tanzania 1967, vol. I, Director, General by Countries, W.S., I.2, LWF.

95 Letter from Bruno Muetzelfeldt, April 2, 1964, Mwesi Highland . . . Budget 1964, Tanzania 1964, Director, General by Countries, W.S., I.2, LWF.

96 On "thick" versus "thin" citizenship and "processes of 'thickening' or 'thinning'" in which citizens are continually engaged, see Cooper, "Postscript," 291.

97 Nugent and Asiwaju, "Introduction," 11.

6. CONFLICTING SOVEREIGNTIES

1 Cable from Dar es Salaam to Legal Division, Geneva, May 9, 1970, 6/1/TAN, File V, folder IV, box 167, fonds 11, series 1, UNHCR.

2 The area of the Mwesi Highlands Rwandan Refugee camp is known today as Mwese.

3 Chaulia, "Politics of Refugee Hosting," 159.

4 Malkki refers to this as "national cosmology." Malkki, *Purity and Exile.*

5 Indeed, Rwandan refugees' evolving ambitions to form a Rwandan nation-state in accordance with their notions of the appropriate political structure of postcolonial Rwanda led to the 1990 invasion by the Rwandan Patriotic Front (RPF) and subsequent civil war.

6 Bogaerts and Raben, *Decolonization of African,* 3.

7 Refugee camps and settlements thus use social technology such as "rules, techniques and physical structures and arrangements . . . [to] . . . curb the potential threat posed by refugees to the order created around the nation state." Jaji, "Social Technology," 222–23. Harrell-Bond notes that while empowerment is part "of the *doxa* of 'humanitarian speak,'" the reality of aid as a technology of control undermines the legitimacy of refugee aid. Harrell-Bond, "Can Humanitarian Work," 55n22.

8 Legislation that increased the power of the central state during this time included abolishment of the native authorities system (1963), Preventative Detention Act (1963), creation of the one-party state (1967), and Ward Development Committees Act (1969), which granted local officials power to compel citizens to work on development schemes. Jennings, "'Very Real War,'" 91; Ghai, "Notes towards a Theory," 69.

9 During the late 1960s the state became more nonaligned in terms of Cold War politics. In Nyerere's "Principles and Development" memo (June 1966), he noted that offers of foreign aid would be carefully considered to ensure "that they would really contribute to the kind of society Tanzania was attempting to build." Picciotto, "Tanzania's Foreign Policy," 99.

10 According to Jennings, the "rise of statism throughout the 1960s, culminating in its fully fledged appearance by 1969, was a response to this need to establish full

Notes to Chapter 6 · 247

control over development planning and implementation. . . . By the early 1970s, authoritarianism had emerged as the answer." Jennings, *Surrogates of the State*, 33.

11 Hilhorst and Jansen, "Humanitarian Space," 1137.

12 The UNHCR policy was to offer the "vital minimum" to meet refugees' "basic vital needs"—a concept that was ill defined. Memorandum from V. A. Temnomeroff to UNHCR, "Interagency Cooperation," March 20, 1963, 15/SA, box 259, fonds 11, series 1, UNHCR.

13 This statement is based largely on the archival evidence surrounding this refugee group, which is limited to refugee leaders.

14 The reasons for this refusal remain unclear. Both UNHCR and LWF officials blamed the refugees' intransigence on the "Red Chinese influence," although it seems more likely that the ability to move relatively unencumbered in Burundi, as opposed to the more restrictive environment in Tanzania, had a decisive influence. Muetzelfeldt to Empie, September 11, 1964, Mwesi Highland Settlements, Tanzania 1964, Director, General by Countries, W.S., I.2, LWF. Refugee leaders were also concerned about the group's dispersal, and subsequent weakening, in several countries and settlements. "Interview with Dr. Medard Gahiga," October 1, 1964, 15/GEN/RWA, box 252, fonds 11, series 1, UNHCR.

15 Bruno Muetzelfeldt to Brian Neldner, September 9, 1964, Mwesi Highland Settlements, Tanzania 1964, Director, General by Countries, W.S., I.2, LWF.

16 Farquharson noted that these were the first words Jamieson said to him upon their introduction at a reception in Dar es Salaam. George Farquharson to Bruno Muetzelfeldt, March 29, 1964, Program Director, Personnel, Christian Council . . . 1964; Mwesi Highland Settlements . . . 1964, Tanzania 1964, Director, General by Countries, W.S., 1.2, LWF.

17 Accordingly, the UNHCR acted if the situation were of a magnitude or character that justified special action by the international community. "Attitude of the High Commissioner's Office in New Refugee Situations," March 29, 1963, 15/SA, box 259, fonds 11, series 1, UNHCR.

18 Office of UNHCR, Geneva, "Kivu Tanganyika Airlift of Rwandese Refugees under Way," November 5, 1964, Mwesi Highland Settlements. . . . 1964, Tanzania 1964, Director, General by Countries, W.S., I.2, LWF.

19 Bernie Confer to Bruno Muetzelfeldt, July 28, 1964, Mwesi Highland Settlements . . . 1964, Tanzania 1964, Director, General by Countries, W.S., I.2, LWF.

20 Felix Schnyder to Bruno Muetzelfeldt, September 22, 1964, 15/GEN/RWA, box 252, fonds 11, series 1, UNHCR.

21 "Watusi Tribe Will Dance Again," *Viewpoint*, August 16, 1964; "Watusis Moved to Tanganyika," *Discover*, August 30, 1964, *Discover*, Reports, Tanzania 1964, Director, General by Countries, W.S., I.2, LWF.

22 "Progress Report—Mwesi Highland Settlement: For the Period up to and Including 31 July 1964," appendix A, 16, Reports, Tanzania 1964, Director, General by Countries, W.S., I.2, LWF.

23 Schnyder to Muetzelfeldt, September 22, 1964. Administrators also surmised that rumors of malnutrition at Muyenzi may have impacted the decision. George Farquharson to Bruno Muetzelfeldt, September 20, 1964, General Program

Director, . . . Muyenzi Settlements 1964, Tanzania 1964, Director, General by Countries, W.S., I.2, LWF.

24 Bruno Muetzelfeldt to Mr. B. Confer, Secretary Deputy, Lutheran World Service, "Re: Tanganyika," September 11, 1964, Mwesi Highland Settlements . . . , 1964, Tanzania 1964, Director, General by Countries, W.S., I.2, LWF.

25 Muetzelfeldt to Confer, "Re: Tanganyika."

26 The Kikuyu were themselves refugees, fleeing from British Kenya during the Mau emergency of the 1950s. Many Kikuyu were moved from their original settlement at Katuma, which was in a lowland malaria zone, to Mwesi, in anticipation of the refugee settlement. Interview with Brian Neldner, Skype, November 10, 2013. See Moskowitz, "Sons and Daughters of the Soil."

27 "Mwesi Highland Settlement, 2nd Report," August 25, 1964, Reports, Tanzania 1964, Director, General by Countries, W.S., 1.2, LWF.

28 Philip A. Johnson, Executive Secretary, Division of Public Relations, National Lutheran Council, to Bruno Muetzelfeldt, July 14, 1964, Film Projects . . . 1964, Tanzania 1964, Director, General by Countries, W.S., 1.2, LWF. Muetzelfeldt was also concerned that a potential film made by the Catholic World Service would mislead audiences regarding the true operational agency. Bruno Muetzelfeldt to George Farquharson, March 4, 1964, Film Projects . . . 1964, Tanzania 1964, Director, General by Countries, Tanzania, W.S., 1.2, LWF.

29 "Proceedings of the Brief Discussion Held on 25th September, 1964, between Hon. Sijaona, Minister of State (V.P.), and Mr. Jaeger of U.N.H.C.R.," Mwesi Highland . . . , 1964, Tanzania 1964, Director, General by Countries, W.S, 1.2, LWF.

30 Rwandan refugees in Leopoldville (not Kivu) requested UNHCR intercession following Decision No. 1650 of August 18, 1964, which stated that Rwandan refugees and other foreigners had to be evacuated to Bamu island, and the subsequent Radio Leopoldville broadcast on August 25 or 26 that all Rwandans had to report to the Rwandan embassy on September 1, 1964, for registration. J. Cuenod to High Commissioner, "Situation of Rwandese Refugees in Leopoldville," September 26, 1964, 15/GEN/RWA, box 252, fonds 11, series 1, UNHCR.

31 Bruno Muetzelfeldt to G. Farquharson, "Re: Mwesi and New Refugee Situation," September 9, 1964, Mwesi Highland Settlements . . . , 1964, Tanzania 1964, Director, General by Countries, W.S., I.2, LWF.

32 Office of UNHCR, "Kivu Tanganyika Airlift of Rwandese Refugees under Way."

33 All people who spoke Kinyarwanda and were perceived to be of Rwandan ancestry (whether refugees of the Rwandan nation-state or not) were both actors in and victims of the rebellions and violence in eastern Congo in the 1960s and later.

34 It is telling that in August 1967, when "the situation in Kivu seems to be disastrous," no plans for evacuation were developed. "Meeting with Dr. Vojislav Jerkovic, Resident Representative of UNDP in Kigali, Rwanda, on 15 August 1967," August 21, 1967, 21/GEN/RWA, box 322, fonds 11, series 1, UNHCR.

35 Felix Schnyder, High Commissioner for Refugees, to David Morse, Director General, International Labour Office, March 28, 1963, 15/SA, box 259, fonds 11, series 1, UNHCR.

36 Pierre Coat, Goma, to High Commissioner, "Bibwe," December 22, 1964, 15/KIVU/RWA, [1], box 258, fonds 11, series 1, UNHCR.

37 Office of UNHCR, "Kivu Tanganyika Airlift of Rwandese Refugees under Way."

38 Bruno Muetzelfeldt to Paul Empie, National Lutheran Council, "Re: Tanganyika Airlift," November 13, 1964, Mwesi Highland Settlement . . . , 1964, Tanzania 1964, Director, General by Countries, W.S., I.2, LWF.

39 George Farquharson to Bruno Muetzelfeldt, July 20, 1964, Tanzania, Personnel 1964, Director, General by Countries, W.S., 1.2, LWF. Tellingly, Farquharson noted that while using Mwesi to resettle Tanzanians would increase local living standards and develop the highlands, "it might not be so acceptable to those who have committed resources to the scheme, but surely we would be able to present them with proposals which would not cause them to withdraw their commitments entirely." Farquharson to Muetzelfeldt, September 9, 1964. The circumstances around Farquharson's request to leave the TCRS are ambiguous and seemingly involved "medical problems," although his close relationship with the Tanzanian government may have been a factor.

40 Muetzelfeldt agreed that if the original Rwandan refugees did not move to Mwesi, the settlement should be used for Tanganyikan development. Bruno Muetzelfeldt to Bernie Confer, June 23, 1964, Mwesi Highland Settlements . . . , Tanzania 1964, Director, General by Countries, W.S., 1.2, LWF.

41 Prince Sadruddin Aga Khan (Deputy High Commissioner) to Hon. R. M. Kawawa, February 13, 1965, Mwesi Highland, Airlift . . . Congolese Francs, Tanzania 1964, Director, General by Countries, W.S., I.2., LWF.

42 "Notes on the Discussion Concerning the Mwesi Settlement Held the Afternoon of 12th October . . . ," 3, Film and Water . . . , Reports, Tanzania 1964, Director, General by Countries, W.S., 1.2., LWF.

43 Jorgen Norredam to Bruno Muetzelfeldt, November 12, 1964, General . . . 1964, Tanzania 1964, Director, General by Countries, W.S., I.2, LWF.

44 The assumption that wealthier-looking refugees would have connections to such groups and that criminals and missionaries would be related bears thought. Coming from Rwanda, these refugees probably would have been Catholic. The area commissioner in Mpanda later alleged that a local Catholic priest had dispensed medicines and sweets "in such a manner that some refugees complained that the Catholics were a privileged class." Brian Neldner to Rev. B. Muetzelfeldt, December 21, 1964, Mwesi Highland Settlements . . . , 1964, Tanzania 1964, Director, General by Countries, W.S., I.2, LWF.

45 R. C. Kohaut, UNHCR Tabora, to UNHCR Representative for Tanzania, "Airlift Operation Statistical Data," May 31, 1965, Mwesi Highland, Airlift . . . Congolese Francs 1965, Tanzania 1965, Director, General by Countries, W.S., I.2, LWF.

46 Indeed, in June 1965 a UNHCR representative reported that the Kivu situation "can be considered as being under control." Gilbert Jaeger to Dr. E. Schlatter, UNHCR Representative, Leopoldville, June 17, 1965, 15/KIVU/RWA [2], box 258, fonds 11, series 1, UNHCR. Ironically, refugees who remained in Kivu, many of

250 · Notes to Chapter 6

whom were indistinguishable from older migrants, continue to live in a precarious and violent environment.

47 Norredam seemed unconcerned by many of these issues, flying to Nairobi to buy furniture for the house he was building, at some expense, for his family. Norredam became central to much of the tension at Mwesi, even within his own organization. By the end of 1964, the situation had reached a breaking point, with the WS-LWF director refusing to communicate directly with his own program officer. Unable to fire Norredam due to his Danish nationality and the donations of Danish charities, Muetzelfeldt inquired whether the Tanzanian government would be willing to request his removal. A few months later, Norredam died in a plane accident. However, the high rate of turnover in TCRS directors for Mwesi—three in as many years—continued to hinder the operation.

48 David Johnson to Bruno Muetzelfeldt, November 11, 1964, Muyenzi Settlement 1964, Tanzania 1964, Director, General by Countries, W.S., 1.2, LWF.

49 David Johnson to Bruno Muetzelfeldt, Director World Service, November 25, 1964, Mwesi Highland Settlements . . . ,1964, Tanzania 1964, Director, General by Countries, W.S., I.2, LWF.

50 From late 1965 until 1968, the Tanzanian governments broke off relations with the UK. Lal, *African Socialism*, 57.

51 This suspicion apparently stemmed from the fact that the pilot had previously worked for Congolese prime minister Tshombe. Eugine Ries to Rev. Ove. R. Nilsen, Assistant Executive Secretary, Lutheran World Relief Inc., January 27, 1965, Mwesi Highland, Airlift, . . . , Congolese Francs, Tanzania 1964, Director, General by Countries, W.S., I.2, LWF.

52 Starting in late October, officials had hoped to move 250 refugees twice a week. B. Muetzelfeldt to J. Norredam, December 7, 1964, 3, Mwesi Highland Settlements . . . , 1964, Tanzania 1964, Director, General by Countries, W.S., I.2, LWF.

53 Bernard A. Confer, Executive Secretary, Lutheran World Relief Inc., to the Rev. Eugene Ries, Secretary, Resettlement and Material Relief, LWF, February 8, 1965, Mwesi Highland, Airlift . . . , Congolese Francs, Tanzania 1964, Director, General by Countries, W.S., I.2, LWF.

54 Interview with Brian Neldner.

55 Jorgen Norredam, "Field Officer's Diary," October 31, 1964, 33, Mwesi Highlands Settlement . . . (Tractor) 1964, Tanzania 1964, Director, General by Countries, W.S., 1.2, LWF.

56 Memorandum from Jorgen Norredam to Dr. Bruno Muetzelfeldt, "A Lion without Teeth," December 26, 1964, Mwesi Highland Settlements . . . , 1964, Tanzania 1964, Director, General by Countries, W.S., I.2, LWF.

57 Brian Neldner to Bruno Muetzelfeldt, May 7, 1966, Tanzania 1966 vol. I, Director, General Correspondence, W.S., I.2, LWF.

58 For example, a TCRS official wrote that the transport delay in early November 1964 was due to bad weather and the "continued resistance to the movement on the part of regional headquarters in Tabora." David Johnson to Bruno Muetzelfeldt, November 25, 1964.

Notes to Chapter 6 · 251

59 Norredam, "Field Officer's Diary," October 31, 1964, 33, 35. The colonial attitude toward refugees and locals was continued by UNHCR and LWF officials who, mimicking Belgian colonial discourse, continually described the Tutsi refugees as a "Nilotic race" of "superior intelligence." "Brief for Mr. Ghosh," April 11, 1963, 15/SA, box 259, fonds 11, series 1, UNHCR.

60 Brian Neldner to Bruno Muetzelfeldt, December 6, 1964, General, Programme Director, Tanzania 1964, Director, General by Countries, W.S., I.2, LWF.

61 "Notes on the Discussion Concerning the Mwesi Settlement Held the Afternoon of 12th October. . . ."

62 "Notes on the Discussion Concerning the Mwesi Settlement Held the Afternoon of 12th October . . ."; interview with Brian Neldner.

63 Norredam, "Field Officer's Diary," October 31, 1964.

64 G. de Bosch Kemper, Representative, Dar es Salaam, to High Commissioner, Geneva, "Operation 'Armand Kuijpers'—Resumption of Airlift—Staffing at Mwesi," February 26, 1965, Mwesi Highlands, Tanzania 1965, Director, General by Countries, W.S., I.2, LWF.

65 The dislike apparently went both ways, as one UNHCR official complained that "discussion . . . with the 'competent' authorities in Tanzania becomes more and more difficult." J. Cuenod to High Commissioner, "UNA Volunteers in Central Africa," December 19, 1964, 15-TAN-RWA, box 260, fonds 11, series 1, UNHCR.

66 Brian Neldner to Bruno Muetzelfeldt, December 21, 1964, 3, Mwesi Highlands Settlement, Tanzania 1964, Director, General Correspondence by Countries, W.S., I.2, LWF.

67 See, for example, Field Officer's Diary, November 7, 1964, 33, Mwesi Highlands Settlement, General Tripartite Agreement, Tanzania 1964, Director, General Correspondence by Countries, W.S., I.2, LWF.

68 On town and *shamba* (farm) groups within the settlement community and the former's eventual turn to agricultural work, see Settlement Commandant, Mwesi Highlands Settlement, to Principle Secretary, 2nd Vice President's Office, Dar es Salaam, September 30, 1966, Tanzania 1966 vol. I, Director, General by Countries, W.S., I.2, LWF.

69 On local concerns about international "overprotection" of refugee settlers, see Brian Neldner to Bruno Muetzelfeldt, February 24, 1965, Mwesi Highland-General 1965, Tanzania 1965, Director, General by Countries, W.S., I.2, LWF. Regarding tensions between TCRS and government staff, see Jorgen Norredam to Brian Neldner, February 21, 1965, Mwesi Highland-General, 1965, Tanzania 1965, Director, General by Countries, W.S., I.2, LWF.

70 The provision of supplemental food to vulnerable populations in the refugee community continued. "Report on Integration of Project: Mwesi Highlands Refugee Settlement," March 20, 1968, 3, Tanzania 1968, vol. II, Director, General by Countries, W.S., I.2, LWF.

71 BW Neldner to Bruno Muetzelfeldt, November 2, 1966, Tanzania 1966, vol. I, Director, General by Countries, W.S., I.2, LWF.

252 · Notes to Chapter 6

72 As Neldner noted in 1966, "The refugees ask me about cattle on every visit." Brian Neldner to Rev. E. Ries, "Mwesi Settlement," January 11, 1966, 6, Tanzania 1966, vol. I, Director, General by Countries, W.S., I.2, LWF. See also Gasarasi, "Tripartite Approach," 107.

73 Daley, "Politics of the Refugee Crisis," 145n6.

74 The OAU expanded the 1951 definition to include people who seek refuge due to "external aggression, occupation, foreign domination or events seriously disturbing the public order." The act also required asylum countries, "for reasons of security," to "settle refugees at a reasonable distance from the frontier of their country of origin." For the prohibition of subversive activities, see Article III. OAU Convention Governing the Specific Aspects of Refugee Problems in Africa, September 10, 1969, https://www.unhcr.org/en-us/about-us/background/45dc1a682/oau-convention -governing-specific-aspects-refugee-problems-africa-adopted.html.

75 Specific concerns centered on refugee deportation and detention and the increasing power of settlement commandants. Rosenthal, "'From a Place of Misery,'" 109–10.

76 Rep. for Tanzania to High Commissioner (Att. Dr. P. Weis), "Refugee (Control) Act 1965 Tanzania," November 18, 1965, 6/1/TAN, folder I, box 167, fonds 11, series 1, UNHCR.

77 Rep. for Tanzania to High Commissioner (Att. Dr. P. Weis), "New Refugee (Control) Act 1965," November 23, 1965, 6/1/TAN, folder I, box 167, fonds 11, series 1, UNHCR.

78 Dr. P. Weis to UNHCR Representative for Tanzania, "Refugees (Control) Bill," December 21, 1965, 6/1/TAN, folder I, box 167, fonds 11, series 1, UNHCR.

79 Special Provisions 11i of the 1965 Refugee (Control) Act required refugee permits.

80 Neldner informed the UNHCR about the permit issue in Mwesi on February 7, 1968, at which point the situation had "existed for more than eight months and was becoming critical." Representative for Tanzania to UNHCR Headquarters, "Mwesi Refugee Settlement," March 19, 1968, 6/1/TAN, file 2, part I, fonds 11, series 1, UNHCR.

81 Representative for Tanzania to UNHCR Headquarters, "Mwesi Refugee Settlement," March 19, 1968. The permit crisis also affected Muyenzi, where the government repeatedly threatened to send two thousand troublemakers to Mwesi. Officials decided against the move, fearing that the refugees from Muyenzi would exacerbate the situation in Mwesi.

82 Representative for Tanzania to UNHCR Headquarters, "Mwesi Refugee Settlement," March 19, 1968.

83 Representative for Tanzania to UNHCR Headquarters, "Mwesi Refugee Settlement," March 19, 1968. One refugee died en route to Tabora. Of those imprisoned, one accepted the permit and returned to Mwesi in July 1968. Representative for Tanzania to UNHCR, Geneva, "Rwandese Detainees at the Central Prison Tabora, Uyui," October 25, 1968, 6/1/TAN, file IV, folder V, fonds 11, series 1, UNHCR. Refugee leaders at Muyenzi were arrested and sent to prison in Bukoba. Most of these leaders returned to Muyenzi by June 1970. G. Gobius,

Notes to Chapter 6 · 253

"Note for the File 25 June 1970 Meeting with the Second Vice-President, the Hon. R. M. Kawawa," 6/1/TAN, file VI, folder V, fonds 11, series 1, UNHCR.

84 Representative for Tanzania to UNHCR, "Rwandese Detainees at the Central Prison Tabora, Uyui."

85 A. Rorholt to Mr. T. Jamieson, "Refugee Detainees in Tanzania," November 18, 1968, 6/1/TAN, file IV, fonds 11, series 1, UNHCR.

86 Principal Secretary, Second Vice President's Office, Dar es Salaam, to Resident Representative UNHCR, Dar es Salaam, "Rwandese Refugees in Detention at Tabora," November 7, 1968, 6/1/TAN, file IV, fonds 11, series 1, UNHCR.

87 Thomas Jamieson to Mr. A. Rorholt, "Refugee Detainees in Tanzania," November 12, 1968, 6/1/TAN, file I, fonds 11, series 1, UNHCR. On the detailed and repeated attempts by the second vice president to extradite the refugees, see Rosenthal, "'From a Place of Misery,'" 112–13.

88 Nils G. Gussing, Representative for Tanzania, to UNHCR, Geneva, "Refugee Permits at Mwesi Settlement," March 26, 1970, 6/1/TAN, file VI, fonds 11, series 1, UNHCR. This time, the incarcerated refugees were those who had signed any of three letters sent to the TCRS settlement commandant during March that read: "Again we tell you personaly [sic] that we shall not take 'permits' what ever the case may be happened to us we are ready to *die* instead of staying in Tanzania. Please take us any time." Nils G. Gussing, Representative for Tanzania, Note for the File, "Non-Permit Holders at Mwesi Settlement," April 8, 1970, 6/1/TAN, file VI, fonds 11, series 1, UNHCR.

89 Gussing to UNHCR, "Refugee Permits at Mwesi Settlement," March 26, 1970.

90 The original "'legal' problem" thus became an "'agricultural' concern . . . caused by the stubbornness of the non permit holders," which then impacted the whole community and eventually led to an increased "potential towards larceny." Representative for Tanzania to UNHCR, Geneva, January 29, 1969, 6/1/TAN, file IV, fonds 11, series 1, UNHCR.

91 Representative for Tanzania to UNHCR, January 29, 1969.

92 UNHCR Legal Officer for Eastern and Southern Africa to UNHCR Headquarters, January 29, 1969, 6/1/TAN, file IV, fonds 11, series 1, UNHCR. Regarding the government's "lack of co-operation" on legal protection, see C. Brink-Petersen to UNHCR, Geneva, received April 14, 1970, 6/1/TAN, file VI, fonds 11, series 1, UNHCR.

93 Representative for Tanzania to UNHCR, January 29, 1969. Since at least 1967, TCRS officials had been concerned about the UNHCR's reduction of the Mwesi budget. B. W. Nelder to B. Muetzelfeldt, December 15, 1967, Tanzania 1967, vol. II, Director, General Correspondence by Countries, W.S., I.2, LWF.

94 Representative for Tanzania to UNHCR, Geneva, November 14, 1968, 6/1/TAN, file IV, box 167, fonds 11, series 1, UNHCR.

95 A. Rorholt to T. Jamieson, November 18, 1968.

96 Brian Neldner to Bruno Muetzelfeldt, March 1, 1968, Tanzania 1968, vol. II, Director, General by Countries, W.S., I.2, LWF. For details of agricultural noncooperation see Rosenthal, "'From a Place of Misery,'" 114.

254 · Notes to Chapter 6

97 Interview with Brian Neldner.

98 A. Rorholt to UNHCR Representative for Tanzania, "Situation in Mwesi Settlement," April 23, 1968, 6/1/TAN, file II, part I, fonds 11, series 1, UNHCR. The UNHCR was concerned about such detentions "for their own sakes and because of the fact that these detentions are becoming internationally known." A. Rorholt, Director, Legal Division, to Representative, UNHCR Branch Office for Tanzania, August 14, 1968, 6/1/TAN, file 3, folder III, fonds 11, series 1, UNHCR.

99 Representative for Tanzania to UNHCR, Geneva, "Refugee-Permits-Mwesi," February 22, 1969, 6/1/TAN, folder IV, fonds 11, series 1, UNHCR. Interestingly the representative describes these "groups" as not having "any ambition to restore, by means of militant operations, the former conditions in their country of origin."

100 Representative for Tanzania to UNHCR, "Refugee-Permits-Mwesi," February 22, 1969.

101 O. Goundiam to P. Mitha, "Tanzania re: Rwandese Refugees in Tabora Prison," April 23, 1969, 6/1/TAN, file IV, fonds 11, series 1, UNHCR.

102 Goundiam to Mitha, "Tanzania re: Rwandese Refugees in Tabora Prison," April 23, 1969.

103 An exception is a letter from the UNHCR's legal officer, who conveyed the feeling of the senior magistrate in Tabora that the refugees' refusal was "politically motivated" and "obviously presented the Government with a nasty political problem." Tellingly, the politics of the situation surfaced only through the observations of the Tanzanian magistrate. UNHCR Legal Officer for Eastern and Southern Africa, Note for the File, "Interview of the 72 Rwandan Refugees in Tabora Prison," November 11, 1968, 6/1/TAN, file IV, fonds 11, series 1, UNHCR.

104 Representative for Tanzania to UNHCR, "Rwandese Detainees at the central Prison Tabora, Uyui," October 25, 1968.

105 Representative for Tanzania to United Nations High Commissioner, "Situation in the Mwesi Highlands Refugee Settlement—1st March 1969, Trip to Mwesi . . . Friday 28th February 1969," 6, 6/1/TAN, file IV, fonds 11, series 1, UNHCR; emphasis in original. The idea that if refugee leaders were forced to perform manual labor they would change their minds about signing the refugee permits pervades UNHCR correspondence on the issue, even though the UNHCR legal division continually bemoaned the lack of refugee rights in Tanzania. The UNHCR legal officer for eastern and southern Africa even suggested that the refugee leaders be "retried in the ordinary courts and sentenced to imprisonment with hard labour." Kwame Amoo-Adare, UNHCR Legal Officer for Eastern and Southern Africa, to Principal Secretary, Office of the Second Vice President, "Petition for Trial in Court of the 72 Rwandese Refugees Presently in Tabora Prison," January 28, 1969, 6/1/TAN, file IV, fonds 1, series 2, 6, UNHCR.

106 Nils G. Gussing, Representative for Tanzania, to Dr. O. Bayer, Acting Director, Legal Division, Geneva, April 30, 1970, 6/1/TAN, folder VI, fonds 11, series 1, UNHCR.

107 Nils Gussing to UNHCR, Geneva, March 26, 1970, 6/1/TAN/IV, box 167, fonds 11, series 1, UNHCR.

108 Gussing to Bayer, April 30, 1970.

109 "Report on the Visit of Mr. Gussing to Dabalo on 12 May 1970," 6/1/TAN, file IV, fonds 11, series 1, UNHCR.

110 Scott, *Seeing Like a State*, 20, 13.

111 Ferguson, *Anti-Politics Machine*, xiv–xv.

112 Armstrong, "Aspects of Refugee," 59.

113 Hack, "Decolonization and Violence," 141.

114 Kibraeb, "Revisiting the Debate," 11.

115 As I was unable to interview many former refugees at Mwesi, these conclusions are drawn from archival material.

116 Metcalfe, "Effects of Refugees," 77.

117 This was an "embarrassing" situation for both TCRS and UNHCR, with Muetzelfeldt later noting that "TCRS should watch out for [budget considerations so] that we do not have a repetition of the Mwesi situation." Brian Neldner to Roman Ritter, Finance Comptroller, July 27, 1965, Tanzania, Mbamba Bay . . . UNHCR Budget and Agreement 1965, Director, General by Countries, W.S., I.2, LWF.

118 *Number and Movement of Refugees of Concern to UNHCR in 1975, Country: Tanzania*, 100/TAN/GEN, folder I, box 187, fonds 11, series 2, UNHCR.

7. OF "NATURAL" CITIZENS AND "NATURAL" ILLEGALITY

1 Interview with Marco Bautbula, Munweje, June 27, 2012.

2 Attention to *ujamaa* has often overshadowed other important processes and events in Tanzanian history. Jennings, "'Very Real War,'" 76.

3 I use the term *ujamaa* to refer to both state-led voluntary villagization during the late 1960s and early 1970s and compulsory villagization during 1973–1975. The term also refers generally to Tanzanian policies of African socialism, as elucidated by President Julius Nyerere, during the late 1960s and 1970s. Lawi, "Tanzania's Operation Vijiji," 73.

4 Although this chapter does not reify state discourse or imagine the state as a consolidated, unified organ of governance (see Lal, "Self-Reliance and the State," 214), I use *the state* to analyze how national leaders' discourse, particularly Nyerere's, filtered into Ngaran lives and imaginations.

5 On the idea of familyhood linked to the nation and national land, see Bjerk, *Building a Peaceful Nation*, 99–104. Lal notes the tension between state attempts to transform "fluid" family institutions into nuclear units while simultaneously celebrating an "abstracted version of kinship as an adhesive binding diffuse populations into a national unit." Lal, *African Socialism*, 120.

6 Hydén, *Beyond Ujamaa*.

7 Nyerere, *Uhuru na Ujamaa*, 385.

8 Thus, the idea of development became "essential to the definition of the citizen" and integral to state claims of both legitimacy and proper citizenship. Jennings, "'Very Real War,'" 76.

256 · Notes to Chapter 6

9 Nyerere, *Uhuru na Ujamaa*, 407.

10 Nyerere's September 1967 policy paper *Ujamaa Vijijini* and his October 1968 policy paper *Freedom and Development* emphasize that these factors are essential to successful rural development through communal villages. Schneider notes Nyerere's central role in crafting *ujamaa* policy and, later, extending that policy "toward its coercive realities." Schneider, "Freedom and Unfreedom," 346. Two members of parliament from WLR "who protested against a coercive villagization campaign" were expelled from TANU and labeled "'enemies of the People.'" Schneider, "Colonial Legacies," 113. On the sidelining of "moderate" TANU members during the 1970s, see Roberts, *Revolutionary State-Making*, chap. 7.

11 Jennings, "'Very Real War,'" 94. Bureaucratic rhetoric about overcoming laziness, a characteristic inimical to the qualities of good citizens, existed throughout the 1960s, as did district officials' requests to legitimize compulsion. Jennings, "'Very Real War,'" 90. Boesen writes that due to the dearth of *ujamaa* villages in the region, "West Lake authorities received the changing signals from the centre in 1973–75" with "clear relief." Some initially interpreted the new villagization program as "having nothing to do with ujamaa" and only later learned "to include ujamaa rhetoric when talking about the call for villagization." Boesen, "Tanzania: From Ujamaa," 136.

12 District and regional officials perceived as too slow in implementing policies were often replaced. Schneider, "Freedom and Unfreedom," 367–68.

13 For example, houses were constructed in straight lines along roads according to officials' understanding of "modern" villages. Freund, "Class Conflict," 491. See also Scott, *Seeing Like a State*, chap. 7.

14 Schneider, "Freedom and Unfreedom," 368.

15 For example, Bernhard Staub noted that, due to the shortage of petrol in the country, acquiring even twenty liters required a permit from the district commissioner. Interview with Bernhard Staub, Dar es Salaam, February 14, 2012.

16 Interview with Bernhard Staub.

17 See Freund, "Class Conflict."

18 Lal, *African Socialism*, 197.

19 Interview with Bernhard Staub.

20 Interview with Etafodi Rumisi, Ntobeye, July 25, 2012.

21 Officials often built villages in proximity to existing roads from the colonial period in an effort to connect administrative centers quickly and cheaply. Such roads, however, often passed through dry areas far from good agricultural land and water sources. Boesen, "Tanzania: From Ujamaa," 137.

22 Interview with Crispin Ubuzutwe, Mugoma, July 12, 2012.

23 Interview with Peter Kato, Keza, July 17, 2012.

24 Interview with Simon Ndyaderi, Keza, July 17, 2012.

25 Interview with Father Lazarus, Diocese Vicar General, Rulenge, July 19, 2012.

26 Interview with Jacob Butabiya, Kanyinya, July 19, 2012. This is consistent with findings in other areas of Tanzania. See Hunter, "Revisiting Ujamaa"; Lal, "Self-Reliance and the State."

Notes to Chapter 7 · 257

27 Boesen and coauthors' study of voluntary *ujamaa* villages in WLR during 1968–1972 notes that, particularly in Bugufi division, families retained plots of land in traditional villages while utilizing *ujamaa* village land for production. During these early years, when resettlement was voluntary, often "only the man" moved to the *ujamaa* village, and even then only after bureaucratic pressure. Boesen, Storgaard, and Moody, *Ujamaa*, 64, 67. The relative success of Ntobeye *ujamaa* village in Bugufi was due to its proximity to traditional villages, which provided social support. Ntobeye also helped alleviate land pressure, perpetuating the age-old "farm family cycle" whereby fathers provide land to their sons, thus decreasing the patriarch's original landholdings. Even this "successful" village, however, achieved a standard of living that equaled, rather than surpassed, that of surrounding traditional villages. See Boesen Storgaard, and Moody, *Ujamaa*, chap. 4.

28 Interview with Samson Sankuale, Ntobeye, June 21, 2012.

29 Boesen, "Tanzania: From Ujamaa," 128. According to many Ngarans, popular resistance to villagization also sprang from human nature, which tends to resist change and desires personal accumulation. In the words of Justice Ksuma Numyogoro, a government official in Muyenzi, "If some guy has a good *shamba* with water nearby and he is told to move to a barren place it is hard to stomach." Justice's own family was forced to move to *ujamaa* villages with poor water availability. Interview with Justice Ksuma Numyogoro, Muyenzi, June 27, 2012.

30 Interview with Father Lazarus; interview with Edward Teadi, Mugoma, July 12, 2012; interview with Thomas Kapondo, Mbuba, July 19, 2012.

31 Interview with David Natori, Rulenge, June 17, 2012.

32 Interview with Adrian Mudende, Rulenge, July 11, 2012; interview with Joseph Bwizi, Shanga, June 20, 2012.

33 These individuals thus echoed state nationalist discourse around the perils of laziness and idleness. Hunter, "Revisiting Ujamaa"; interview with Charles Baringe, Chivu, June 14, 2012.

34 Interview with Leonad Kanyeshamba, Muyenzi, July 18, 2012.

35 Villagers often cooperate in economic endeavors. Women in particular often participate in rotating savings and credit groups, with some individuals taking part in multiple associations. There is also a communal aspect to most people's lives in Ngara. Extended families often pitch in during times of celebration or crisis, providing a social safety net based on ideals of generosity and reciprocity. Lal suggests that comments on the longevity of *ujamaa* reflect the ongoing relevance of such "forms of sociability and mutual assistance." Lal, *African Socialism*, 224.

36 Interview with Bernard Kadene, Shanga, July 9, 2012.

37 Tripp, *Changing the Rules*, 65. In 1976 the government abolished cooperative unions, which were replaced with "cumbersome, inefficient crop authorities." Tripp, *Changing the Rules*, 66.

38 Tripp, *Changing the Rules*, 63. Sarris and Van den Brink question official estimates of increased food production during 1966–1989, as survey estimates, malnutrition rates, and grain imports (among other factors) contradict official data. Sarris and Van den Brink, *Economic Policy*, 144.

39 Tanzanian expenditures on oil imports rose from 7–8 percent of imports in 1980 to 23 percent in 1982. Tripp, *Changing the Rules*, 64.

40 Tripp, *Changing the Rules*, 64. Most respondents noted that, aside from economics, the border war did not impact their lives.

41 Freund, "Class Conflict," 488.

42 Recurrent famine also impacted food shortages in Ngara. In 1969 Rulenge missionary authorities approached the UNHCR representative to request food assistance to fight tuberculosis and malnutrition in Ngara (among refugees and locals alike). Copy of letter from Second Vice President (S. C. Mwakang'ata for Principal Secretary) to Area Commissioner and District Medical Officer of Ngara district, "Incidence of Malnutrition and Tuberculosis in Ngara District," March 5, 1969, 100-TAN-RWA, box 188, fonds 11, series 2, UNHCR.

43 Semboja and Rugumisa, "Price Control."

44 Hydén, *Beyond Ujamaa*, 132; Sarris and Van den Brink, *Economic Policy*, 119.

45 Hydén, *Beyond Ujamaaa*, 133.

46 Semboja and Rugumisa note that price controls led to greater inequality due to unequal access to goods. Semboja and Rugumisa, "Price Control," 50.

47 It is unclear how "powerful" such people had to be to receive preferential access to goods. In Ngara, it seems that government employment at any level ensured that one "could get more than others" from communal shops. Interview with Wilfrida Pexto, Shanga, July 9, 2012; interview with Adrian Mudende.

48 Sarris and Van den Brink, *Economic Policy*, 48. Sarris and Van den Brink estimate that the "second economy" grew rapidly in the early 1970s, fluctuating between 35 and 52 percent of "real official GDP [gross domestic product]" from 1977 to 1993. Sarris and Van den Brink, *Economic Policy*, 48, 54.

49 According to one respondent, after Nyerere announced that people had to tighten their belts in 1979, the whole government failed and "endemic corruption began." Interview with Leon Gespary, Rulenge, June 25, 2012.

50 Many people also thought economic hardship resulted from the actions of *wahujume*, or economic saboteurs, discussed later.

51 Literally "mouse" routes, or "shortcuts."

52 Interview with Bernard Kadene.

53 Interview with Nasan Nkurikie, Shanga, July 9, 2012. Cross-border trade was also used to procure used products, such as secondhand clothes, which were outlawed in Tanzania. Interview with Leon Gespary.

54 Interview with Samwel Rwanzi, Shanga, July 9, 2012.

55 The area commissioner in Karagwe noted in 1963 that Rwandan refugees "sell things which they get free" to local people to "obtain money for their personal use." Area Secretary for the Area Commissioner Karagwe to Administrative Secretary Regional Commissioner's Office, West Lake Region, May 6, 1963, A.4/1/III, 527, TNA.

56 Interview with Celestine Kaheri, Kanyinya, June 28, 2012.

57 Interview with David Natori.

58 Interview with Jacob Butabiya.

59 Scott, *Domination and the Arts.*

60 Hydén, *Beyond Ujamaa.*

61 Tripp, *Changing the Rules,* 10. Tripp argues that in addition to understanding informal economies in their social, political, and historical contexts, it is necessary to distinguish between productive illegality, which can create new resources, and illegal trade that diverts state resources. Tripp, *Changing the Rules,* 20.

62 There is a long historiography of resistance in African studies, which stems from the social turn of the 1970s and 1980s and an exploration of the lived experiences of peasants, mine workers, domestic laborers, and women, among others.

63 MacGaffey, *Entrepreneurs and Parasites;* Roitman, *Fiscal Disobedience;* Tripp, *Changing the Rules.*

64 I am not suggesting a straightforward reading of oral histories, as memories must always be situated within the subjective fields of both interviewer and interviewee. However, in theorizing the actions of marginalized peoples, Western scholars are perhaps too quick to attribute meanings derived from subjective agendas. In the process, the words and perceptions of individuals often become lost in a haze of liberal, albeit well-intentioned dramatization. While analysis is a necessary precondition of scholarship, there is something off (even imperial) about replacing or subsume Africans' words and explanations with the author's.

65 Interview with Deus Rwanzo, Kumnazi, August 4, 2012.

66 Just as it is important not to give undue meaning to *magendo,* it is important not to think of the state as an all-encompassing entity of undue strength. I like Priya Lal's suggestion that Tanzanians experienced "the consolidation and fragmentation of the national state as part of a single process" whereby the state was not excessively weak or excessively strong. Lal, "Self-Reliance and the State," 214. On "moral expectation and responsibilities" outside of the state and economy, see Giblin, *History of the Excluded,* 7.

67 In response to such critiques, Scott posits "the messy encounter between tangled and ineffective state plans, on the one hand, and local forms of resistance and accommodation, on the other hand, that produce, yes, contingent hybrid confections that meet no one's pristine vision." Scott, "Afterword," 399.

68 Interview with Leon Gespary.

69 Interview with Stephen Joseph Gwaho, Muruvyagira, June 5, 2012. According to Peter Kato, *uhujume* meant buying and collecting many goods in a store and later reselling them at a higher price than the government. The result was that small traders could not acquire goods hoarded by rich traders. Interview with Peter Kato.

70 I have found no reference to *uhujume* in secondary literature and only marginal explorations of Tanzanian economic sabotage—mostly in the writings of economists and political scientists. An exception is Ronald Aminzade's *Race, Nation, and Citizenship,* a sociological study of nationalism in Tanzania.

71 Aminzade, *Race, Nation, and Citizenship,* 230–31.

72 Aminzade, *Race, Nation, and Citizenship,* 232.

73 For example, interview with Jacob Butabiya.

260 · Notes to Chapter 7

74 Interview with Thomas Kapondo.

75 Aminzade, *Race, Nation, and Citizenship*, 233. As a TCRS employee in Dar es Salaam noted in 1983, "The search for hoarders, saboteurs, etc. is questionable as only 4 party members among those accused. Big boys are still left alone. People expect items formerly scarce to now be available, but actually it has merely driven black market deeper so it is even more difficult to get item on black market." Arthur E. Storhaug, "Note to File," July 5, 1983, EAT/1, vol. I, Tanzania 1983, W.S., Y.O., LWF.

76 Interview with Deus Rwanzo. Almost everyone interviewed misremembered that Sokoine died in a plane crash, not a car crash, perhaps elevating the circumstances of his death in a way that matched the retrospective importance of the event.

77 Tripp, *Changing the Rules*, xii.

78 Aminzade, *Race, Nation, and Citizenship*, 3. Aminzade primarily references these contradictions in terms of the state's policies and ideologies surrounding race in Tanzania. On the contradictory role of Pan-Africanist and nationalist ideologies in Tanzania, see Lal, *African Socialism*, 65–66.

79 Nyerere, *Uhuru na Ujamaa*, 347.

80 Aminzade suggests that this ambiguity, or contradiction, in national policy stemmed from shifting political power between state and party officials, as well as between "capital accumulation in a global economy and political legitimation in a nation-state." Aminzade, *Race, Nation, and Citizenship*, 10, 12.

81 Indeed, Nyerere's writings and speeches were full of references to "the equality of man" as "the first principle of socialism," a principle that racialism "absolutely and fundamentally" contradicted. Nyerere, *Uhuru na Ujamaa*, 30.

82 Nyerere quoted in Aminzade, *Race, Nation, and Citizenship*, 18.

83 Nyerere, *Uhuru na Ujamaa*, 144.

84 Nyerere, *Uhuru na Ujamaa*, 63.

85 Nyerere, *Uhuru na Ujamaa*, 352.

86 Those who did not share the cultural values of national socialism were often denounced "as enemies of the nation . . . their loyalty to the nation was questionable." Aminzade, *Race, Nation, and Citizenship*, 3.

87 Interview with A. Nzuri, Rulenge, June 25, 2012.

88 Interview with Celestine Kaheri. Other respondents noted that only a few Rwandan refugees were part of villagization.

89 A state village (or *ujamaa* village of the mandatory variety) was created close to the initial Muyenzi refugee camp. The village bears the same name.

90 Before conducting interviews in Busubi, I had to obtain the permission of local government officers. Thankfully, my research assistant was familiar with the local official based in Muyenzi, who initially insisted on finding people for me to interview and often attended these meetings himself. As a result, when I arrived in villages, there would often be three to seven people waiting to speak with me. At my first interview in Muyenzi village, I found four men sitting together, which made the interviews more public than usual. Each man listened to the others'

Notes to Chapter 7 · 261

responses, and a small crowd gathered to watch the odd spectacle of a *mzungu* in their midst—made even odder by my obsession with the past, my tape recorder, and my official escort.

91 Interview with Roland Ndurande, Muyenzi, June 7, 2012. People remarked that while refugees could live in *ujamaa* villages, Ngarans were suspicious of them, wondering "why they would choose to join us." Interview with Father Lazarus. Others noted that only Rwandans who became citizens lived in *ujamaa* villages. Interview with Leonad Kanyeshamba, Muyenzi, July 18, 2012. The few former refugees I interviewed did not live in state villages, so I have little evidence whether the refugees who joined villages did so voluntarily.

92 According to the director of TCRS, who attended the Mwesi ceremony, "The people were happy and contented, happy for the occasion." Egil Nilssen to Mr. B. W. Neldner, "Naturalization of Rwandese in Mwese Settlement," October 17, 1980, EAT 1–2, vol. I, Tanzania 1980, W.S., Y.O., LWF.

93 According to the UNHCR, in 1980 the populations of Mwesi, Muyenzi, and Karagwe/Kimuli all decreased to zero due to naturalization. "Information Required for the Countries in Column B, Number and Movement of Refugees of Concern to UNHCR in 1980," Country: Tanzania, 120-TAN [vol. 2], box 388, fonds 11, series 2, UNHCR. It is unclear how the UNHCR came up with the number of thirty-seven thousand Rwandan refugees. Throughout the 1970s the agency had noted increases in Rwandan refugees from Rwanda, Burundi, Uganda, and Zaire in Tanzania. Clearly, these "new" refugees would not have been eligible for naturalization. In spite of this, the numbers used by both the government and the UNHCR for Rwandan refugees eligible for naturalization consistently exceeded thirty thousand. Hugu Idoyaga, Representative for Tanzania, to UNHCR headquarters, Geneva, "Number and Movement of Refugees of Concern to UNHCR in 1974," February 20, 1975, 120-TAN [vol. 2], box 388, fonds 11, series 2, UNHCR.

94 Indeed, the UNHCR would later acknowledge that the failure to resolve the 1960s Rwandan refugee caseload "'contributed substantially to the cataclysmic violence of the 1990s.'" Quoted in Loescher and Milner, "Protracted Refugee Situations," 3.

95 Representative UNHCR Field Office for Tanzania, Dar es Salaam, "Naturalization of Rwandese Refugees," February 9, 1984, 656.TAN, box 1292, fonds 11, series 2, UNHCR.

96 Clearly, the government's fear of de-territorialization was "not uniformly manifested" among average citizens; however, resentment of refugees may have been linked to this discourse. Lal, *African Socialism*, 67, 123–24.

97 Note for the File, "The Director of Assistance Mr. M. L. Zollner met Tanzanian delegation to EXCOM headed by H.E. Mr. S. Amour, Minister of Home Affairs on 17 October 1984," 100-TAN-GEN [vol. 2], box 187, fonds 11, series 2, UNHCR.

98 Interview with Leon Gespary. Additional reports from Zaire of Rwandan refugees "trying to prepare for an armed action directed against Rwanda" troubled UNHCR officials. UNHCR Branch Office, Kigali, May 20, 1976, "Meeting with the Zairean Ambassador (19.5.76)," 100.GEN.RWA [vol. 3], box 30, fonds 11, series

2, UNHCR. On the impossibility of monitoring refugee movements, see Gunnar Kaellenius, Representative for Tanzania, Dar es Salaam, to UNHCR, Geneva, "Refugee Population at Mwesi Settlement," May 2, 1972, 100-TAN-GEN [vol. 2], box 187, fonds 11, series 2, UNHCR.

99 There was never a "firm request" from the Tanzanian government regarding "the resettlement of up to a million people from Ruanda" in Tanzania, a subject that "has been raised a number of times." B. W. Neldner to Mr. Egil S. W. Nilssen, "Tanzanian Delegation to UNHCR EXCO in October 1979," January 7, 1980, EAT 1–2, Tanzania 1980, W.S., Y.O., LWF. In 1980 "the Tanzanian and Ruandese Government officials . . . [had] frequent meeting[s] on this issue." Egil S. W. Nilssen to Mr. Brian W. Neldner, "Ruandese Resettlement," February 26, 1980, EAT/r20–r21, vol. IV, Tanzania 1980, W.S., Y.O., LWF.

100 On violence against Rwandan refugees in Uganda, see T. M. Unwin, Representative for Uganda, to High Commissioner, "Rwandan Refugees in Uganda," February 8, 1982, 100-UGA.RWA [vol. 2], box 206, fonds 11, series 2, UNHCR.

101 TCRS officials were similarly elated at the idea of mass naturalization because "the acceptance of Tanzania to this group receiving citizenship is regarded as the single largest group citizenship given in the world history. With this TCRS has seen the third large refugee problem solved, first the repatriation of the Mozambique refugees, then the repatriation of the Ugandan refugees and now the naturalization of the Rwandese refugees." Ironically, in time, all three of these "solved" refugee problems would prove to be anything but. LWF/TCRS Quarterly Report July–September 1980, EAT 1–2, vol. I, Tanzania 1980, W.S., Y.O., LWF.

102 "Extract from Report to Southern Africa from 9 March to 29 April by UNHCR Mission," 6/12/TAN, box 204, fonds 11, series 1, UNHCR. Additionally, even those who enthusiastically applied for and received citizenship often faced discrimination, revealing "the fragility of citizenship by naturalization." Rubagumya, *Son of Two Countries*, 114.

103 Mendel, "Refugee Law," 44.

104 A. B. M. Saied, Representative UNHCR B.O. for Tz to Ndugu Lt. Col. Nsa-Kaisi, Regional Commissioner, Kagera Region, February 16, 1984, 656.TAN, box 1292, fonds 11, series 2, UNHCR.

105 This included those who had entered from Burundi and Uganda and those who had fled the 1973 military coup in Rwanda. Rwandan sources, as well as UNHCR statistics, note increases in Rwandan settlements in Ngara and elsewhere during 1974. It is likely that at the least eleven thousand additional Rwandans entered Tanzania in the mid-1970s alone. "Number and Movement of Refugees of Concern to UNHCR in 1974." On refugees fleeing the violence of Obote's regime, see Peter C. Matovu, UNHCR Senior Counsellor, 22.4.81, 100-UGA.RWA [vol. 1], box 205, fonds 11, series 2, UNHCR.

106 In addition to targeting Asian groups as inimical to national development, nationalists "targeted pastoralist groups, such as the Wamaasai, whose 'backward' cultures were denounced as inimical to modernity and whose migratory behavior challenged the borders of the nation-state." Aminzade, *Race, Nation,*

Notes to Chapter 7 · 263

and Citizenship, 9n22. It is likely that Tutsi pastoralists would have fallen into a similar category of "nomadic" peoples.

107 Indeed, many Ngarans did not consider these later arrivals to be refugees because they did not arrive in large groups or receive external aid. Rather, they stayed with relatives and friends until they became self-sufficient. Interview with David Natori.

108 Gasarasi, "Mass Naturalization," 96. According to Gasarasi, refugees "jealously monitored the distribution of refugee permits to allegedly non-qualifying migrants from Rwanda and Burundi," and during 1973–1976 they complained that settlement commandants sold refugee permits to nonqualifying individuals. Gasarasi, "Mass Naturalization," 93.

109 "Speech Delivered by the Regional Commissioner of Kagera, Ndugu P. N. Kafanabo, on the Occasion of Naturalising the Ruandese Refugees of Kimuli and Muyenzi Settlements on 13-12-1980," 1A-1B vol. 1, Tanzania 1981, W.S., Y.O., LWF.

110 "Speech Delivered by the Regional Commissioner of Kagera, Ndugu P. N. Kafanabo, on the Occasion of Naturalising the Ruandese Refugees of Kimuli and Muyenzi Settlements on 13-12-1980." This echoes the attitude of the principal secretary for the Ministry of Home Affairs, who, in response to the continued detention of Rwandan refugees from Mwesi settlement, "seemed to be in favour of just pushing them [the detained refugees] over the border to Rwanda." Gunnar Kaellenius, Representative for Tanzania, to UNHCR, Geneva, "Detained Rwandese Refugees," February 21, 1973, 100-TAN-RWA, box 188, fonds 11, series 2, UNHCR.

111 Interview with Jacob Kanani, former chairman of Muyenzi village, Rulenge, June 25, 2012; interview with A. Nzuri.

112 Interview with David Natori.

113 Hunter, "Revisiting Ujamaa," 471.

114 B. Mbawala for Principal Secretary, Ministry of Home Affairs, to Representative UNHCR Dar es Salaam, "Final Financial Statement of Naturalization of Rwandese Refugees and Narrative Report," February 14, 1984, 656.TAN, box 1292, fonds 11, series 2, UNHCR.

115 Representative UNHCR Field Office for Tanzania, Dar es Salaam, to UNHCR headquarters, Geneva, "Finalization of Naturalization of Rwandese Refugees," February 23, 1984, 656.TAN, box 1292, fonds 11, series 2, UNHCR.

116 UNHCR Field Office, "Naturalization of Rwandese Refugees," February 9, 1984.

117 I. Tanzil, Southern Africa Regional Section, Note for the File, "Imprisoned Refugees and Rwandese Refugees," May 18, 1981, 110-TAN, box 323, fonds 11, series 2, UNHCR.

118 "Report on UNHCR Activities in Tanzania 1983/84," 120-TAN [vol. 2], box 188, fonds 11, series 2, UNHCR. The UNHCR had allocated (at least) $100,000 to the naturalization program. B. Mbawala to Representative UNHCR Dar es Salaam, "Final Financial Statement of Naturalization of Rwandese Refugees and Narrative Report."

119 Local conceptions of citizenship are thus a result of national discourses as perceived through "village-level politics and a range of discourses and material processes at mixed subnational and supranational levels." Lal, *African Socialism*, 209.

120 Chipkin, "'Functional' and 'Dysfunctional Communities,'" 69.

121 *Ujamaa* was not officially abandoned as a national policy until 1991, but "authorities announced in the 1980s" that villagers could return to their previous homes. Lal, *African Socialism*, 219–20.

122 Kaiser, "Structural Adjustment," 231.

123 Tripp, *Changing the Rules*, 75.

124 Tony Waters cautions us about structural adjustment in Tanzania, as such programs often only marginally impacted local livelihoods. Nevertheless, under IMF-brokered programs, the Tanzanian shilling dropped from 17 per dollar in 1985 to over 520 per dollar in 1995. Waters, "Beyond Structural Adjustment," 59–60.

125 Lal, *African Socialism*, 210.

126 Rwandan refugees' "right of return" was affirmed at the 1985 World Congress of Rwandan refugees in Washington, DC. Prunier, *Rwanda Crisis*, 74.

8. COMPETITION AND BACKSTABBING

1 Avent Appeal 1995, Tanzania 1997, DWS, Y.1, LWF.

2 The team involved in Study 3 of the Joint Evaluation of Emergency Assistance to Rwanda estimated that from April to December 1994, the international community spent $1.4 billion in aid on the Rwanda crisis (one-third in Rwanda and two-thirds in neighboring countries). Borton, Brusset, and Hallam, "International Response to Conflict and Genocide: Study 3," 5 (hereafter, Study 3). The report later estimated that 15.37 percent of the $1.29 billion spent by the international community during this time was allocated to Tanzania, largely within Ngara district (there is no explanation of the different aid amounts—$1.4 billion versus $1.29 billion). Study 3, fig. 2, 28. The joint study was a novel effort undertaken by scholars, aid practitioners, and government officials to analyze the factors that led to the Rwandan genocide, to examine the unprecedented scale of the humanitarian response and the allocation of aid, and to provide suggestions for future international aid efforts during subsequent "complex emergencies." Study 3, 5.

3 This was the first time the UN Security Council discussed refugee camp security "as a peacekeeping matter," although it never came to a conclusion on how to carry out such peacekeeping. Adelman and Suhrke, "International Response to Conflict and Genocide: Study 2," 57 (hereafter, Study 2).

4 This chapter focuses on TCRS activities and personnel due to the availability of archival information and the prohibitive task of analyzing the more than twenty agencies involved in Ngara district. Study 3 attempted a comprehensive evaluation of the more than 235 donor, UN, NGO, and government agencies involved in the Rwandan refugee crisis—noting the near impossibility of a comprehensive analysis due to the costs, the availability and willingness of agencies and personnel, and the sheer number of people involved. To understand the humanitarian response in Ngara beyond the actions of the TCRS and its relationship with the UNHCR, I utilized Study 3, which involved on-site and international

Notes to Chapter 8 · 265

interviews with 245 aid personnel and donors, as well as 140 interviews with beneficiaries. In particular, I relied on the findings of Johan Pottier, the Study 3 anthropologist who conducted research in both Ngara district and North Kivu Province, Zaire, during 1994 and 1995.

5 In 1996 a TCRS official noted that the agency was not "supportive" of having "all NGOS specializing in specific activities," as it preferred "a healthy mix of activities." Email from Bernhard Staub to Admasu Simeso, "UNHCR and Karagwe," March 10, 1996, DWS, Y.1, Country Programs, Tanzania 1995, LWF.

6 There has been an outpouring of scholarship that attempts to explain, detail, and analyze the events preceding, during, and following the 1994 Rwandan genocide. The best of this scholarship comes from those who had long studied events in Rwanda and the region. See, for example (in English), Uvin, *Aiding Violence*; Des Forges, *"Leave None to Tell"*; Newbury and Newbury, "Bringing the Peasants"; Pottier, *Re-imagining Rwanda*; Longman, *Christianity and Genocide*.

7 On the complexity of "home" as a concept in the region, see Newbury, "Returning Refugees."

8 It is impossible to know exactly how many descendants of the first refugees joined the RPF. From interviews in Ngara, it is clear that there was much support for the movement and that many former refugees joined the RPF, while others sent monetary support. Rubagumya, a former Rwandan refugee living then in Dar es Salaam, notes that there was some pressure on Rwandans in Tanzania to join the RPF. Rubagumya, *Son of Two Countries*, 62.

9 Des Forges, *"Leave None to Tell,"* 37.

10 For the Tanzanian state's role in the Arusha Accords, see Rutinwa, "Tanzania Government's Response." On the peace accords themselves, see Newbury, "Background to Genocide"; Lemarchand "Consociationalism."

11 Scholars have noted that the post–Cold War UN-led effort to impose Western-style democratization on African nations, without considering the political, economic, and cultural realities in those nations, hastened the forces of violence in the Great Lakes region. See, for example, Prunier, *Africa's World War*, xxxii–xxxiii. On the incredibly high level of poverty, inequality, and scarcity in Rwanda during the late 1980s and early 1990s, see Uvin, *Aiding Violence*, chap. 6.

12 Des Forges, *"Leave None to Tell."* In particular, the Coalition for the Defense of the Republic (CDR) formed in 1992.

13 The Arusha Accords were signed in 1993.

14 Mamdani, *From Victims to Killers*, 203–5. *Internally* displaced persons are increasingly viewed as a "category of concern" by the UNHCR, although, as a group, they are not afforded the same legal protections as refugees.

15 On the Burundian genocide of 1972 and subsequent ethnic violence, see Lemarchand, *Burundi*. On Burundian Hutu refugees' life in exile and ideologies of nationalism, see Malkki, *Purity and Exile*.

16 For a refutation of the influence of RTLM, see Straus, "What is the Relationship."

17 Such individuals included the *Akazu*, a group of politicians and military personnel related to Habyarimana's wife and home region.

266 · Notes to Chapter 8

18 In addition to Burundian president Cyprien Ntaryamira. Fierce debates continue to surround this event, with scholars and politicians arguing that either the RPF or extremist Hutu political elites were responsible for the plane's destruction.

19 Des Forges, "Leave None to Tell," 62.

20 Interview with David Ntahura, Rusumo, July 14, 2012. Many respondents noted that, particularly in early April, small numbers of Rwandan Tutsi entered Ngara.

21 The initial estimate that 300,000 Rwandans entered the district over April 28–29 was later downgraded to 170,000. Study 3, 37. Initial reports were later found to be at least 40 percent inflated, allegedly due to inadequate resources to accurately estimate the size of the refugee population (even though, at this point, the refugees entered Ngara almost exclusively from the Rusumo Bridge). Additional factors that led to the inaccurate figure included the "inflationary pressure" of the media and of the international refugee agencies themselves. Study 3, 128.

22 Initially, the UNHCR elected to fund only twelve of the twenty to thirty NGOs that sent representatives to Ngara. Those not chosen included local NGOs and churches. Waters, *Bureaucratizing the Good Samaritan*, 113.

23 Study 3, 37.

24 Study 3, 37.

25 Repatriation was particularly popular after the extensive Mozambican repatriation from southern Tanzania following the civil war in Mozambique. UNHCR Executive Committee of the High Commissioner's Programme, 42nd Session, Sub-committee on Administrative and Financial Matters, "Voluntary Repatriation Programmes: 1992," September 6, 1991, Tanzania 1990, W.S., Y.O., LWF. The end of the Cold War led to a reduction in refugees' strategic value, with repatriation becoming the preferred "durable solution" for refugees. Hammerstad, "Whose Security?" 394.

26 Bernhard Staub to Admasu Simeso, November 11, 1990, Tanzania 1990, W.S., Y.O., LWF. Burigi first opened in the 1980s for Rwandans from Uganda. Although Burigi had been "started with many good intentions . . . things went wrong," as the Tutsi pastoralists left the settlement with their cattle due to tsetse flies and a general lack of funding. Karin Iljelund, "Tanganyika Christian Refugee Service, Burigi Refugee Settlement Feature Report," December 1990, Tanzania 1990, W.S., Y.O., LWF.

27 F. J. Homann-Herimberg, Acting Director for Assistance, UNHCR, to Dr. Muetzelfeldt, August 1, 1977, Tanzania 1997, vol. 1, W.S., Y.O., LWF.

28 On the cult of accountability in humanitarian aid, see, for example, Hilhorst, "Being Good at Doing Good?" Staff at TCRS often balked at reporting procedures that were "easy to undertake . . . in the case of projects whose results are tangible, e.g. building construction, but rather difficult in the case of service-oriented projects such as education or agricultural extension work whose inputs cannot easily be evaluated against their outcome." B. W. Neldner to Mr. Nils Gussing, August 30, 1977, Tanzania 1977, vol. I., W.S., Y.O., LWF.

29 Note for the File, B. W. Neldner, "Phone Call with Arthur Storhaug, 21.11.77," 22, Tanzania 1977, W.S., Y.O., LWF; Neldner to Gussing, August 30, 1977.

30 Neldner to Gussing, August 30, 1977.

31 Today, many agencies lament that reporting tasks take up an inordinate amount of time and money that would be better spent on actual aid. Interview with Mark Leveri, TCRS director, Dar es Salaam, April 2012.

32 The Singida project represented a shift in TCRS's focus on Tanzanian rather than refugee needs. Admasu Simeso, "Summary of the TCRS Programme (Present Activities and Future Priorities)," Geneva, June 1991, Tanzania 1990, W.S., Y.O., LWF.

33 Memo by A.S., "TCRS Management," May 1996, Tanzania 1996, DWS, Y.1, LWF.

34 Lemarchand, *Burundi.*

35 "Final Report, Repatriation of Burundi Refugees No. 1992—Oct.1993," Reports 1993, Tanzania 1993, DWS, Y.1, LWF.

36 Bernhard Staub to Mr. Doherty, Representative UNHCR, Dar es Salaam, October 13, 1993, Reports 1993, Tanzania 1993, DWS, Y.1, LWF. Other factors hindering repatriation included corruption and bribery at the settlement level. The Burundian government also feared that repatriating refugees would disrupt upcoming elections. Ironically, "the repatriation base was [later] turned into a refugee reception centre." Final Narrative Report, Kibondo Project, October 1993–October 1994, December 6, 1994, LWF.

37 The TCRS was involved primarily in water development and logistics for the Burundian refugee camps in Kigoma region.

38 Admasu Simeso, "Report on the Situation of the Burundian Refugees in Western Tanzania," Geneva, November 26, 1993, Reports 1993, Tanzania 1993, DWS, Y.1, LWF. As always, the official figures and the estimates of the number of Rundi refugees in Tanzania did not match: 380,000 (official) versus 164,000 (estimate).

39 Fax from John Cosgrave, courtesy of UNHCR Kigoma, to Bernhard Staub, "Update 22.1.94," January 22, 1994, Tanzania 1994, DWS, Y.1, LWF.

40 Burundian refugees also strategically engaged in "border straggling," moving across the border of Tanzania and Burundi based on local conditions. Waters, *Bureaucratizing the Good Samaritan,* 174.

41 Many of these refugees would remain in Tanzanian refugee camps well into the 2000s, including Lukole and Lumasi camps in Ngara.

42 Bernhard Staub to Johan Balslev, "Update on the Burundi Refugee Situation," December 6, 1993, Country Programs Tanzania 1992, Reports 1993, Tanzania 1993, DWS, Y.1, LWF.

43 Some funding for local purchases came from the Norwegian government, which already supported development projects in Kigoma. Staub to Balslev, "Update on the Burundi Refugee Situation."

44 The food situation was somewhat relieved by the camps' proximity to Burundi as refugees were able to acquire "what little food they might find" across the border. In addition, because there was no drought in western Tanzania, local farmers often employed refugees as casual labor and allowed them to cultivate their own "small plots of land." Simeso, "Report on the Situation of the Burundian Refugees," November 26, 1993.

45 Interview with Roberti Shabani, Kasulo/Benaco, July 30, 2012.

46 This was particularly the case for the Lukole (A and B) and Lumasi refugee camps. Lukole A was established in January 1994 for Burundian refugees. In 1995–1996 many Burundians and Rwandans were sent to the Keza and Kitali Hills camps, but following the forced repatriation of Rwandans, they were resettled in Lukole A and B. Turner, *Politics of Innocence.*

47 Interview with Tony Waters, Skype, May 16, 2014.

48 Twenty-five hours after the bridge was opened by the Rwandan army, an RPF platoon arrived at the border and halted the refugees' exodus by closing the bridge. Study 3, 37.

49 Initially, the area was surveyed in anticipation of additional Burundian refugees. Waters, *Bureaucratizing the Good Samaritan*, 106. The name Benaco came from the Italian construction agency that built the major road from Rusumo to Ngara.

50 This statement gains relevance given Simeso's long experience in refugee relief, including with Ethiopian "famine refugees" in the mid-1980s. Admasu Simeso, "Ngara Tanzania, Wednesday 04 May 1994," Tanzania 1994, DWS, Y.1, LWF.

51 Simeso, "Ngara Tanzania, Wednesday 04 May 1994."

52 Simeso, "Ngara Tanzania, Wednesday 04 May 1994."

53 One of the TCRS's first responsibilities in the UNHCR's sectoral approach was the removal of bodies from Rusumo Falls, a job that was essential but underappreciated by the media. The project eventually removed the bodies of more than nine hundred people, who were then buried in a small memorial.

54 Simeso, "Ngara Tanzania, Wednesday 04 May 1994."

55 Simeso, "Ngara Tanzania, Wednesday 04 May 1994."

56 Simeso, "Ngara Tanzania, Wednesday 04 May 1994."

57 Bernhard Staub to Johan Balslev, "Rwandese Refugee Influx," May 4, 1994, Tanzania 1994, DWS, Y.1, LWF.

58 This statement referred specifically to Rwandan refugee camp organization and management in Karagwe district, which received an initial influx of refugees. Memo from Admasu Simeso to Brian Neldner, "Update on the Burundian and Rwandese Refugees in Western Tanzania," April 30, 1994, Tanzania 1994, DWS, Y.1, LWF.

59 Mr. Staub's Resident, "Benaco Logistics on the Twelfth Day," 3, Tanzania 1994, DWS, Y.1 LWF.

60 Report by Bernhard Staub, Director, TCRS, "Benaco Refugee Camp," May 21, 1994, Tanzania 1994, DWS, Y.1. LWF.

61 Simeso, "Ngara Tanzania, Wednesday 04 May 1994." The UNHCR, In addition to some implementing NGOs, hired "media specialists" in an attempt to capitalize on news coverage. Waters, *Bureaucratizing the Good Samaritan*, 114.

62 The influx into North and South Kivu was precipitated in part by the French implementation of Zone Turquoise during the last weeks of the genocide. This operation has been roundly criticized for prolonging the genocide and for giving *génocidaires* and the Rwandan government a safe escape route into Zaire, where they were then (re)militarized and formed the Front for the Liberation of Rwanda (FDLR), a militia group composed of hard-line Hutu power extremists and others who were co-opted or joined voluntarily. Study 2, 53–54.

Notes to Chapter 8 · 269

63 Study 3, 180, 184.

64 See, for example, Gary Sibson, Project Coordinator, "TCRS Rwandese Refugee Emergencies Project, Project Coordinator Handover Notes," October 26, 1994, 5, Tanzania 1994, DWS, Y.1, LWF. Aid workers in Ngara noted that they lost some funding when media attention shifted to Goma. Nevertheless, during these early months of the emergency, the UNHCR acted "without care for money" in terms of financing the needs of refugees in Ngara. Interview with Tony Waters.

65 On donors' influence on repatriation, see Waters, *Bureaucratizing the Good Samaritan*, 169. Tanzanian president Ali Hasan Mwinyi suggested resettling the refugees along the southern border, but given the enormous logistical costs and lack of political will, the plan never went far. Waters, *Bureaucratizing the Good Samaritan*, 127.

66 "Report on the Rwanda Refugee Situation in Ngara and Karagwe District," October 10, 1994, Tanzania 1994, DWS, Y.1, LWF.

67 "Rwandese Refugee Situation in Tanzania," n.d., Tanzania 1994, DWS, Y.1, LWF.

68 It was estimated that as of September 23, 1994, Ngara district held a total of 373,892 refugees among four refugee camps (including Lukole camp, built by the UNHCR to decongest Benaco camp, Lumasi camp, and Msuhura Hill). Kagera region as a whole had 516,870 refugees. Between September 17 and 23, UNHCR reports noted a decrease in new refugee arrivals in Ngara, down from the peak of 5,000 people a day in July to 940 a day, as well as the spontaneous repatriation of 565 "Tutsis or those of mixed Hutu Tutsi heritage" to Rwanda. By October, the number of new refugees per day had increased to 1,200 in Ngara. "Report on the Rwanda Refugee Situation in Ngara and Karagwe District," October 10, 1994.

69 "Report on the Rwanda Refugee Situation in Ngara and Karagwe District," October 10, 1994.

70 Admasu Simeso, "Report from Ngara, Tanzania," September 5, 1996, Tanzania 1996, DWS, Y.1, LWF; Admasu Simeso, "Ngara Revisted (A Field Visit Report to TCRS Tanzania)," Geneva, May 3, 1996, Tanzania 1996, DWS, Y.1, LWF.

71 Ministry of Foreign Affairs and International Cooperation, Dar es Salaam, "Government Statement on the Current Situation in Burundi," March 31, 1995, Tanzania 1995, DWS, Y.1, LWF.

72 The government also argued that Tanzania was not obligated under refugee law to accept Rwandan refugees seeking a second country of asylum after passing through Burundi. "Government Statement on the Current Situation in Burundi," by the Ministry of Foreign Affairs and International Cooperation, Dar es Salaam, 31.2.95, County Programs, Tanzania, 1995, DWS, Y.1, LWF.

73 Lisa Henry (DanChurch Aid), "Monitoring Visit to Tanzania September 2–12, 1995," September 19, 1995, 2, Tanzania 1995, DWS, Y.1, LWF. On changing Tanzanian perceptions of Rwandan refugees following the murder of a Tanzanian evangelist in Benaco, see Waters, *Bureaucratizing the Good Samaritan*, 127.

74 ACT-TCRS Rwanda/Burundi Refugee Program 1995B, Tanzania 1995, DWS, Y.1, LWF.

75 Interview with Thomas Barondo, Keza, July 17, 2012.

76 This overestimation of the number of refugees likely stems from both the significant impact on local communities and the enormous number of refugees in the district generally.

77 Interview with Thomas Barondo. According to Simon Ndyaderi, "very dangerous" refugees often left weapons near the border and later went back to retrieve them. Interview with Simon Ndyaderi, Keza, July 17, 2012. Peter Kato recalled that the refugees singled out those who looked Tutsi and marked them for death. Interview with Peter Kato, Keza, July 17, 2012.

78 Other sectors operated by various agencies under UNHCR coordination included camp management, medical service, education, vector control, food distribution, and central storage, among others. Sibson, "TCRS Rwandese Refugee Emergencies."

79 Having previously been the "privileged" implementing partner of the UNHCR, it must have been difficult to take on such "unattractive" sectors of the aid operation. Interview with Duane Poppe, Geneva, November 4, 2011.

80 "Report on the Rwanda Refugee Situation in Ngara and Karagwe District," October 10, 1994, 3.

81 J. H. Aantjes, Emergency Coordinator, Rwanda and Burundi Refugees, TCRS Dar es Salaam, "Report on the Project Visit to Ngara and Karagwe Districts, the Rwanda Refugee Project, 08–12 November 1994," 8, 1994, DWS, Y.1, LWF.

82 Aantjes, "Report on the Project Visit to Ngara and Karagwe Districts," 8.

83 Simeso, "Ngara Revisited (A Field Report to TCRS Tanzania)," May 3, 1996. Five million liters of diesel was equivalent to "about Tsh 1.6 billion or $3 million." Tony Waters, TCRS, Ngara, "The Billion Shilling Man: Stein Jensen and the Ngara Fuel Business," August 1995, Tanzania 1995, DWS, Y.1, LWF.

84 Charles Franzen, "Report of Visit to Ngara/Karagwe/Kibondo Projects by Interim Emergency Refugee Coordinator, 2–14 February 1995," February 17, 1995, Tanzania 1995, DWS, Y.1, LWF.

85 Waters, "Billion Shilling Man," 3.

86 There were also more ambitious thieves, such as the truck driver who attempted to steal seven thousand liters of fuel in June 1995 by pretending that he had offloaded the entire load. Most truckers stole "a few hundred liters off their 50,000 liter loads." Waters, "Billion Shilling Man," 3. In June 1995 a "turnboy" was found with eighty liters of fuel in his tent at K9. "Minutes of Senior Staff Meeting," June 21, 1995, Tanzania, 1995, DWS, Y.1, LWF.

87 Aantjes, "Report on the Project Visit to Ngara and Karagwe Districts," 5.

88 Franzen, "Report of Visit to Ngara/Karagwe/Kibondo Projects." Employees of TCRS were also implicated in a fuel theft. "Minutes of Senior Staff meeting," June 21, 1995.

89 Henry, "Monitoring Visit to Tanzania September 2–12, 1995," 5.

90 Aantjes, "Report on the Project Visit to Ngara and Karagwe Districts," 8–9.

91 As Jaap Aantjes, TCRS emergency coordinator, noted in November 1994, "TCRS activities are now growing at a tremendous pace, to such extend [sic] even that we should pause for a few seconds and ask ourselves how much can TCRS handle. . . .

Notes to Chapter 8 · 271

It has to be kept in mind that we are taking over activities and equipment designed for the emergency phase while we are gradually moving towards a semipermeanent situation . . . any small disruption causes an emergency with the potential for disaster." Aantjes, "Report on the Project Visit to Ngara and Karagwe Districts."

92 By February 1995, international fuel usage in Ngara had climbed to twelve thousand liters per day, leading UNHCR officials to impose "strict rationing" for each agency, according to need. Franzen, "Report of Visit to Ngara/Karagwe/Kibondo Projects."

93 In May 1995 the UNHCR owed the LWF more than $2 million for the year, leading TCRS officials to threaten to halt operations. Peter Tyler, Secretary for Finance and Administration, TCRS, to Mr. Karl Stenacker, Officer in Charge, UNHCR, Ngara, May 12, 1995, Tanzania 1995, DWS, Y.1, LWF.

94 Bernhard Staub to Peter Tyler, "UNHCR Funding for Ngara," May 13, 1995, Tanzania 1995, DWS, Y.1, LWF.

95 The shortcomings of "emergency" aid in situations that become "permanent" were already on display in reporting on Muyenzi in 1963. Such issues have only increased. See Loescher and Milner, "Protracted Refugee Situations."

96 Study 3, 92.

97 Aantjes, "Report on the Project Visit to Ngara and Karagwe Districts."

98 Fax from Bernhard Staub to Johan Balslev, "Government Statement on Situation in Burundi," April 24, 1995, Tanzania 1995, DWS, Y.1, LWF.

99 Cosgrave to Staub, "Update 22.1.94."

100 The lake initially provided 60 percent of the refugees' water needs. ACT-TCRS Rwanda/Burundi Refugee Program 1995B. Waters notes that the lake did not dry up completely due to the presence of local springs in the area. Waters, *Bureaucratizing the Good Samaritan*, 185.

101 ACT-TCRS Rwanda/Burundi Refugee Program 1995B. On the many expensive and eventually useless water schemes the UNHCR envisioned (and enacted) in 1994, see Waters, *Bureaucratizing the Good Samaritan*, 182–83.

102 ACT-TCRS Rwanda/Burundi Refugee Program 1995B.

103 Franzen, "Report of Visit to Ngara/Karagwe/Kibondo Projects."

104 Franzen, "Report of Visit to Ngara/Karagwe/Kibondo Projects."

105 ACT-TCRS Rwanda/Burundi Refugee Program 1995B.

106 Staub to Balslev, "Government Statement on Situation in Burundi."

107 Study 3, 93.

108 Study 3, 103.

109 Quoted in Study 3, 93.

110 Staub noted that even though the TCRS had a "temporary low performance," it was still able to transport food, water, and material aid without major halts in distribution. Bernhard Staub to Representative UNHCR, Dar es Salaam, "Re: UNHCR/TCRS Partnership in Ngara UNHCR Financial Constraints," February 6, 1996, Tanzania 1996, DWS, Y.1, LWF.

111 According to Staub, "The main problem between UNHCR and TCRS in Ngara was that after the difficult months of Jan–April 1995 UNHCR was so used to blame and ride on TCRS that it just did not accept that TCRS had sorted it self out and

272 · Notes to Chapter 8

continued to have a negative attitude despite the very obvious positive things that TCRS was doing." Email from Bernhard Staub to Rudolf Hinz, "TCRS UNHCR Funding and Cooperation," January 3, 1996, Tanzania 1995, DWS, Y.1, LWF.

112 Staub to Representative UNHCR, "Re: UNHCR/TCRS Partnership in Ngara," February 6, 1996.

113 Staub noted, "UNHCR are always referring to what went wrong . . . without taking into consideration that no other agency could and would have been able to do it better." Bernhard Staub to Admasu Simeso, January 16, 1996, Tanzania 1996, DWS, Y.1, LWF.

114 John Cosgrave to Bernhard Staub, "Confidential: UNHCR and TCRS," February 16, 1996, Tanzania 1996, DWS, Y.1, LWF.

115 Bernhard Staub to Kaanaeli Makundi, "Rwandese Refugees in Tanzania Scenario if Funding Is Not Forthcoming," February 8, 1996, Tanzania 1995, DWS, Y.1, LWF. Similarly, Staub noted that TCRS's budget in Kagera was financed 66 percent from UNHCR and 34 percent from LWF sources and that "UNHCR like to think that they are financing at least 90% and certainly give the impression to the general public that it is their show." Bernhard Staub to Peter Tyler, "UNHCR Funding and Budget for 1996," January 18, 1996, Tanzania 1996, DWS, Y.1, LWF.

116 Email from Bernhard Staub to Admasu Simeso, "UNHCR and Karagwe," March 10, 1996.

117 Staub to Simeso, "UNHCR and Karagwe."

118 Email from Jaap Aantjes to Admasu Simeso, "TCRS Karagwe Involvement," September 23, 1996, Tanzania 1996, DWS, Y.1, LWF.

119 Admasu Simeso to Relags, "Report from Ngara, Tanzania," September 5, 1996, Tanzania 1996, DWS, Y.1, LWF. As Staub put it, "TCRS would like a healthy mix of activities and was not supportive of UNHCR initiatives to have all NGOs specializing in specific activities." Staub to Simeso, "UNHCR and Karagwe."

120 "TCRS Ngara Project Mechanical Workshop End of Contract Report, 1995–97," Tanzania 1997, DWS, Y.1, LWF.

121 In 1988, the Ngaran population was estimated at 192,000. "Assistance to Local Communities in Refugee Impacted Areas, Kagera Region, Tanzania," Country Programs, Tanzania, 1996, DWS, Y.1, LWF.

9. OF *GÉNOCIDAIRES* AND HUMANITARIANS

1 Fax from Admasu Simeso to Mr. John Halverson, ELCA, May 17, 1994, Tanzania 1994, DWS, Y.1, LWF.

2 J. H. Aantjes, Emergency Coordinator, TCRS, "Report on the Project Visit to Ngara and Karagwe Districts, the Rwanda Refugee Project, 08–12 November 1994," 1994, DWS, Y.1, LWF.

3 Aantjes, "Report on the Project Visit to Ngara and Karagwe Districts."

4 The principle of *non-refoulement* "constitutes the corner stone of international refugee protection" and is guaranteed by Article 33 of the 1951 Convention.

Notes to Chapter 9 · 273

UNHCR, "Advisory Opinion on the Extraterritorial Application of *Non-Refoulement* Obligations under the 1951 Convention Relating to the Status of Refugees and Its 1967 Protocol," https://www.unhcr.org/4d9486929.pdf.

5 Relief work continued at the Burundian refugee camps of Lukole A and B and the transit camp at Mbuba. As of January 2000, there were 88,542 Burundian refugees at Lukole A and B and 21,421 Rwandans at Lukole B. By this point, Burundians and Rwandans were separated in transit camps and sent to different settlement camps. Akarro, "Population Issues in Refugee Settlements," 30, table 2.

6 Interview with David Magwi, Benaco, July 23, 2012.

7 See, for example, Jaspers, *Rwandan Refugee Crisis*; Whitaker, "Refugees in Western Tanzania"; Alix-Garcia and Saah, "Effect of Refugee Inflows." A notable exception is Waters, "Assessing the Impact."

8 Whitaker, "Refugees in Western Tanzania."

9 Nugent and Asiwaju, "Introduction," 10. Ironically, as Loren Landau has demonstrated in other refugee hosting areas of Tanzania, this entrenchment of nationalism took place during a time of diminishing state presence and resources in the district. Landau, "Beyond the Losers." Following structural adjustment reforms and increased perceptions of governmental corruption, state resources expended in Ngara district for Tanzanians were at an all-time low during the mid-1990s. That Ngarans nevertheless identified with a beneficent Tanzania (despite official corruption) indicates the powerful influence of refugee experiences on local perceptions of self and state. This chapter refutes Landau's claim that "only four years after camp closures in Kagera Region, even the campsites themselves have been 'reclaimed' and are largely indistinguishable from their surroundings." Landau, "Beyond the Losers," 28. Based on research conducted in Ngara during 2012 and 2015, this assertion could not be further from the truth.

10 Interview with David Ntahura, Rusumo, July 14, 2012.

11 Based on interviews, it seems likely that violence between Hutu and Tutsi, as well as among members of these ethnic groups, took place in the refugee camps.

12 Interview with David Ntahura.

13 Interview with Deus Rwanzo, Kumnazi, August 4, 2012.

14 Interview with Danieli Mdenda, Rusumo, July 12, 2012. Answers like these, which place the start of the war in Rwanda at varying points, including 1990 (the year the RPF invaded Rwanda from Uganda), 1991, 1992, and 1994, emphasize the difficulty in pinpointing the start of wars that have fixed dates in media and scholarship. They also reveal the ongoing nature of violence and trauma; if a war starts before its "historical" date, it might end well after its closing date. Such wars do not have defined beginnings and ends, despite the events we use to mark their occurrences (e.g., a plane crash on April 6, 1994, an RPF takeover in July). It is not just memory and trauma that make wars ongoing but also the violent incidents that continue to affect people's lives and defy simple teleologies, as Mdenda and others elaborated on.

15 Interview with Danieli Mdenda.

16 Interview with Danieli Mdenda.

17 Unlike David Ntahura, Danieli Mdenda remembered that the price of food remained high throughout the refugees' stay in Ngara, including 1995–1996. There are no simple, easy narratives in oral history—memory is a fickle thing, and there is no single common experience of the refugee emergency to call on. Each person remembers in his or her own way.

18 The local word is *kuosha*, which means here "washing the house."

19 Interview with Julien Rundadi, Benaco, July 23, 2012.

20 As one TCRS official wrote in June 1994, "Considering such a large camp and the concentration of people it is remarkable that the camp is under such good control vis a vis nutrition, health and security." Gary Sibson, Project Coordinator, to Johan Balsev, TCRS Emergency Coordinator, "Travel Report Tanzania Uganda Rwanda-Rwanda Crises, May 30th–June 9th," Tanzania 1994, DWS, Y.1, LWF.

21 In late May Staub wrote of Benaco, "The uncanny thing about Benaco is the peaceful attitude around the whole camp. People are standing in line and waiting their turn to be issued with food, standing in line at the medical centers and mingling around at the market place along the tarmac road." Bernhard Staub, Director, TCRS, "Benaco Refugee Camp," May 21, 1994, Tanzania 1994, DWS, Y.1, LWF.

22 "It was reported that 2 Rwandese staff members from the organization CARE were killed in the event." "Report on the Rwanda Refugee Situation in Ngara and Karagwe District," October 10, 1994, Tanzania 1994, DWS, Y.1, LWF.

23 The manipulation of the refugee crisis and international aid for the benefit of militias and the Rwandan military was more acute in Zaire, where the instability of the government led to some cooperation between the *génocidaires* and Zairean forces. The refugee community in Zaire also had a larger population of militia and army members, as well as a larger refugee population in general, which made it even more difficult for refugee agencies to control the population. Borton, Brusset, and Hallam, "International Response to Conflict and Genocide: Study 3" (hereafter, Study 3). Nevertheless, as one scholar with long experience in the region noted, Benaco was a place of extreme violence and fear. David Newbury, email to author, July 16, 2019; interview with former UNHCR worker Samson Bayashamba, Ngara, August 4, 2012.

24 Study 3, 117.

25 According to a TCRS report, "The wealthier refugees, those with cars or trucks, brought everything their transport could carry. There is a car park near the camp full of cars and trucks. When the Rwandan government troops fled from the border there was a queue 8 km long waiting to cross." Many of the elite found jobs with relief agencies. Mr. Staub's Resident, "Benaco Logistics on the Twelfth Day," Tanzania 1994, DWS, Y.1, LWF.

26 Study 3, 39; Adelman and Suhrke, "International Response to Conflict and Genocide: Study 2," 57 (hereafter, Study 2); Waters, *Bureaucratizing the Good Samaritan*, 120–23.

27 Interview with former UN coordinating official in Ngara in Study 2, 96n121. On the differences in camp management in the Lumasi Rwandan refugee camp, see Pottier, "Relief and Repatriation."

Notes to Chapter 9 · 275

28 Michael Hyden, a TCRS program manager, recalled that K9 was a "symbol of Westerners." Interview with Michael Hyden, Geneva, October 28, 2011.

29 Some of this infrastructure was later successfully handed over to local organizations and governments in Ngara; others, such as the staff houses built out of shipping containers, continued to house TCRS staff involved in development projects in Ngara. Lisa Henry (DanChurch Aid), "Monitoring Visit to Tanzania September 2–12, 1995," September 19, 1995, 4, Tanzania 1995, DWS, Y.1, LWF.

30 Jaap Aantjes to Bernhard Staub, "Subject: Memorandum Colin Pryce UNHCR-Ngara," March 6, 1995, Tanzania 1995, DWS, Y.1, LWF.

31 Colin Pryce, Senior Logistics Officer, UNHCR, Ngara, to Charles Franzen, Project Coordinator, TCRS, Ngara, "Areas of Management Causing Concern," March 4, 1995, Tanzania 1995, DWS, Y.1, LWF. Aantjes responded to Pryce's letter by noting that complaints about delays in construction of the workshop at K9 were "interesting to hear, because it was exactly the indecisiveness of UNHCR about where to put the workshop, that led us to lean heavily on Colin, to make up his mind about the site." The TCRS was concerned about the mud at K9, and Pryce had apparently given permission to build the permanent workshop at Ngara town, as long as there was a mobile workshop unit operational at K9. Aantjes to Staub, "Subject: Memorandum Colin Pryce."

32 Interview with Deus Rwanzo.

33 One example was TCRS's decision to move all ex-TCRS drivers from the Katumba Burundian refugee camp to Ngara. Bernhard Staub to Johan Balslev, "Rwandese Refugee Update," May 23, 1994, Tanzania 1994, DWS, Y.1, LWF.

34 Fax from Bernhard Staub to Johan Balslev, "Government Statement on Situation in Burundi," April 24, 1995, Tanzania 1995, DWS, Y.1, LWF. By the fall of 1995, the TCRS employed 330 Tanzanian, 12 expatriate, and 30 refugees in Ngara, in addition to Ngarans hired as day laborers. Henry, "Monitoring Visit to Tanzania September 2–12, 1995," 3.

35 Charles Franzen, "Report of Visit to Ngara/Karagwe/Kibondo Projects by Interim Emergency Refugee Coordinator, 2–14 February 1995," February 17, 1995, 9, Tanzania 1995, DWS, Y.1, LWF.

36 Aantjes, "Report on the Project Visit to Ngara and Karagwe Districts."

37 Aantjes, "Report on the Project Visit to Ngara and Karagwe Districts."

38 Franzen, "Report of Visit to Ngara/Karagwe/Kibondo Projects."

39 Pryce to Franzen, "Areas of Management Causing Concern," 5.

40 Marfleet, "Refugees and History," 139.

41 Henry, "Monitoring Visit to Tanzania September 2–12, 1995." Study 3 noted that during the initial influx of refugees, local crops were trampled or stolen, and doors, window frames, and furniture were removed form schools and health posts to be used for firewood. Study 3, 177n4.

42 Henry, "Monitoring Visit to Tanzania September 2–12, 1995."

43 Tony Waters to Director, "Repatriation News," August 31, 1995, 2, Tanzania 1995, DWS, Y.1, LWF.

44 Interview with David Magwi, Benaco, July 23, 2012. Another woman who worked with the Red Cross supplying food in Benaco recalled that when she lived near the camp, she was attacked by "bombs"; after she moved to K9, some problems continued. Interview with Mary Sidado, Benaco, July 23, 2012.

45 Interview with Pastory Natore, K9, June 19, 2012.

46 Interview with Pastory Natore. Pastory made a list of all those who lost property during the construction of the Benaco camp; however, he and other community members claimed they were never compensated. Michael Hyden also recalled that Ngarans attempted to contact aid agencies about theft. Interview with Michael Hyden.

47 Admasu Simeso, "Ngara Revisited (A Field Report to TCRS Tanzania)," May 3, 1996, Tanzania 1996, DWS, Y.1, LWF.

48 Interview with Selma Amani, Kasulo, July 24, 2012.

49 Hyden remembered frequent "hijackings" along the Ngara-Karagwe road.

50 According to Thomas Kapondo, the refugees were given "more services" than the locals, who felt "totally frustrated." Interview with Thomas Kapondo, Rulenge, June 28, 2012.

51 Interview with Marco Bautbula, Munweje, June 27, 2012. See also Whitaker, "Refugees in Western Tanzania," 343.

52 Whitaker estimates that more than 50 percent of the health center staff and 35 percent of dispensary workers left government work for relief agency employment. There were also severe drug shortages in the district, outside of the refugee camps. Whitaker, "Refugees in Western Tanzania," 343. Although not nearly as severe as in Goma, there were cholera outbreaks in Benaco during December 1994 and February 1995, and cases of bloody diarrhea occurred in the refugee camps, which likely impacted nearby populations. Study 3, 82, 91.

53 Interview with Julien Rundadi. Rundadi worked for Norwegian People's Aid at a dispensary in Kasulu, the village next to Benaco.

54 Whitaker, "Refugees in Western Tanzania," 343.

55 Whitaker, "Refugees in Western Tanzania," 345. Women were generally responsible for obtaining firewood. Whitaker notes that some women were able to start small businesses and hire refugee laborers. Thus, although the refugee presence "may have reduced the power of some women, it afforded others" opportunities "to gain a degree of economic independence." Whitaker, "Refugees in Western Tanzania," 346. The most vulnerable were single mothers and the elderly. One notable instance of women increasing their economic standing was those who were able to thrive in the Benaco market. Interview with Tony Waters, Skype, May 16, 2014.

56 Maize was supplied by WFP donors who were unwilling to cover the milling costs. The grain was unfamiliar and required additional cooking time, which likely led to increased refugee consumption of firewood and contributed to deforestation in the areas around Benaco. Study 3, 116.

57 In 1994 Susanne Jaspers, a UNHCR food coordinator during the first few weeks of the Ngara operation, noted that of the five markets operated in Benaco, four were large maize collection sites for traders. "Tanzanian traders came from far and often returned maize to the towns from which WFP had transported it to the camp. In

some cases, the same trucks were even used, in which case the traders paid the WFP drivers to take food out of the camp again." Jaspers, *Rwandan Refugee Crisis*, 22.

58 On the decreased price and local surplus of beans and maize, see Whitaker, "Refugees in Western Tanzania," 341.

59 Rutinwa, "Tanzanian Government's Response," 297.

60 Interview with Esther Philo, Ngara, August 7, 2012.

61 Interview with Samson Bayashamba.

62 Interview with Roberti Shabani, Benaco, July 30, 2012.

63 Interestingly, the men in more distant villages did not remember the price of food increasing, but the women often did. Interview with Mary Roberti, Mugoma, July 12, 2012. In Muyenzi, where there were few refugees, the price of food was immaterial in 1994, as few people had any money with which to buy food. Interview with Sylvia Rwabani, Muyenzi, June 18, 2012. Sylvia also remembered soldiers around the 1994–1996 camps.

64 Interview with Bernard Kadene, Shanga, July 9, 2012.

65 Interview with Samwel Rwanzi, Shanga, July 9, 2012.

66 Interview with Edward Teadi, Mugoma, July 12, 2012.

67 Interview with Leora Mudard, Kumnazi, July 30, 2012.

68 Interview with Sarah Mzee, Kumnazi, July 30, 2012.

69 Interview with Gasper Buneza, Kumnazi, August 4, 2012. Gasper thought the local police might have collaborated with refugees in theft.

70 Interview with Nicholas Kanuma, Rulenge, June 25, 2012.

71 ACT/TCRS Tanzania, 1996 Rwanda/Burundi Refugee Program, Tanzania 1996, DWS, Y.1, LWF.

72 Interview with Thomas Barondo, Keza, July 17, 2012.

73 ACT/TCRS Tanzania, 1996 Rwanda/Burundi Refugee Program.

74 ACT/TCRS Tanzania, 1996 Rwanda/Burundi Refugee Program.

75 In 1996 there were an estimated 414,960 Rwandan refugees in Ngara, with "some observers" estimating 500,000. ACT/TCRS Tanzania, 1996 Rwanda/Burundi Refugee Program.

76 Waters contends that the Jesuit Refugee Service "resisted UNHCR efforts to focus" on repatriation. Waters, *Bureaucratizing the Good Samaritan, 153.*

77 Interview with William Bumbaya, Ngara, July 20, 2012.

78 Interview with Leora Mudard, Kumnazi, July 30, 2012.

79 Email from Jaap Aantjes to WCC (World council of Churches), Geneva, December 7, 1996, Tanzania 1996, W.S., Y.O., LWF. The announcement was a joint statement with the UNHCR. Senior government officials and UNHCR representatives had announced the new policy in Karagwe "a few days earlier." Whitaker, "Changing Priorities," 328n2.

80 Email from Jaap Aantjes to WCC, Geneva, "Reported Refugee Movement in Karagwe," December 9, 1996, Tanzania, 1996, W.S., Y.O., LWF.

81 Jaap Aantjes, TCRS Head Office, DSM, "Rwandan Refs in Tanzania 12/13/1996 Jaap," Tanzania 1996, W.S., Y.O., LWF.

82 Aantjes, "Rwandan Refs in Tanzania."

83 Lazarus Mezza, TCRS, Ngara Project, "Repatriation," December 13, 1996, Tanzania 1996, W.S., Y.O., LWF.

84 Mezza, "Repatriation."

85 One former UNHCR aid worker recalled that children were sometimes left behind in Benaco, some of whom committed suicide. Interview with Samson Bayashamba.

86 Exceptions included the IFRC and Oxfam, both of which distributed water to the refugees. Note for the File, "Re: Rwandese Refugee Movement from Western Tanzania," December 16, 1996, Tanzania 1996, W.S., Y.O., LWF.

87 Such allegations continued for several years. As noted by TCRS personnel in 1998, "The Rwanda government continues to make charges that rebel Rwandan forces are taking sanctuary in western Tanzania." TCRS-DAR to LWFDOMAIN.LWF, "LWF/WS Tanzania Programme Update March 1998," April 2, 1998, Tanzania 1998, DWS, Y.1, LWF.

88 One TCRS official wrote, "Resistance groups are beginning to use Benaco as a site for launching attacks on the RPF government inside Rwanda, a situation which jeopardizes the security of Tanzania and the Rwanda refugees." "Rwandese Refugee Situation in Tanzania," n.d., Tanzania 1994, W.S., Y.O., LWF. Other personnel maintain that the extent to which the refugees at Benaco were "held hostage" was exaggerated by the UNHCR. Interview with Tony Waters. One aid worker noted that the refugees did not want to return to "Tutsi land." Interview with Sabas Nicolaus, Ngara, August 11, 2012.

89 Aantjes, "Report on the Project Visit to Ngara and Karagwe Districts."

90 See Prunier, *Africa's World War*, 38–42.

91 The UNHCR itself suppressed an internal report commissioned in September 1994 to assess the appropriateness of repatriation efforts (known as the Gersony Report). It claimed evidence of "an unmistakable pattern of killings and persecution" by the RPF. Later, sections of the report were leaked to the press and likely made their way to refugees in Ngara, who remained vigilant in their search for information on conditions in Rwanda. See Study 3, 53. Additionally, throughout the end of 1994, three to five bodies a day were found in the Kagera River, "some of which have been the victims of execution type slayings. Such observations suggest that hopes for a massive repatriation of the Hutu refs . . . are dwindling." "Rwandese Refugee Situation in Tanzania."

92 Lucky employees were transferred to work at the Burundian refugee camps. Interview with Esther Philo.

93 Interview with Pastory Natore.

94 Bernhard Staub, Director, TCRS, to Ms. Maureen Connelly, UNHCR, Senior Emergency Officer, Kagera Region, "Program Planning," May 20, 1994, Tanzania 1994, DWS, Y.1, LWF.

95 "TCRS Advisory Committee Held on 13/11/1995 at Bishop Sendero's Office Luther House DSM," Tanzania 1995, DWS, Y.1, LWF.

96 Tony Waters, Program Officer, and Bodil Torp, Project Coordinator (Acting), TCRS, "Ref: Implementation Status Report on Donor Supported Programmes in Refugee Affected Areas in Kagera Region," July 5, 1995, Tanzania 1995, DWS, Y.1, LWF.

Notes to Chapter 9 · 279

97 By 1996, the TCRS had repaired ten kilometers of roads in Ngara town, distributed two thousand tree seedlings, conducted management training for sixty village and church leaders, stocked six fishponds, and handed over one village well in Keza for five hundred villagers. Email from TCRS-DAR to LWFDOMAIN. LWF (Ide), "LWF/DWS Tanzania Programme Update June/July 1998," August 3, 1998, Tanzania 1998, DWS, Y.1, LWF.

98 Waters and Torp, "Ref: Implementation Status Report on Donor Supported Programmes." Study 3 found that in Ngara, "UNHCR appears to have been over-legalistic in the application of its mandate, with local residents having been treated as second-class citizens in relation to the refugees." An example was the UNHCR's use of planes to spray refugee camps for vector control, but the planes "turned off" the spray as they flew over adjoining Tanzanian villages. Study 3, 179.

99 Edwin Ramathal, Project Coordinator, to Bernhard Staub, Director, TCRS, "Comments on PMS—Our Clarifications," July 8, 1997, Tanzania 1997, DWS, Y.1, LWF.

100 Email from J-AANTJES@maf.org to LWFDOMAIN.LWF, "Situation Report Emergency Department TCRS—April 1997," May 16, 1997, Tanzania 1997, DWS, Y.1, LWF; emphasis in original.

101 TCRS-DAR to LWFDOMAIN.LWF (Ide), "Tanzania Programme Update June/July 1998."

102 A few agencies, such as Concern and NPA, did remain in the district—albeit with drastically scaled down programs. The UNHCR eventually funded the rehabilitation of roads in Ngara, as well as some health care and education initiatives. Karren L. K. Washoma, "Executive Summary—Refugee Impact in NW Tanzania," August 2003, https://repositories.lib.utexas.edu/bitstream/handle/2152/4679/3765.pdf?sequence=1.

103 Mezza, "Repatriation."

104 There is a large scholarship on peacekeeping failures in Rwanda. For an introduction, see Des Forges, *"Leave None to Tell the Story,"* 408–57.

105 Generally, Ngarans spoke of the need for refugee agencies to help host communities, often prioritizing aid to rebuild water resources, provide health care, and promote reforestation. While some Ngarans mentioned that humanitarian agencies had assisted their communities, the vast majority of interviewees expressed frustration at their precipitous departure.

CONCLUSION

1 Admasu Simeso, "Ngara Tanzania, Wednesday 04 May 1994," Tanzania 1994, DWS, Y.1, LWF.

2 Marfleet, "Refugees and History," 139. For example, as of 2011, internally displaced persons (IDPs) and stateless persons were recognized as UNHCR categories of concern.

3 On similar UNHCR views toward Angolan refugees, see Rich, "Victims or Burdens?" On the legacy of colonialism in humanitarian organizations, see Baughan, "Rehabilitating an Empire."

4 Hunter, "Introduction," 5.

5 Tripp, *Changing the Rules*, 10.

6 Adelman, "Age of Imperial Revolutions," 323.

7 Integrated Regional Information Network (IRIN), UN Office for the Coordination of Humanitarian Affairs, "Rwanda-Tanzania: IRIN Focus on Rwandan Refugees in Tanzania," May 16, 2002, http://pambazuka.org/en/category/refugees /7482.

8 Southern Africa Documentation and Cooperation Centre (SADOCC), "Tanzania: Last Group of Rwandans Leaves," January 3, 2003, http://www.sadocc.at/news /2003-006.shtml,.

9 IRIN, "Rwanda-Tanzania: Thousands Expelled from Tanzania," March 5, 2007, http://www.irinnews.org/report/70510/rwanda-tanzania-thousands-expelled -from-tanzania.

10 IRIN, "Rwanda-Tanzania: Thousands Expelled from Tanzania."

11 The government reported that these people were deported after refusing to naturalize or acquire residence permits. IRIN, "Humanitarian Crisis Looms for Migrants Expelled by Tanzania," September 19, 2013, http://www.irinnews.org /report/98789/humanitarian-crisis-looms-for-migrants-expelled-by-tanzania.

12 Among those deported, many claimed they had been born and lived their entire lives in Tanzania and thought their birth certificates identified them as Tanzanians, which they felt themselves to be. As one deported woman noted, "'Even some of those leaders don't have the documents they were asking from us to prove our citizenship.'" British Broadcasting Corporation (BBC), "Why Has Tanzania Deported Thousands to Rwanda?" September 2, 2013, http://www.bbc.com /news/world-africa-23930776.

13 IRIN, "Humanitarian Crisis Looms." Immigrant round-ups and deportations continued into 2021. Meddy Mulisa, "Tanzania: Immigration Nets 25 Prohibited Immigrants in Kagera," *Tanzania Daily News*, February 18, 2021, https://allafrica .com/stories/202102190596.html.

14 BBC, "Why Has Tanzania Deported Thousands to Rwanda?"

15 As Tague notes, during decolonization, "citizenship and refugeedom consisted of gradations of gray, reflective of African in/abilities to call on and acquire the rights, privileges, and protections" of the nation-state. Tague, *Displaced Mozambicans*, 14. I argue that this situation continues beyond that era.

16 "Rwanda Press Viewed Trashed," *Daily News*, August 22, 2013, http://www .dailynews.co.tz/index.php/local-news/21355-rwanda-press-views-trashed.

17 "Rwanda Press Viewed Trashed."

18 "Tanzania President Kikwete Married to Habyarimana Cousin," *News of Rwanda*, August 19, 2013.

19 The World Bank's Board of Executive Directors approved US$340 million of the projected US$468.6 million needed to implement the project. The project

Notes to Conclusion · 281

is the first under the World Bank Group Great Lakes Regional Initiative, begun in May 2013. "World Bank Approves Rusumo Falls Hydropower Plant," press release, August 6, 2013, http://www.worldbank.org/en/news/press-release/2013 /08/06/world-bank-approves-rusumo-falls-hydropower-plant.

20 Artelia Eau & Environment, "Rusumo Falls Hydroelectric Project—Dam & Powerplan Component: Environmental and Social Impact Assessment (ESIA), Volume 1: Main Report," Draft Final Report—Revision 1, Nile Basin Initiative (NBI)/Nile Equatorial Lakes Subsidiary Action Program (NELSAP), February 2013, http://www-wds.worldbank.org/external/default/WDSContentServer /WDSP/IB/2013/03/01/000442464_20130301113925/Rendered/PDF/E4144v10Rwa ndao2028020130Box374348B.pdf.

21 There are some who question the efficacy of the project in relation to mining interests (including the UK-based Kabanga Nickel Ltd.) and the potential effects on local environments. Zachary Hurwitz, "Multilateral Development Banks: Projects to Watch," International Rivers, July 17, 2013, http://www.internationalrivers .org/blogs/258/multilateral-development-banks-projects-to-watch.

22 The EAC was (re)established in 2000 as an economic and intergovernmental association that includes Burundi, the Democratic Republic of Congo, Kenya, Rwanda, South Sudan, Tanzania, and Uganda.

23 Inter-Agency Operational Update on the Burundi Refugee Situation, Tanzania, January 31, 2017, UNHCR, https://data2.unhcr.org/en/documents/download/60876.

24 Samuel Okiror, "Tanzania President under Fire for Urging Refugees to Return to 'Stable' Burundi," *Guardian*, July 29, 2017, https://www.theguardian.com /global-development/2017/jul/29/tanzania-president-under-fire-for-urging -refugees-return-stable-burundi-john-magufuli.

25 At the time of the meeting, 170,000 Burundians had been granted citizenship, with 30,000 still waiting. However, plans for new citizens to be granted the right to migrate within the country have stalled. A few months earlier, Tanzania also halted Burundians' "automatic refugee status." "As Risks Rise in Burundi, Refuge in Tanzania Is No Longer Secure," *New Humanitarian*, May 8, 2018, https://www .thenewhumanitarian.org/feature/2018/05/08/risks-rise-burundi-refuge-tanzania -no-longer-secure.

26 Milner, "Can Global Refugee Policy"; Kweka, "Citizenship without Integration"; Amelia Kuch, "Lessons from Tanzania's Historic Bid to Turn Refugees to Citizens, "*New Humanitarian*, February 22, 2018, https://deeply.thenewhumanitarian .org/refugees/community/2018/02/22/lessons-from-tanzanias-historic-bid-to -turn-refugees-to-citizens.

27 Startlingly, a 2019 World Bank study found preliminary evidence of intergenerational trauma in Ngara. The report indicates that mothers who lived near refugee camps in their early childhoods were more likely to have stunted and shorter children. This calls for further research into the ongoing nature of refugee crises in host communities. Soazic Elise Wang Sonne and Paolo Verme, "Intergenerational Impact of Population Shocks on Children's Health: Evidence from the 1993–2001 Refugee Crisis in Tanzania," Policy Research Working Paper 9075,

282 · Notes to Conclusion

World Bank Group, December 2019, https://documents1.worldbank.org/curated /en/520491575397140628/pdf/Intergenerational-Impact-of-Population-Shocks-on -Childrens-Health-Evidence-from-the-1993–2001-Refugee-Crisis-in-Tanzania .pdf.

28 Interview with Deus Rwazo, Kumnazi, August 4, 2012.

29 Interview with Bernhard Staub, Dar es Salaam, February 14, 2012; Rubagumya, *Son of Two Countries*, 77.

30 Given the constraints of research, I was able to interview few former Rwandan refugees. On the need for scholarship that listens to, includes, and celebrates the diversity of refugee voices (and is written by refugees), see Banko et al., "What Is Refugee History."

31 Hunt, *Inventing Human Rights*; Okafor, *African Human Rights System*; De Waal, *Famine Crimes*, 219–20; Harrell-Bond, "Can Humanitarian Work," 52. The Sphere Project, begun by NGOs in 1997, has attempted to redress some of these concerns by creating universal, minimum humanitarian standards for aid agencies. See Sphere Standards, "Interactive Handbook," https://spherestandards.org /contribute/. Membership is, of course, voluntary.

32 Polzer and Hammond, "Invisible Displacement," 422.

33 De Waal, *Famine Crimes*, 124.

34 De Waal, *Famine Crimes*, 138–39.

35 For a similar analysis of Protestant aid workers in the Democratic Republic of the Congo, see Rich, *Protestant Missionaries*.

36 Interview with Brian Neldner, Skype, November 10, 2013.

37 To this end, the UNHCR has revamped the zonal development projects used in the 1960s in Burundi and Zaire and implemented them in places like Uganda. Unfortunately, due to budgetary constraints, many of these projects are underfunded. UNHCR, "UNHCR's Grandi Calls for Renewed High-Level Engagement to Advance Uganda's Comprehensive Refugee Response," March 9, 2021, https://www .unhcr.org/afr/news/press/2021/3/60479cde4/unhcrs-grandi-calls-for-renewed -high-level-engagement-to-advance-ugandas.html.

38 Cooper, "Postscript," 286.

39 Tague, *Displaced Mozambicans*, 14.

40 *Sometimes in April*, directed by Raoul Peck (New York: HBO Home Video, 2005), DVD.

Notes to Conclusion · 283

BIBLIOGRAPHY

Adelman, Howard, and Astri Suhrke. "The International Response to Conflict and Genocide: Lessons from the Rwanda Experience: Study 2, Early Warning and Conflict Management." Steering Committee of the Joint Evaluation of Emergency Assistance to Rwanda, March 1996.

Adelman, Jeremy. "An Age of Imperial Revolutions." *American Historical Review* 113, no. 2 (2008): 319–40.

Agamben, Giorgio. *Homo Sacer: Sovereign Power and Bare Life.* Palo Alto, CA: Stanford University Press, 1998.

Akarro, Rocky. "Population Issues in Refugee Settlements of Western Tanzania." *Tanzanian Journal of Population Studies and Development* 8, no. 1–2 (2001): 27–42.

Alix-Garcia, Jennifer, and David Saah. "The Effect of Refugee Inflows on Host Communities: Evidence from Tanzania." *World Bank Economic Review* 24, no. 1 (2009): 148–70.

Alonso, Ana María. "The Politics of Space, Time and Substance: State Formation, Nationalism and Ethnicity." *Annual Review of Anthropology* 23 (1994): 379–405.

Aminzade, Ronald. *Race, Nation, and Citizenship in Post-Colonial Africa: The Case of Tanzania.* Cambridge: Cambridge University Press, 2013.

Anacleti, Odhiambo. "The Regional Response to the Rwandan Emergency." *Journal of Refugee Studies* 9, no. 3 (1996): 303–11.

Anderson, Benedict. *Imagined Communities: Reflections on the Origin and Spread of Nationalism.* New York: Verso Books, 2006.

Anderson, James, and Liam O'Dowd. "Imperialism and Nationalism: The Home Rule Struggle and Border Creation in Ireland, 1885–1925." *Political Geography* 26, no. 8 (2007): 934–50.

Anghie, Antony. "Colonialism and the Birth of International Institutions: Sovereignty, Economy, and the Mandate System of the League of Nations." *New York University Journal of International Law and Politics* 34 (2001–2002): 513.

Anghie, Antony. "The Evolution of International Law: Colonial and Postcolonial Realities." *Third World Quarterly* 27, no. 5 (2006): 739–53.

Arendt, Hannah. *The Origins of Totalitarianism.* London: Houghton Mifflin Harcourt, 1973.

Armstrong, Allen. "Aspects of Refugee Wellbeing in Settlement Schemes: An Examination of the Tanzanian Case." *Journal of Refugee Studies* 1, no. 1 (1988): 57–73.

Axworthy, Lloyd. "Human Security and Global Governance: Putting People First." *Global Governance* 7, no. 1 (2001): 19–23.

Baez, Javier E. "Civil Wars beyond Their Borders: The Human Capital and Health Consequences of Hosting Refugees." *Journal of Development Economics* 96, no. 2 (2011): 391–408.

Bakewell, Oliver. "Uncovering Local Perspectives on Humanitarian Assistance and Its Outcomes." *Disasters* 24, no. 2 (2000): 103–16.

Banko, Lauren, Katarzyna Nowak, and Peter Gatrell. "What Is Refugee History, Now?" *Journal of Global History* 17, no. 1 (2022): 1–19.

Barnett, Michael. *Empire of Humanity: A History of Humanitarianism*. Ithaca, NY: Cornell University Press, 2011.

Barnett, Michael. "Humanitarianism with a Sovereign Face: UNHCR in the Global Undertow." *International Migration Review* 35, no. 1 (2001): 244–77.

Baughan, Emily. "Rehabilitating an Empire: Humanitarian Collusion with the Colonial State during the Kenyan Emergency, ca. 1954–1960." *Journal of British Studies* 59, no. 1 (2020): 57–79.

Berger, Mark T. "From Nation-Building to State-Building: The Geopolitics of Development, the Nation-State System and the Changing Global Order." *Third World Quarterly* 27, no. 1 (2006): 5–25.

Bjerk, Paul. *Building a Peaceful Nation: Julius Nyerere and the Establishment of Sovereignty in Tanzania, 1960–1964*. Rochester, NY: University of Rochester Press, 2015.

Bjerk, Paul. "Postcolonial Realism: Tanganyika's Foreign Policy under Nyerere, 1960–1963." *International Journal of African Historical Studies* 44, no. 2 (2011): 215–47.

Black, Richard. "Fifty Years of Refugee Studies: From Theory to Policy." *International Migration Review* 35, no. 1 (2001): 57–78.

Boesen, Jannik. "Tanzania: From Ujamaa to Villagization." In *Towards Socialism in Tanzania*, edited by B. U. Mwansasu and Cranford Pratt, 125–44. Toronto: University of Toronto Press, 1979.

Boesen, Jannik, Madsen Birgit Storgaard, and Tony Moody. *Ujamaa: Socialism from Above*. Uppsala, Sweden: Nordic Africa Institute, 1977.

Bogaerts, Els, and Remco Raben. *The Decolonization of African and Asian Societies, 1930s–1960s*. Leiden, Netherlands: KITLV Press, 2012.

Borton, John, Emery Brusset, and Alistair Hallam. "The International Response to Conflict and Genocide: Lessons from the Rwanda Experience: Study 3: Humanitarian Aid and Effects." Steering Committee of the Joint Evaluation of Emergency Assistance to Rwanda, March 1996.

Brennan, James R. "Blood Enemies: Exploitation and Urban Citizenship in the Nationalist Political Thought of Tanzania, 1958–75." *Journal of African History* 47, no. 3 (2006): 389–413.

Burton, Andrew, and Michael Jennings. "Introduction: The Emperor's New Clothes? Continuities in Governance in Late Colonial and Early Postcolonial East Africa." *International Journal of African Historical Studies* 40, no. 1 (2007): 1–25.

Callahan, Michael D. *Mandates and Empire: The League of Nations and Africa, 1914–1931*. Portland, OR: Sussex Academic Press, 1999.

Callahan, Michael D. *A Sacred Trust: The League of Nations and Africa, 1929–1946.* Portland, OR: Sussex Academic Press, 2004.

Cameron, Donald, Sir. *My Tanganyika Service and Some Nigeria.* Washington, DC: George Allen and Unwin, 1939.

Castryck, Geert. "Introduction: The Bounds of Berlin's Africa: Space-Making and Multiple Territorialities in East and Central Africa." *International Journal of African Historical Studies* 52, no. 1 (2019): 1–10.

Chatty, Dawn, and Philip Marfleet. "Conceptual Problems in Forced Migration." *Refugee Survey Quarterly* 32, no. 2 (2013): 1–13.

Chaulia, Sreeram Sundar. "The Politics of Refugee Hosting in Tanzania: From Open Door to Unsustainability, Insecurity and Receding Receptivity." *Journal of Refugee Studies* 16, no. 2 (2003): 147–66.

Chidzero, B. T. G. *Tanganyika and International Trusteeship.* London: Oxford University Press, 1961.

Chimni, Bupinder. S. "From Resettlement to Involuntary Repatriation: Towards a Critical History of Durable Solutions." *Refugee Survey Quarterly* 23, no. 3 (2004): 55–73.

Chipkin, Ivor. "'Functional' and 'Dysfunctional' Communities: The Making of National Citizens." *Journal of Southern African Studies* 29, no. 1 (2003): 63–82.

Chrétien, Jean-Pierre. *The Great Lakes of Africa: Two Thousand Years of History.* New York: Zone Books, 2003.

Chrétien, Jean-Pierre. "The Slave Trade in Burundi and Rwanda, 1890–1906." In *Slavery in the Great Lakes Region of East Africa,* edited by Henri Médard and Shane Doyle, 210–30. Oxford: James Currey, 2007.

Cooper, Frederick. *Colonialism in Question: Theory, Knowledge, History.* Berkeley, CA: University of California Press, 2005.

Cooper, Frederick. *Decolonization and African Society: The Labor Question in French and British Africa.* Cambridge: Cambridge University Press, 1996.

Cooper, Frederick. "Possibility and Constraint: African Independence in Historical Perspective." *Journal of African History* 49, no. 2 (2008): 167–96.

Cooper, Frederick. "Postscript." In *Citizenship, Belonging, and Political Community in Africa: Dialogues between Past and Present,* edited by Emma Hunter, 282–97. Athens: Ohio University Press, 2016.

Cooper, Frederick. "Review: Mahmood Mamdani." *International Labor and Working-Class History* 52 (1997): 156–60.

Cooper, Frederick, and Ann L. Stoler. "Introduction Tensions of Empire: Colonial Control and Visions of Rule." *American Ethnologist* 16, no. 4 (1989): 609–21.

Coulson, Andrew. "Agricultural Policies in Mainland Tanzania." *Review of African Political Economy* 10 (1977): 74–100.

Crisp, Jeffrey. "Mind the Gap! UNHCR, Humanitarian Assistance and the Development Process." *International Migration Review* 35, no. 1 (2001): 168–91.

Daley, Patricia. "From the Kipande to the Kibali: The Incorporation of Refugees and Labour Migrants in Western Tanzania, 1900–1987." In *Geography and Refugees: Patterns and Processes of Change,* edited by Richard Black and Vaughan Robinson, 17–32. London: Bellhaven Press, 1993.

Daley, Patricia. "The Politics of the Refugee Crisis in Tanzania." In *Tanzania and the IMF: The Dynamics of Liberalization*, edited by Horace Campbell and Howard Stein, 125–46. London: Routledge, 1992.

de Haas, Michiel. "Moving beyond Colonial Control? Economic Forces and Shifting Migration from Ruanda-Urundi to Buganda, 1920–60." *Journal of African History* 60, no. 3 (2019): 379–406.

Des Forges, Alison. *Defeat Is the Only Bad News: Rwanda under Musinga, 1896–1931*. Edited by David Newbury. Madison: University of Wisconsin Press, 2011.

Des Forges, Alison. *"Leave None to Tell the Story": Genocide in Rwanda*. New York: Human Rights Watch, 1999.

Des Forges, Alison. Preface to *Defeat Is the Only Bad News: Rwanda under Musinga, 1896–1931*. Edited by David Newbury, xv–xvi. Madison: University of Wisconsin Press, 2011.

De Waal, Alexander. *Famine Crimes: Politics & the Disaster Relief Industry in Africa*. Bloomington: Indiana University Press, 1997.

Duara, Prasenjit. "Introduction: The Decolonization of Asia and Africa in the Twentieth Century." In *Decolonization: Perspectives from Now and Then*, edited by Prasenjit Duara, 1–20. London: Routledge, 2004.

Dumbaya, Peter A. *Tanganyika under International Mandate, 1919–1946*. Lanham, MD: University Press of America, 1995.

Eckert, Andreas. "Useful Instruments of Participation? Local Government and Co-operatives in Tanzania, 1940s to 1970s." *International Journal of African Historical Studies* 40, no. 1 (2007): 97–118.

Edelman, Marc, and Angelique Haugerud. "Introduction: The Anthropology of Development and Globalization." In *The Anthropology of Development and Globalization: From Classical Political Economy to Contemporary Neoliberalism*, edited by Marc Edelman and Angelique Haugerud, 1–74. Malden, MA: Blackwell Publishing, 2005.

Elmer, Jonathan. *On Lingering and Being Last: Race and Sovereignty in the New World*. New York: Fordham University Press, 2008.

Escobar, Arturo. *Encountering Development: The Making and Unmaking of the Third World*. Princeton, NJ: Princeton University Press, 2011.

Etzioni, Amitai. "Sovereignty as Responsibility." *Orbis* 50, no. 1 (2006): 71–85.

Fair, Laura. "Drive-in Socialism: Debating Modernities and Development in Dar es Salaam, Tanzania." *American Historical Review* 188, no. 4 (2013): 1077–104.

Falola, Toyin, and Mathew Heaton. *A History of Nigeria*. Cambridge: Cambridge University Press, 2008.

Fassin, Didier. *Humanitarian Reason: A Moral History of the Present*. Berkeley: University of California Press 2012.

Ferguson, James. *The Anti-Politics Machine: "Development," Depoliticization, and Bureaucratic Power in Lesotho*. Minneapolis: University of Minnesota Press, 1994.

Ferguson, James, and Akhil Gupta. "Spatializing States: Toward an Ethnography of Neoliberal Governmentality." *American Ethnologist* 29, no. 4 (2002): 981–1002.

Fouéré, Marie-Aude. "Julius Nyerere, Ujamaa, and Political Morality in Contemporary Tanzania." *African Studies Review* 57, no. 1 (2014): 1–24.

Fresia, Marion. "Building Consensus within UNHCR's Executive Committee: Global Refugee Norms in the Making." *Journal of Refugee Studies* 27, no. 4 (2014): 514–33.

Freund, W. M. "Class Conflict, Political Economy and the Struggle for Socialism in Tanzania." *African Affairs* 80, no. 321 (1981): 483–99.

Gasarasi, Charles P. "The Mass Naturalization and Further Integration of Rwandese Refugees in Tanzania: Process, Problems and Prospects." *Journal of Refugee Studies* 3, no. 2 (1990): 88–109.

Gasarasi, Charles P. *The Tripartite Approach to Rural Refugees in Tanzania.* Research Report no. 71. Uppsala: The Scandinavian Institute of African Studies, 1984.

Gatrell, Peter. *The Making of the Modern Refugee.* Oxford: Oxford University Press, 2013.

Geschiere, Peter. *The Perils of Belonging: Autochthony, Citizenship, and Exclusion in Africa & Europe.* Chicago: University of Chicago Press, 2009.

Ghai, Yash. "Notes towards a Theory of Law and Ideology—Tanzanian Perspectives." *African Law Studies* 13 (1976): 31–105.

Gibbs, David. "The United Nations, International Peacekeeping and the Question of 'Impartiality': Revisiting the Congo Operation of 1960." *Journal of Modern African Studies* 38, no. 3 (2000): 359–82.

Giblin, James. *A History of the Excluded: Making Family a Refuge from State in Twentieth-Century Tanzania.* Oxford: James Currey, 2005.

Glynn, Irial. "The Genesis and Development of Article 1 of the 1951 Refugee Convention." *Journal of Refugee Studies* 25, no. 1 (2012): 134–48.

Goody, Jack. "Feudalism in Africa?" *Journal of African History* 4, no. 1 (1963): 1–18.

Gupta, Akhil, and James Ferguson. "Beyond 'Culture': Space, Identity, and the Politics of Difference." *Cultural Anthropology* 7, no. 1 (1992): 6–23.

Hack, Karl. "Decolonization and Violence in Southeast Asia: Crises of Authority and Identity." In *Beyond Empire and Nation: Decolonizing Societies in Africa and Asia, 1930s–1970s,* edited by Els Bogaerts and Remco Raben, 137–66. Leiden, Netherlands: KITLV Press, 2012.

Hammerstad, Anne. "Whose Security? UNHCR, Refugee Protection and State Security after the Cold War." *Security Dialogue* 31, no. 4 (2000): 391–403.

Harrell-Bond, Barbara. "Can Humanitarian Work with Refugees Be Humane?" *Human Rights Quarterly* 24, no. 1 (2002): 51–85.

Harrell-Bond, Barbara. *Imposing Aid: Emergency Assistance to Refugees.* Oxford: Oxford University Press, 1986.

Harrell-Bond, Barbara, Eftihia Voutira, and Mark Leopold. "Counting the Refugees: Gifts, Givers, Patrons and Clients." *Journal of Refugee Studies* 5, no. 3–4 (1992): 205–22.

Helleiner, Gerard. "Trade, Aid and Nation Building in Tanzania." In *National-Building in Tanzania: Problems and Issues,* edited by Anthony H. Rweyemamu, 61–78. Nairobi: East African Publishing House, 1970.

Herbst, Jeffrey. "The Creation and Maintenance of National Boundaries in Africa." *International Organization* 43, no. 4 (1989): 673–92.

Hilhorst, Dorothea. "Being Good at Doing Good? Quality and Accountability of Humanitarian NGOs." *Disasters* 26, no. 3 (2002): 193–212.

Hilhorst, Dorothea, and Bram J. Jansen. "Humanitarian Space as Arena: A Perspective on the Everyday Politics of Aid." *Development and Change* 41, no. 6 (2010): 1117–39.

Holborn, Louise. *Refugees, a Problem of Our Time: The Work of the United Nations High Commissioner for Refugees, 1951–1972*. Lanham, MD: Scarecrow Press, 1975.

Hunt, Lynn. *Inventing Human Rights: A History*. New York: W. W. Norton, 2007.

Hunter, Emma. "Introduction." In *Citizenship, Belonging, and Political Community in Africa: Dialogues between Past and Present*, edited by Emma Hunter, 1–16. Athens: Ohio University Press, 2016.

Hunter, Emma. "'Our Common Humanity': Print, Power, and the Colonial Press in Interwar Tanganyika and French Cameroun." *Journal of Global History* 7, no. 2 (2012): 279–301.

Hunter, Emma. *Political Thought and the Public Sphere in Tanzania*. Cambridge: Cambridge University Press, 2015.

Hunter, Emma. "Revisiting Ujamaa: Political Legitimacy and the Construction of Community in Post-Colonial Tanzania." *Journal of Eastern African Studies* 2, no. 3 (2008): 471–85.

Hydén, Göran. *Beyond Ujamaa in Tanzania: Underdevelopment and an Uncaptured Peasantry*. Berkeley: University of California Press, 1980.

Hydén, Göran. *Political Development in Rural Tanzania: Tanu Yajenga Nchi*. Nairobi: East African Publishing House, 1969.

Hyndman, Jennifer. *Managing Displacement: Refugees and the Politics of Humanitarianism*. Minneapolis: University of Minnesota Press, 2000.

Iliffe, John. "Breaking the Chain at Its Weakest Link: TANU and the Colonial Office." In *In Search of a Nation: Histories of Authority & Dissidence in Tanzania*, edited by Gregory Maddox and James Giblin, 168–97. Oxford: James Currey, 2005.

Iliffe, John. *A Modern History of Tanganyika*. Cambridge: Cambridge University Press, 1979.

Ivaska, Andrew. "Of Students, 'Nizers,' and Struggle over Youth: Tanzania's 1966 National Service Crisis." *Africa Today* 51, no. 3 (2005): 83–107.

Jackson, Stephen. "Sons of Which Soil? The Language and Politics of Autochthony in Eastern D.R. Congo." *African Studies Review* 49, no. 2 (2006): 95–124.

Jaji, Rose. "Social Technology and Refugee Encampment in Kenya." *Journal of Refugee Studies* 25, no. 2 (2012): 221–38.

Jaspers, Susanne. *The Rwandan Refugee Crisis in Tanzania: Initial Successes and Failures in Food Assistance*. Relief and Rehabilitation Network Paper 6. London: Overseas Development Institute, 1994.

Jennings, Michael. "Building Better People: Modernity and Utopia in Late Colonial Tanganyika." *Journal of Eastern African Studies* 3, no. 1 (2009): 94–111.

Jennings, Michael. *Surrogates of the State: NGOs, Development, and Ujamaa in Tanzania*. West Hartford, CT: Kumarian Press, 2008.

Jennings, Michael. "'A Very Real War': Popular Participation in Development in Tanzania during the 1950s & 1960s." *International Journal of African Historical Studies* 40, no. 1 (2007): 71–95.

Kaiser, Paul. "Structural Adjustment and the Fragile Nation: The Demise of Social Unity in Tanzania." *Journal of Modern African Studies* 34, no. 2 (1996): 227–37.

Kamanga, Khoti. "The (Tanzania) Refugees Act of 1998: Some Legal and Policy Implications." *Journal of Refugee Studies* 18, no. 1 (2005): 100–116.

Kelly, John D., and Martha Kaplan. "'My Ambition Is Much Higher than Independence': US Power, the UN World, the Nation-State, and Their Critics." In *Decolonization: Perspectives from Now and Then*, edited by Prasenjit Duara, 149–69. London: Routledge, 2004.

Khadiagala, Gilbert M. "Boundaries in East Africa." *Journal of Eastern African Studies* 4, no. 2 (2010): 266–78.

Kibreab, Gaim. "Revisiting the Debate on People, Place, Identity and Displacement." *Journal of Refugee Studies* 12, no. 4 (1999): 384–410.

Kiwanuka, M. S. M. "The Empire of Bunyoro Kitara: Myth or Reality?" *Canadian Journal of African Studies* 2, no. 1 (1968): 27–48.

Konings, Piet, and Francis Nyamnjoh. "The Anglophone Problem in Cameroon." *Journal of Modern African Studies* 35, no. 2 (1997): 207–29.

Kopytoff, Igor. *The African Frontier: The Reproduction of Traditional African Societies.* Bloomington: Indiana University Press, 1987.

Kushner, Tony. *Remembering Refugees: Then and Now.* Manchester, UK: Manchester University Press, 2006.

Kweka, Opportuna. "Citizenship without Integration: The Case of 1972 Burundian Refugees in Tanzania." *African Review: A Journal of African Politics, Development and International Affairs* 42, no. 2 (2015): 76–93.

Lal, Priya. *African Socialism in Postcolonial Tanzania.* Cambridge: Cambridge University Press, 2015.

Lal, Priya. "Self-Reliance and the State: The Multiple Meanings of Development in Early Post-Colonial Tanzania." *Africa* 82, no. 2 (2012): 212–34.

Landau, Loren B. "Beyond the Losers: Transforming Governmental Practice in Refugee-Affected Tanzania." *Journal of Refugee Studies* 16, no. 1 (2003): 19–43.

Landau, Loren B. "Challenge without Transformation: Refugees, Aid and Trade in Western Tanzania." *Journal of Modern African Studies* 42, no. 1 (2004): 31–59.

Lawi, Yusufu. "Tanzania's Operation Vijiji and Local Ecological Consciousness: The Case of Eastern Iraqwland, 1974–1976." *Journal of African History* 48, no. 1 (2007): 69–93.

Lefebvre, Camille. *Frontières de Sable, Frontières de Papier. Histoires de Territoires et de Frontières, du Jihad de Sokoto à la Colonisation Française du Niger, XIXe–XXe siècles.* Paris: Publications de la Sorbonne, 2015.

Lefebvre, Camille. "We Have Tailored Africa: French Colonialism and the 'Artificiality' of Africa's Borders in the Interwar Period." *Journal of Historical Geography* 37, no. 2 (2011): 191–202.

Lemarchand, René. *Burundi: Ethnic Conflict and Genocide.* Cambridge: Cambridge University Press, 1996.

Lemarchand, René. "Consociationalism and Power Sharing in Africa: Rwanda, Burundi, and the Democratic Republic of the Congo." *African Affairs* 106, no. 422 (2006): 1–20.

Lemarchand, René. *Rwanda and Burundi*. Westport, CT: Praeger Publishers, 1970.

Leys, Colin. *The Rise and Fall of Development Theory*. Bloomington: Indiana University Press, 1996.

Li, Tania Murray. *The Will to Improve: Governmentality, Development, and the Practice of Politics*. Durham, NC: Duke University Press, 2007.

Linden, Ian, and Jane Linden. *Church and Revolution in Rwanda*. Manchester, UK: Manchester University Press, 1977.

Loescher, Gil. *Beyond Charity: International Cooperation and the Global Refugee Crisis*. New York: Oxford University Press, 1993.

Loescher, Gil. *The UNHCR and World Politics: A Perilous Path*. Oxford: Oxford University Press, 2001.

Loescher, Gil. "The UNHCR and World Politics: State Interests vs. Institutional Autonomy." *International Migration Review* 35, no. 1 (2001): 33–56.

Loescher, Gil, and James Milner. "Protracted Refugee Situations: Domestic and International Security Implications." In *Adelphi Paper 375*. London: Routledge, 2007.

Long, Katy. "Rwanda's First Refugees: Tutsi Exile and International Response 1959–64." *Journal of Eastern African Studies* 6, no. 2 (2012): 211–29.

Longman, Timothy. *Christianity and Genocide in Rwanda*. Cambridge: Cambridge University Press, 2009.

Lonsdale, John, and Bruce Berman. "Coping with the Contradictions: The Development of the Colonial State in Kenya, 1895–1914." *Journal of African History* 20, no. 4 (1979): 487–505.

Louis, William Roger. "The United Kingdom and the Beginning of the Mandates System, 1919–1922." *International Organization* 23, no. 1 (1969): 73–96.

Louis, William Roger, and Ronald Robinson. "Empire Preserv'd: How the Americans Put Anti-Communism before Anti-Imperialism." In *Decolonization: Perspectives from Now and Then*, edited by Prasenjit Duara, 152–61. London: Routledge, 2003.

Low, D. A., and J. M. Lonsdale. "Introduction: Towards the New Order, 1945–63." In *History of East Africa*, vol. 3, edited by D. A. Low and Alison Smith. Oxford: Clarendon Press, 1976.

Lugard, Frederick. *The Dual Mandate in British Tropical Africa*. London: Routledge, 1922.

Lui, Robyn. "The International Government of Refugees." In *Global Governmentality: Governing International Spaces*, edited by Larner Wendy and William Walters, 116–35. New York: Routledge, 2004.

MacArthur, Julie. *Cartography and the Political Imagination: Mapping Community in Colonial Kenya*. Athens: Ohio University Press, 2016.

MacGaffey, Janet. *Entrepreneurs and Parasites*. Cambridge: Cambridge University Press, 1987.

Malkki, Liisa. "National Geographic: The Rooting of Peoples and the Territorialization of National Identity among Scholars and Refugees." *Cultural Anthropology* 7, no. 1 (1992): 24–44.

Malkki, Liisa. *The Need to Help: The Domestic Arts of International Humanitarianism*. Durham, NC: Duke University Press, 2015.

Malkki, Liisa. *Purity and Exile: Violence, Memory, and National Cosmology among Hutu Refugees in Tanzania.* Chicago: University of Chicago Press, 1995.

Malkki, Liisa. "Refugees and Exile: From 'Refugee Studies' to the National Order of Things." *Annual Review of Anthropology* 24 (1995): 495–523.

Mamdani, Mahmood. *Citizen and Subject: Contemporary Africa and the Legacy of Late Colonialism.* Princeton, NJ: Princeton University Press, 1996.

Mamdani, Mahmood. *When Victims Become Killers: Colonialism, Nativism, and the Genocide in Rwanda.* Princeton, NJ: Princeton University Press, 2014.

Maquet, Jacques J. *The Premise of Inequality in Ruanda: A Study of Political Relations in a Central African Kingdom.* London: Routledge, 1961.

Marfleet, Philip. "Explorations in a Foreign Land: States, Refugees, and the Problem of History." *Refugee Survey Quarterly* 32, no. 2 (2013): 14–34.

Marfleet, Philip. "Making States, Making Refugees: A Review of Displacement and Dispossession in the Modern Middle East." *American Historical Review* 118, no. 5 (2013): 1403–29.

Marfleet, Philip. "Refugees and History: Why We Must Address the Past." *Refugee Survey Quarterly* 26, no. 3 (2007): 136–48.

Marriage, Zoe. *Challenging Aid in Africa. Principles, Implementation, and Impact.* New York: Palgrave Macmillan, 2006.

Mazower, Mark. *No Enchanted Palace: The End of Empire and the Ideological Origins of the United Nations.* Princeton, NJ: Princeton University Press, 2013.

Mbembe, Achille, and Steven Randall. "At the Edge of the World: Boundaries, Territoriality, and Sovereignty in Africa." *Public Culture* 12, no. 1 (2000): 259–84.

Médard, Henri, and Ikram Kidari. "The Kagera River and the Making of a Contested Boundary: Territorial Legacies and Colonial Demarcations in Buganda." *International Journal of African Historical Studies* 52, no. 1 (2019): 11–30.

Mendel, Toby D. "Refugee Law and Practice in Tanzania." *International Journal of Refugee Law* 9, no. 1 (1997): 35–59.

Metcalfe, George. "Effects of Refugees on the National State." In *Refugees South of the Sahara: An African Dilemma,* edited by Hugh C. Brooks and Yassin El-Ayouty. Westport, CT: Negro Universities, 1970, 73–85.

Miller, Norman N. "Tanzania: Documentation in Political Anthropology—the Hans Cory Collection." *African Studies Bulletin* 11, no. 2 (1968): 195–96.

Milner, James. "Can Global Refugee Policy Leverage Durable Solutions? Lessons from Tanzania's Naturalization of Burundian Refugees." *Journal of Refugee Studies* 27, no. 4 (2014): 553–73.

Mongia, Radhika Viyas. *Indian Migration and Empire: A Colonial Genealogy of the Modern State.* Durham, NC: Duke University Press, 2018.

Mongia, Radhika Viyas. "Race, Nationality, Mobility: A History of the Passport." *Public Culture* 11, no. 3 (1999): 527–55.

Moore, Sally Falk. *Social Facts and Fabrications: "Customary" Law on Kilimanjaro.* Cambridge: Cambridge University Press, 1986.

Moskowitz, Kara. *Seeing Like a Citizen: Decolonization, Development, and the Making of Kenya, 1945–1980.* Athens: Ohio University Press, 2019.

Moskowitz, Kara. "Sons and Daughters of the Soil: Politics and Protest of Kenyan Resettlement to Tanzania, 1961–1968." *Past and Present* 531, no. 1 (2021): 301–37.

Mosse, David. *Cultivating Development: An Ethnography of Aid Policy and Practice.* New York: Pluto Press, 2005.

Mutahaba, Gelase. "Decentralized Administration in Tanzania: Bukoba and Ngara District Councils, 1962–69." PhD diss., University of California, 1973.

Mutahaba, Gelase. "Local Autonomy and National Planning: Complementary or Otherwise? Case Study from Tanzania." *African Review: A Journal of African Politics, Development and International Affairs* 4, no. 4 (1974): 509–30.

Newbury, Catharine. "Background to Genocide: Rwanda." *African Issues* 23, no. 2 (1995): 12–17.

Newbury, Catharine. *The Cohesion of Oppression: Clientship and Ethnicity in Rwanda, 1860–1960.* New York: Columbia University Press, 1993.

Newbury, David. *Kings and Clans: Ijwi Island and the Lake Kivu Rift, 1780–1840.* Madison: University of Wisconsin Press, 1991.

Newbury, David. *The Land Beyond the Mists: Essays on Identity and Authority in Precolonial Congo and Rwanda.* Athens: Ohio University Press, 2009.

Newbury, David. "Precolonial Burundi and Rwanda: Local Loyalties, Regional Royalties." *International Journal of African Historical Studies* 34, no. 2 (2001): 255–314.

Newbury, David. "Returning Refugees: Four Historical Patterns of 'Coming Home' to Rwanda." *Comparative Studies in Society and History* 47, no. 2 (2005): 252–85.

Newbury, David. "The 'Rwakayihura' Famine of 1928–1929: A Nexus of Colonial Rule in Rwanda." In *Histoire Sociale de l'Afrique de l'Est (Xix–Xx Siecle). Actes du Colloque de Bujumbura (17–24 octobre 1989):* 269–85. Paris: Department d'Histoire de l'Universite du Burundi, 1991.

Newbury, David, and Catharine Newbury. "Bringing the Peasants Back In: Agrarian Themes in the Construction and Corrosion of Statist Historiography in Rwanda." *American Historical Review* 105, no. 3 (2000): 832–77.

Njung, George N. "Refugee Exchanges between Cameroon and Equatorial Guinea, and Their Socio-economic Relevance, from the First World War to Immediate Post-Independence." *Canadian Journal of African Studies* 55, no. 3 (2021):453–74.

Nugent, Paul. "Arbitrary Lines and the People's Minds: A Dissenting View on Colonial Boundaries in West Africa." In *African Boundaries: Barriers, Conduits and Opportunities,* edited by Paul Nugent and A. I. Asiwaju, 35–67. London: Centre of African Studies, University of Edinburgh, 1996.

Nugent, Paul, and A. I. Asiwaju. "Introduction." In *African Boundaries: Barriers, Conduits and Opportunities,* edited by Paul Nugent and A. I. Asiwaju, 1–17. London: Centre of African Studies, University of Edinburgh, 1996.

Nyang'oro, Julius. "The Challenge of Development in Tanzania: The Legacy of Julius Nyerere." In *The Legacies of Julius Nyerere: Influences on Development Discourse and Practice in Africa,* edited by David Alexander McDonald and Eunice Nijeri Sahle, 27–38. Nairobi: Africa World Press, 2002.

Nyerere, Julius K. *Uhuru na Ujamaa: Freedom and Socialism: A Selection from Writings and Speeches, 1965–1967.* Oxford: Oxford University Press, 1968.

Nzongola-Ntalaja, Georges. *The Congo from Leopold to Kabila: A People's History*. New York: Zed Books, 2002.

"Obituary: Hans Cory, O.B.E. 1889–1962." *African Music: Journal of the International Library of African Music* 3, no. 1 (1962): 111.

Okafor, Obiora Chinedu. *The African Human Rights System, Activist Forces and International Institutions*. Cambridge: Cambridge University Press, 2007.

Packard, Randall M. *Chiefship and Cosmology: An Historical Study of Political Competition*. Bloomington: Indiana University Press, 1981.

Pandey, Gyanendra. *Remembering Partition: Violence, Nationalism and History in India*. Cambridge: Cambridge University Press, 2001.

Panikos, Panayi, and Pippa Virdee. "Preface: Key Themes, Concepts and Rationale." In *Imperial Collapse and Forced Migration in the Twentieth Century*, edited by Panayi Panikos and Pippa Virdee, vii–xxiv. New York: Palgrave Macmillan, 2011.

Parsons, Timothy. *The 1964 Army Mutinies and the Making of Modern East Africa*. Westport, CT: Praeger Publishers, 2003.

Pedersen, Susan. *The Guardians: The League of Nations and the Crisis of Empire*. Oxford: Oxford University Press, 2015.

Peterson, Derek. *Ethnic Patriotism and the East African Revival: A History of Dissent, 1935–1972*. New York: Cambridge University Press, 2012.

Picciotto, Catherine. "Tanzania's Foreign Policy." In *Nation-Building in Tanzania: Problems and Issues*, edited by Anthony H. Rweyemamu, 90–109. Nairobi: East African Publishing House, 1970.

Polzer, Tara, and Laura Hammond. "Invisible Displacement." *Journal of Refugee Studies* 21, no. 4 (2008): 417–31.

Pottier, Johan. *Re-imagining Rwanda: Conflict, Survival and Disinformation in the Late Twentieth Century*. Cambridge: Cambridge University Press, 2002.

Pottier, Johan. "Relief and Repatriation: Views by Rwandan Refugees; Lessons for Humanitarian Aid Workers." *African Affairs* 95, no. 380 (1996): 403–29.

Pratt, Cranford. *The Critical Phase in Tanzania: 1945–1968; Nyerere and the Emergence of a Socialist Strategy*. Cambridge: Cambridge University Press, 1976.

Prunier, Gérard. *Africa's World War: Congo, the Rwandan Genocide, and the Making of a Continental Catastrophe*. Oxford: Oxford University Press, 2008.

Prunier, Gérard. *The Rwanda Crisis: History of a Genocide*. New York: Columbia University Press, 1997.

Rich, Jeremy. *Protestant Missionaries & Humanitarianism in the DRC: The Politics of Aid in Cold War Africa*. Rochester, NY: Boydell and Brewer, 2020.

Rich, Jeremy. "Victims or Burdens? Angolan Refugees and Humanitarian Aid Organizations in the Democratic Republic of Congo, 1961–1963." *International History Review* 43, no. 5 (2021): 1001–17.

Richards, Audrey Isabel, Jean M. Fortt, and A. B. Mukwaya. *Economic Development and Tribal Change: A Study of Immigrant Labour in Buganda*. Oxford: Oxford University Press, 1973.

Roberts, George. *Revolutionary State-Making in Dar es Salaam: African Liberation and the Global Cold War, 1961–1974*. Cambridge: Cambridge University Press, 2021.

Roitman, Janet Lee. *Fiscal Disobedience: An Anthropology of Economic Regulation in Central Africa*. Princeton, NJ: Princeton University Press, 2005.

Rosenthal, Jill. "From 'Migrants' to 'Refugees': Humanitarian Aid, Development, and Nationalism in Ngara District, Tanzania (1940–2000)." PhD diss., Emory University, 2014.

Rosenthal, Jill. "From 'Migrants' to 'Refugees': Identity, Aid, and Decolonization in Ngara District, Tanzania." *Journal of African History* 55, no. 2 (2015): 261–79.

Rosenthal, Jill. "'From a Place of Misery to a Place of Deeper Misery': Development, Authority, and Conflict in the Mwesi Highlands Rwandan Refugee Settlement." *International Journal of African Historical Studies* 50, no. 1 (2017): 99–120.

Rubagumya, Casmir Mushongore. *A Son of Two Countries: The Education of a Refugee from Nyarubuye*. Dar es Salaam: Mkuki na Nyota Publishers, 2017.

Russell, Aidan. "Punctuated Places: Narrating Space in Burundi." *International Journal of African Historical Studies* 52, no. 1 (2019): 133–58.

Rutinwa, Bonaventure. "The Tanzanian Government's Response to the Rwandan Emergency." *Journal of Refugee Studies* 9, no. 3 (1996): 291–302.

Rweyemamu, Anthony H. "An Overview of Nation-Building: Problems and Issues." In *Nation-Building in Tanzania: Problems and Issues*, edited by Anthony H. Rweyemamu, 1–8. Nairobi: East African Publishing House, 1970.

Salvatici, Silvia. "'Help the People to Help Themselves': UNRRA Relief Workers and European Displaced Persons." *Journal of Refugee Studies* 25, no. 3 (2012): 428–51.

Sanders, Edith R. "The Hamitic Hypothesis: Its Origin and Functions in Time Perspective." *Journal of African History* 10, no. 4 (1969): 521–32.

Sarris, Alexander, and Rogerius Van den Brink. *Economic Policy and Household Welfare during Crisis and Adjustment in Tanzania*. New York: New York University Press, 1993.

Scalettaris, Giulia. "Refugee Studies and the International Refugee Regime: A Reflection on a Desirable Separation." *Refugee Survey Quarterly* 26, no. 3 (2007): 36–50.

Schneider, Leander. "Colonial Legacies and Postcolonial Authoritarianism in Tanzania: Connects and Disconnects." *African Studies Review* 49, no. 1 (2006): 93–118.

Schneider, Leander. "Freedom and Unfreedom in Rural Development: Julius Nyerere, Ujamaa Vijijini, and Villagization." *Canadian Journal of African Studies* 38, no. 2 (2004): 344–92.

Schoenbrun, David. "Cattle Herds and Banana Gardens: The Historical Geography of the Western Great Lakes Region, ca AD 800–15000." *African Archaeological Review* 11 (1993): 39–72.

Schoenbrun, David. *A Green Place, a Good Place: Agrarian Change, Gender, and Social Identity in the Great Lakes Region to the 15th Century*. Portsmouth, NH: Heinemann, 1988.

Scott, James. "Afterword to 'Moral Economies, State Spaces, and Categorical Violence.'" *American Anthropologist* 107, no. 3 (2005): 395–402.

Scott, James. *Domination and the Arts of Resistance: Hidden Transcripts*. New Haven, CT: Yale University Press, 1999.

Scott, James C. *Seeing Like a State: How Certain Schemes to Improve the Human Condition Have Failed*. New Haven, CT: Yale University Press, 1998.

Semboja, Joseph, and S. M. H. Rugumisa. "Price Control in the Management of an Economic Crisis: The National Price Commission in Tanzania." *African Studies Review* 31, no. 1 (1988): 47–65.

Shadle, Brett L. "Reluctant Humanitarians: British Policy toward Refugees in Kenya during the Italo-Ethiopian War, 1935–1940." *Journal of Imperial and Commonwealth History* 47, no. 1 (2019): 167–86.

Sheehan, James. "The Problem of Sovereignty in European History." *American Historical Review* 111, no. 1 (2006): 1–15.

Soguk, Nevzat. *States and Strangers: Refugees and Displacements of Statecraft.* Minneapolis: University of Minnesota Press, 1999.

Sommers, Marc. *Fear in Bongoland: Burundi Refugees in Urban Tanzania.* New York: Berghahn Books, 2001.

Stephens, Hugh W. *The Political Transformation of Tanganyika: 1920–67.* New York: Frederick A. Praeger, 1968.

Straus, Scott. "What Is the Relationship between Hate Radio and Violence? Rethinking Rwanda's 'Radio Machete.'" *Politics and Society* 35, no. 4 (2007): 609–37.

Sundkler, Bengt. *Bara Bukoba: Church and Community in Tanzania.* London: C. Hurst, 1980.

Tague, Joanna T. *Displaced Mozambicans in Postcolonial Tanzania: Refugee Power, Mobility, Education, and Rural Development.* New York: Routledge, 2019.

Terretta, Meredith. "'God of Independence, God of Peace': Village Politics and Nationalism in the Maquis of Cameroon, 1957–71." *Journal of African History* 46, no. 1 (2001): 75–101.

Terretta, Meredith, and Philip Janzen. "Historical Perspectives on Contemporary Refuge Seeking in Africa." *Canadian Journal of African Studies* 55, no. 3 (2021): 445–51.

Terry, Fiona. *Condemned to Repeat? The Paradox of Humanitarian Action.* Ithaca, NY: Cornell University Press, 2002.

Tripp, Aili Mari. *Changing the Rules: The Politics of Liberalization and the Urban Informal Economy in Tanzania.* Berkeley: University of California Press, 1997.

Trouillot, Michel-Rolph. *Silencing the Past: Power and the Production of History.* Boston: Beacon Press, 1995.

Turner, Simon. *Politics of Innocence: Hutu Identity, Conflict, and Camp Life.* New York: Berghahn Books, 2010.

Turner, Simon. "Suspended Spaces—Contesting Sovereignties in a Refugee Camp." In *Sovereign Bodies*, edited by Thomas Blom Hansen and Finn Stepputat, 312–32. Princeton, NJ: Princeton University Press, 2009.

Turner, Simon. "Under the Gaze of the 'Big Nations': Refugees, Rumours and the International Community in Tanzania." *African Affairs* 103, no. 411 (2004): 227–47.

Turton, David. "Conceptualizing Forced Migration." Working Paper 12. Refugee Studies Centre, 2003.

Turton, David. "The Meaning of Place in a World of Movement: Lessons from Long-Term Field Research in Southern Ethiopia." *Journal of Refugee Studies* 18, no. 3 (2005): 258–80.

Uvin, Peter. *Aiding Violence: The Development Enterprise in Rwanda*. West Hartford: CT: Kumarian Press, 1998.

Van Asten, Piet, et al. "Agronomic and Economic Benefits of Coffee-Banana Intercropping in Uganda's Smallholder Farming Systems." *Agricultural Systems* 104, no. 4 (2011): 326–34.

Van der Meeren, Rachel. "Editorial Introduction." *Journal of Refugee Studies* 9, no. 3 (1996): 233–35.

Van der Meeren, Rachel. "Three Decades in Exile: Rwandan Refugees 1960–1990." *Journal of Refugee Studies* 9, no. 3 (1996): 252–67.

Van Hoyweghen, Saskia. "Mobility, Territoriality and Sovereignty in Post-Colonial Tanzania." *Refugee Survey Quarterly* 21, no. 1–2 (2002): 300–27.

Vansina, Jan. *Antecedents to Modern Rwanda: The Nyiginya Kingdom*. Madison: University of Wisconsin Press, 2005.

Verdirame, Guglielmo. "Human Rights and Refugees: The Case of Kenya." *Journal of Refugee Studies* 12, no. 1 (1999): 54–77.

Vidal, Claudine. "Alexis Kagame entre Memoire et Historie." *History in Africa* 15 (1988): 493–504.

Walkup, Mark. "Policy Dysfunction in Humanitarian Organizations: The Role of Coping Strategies, Institutions, and Organizational Culture." *Journal of Refugee Studies* 10, no. 1 (1997): 37–60.

Waters, Tony. "Assessing the Impact of the Rwandan Refugee Crisis on Development Planning in Rural Tanzania, 1994–1996." *Human Organization* 58, no. 2 (1999): 142–52.

Waters, Tony. "Beyond Structural Adjustment: State and Market in a Rural Tanzanian Village." *African Studies Review* 40, no. 2 (1997): 59–89.

Waters, Tony. *Bureaucratizing the Good Samaritan: The Limitations of Humanitarian Relief Operations*. Boulder, CO: Westview Press, 2001.

Watson, Catherine L. "Exile from Rwanda: Background to an Invasion." US Committee for Refugees, Issue Paper, February 1991. American Council for Nationalities Service.

Webel, Mari. "Ziba Politics and the German Sleeping Sickness Camp at Kigarama, Tanzania, 1907–1914." *International Journal of African Historical Studies* 47, no. 3 (2014): 399–423.

Weiskopf, Julie M. "Living in 'Cold Storage': An Interior History of Tanzania's Sleeping Sickness Concentrations, 1933–1946." *International Journal of African Historical Studies* 49, no. 1 (2016): 1–22.

Weitzberg, Keren. *We Do Not Have Borders: Greater Somalia and the Predicaments of Belonging in Kenya*. Athens: Ohio University Press, 2017.

Whitaker, Beth Elise. "Changing Priorities in Refugee Protection: The Rwandan Repatriation from Tanzania." *Refugee Survey Quarterly* 21, no. 1–2 (2002): 328–44.

Whitaker, Beth Elise. "Refugees in Western Tanzania: The Distribution of Burdens and Benefits among Local Hosts." *Journal of Refugee Studies* 15, no. 4 (2002): 339–58.

Williams, Christian. *National Liberation in Postcolonial Southern Africa: A Historical Ethnography of SWAPO's Exile Camps*. New York: Cambridge University Press, 2015.

Yuval-Davis, Nira. "Citizenship, Autochthony, and the Question of Forced Migration." *Refugee Survey Quarterly* 32, no. 2 (2013): 53–65.

Zamindar, Vazira Fazila-Yacoobali. *The Long Partition and the Making of Modern South Asia: Refugees, Boundaries, Histories.* New York: Columbia University Press, 2007.

Zolberg, Aristide R. "The Formation of New States as a Refugee-Generating Process." *Annals of the American Academy of Political and Social Science* 467 (1983): 24–38.

INDEX

abatungwa (ritualists), 31
accountability: in adulthood, 50; culture of, 163; and humanitarian rights, 200; issues with NGOS, 164
African socialism, 97, 106, 141, 150, 157
agentive individuals, 4
agriculture: African attitudes toward, 64; colonial development of, 49, 54, 64–65, 69; commercial, 145; communal, 141, 202
aid agencies: and change in Ngara, 4, 73, 97, 180, 189–91, 199, 202; lack of oversight, 13, 201; limitations of, 18, 181, 200–201; and local staff, 183, 186; and policy creation, 169, 181, 191; relations with Africans, 4, 17, 96, 111, 175, 181, 183; relationship to states, 7, 14, 73, 96, 188, 200; and resources, 186; in Tanzanian refugee camps, 1, 158, 160, 175, 179–81, 188–90, 201; tensions between, 160, 167
airlift, 114, 122–25
aliens, 90, 112, 128, 154, 182
Allushula, Mannington, 125
Aminzade, Ron, 149
anger: at refugees, 154, 199; at Tutsi elite, 79; over refugee aid, 115; over repatriation, 199; over taxes, 49
Anghie, Antony, 25
Anglo–Belgian Boundary Commission, 34
Angola, 86
antagonism: between locals and refugees, 102; racial, 61
apathy, 143
Arabs: and 1965 unrest in Muyenzi, 107; businessmen, 150; trade with Europe, 31
Armee Nationale Congolaise (ANC), 82
Arusha Declaration (1967), 142, 151, 155

Asians, 149–50
Asiwaju, A. I., 4
asylum hearings, 11; history of, 4; and incursions into Rwanda, 79; and integration, 12; and resettlement, 12, 117, 119; and Rwandans, 86, 93–94, 113, 115, 117
autonomy: of Gisaka, 35; of refugees, 114, 131, 194; from Rundi state, 27, 30; and Rwandan monarchy, 31; of Tanzania, 117, 135

Bacwezi, 26, 47
Baha, 34–35
Bahangaza: and Bugufi, 29; and Barundi, 38; elites, 39, 41; and feudalism; and identity, 51, 200; and labor, 56, 63, 88; migrants, 48, 88; and refugee crisis, 177, 200; and Rwanda–Tanzania border, 42, 200; and Tanzanian independence, 97, 200; writings of, 30, 39
Bahutu. *See* Hutu
Balamba I (Bugufi chief), 35
Balamba II (Bugufi chief), 26, 39, 49, 57
Bana, Benson, 197
bananas: beer, 31; as cash crop, 145; cooking, 185; farming, 144; groves, 16; importance of, 30; and intercropping, 65; and refugees, 186; selling, 147; shoots, 105, 107, 110; trees, 2, 30
Bantu, 28, 40
Banyaruanda. *See* Banyarwanda
Banyarwanda, 51, 54, 77–78, 80, 89, 108, 153, 200
Barundi: and Bugufi, 38; and Bahangaza, 38; and Hutu and Tutsi, 34, 48; and identity, 51; and settlement in Ngara, 55; Warundi refugees from, 170, 222n71, 225n101

Basubi: and elephant hunting, 48; and identity, 42, 51, 200; and labor migration, 56, 88; as middlemen, 48; and refugee crisis, 177; and Tanzanian independence, 97

Baswui, 35

Batutsi. *See* Tutsi

batwale (subdistrict chiefs), 30–31, 47–48

beans, 30, 107, 145, 147, 186

Benaco, 166, 168–69, 171–72, 175, 179–82, 184–86, 188, 190, 197

Berlin Conference (1884–85), 31

Biharamulo, 20, 24, 54, 70, 72, 88, 90, 170, 196

boma (administrative center), 46

bribery, 39, 150

bridewealth, 63

British Colonial Office, 34, 36, 39, 43, 67

Browne, G. St. John Orde (Adviser on Colonial Labour to the Secretary of State for Colonies), 52–53

buffalo, 88

Buganda: as attractive alternative to Tanganyika, 50; borders of, 44; coffee production in, 62; labor migration to, 10, 15, 44, 49; use of African supervision of agriculture, 63

Bugufi Coffee Co-operative Union (BCCU), 63, 65

Bukoba Native Co-operative Union (BNCU), 63

bureaucracy: and border creation, 80, 196; and categorization, 13, 84, 198, 202; and coercion, 117; colonial, 45–46, 59–60, 62, 64–66, 73, 196; control, 133–4, 142, 146; and corruption, 142; creation of refugee status, 3, 84; incompetence of, 98, 143; individuals in, 14, 140; inefficiency of, 141, 155; and papers, 126; state, 9, 117, 126, 140, 143, 198, 202; transnational, 7; UNHCR, 12, 84, 133, 168, 171, 198

Burns, Alan, 38

bush pigs, 73, 88, 107

Busubi. *See* Basubi

Cameron, Donald, 36

canalization, 11, 45, 53–54, 56, 82

CARE, 184

Caritas, 165, 174

cash crops: and Baganda farmers, 44; colonial schemes around, 40, 49, 58–62, 64, 70, 73; and cooperatives, 70; and development, 69, 72–73, 120; exports, 40, 145; illicit trade and smuggling of, 72, 74; and independent state, 58–59, 73, 109, 120; interest in, 63–65, 68; labor for, 44; lack of, 59, 72; and land tenure, 48; and migration, 65; reluctance to grow, 63–64; and technology, 59, 61, 64; and *ujamaa* villages, 145; cassava, 107, 186. *See also* coffee; maize; tobacco

catholicism: in Busubi, 90; conversion to, 106; and Hutu politics, 79; missions, 77

cattle: Ankole, 30; and cash economy, 50; control of, 30, 47, 49; disease, 29; exchange of, 147, 199; grazing, 199; herders, 30, 83, 85, 199; and inequality within refugee population, 93; and migration, 77; raids, 29; and refugee agency, 127, 166, 180; and tensions between locals and refugees, 199; theft of, 110, 186; trade in, 48; as tribute, 30–31, 49; and Tutsi identity, 28, 31, 47, 85

Central Africa, 120, 134

centralization: of bureaucracy, 140, 202; decentralization, 64, 155; and elites, 31; and leadership, 58, 111, 142; of parastatals, 145; of refugees, 78, 108; of states, 29, 31, 142

Chabalissa II, 173–4

children: dangers to, 100; and nutrition, 68; as refugees, 77, 95, 100, 165, 191, 196; and repatriation, 160; and schooling, 17, 50, 68, 73

Chipken, Ivor, 156

cholera, 169

christianity: and international donors, 118; missionaries, 105; among Ngaran population, 26

citizenship metaphors, 155

civil war; Burundian, 165; Rwandan, 1, 161, 163, 165;

clans: obligations, 45; royal, 93

clothing distribution, 89, 94, 99, 146–47

Coat, Pierre, 122

coffee: as cash crop, 48, 62, 145; cooperatives, 64; cultivation, 40, 62–64, 91; economy, 63, 65, 68; forced production of, 62; intercropping with bananas, 65; lack of infrastructure, 65; and migrant labor, 44, 50; plantations, 62; smuggling and illicit trade, 65,

147; trials, 62, 64–65. *See also* Bugufi Coffee Co-operative Union (BCCU); Bukoba Native Co-operative Union (BNCU)

Cold War, 5, 13, 60, 78–79, 85–86, 124, 159, 161

colonial agents, 45, 49

colonial camps: and boundaries, 80; comparison to refugee camps, 56; containment, 8, 11, 45, 54, 56, 74, 82; conditioning, 53–54, 56; control, 51, 54; and environmental transformation, 80; labor, 55; and medical intervention, 53, 55; migrant, 53–55; segregation in, 53

colonization: and boundaries, 27, 41; and citizenship, 195; criticism of, 61; and development, 33, 36, 60; and ethnicity, 27–28, 40, 79; funding of, 43; and history, 28–29; and language, 93; and migration, 45; and patronizing attitude toward colonized, 25, 33, 60; and self-rule, 61, 79; and taxation, 49; and wage labor, 43–44

communal citizenship, 155

communal farming, 91, 141, 145, 202

communal living. *See ujamaa* villages

communication: with ancestors (*see* abatungwa); lack of, 99; miscommunication, 95, 99–100; between Ngarans and Rwandans, 112; from officials, 69; among refugees, 105; between refugees and camp administration, 132, 167

communism, 60, 81–82, 85–87, 94

competition: and humanitarian governance, 13, 163, 174; organizational, 159, 174; religious, 106; over resources, 130, 184, 201; over territory, 32, 174; for visibility, 175, 201. *See also* sovereignty

compulsory labor, 48, 113, 130

Confer, Bernard, 124

Congo: Belgian, 81; crisis, 81, 114; government, 120–21, 123–4, 131; migrants from, 51; military training in, 82; mining interests in, 56; rebellions in, 120; refugees in, 113–4, 119, 121–23, 132, 135; and Red Cross, 86; Rwandan incursions into, 197; state formation, 122; Zaïre, 159, 168–69, 181

Congolese, as colonial categorization, 222n71

Congolese government, 120–24, 131. *See also* Barundi

Congolese state formation, 123

Connolly, Maureen, 166

Convention Relating to the Status of Refugees (1951), 12, 85, 127–28, 177, 181

Cooper, Frederick, 23, 61, 202

cooperation: agricultural, 141; and international funding, 104; in East Africa, 151; lack of, 69; noncooperation, 113, 132, 134; refugee, 98, 104; within refugee camps, 140; regional, 197; and relief effort, 160; in *ujamaa*, 141, 150; with UNHCR, 128

corruption, 20, 58, 71–73, 141–44, 146, 148–50, 152, 155, 157, 169, 195

Cory, Hans, 46–49, 51, 55, 63

cotton, 44, 50

courts: illegal, 72; Rwandan monarchical, 28, 30, 35, 55

crop distribution, 146

Cuba, 124

Dabalo, 1, 132

decolonization: acceleration of, 67; advent of, 1; and African socialism, 97; and border enforcement, 82, 94; and Cold War, 79; and competing sovereignties, 8, 19, 79, 194, 202; and creation of nation–states, 3, 80; and creation of refugees, 2, 5–6, 78, 84, 86, 97, 110, 159, 190, 195; and development programs, 53, 87; ideologies of, 108, 178; imagination of, 134; and imagined home, 15; and international bureaucracy, 7, 11, 79, 83, 85, 114, 200; and land ownership, 69; and migration, 19, 58, 73, 110; and national identity, 96, 112, 190, 195, 202; and nation building, 5–6, 82, 96, 116, 178, 190; pace of, 58; politics of, 81, 111; realities of, 72–73, 109; Tanzanian, 5, 14, 79, 94, 96–97, 202; and transnational governance, 19; and violence, 11, 81, 97, 112, 159

Defense (Recruitment of Native Servants) Regulations (1947), 54

deforestation, 169, 175, 185

democracy: representation, 10; in Rwanda, 93, 161–62; in *ujamaa*, 142

detention, 132, 154

deterritorialization, 14

development aid: British, 68; decrease in, 87; foreign, 68; and refugees, 89

diplomacy, 82, 117

Index · 303

discipline; aid agency staff, 183; perceived lack of, 64, 99; refugee, 99

disease: cattle, 29; defense against, 31; human, 29; and immigrants, 52; plant, 72; prevalence in camps, 185

dislocation. *See* displacement

displacement; amelioration of, 85; camps, 83, 85, 161; and genocide, 161; internal, 161, 189; mass, 7; and otherness, 7; representation of, 6

District Commissioner (DC), 54–55, 63, 65, 99, 142

distrust, 8, 59, 85, 100, 102, 107, 155

drought, 55, 68, 145

East Africa, 127, 130, 151

East African Community (EAC), 26, 197

education: adult, 143; colonial, 59; community, 130; competition for, 184; and development, 10; expectations for independence, 68; funding for, 69; government approach to, 69; need for, 68; opportunities, 186; primary, 69; secondary, 69; standards, 187; TANU programs of, 67; university, 69; and wealthy refugees, 93, 133; western, 66

elections: Burundian, 164, 198; and international funding, 161; international pressure for, 66; Mwesi Refugee Council, 134; Ngaran preferences in, 69; in Rwanda and Burundi, 82; Rwandan, 161; and Rwandan refugees, 93; TANU popularity in, 66–67; Tanzanian, 169

elephants, 48

elites: business, 102; and cattle, 30; colonial, 81; creation of Rwandan history, 28; as dictatorial allies, 161; Hutu, 79; and land tenure, 48; literate, 39; monarchical, 31; perception of Rwandan refugees as, 83; power, 47; and redistribution, 31; refugee, 93, 115, 180–81; and Rwandan independence, 109; Tutsi as, 40, 79, 93. *See also* Bahangaza

English (language), 152

environmental hazards, 72

Escobar, Arturo, 60

ethnicity: and citizenship, 10, 68, 87; colonial definitions of, 34–35; origins of, 27, 34; and Rwandan independence, 109; stratification of, 40; and violence, 27, 84, 97, 162, 179; uses of, 40

European Community Humanitarian Organization (ECHO), 173

expatriates: agency staff, 102, 111, 125–26, 133–34, 155, 167–68, 183; disdain for local staff, 182–83; distrust of government officials, 155; as civil servants, 68; as correlates to colonial officials, 125–26, 134; government reliance on, 87; labor, 61, 68; as migrants, 139; perceived expertise, 60, 68, 126, 183; prioritized over locals and refugees, 160, 181–83; and refugee complex, 168, 178; relations with Tabora Refugee Council, 125; Tanzanian, 179

familial relationships: and citizenship, 141; and development, 98, 191; and forced resettlement, 100; husbands, 50–51; marriage, 30, 38, 45, 50, 198; nation as family, 9; necessitating migration, 50; and refugees, 77, 80, 94, 105, 179; royal, 26; spanning borders, 2, 39, 145, 179; wives, 50, 144

famine, alleged, 69; as constant threat, 51; and food security in camps, 186; and mandate state, 40; and refugee burden, 84; and refugee camp management, 106, 110; relief, 164; and Rwandan migration, 55; and subsistence farming, 68

Fassin, Didier, 11

Ferguson, James, 60, 133

ferries: bringing migrants from Rwanda, 77; Kyaka, 54; Muwendo, 54

feudalism: applied to Bahangaza, 48; applied to Bugufi, 46; applied to Busubi, 46; colonial description of Ngara, 46–47; and land laws, 62; led by Tutsi aristocracy, 47; serfdom, 47–48

firewood, 175, 184–85, 187

food distribution, 107, 174, 179–81, 204

food prices, 180, 185

food scarcity, 181

food shortage, 49, 89, 99, 106, 109

forced labor. *See* compulsory labor

forced repatriation, 100, 189, 200

French (language), 93

304 · Index

frustration: with coffee production, 62; of colonial efforts, 49, 54–55, 59, 61; with cross-border migration, 80, 145; and illicit trading, 71; with international agencies, 115; due to lack of understanding, 133–34; with refugees, 92, 94, 154–55, 193; with refugee resettlement, 92; at rejection of local expertise, 102; with Tanzanian government, 132

fuel: agency needs for, 170, 191; consumption, 182; cooking, 185; diesel, 169–70; distribution of, 170; dyeing of, 171; kerosene, 185; petrol, 91, 148, 158, 171; provision of, 160, 169–70, 174; rationing, 171; refugee needs, 171, 191; responsibility for, 169; siphoning, 171; stations, 181; supply, 169–70; theft of, 169–71, 183, 186; transportation of, 169–70, 173–74

Gatete, Jean-Baptiste, 181
genocidaires, 191
geographies of control, 1, 74
German East Africa, 23–25, 32–33
Geschiere, Peter, 5
Gisaka; as disputed territory, 35–36, 38, 41, 55; migration from, 41, 55; migration to, 30
goats, 30, 48, 166, 180
grassroots, 142, 200

Habyarimana, Juvenal, 161–62, 197
hamite, 28, 31, 47
Hamitic hypothesis, 27–28, 40, 47
healthcare, 51–53, 55, 72, 100, 118, 126, 130, 180, 187
historical periodization, 78, 81
historiography, 7
HIV/AIDS, 185
home: ancestral, 145; becoming, 119; building of, 49, 144; homecoming, 153, 157; imagined, 15, 153, 199; as origin, 44, 49, 143–45, 156. See also repatriation
humanitarian aid: changes within, 159; contradictions within, 14, 194; culture of, 183; effects of, 19; history of, 1; distinct from humanitarianism, 13; and human rights, 12; management of, 160; perception of, 114, 118, 174; and Rwandan genocide, 159; for Rwandan refugees, 1; target of, 119; theories of, 200

humanitarian governance, 13
hunger strike, 113, 132
Hunter, Emma, 155
Hutu: colonial understandings of, 34–35, 40, 47–48, 83, 97; deaths during Rwandan independence, 79; definition of, 28, 97; elite, 79; exiles, 161.; extremist narratives, 162; fleeing to Tanzania, 179–80; gaining power, 79, 162; genocide in Burundi, 164; hard-line groups, 161; as identity, 42, 97; and indigeneity, 97; massacres of, 165; migration of Rwandan, 83; militias, 161, 165; moderate, 161–62; oppression of, 40, 47–48, 79; rule, 116. See also Hamitic hypothesis
Hydén, Goran, 147

identity papers, 40, 126, 141, 153, 157
ideological nation building, 4, 9, 18, 178, 195
illegal migration, 45, 145, 196
illegal trade, 9, 72, 88, 111, 140–41, 146–50, 156. See also smuggling
imagination: of borders, 23–26, 37, 44, 78, 140; of colonizers, 64; of decolonization, 134; of history, 93, 161; of home, 15, 153, 199; imagined community, 9, 141; of the nation, 5, 116; political, 10, 25, 27, 114, 116, 153; popular, 3, 78, 96; of refugees, 116, 153; of ujamaa, 143
independence: competing notions of, 108–9; Congo, 81; and cooperatives, 70; and development, 58–59, 67–68; disappointments of, 18–19; East African cooperation after, 151; era in Ngara, 3, 57–59, 67; feelings about, 69; and geographies of control, 74; and governmental rhetoric, 155; and illegal courts, 72; incompleteness of, 94; movement, 73; optimism of, 109; peaceful transition to, 97, 111; periodization of, 74; preparation for, 67; Rwandan, 79, 97, 109; terrain of, 117; and tobacco cultivation, 70; and transformation from migrants to refugees, 19, 78, 81, 110
indigeneity, 47, 79, 122, 149
indirect rule, 40, 43
inflation, 145–46
informal economy, 148, 150

Index · 305

infrastructure: aid funding for, 119; as benefit of refugee crisis, 187; control over, 182, 185, 189; and development, 61; government promise of, 145; lack of, 16, 65, 71, 88, 119, 168–70; lack of funding for, 69, 72; poor, 62; rehabilitation of, 189–90

instability, 6, 81, 90, 120–21

integration: into asylum country, 12; failure, 110, 140; policy, 106; of refugees, 106, 164; regional, 10, 194, 198; and *ujamaa* villages, 140

intercropping, 65

International Federation of Red Cross Societies. *See* Red Cross

international law, 4–5, 25, 33, 44, 80

International Monetary Fund (IMF), 157

intole (landlords), 30–31, 47

invasion: of Bahangaza, 30; and Hamitic hypothesis, 47, 79; repatriation as, 120; Rwandan Patriotic Front (RPF), 160

inyenzi (cockroaches), 79, 90–91, 161

Jesuit Refugee Service, 187

Kafanabo, Ndugu P.N., 154–55

Kagame, Paul, 197

Kagera River: and 1994 genocide, 159, 162, 179; as border, 23, 26, 36, 83, 163; and creation of Bugufi, 26; islands in, 37; as local imaginary, 26; migration in early 1960s, 77; tin discovery, 36

Kaplan, Martha, 8

Karagwe: colonial designation of, 82; as crossing point into Tanganyika, 77; generosity of, 88; permanent settlements in, 90, 106; and precolonial migration, 48; refugee camps in, 169, 173–74, 188, 196; and RPF offensive, 162

Kasulo refugee settlement, 166, 190,

Kasulu, 82, 165, 185, 189

Katavi, 198

Kato, Joseph (WLR), 98, 144

Kawawa, Rashidi Mfaume (Tanganyika second vice president, 1962, 1972–77), 91, 129–30, 132

Kayibanda, Grégoire (president of Rwanda, 1961–1973), 79

Kelly, John D., 8

Kenya, 151

kerosene. *See* fuel

Keza, 15–16, 144–45, 170, 172, 187, 199

Kibondo: as Border Province, 82; and coffee, 70; and TCRS camps, 164–66

Kigali, 83, 159, 161–62

Kigeri IV Rwabugiri (Rwandan king, c. 1865–1895), 29, 35

Kigeri V Ndahindurwa (Rwandan king, 1959–1961), 79

Kigoma: and border creation, 34, 82; and Nyamirembe Native Tobacco Board (NNTB), 70; resettlement project, 166; and Tanganyika Tobacco Board (TTB), 72; and TCRS camps, 165, 198

Kihangaza, 2, 15, 30, 38

Kikuyu, 121, 126

Kikwete, Jakaya, 196–97

Kikwete, Salma, 197

Kimuli/Nkwenda, 90, 152

King's African Rifles (KAR), 82

Kisubi, 5, 15, 30

Kiswahili, 2, 70, 97, 131, 152, 187

Kitali Hills, 170, 172

kodi (taxes), 49. *See also* taxation

kujitegemea (self-reliance), 144

Kumnazi, 186

Kushner, Tony, 6

labor migration, 18, 45, 48, 50, 56

land laws, 46, 62

land scarcity, 102, 161

land tenure, 47–48, 63

laziness, 64, 108, 110

League of Nations, 4, 10–11, 13, 19, 24–25, 32, 34, 37, 41, 58

League of Red Cross Societies (LRCS): aid to Rwandan refugees, 86, 101–3, 105; Dahl, Knud, 102; lack of local knowledge, 102, 104; Makao, R.K., 103; and permanent settlement of refugees, 102–3, 105; rigidity of response, 87, 101; Rohner, Ernst, 102; Tanzanian government contracts with, 101, 104, 106

legibility, 84, 90, 92, 133, 141

lions, 73, 88

livestock: illicit trade in, 148; and refugees, 84, 166, 185; and regional economy, 30, 50

306 · Index

loans, 68, 89

lorries, 15, 45, 54–55, 83, 158, 169, 171

Lutheran World Federation Archives (LWF): and border creation, 7; and development mandate, 105; Muetzelfeldt, Bruno, 105–6, 121–22, 125–26; and origins of TCRS, 105; perception of, 121–22; and refugee settlement, 118–21, 124; Sundkler, Begnt, 105–6; and Tanzanian government contract, 119, 124; and UNHCR, 106

maendeleo (development), 17

magendo (illegal trade). *See* illegal trade

Magufuli, John, 198

maize, 101, 107, 121, 185

malaria, 31, 73

Malkki, Liisa, 44

malnutrition, 100, 106–7, 109

mandate system: Belgian, 10, 23–24; boundaries, 24–25, 27, 36, 39; British, 10, 23–24; and development, 58; famine in, 40; ignorance of local realities, 33; and international law, 25; League of Nations, 24, 32, 37; and technologies of rule, 25, 33–34; transfer of territories, 36, 39; transition to trustee system, 11, 37; and WWI, 25, 32. *See also* Permanent Mandates Commission (PMC)

manpower. *See* labor

Marfleet, Philip, 6

marketing boards, 70

markets: and aid materials, 189; bananas in, 30; and cash crops, 70; closures, 146; coffee, 66; and colonial economy, 44; and interactions with refugees, 147; and lack of infrastructure, 64; petrol in, 158; refugee camp, 179, 181, 185–86; shortages of, 140; sites of, 71; women in, 198

marriage. *See* familial relationships

Mbembe, Achille, 7

meat, 30, 185, 198

Médecins Sans Frontières (MSF), 171

men: Bahangaza, 30; and crime in refugee settlements, 179; and cross-border trade, 147; and labor migration, 10, 45, 50; and marriage eligibility, 50; and multiple wives, 144; and protection of family and property, 50; and regional temporary migration

from refugee camps, 107; and perceptions of wealth during *ujamaa*, 149; in rebel armies, 161; in Rwandan militias, 161; and trade activities, 185

middle class, 130

militias: fleeing from RPF, 162; Hutu, 161–62, 165; massacres by, 165; Tanzanian, 181

milk, 147

Milner-Orts Agreement (1919), 35

mining, 40, 54, 56

Ministry of Agriculture (Tanzania), 92, 103

Mishamo, 164

mobility: economic, 40; social, 31, 40; and state control, 135

modernity: and African backwardness, 61; and cash crops, 60; colonial tutelage of, 25, 32; grievances against, 66; and industrialization, 58; farming initiatives by Tanzanian government, 65, 69; modernization theory, 58; perceived resistance to, 62, 64, 69; political, 60; and popular participation, 58; and science, 61

moral quality of citizenship, 134, 140, 150, 152, 155–57, 178

Mpanda, 114–15, 119, 122–23, 125–27, 129

Musaveni, Yoweri (president of Uganda, 1984–present), 161

Muyenzi: attempts to resettle from, 92, 94, 99–100, 102–3, 111, 170; camp authorities, 93; choice of location, 91; citizenship for refugees, 152, 154; competing sovereignties in, 114, 154; difficulty of travel, 16, 91; expansion of, 92; food shortages, 99, 106, 110; governance within, 99–101, 105, 110, 115; lack of resources, 91–92, 99, 108; land allocation, 91; management of, 106, 110–11, 128; migration from, 95–96, 98–99, 106, 170; negative perceptions of refugees, 98, 101–2, 105, 107–8, 110, 154, 199; and raids into Rwanda, 108, 111; rejection of government control, 128; repatriation from, 107, 111, 199; resistance to control, 134; sanctioning of refugees, 99–100; security in and around, 107; and theft, 93; transition to refugee camp, 90; as *ujamaa* village, 140, 145, 151; water sanitation, 92, 107

Mwambutsa IV (Burundi king, 1915–1966), 30, 38–39, 41

Index · 307

Mwanza: Banyaruanda migration to, 78; infrastructure investment to, 187; international resources to, 168; Ngaran migration to, 70; purchasing fuel from, 170–71; Mwesi Highlands Refugee Settlement; airlift from Kivu province in Congo, 114, 119, 122–24; competing sovereignties in, 114–17, 129–30, 133, 135; conflict among aid organizations, 125, 127; conflict over resources, 125–26; failure of, 114, 118, 121–22, 135; goals of, 114, 117–21, 126; hunger strike in (*see* hunger strike); lack of infrastructure, 119, 125; and political imaginaries of Rwanda, 116, 131; offer of citizenship to refugees, 152; political logics of refugees, 115–17, 127–29, 131, 134; refugee resistance to settlement, 120; rejection of domestic use, 122–23; and self-sufficiency, 127; spirit of noncooperation in, 113, 117, 128, 130, 132, 134; Tanzanian government control over, 114, 118, 129–30, 133

Mwinyi, Ali Hassan, 157

nation building: and ambiguity, 69; and belonging, 5, 200; deliberate, 69; and domestication of borders, 5, 140; and exclusion, 7, 152–53, 156; and global governance, 112; ideological, 18; as ongoing process, 117; and refugees, 5–6, 11, 18, 119, 152, 156, 195, 202; rhetoric of, 73, 97, 153; and *ujamaa* villagization, 122, 140, 151–52, 156

National Economic Survival Programme (1981–1982), 157

national identity, 3, 68

nationality: and borders, 23; changing, 153; and decolonization, 142; and otherness, 178

native authorities, 39–40, 43, 46, 49, 64, 70, 90

naturalization: attempts at, 141, 152, 154, 156, 161, 198; failed, 140, 155; political use of, 154–55; rationales for, 141; and refugee preferences, 153–54, 156, 161; as solution to refugee problem, 152–53, 165, 198

Ndadaye, Melchior, 164

networks, 12, 43, 53, 67, 81

Newbury, David, 8

ngorole (tribute), 31, 48

Nkurunziza, Pierre, 198

noncooperation, 113, 132, 134

Nongovernmental Organization (NGO), 124, 160, 168, 171, 173, 182, 184, 190

Norwegian People's Aid (NPA), 184

Nsoro, Protas (Busubi chief), 49

Ntobeye, 77, 89, 145

Nugent, Paul, 4

Nyerere, Julius (president of Tanzania, 1964–1985): and African socialism, 68, 87, 106, 142; and corruption, 58; and education, 69; failures, 157; ideals of, 2, 87–88, 97, 109, 117, 151; and independence, 66, 68; and national identity, 70; and nation building, 69, 119, 140; and Pan-Africanism, 151; and refugee resettlement, 84, 87–88, 90, 154; relationships with international organizations, 104, 106; and TANU, 66–68, 97; the teacher/*mwalimu*, 57–58, 109; and *ujamaa*, 87, 135, 142–44, 146, 150–51; and war with Uganda (1979), 146

Nyiginya dynasty, 27

Nyamirembe Native Tobacco Board, 70

Obote, Milton (prime minister of Uganda, 1962–1966), 91

Omani traders, 150

Operation Book In (1962–63), 81–82

Operation Maduka (1976), 146

Organization of African Unity (OAU), 124, 127, 181

otherness, 1–2, 6–7, 98, 110

outsiders, 8, 15, 156

Oxfam, 99, 171–72

Pan-Africanism, 84, 151

panya (mouse) routes. *See* smuggling

parasite, 155

parastatals, 145

Paris Peace Conference, 24, 32

Parmehutu (Parti du Mouvement et de l'Emancipation du Hutu), 81

peripherality, 4, 7–8, 29, 41, 44, 60, 81, 84, 148, 187

Permanent Mandates Commission (PMC), 34–37, 74

permits: as commodity, 154; cooperation with, 130, 132; and corruption, 154;

308 · Index

perception as optional, 129; refusal to accept, 117, 128, 131, 134; refusal to sign, 129–32, 134; and Rwandan citizenship, 129, 131; as site of conflict, 131–32, 135, 143; state-mandated, 113, 128, 133, 154; as tool of control, 133–34

pesticide, 72, 129

petrol. *See* fuel

policing; and borders, 78, 82, 197; and control of refugees, 98, 181; and corruption, 148; and decolonization, 72, 82; distrust by refugees, 102, 181; international apparatus role in, 5; in refugee camps, 101, 107; role of UNHCR, 12, 101, 181, 189; and suspicion of refugees, 90; and theft of resources, 171

poll tax, 45

polygamy. *See* familial relationships

pombe (beer), 30, 50, 144

population density, 47, 153

poverty, 59, 62, 68–69, 83, 112, 142, 149, 176

Preventative Detention Act (1962), 129

privilege, 9, 94, 98, 108–11, 191

productivity, 34, 53, 72, 87, 92

protest, 61, 90, 100, 105, 113, 130, 132, 181

Protocol Relating to the State of Refugees (1967), 12, 181

Prunier, Gerard, 197

race: and citizenship, 151; and Hamitic hypothesis, 28, 47; and humanitarianism, 194; and WWII, 37

Radio Kwizera. *See* UNHCR

Radio Tanzania, 187

Radio-Télévision Libre des Milles Collines (RTLM), 161

Randall, Steven, 7

rape, 180, 185

rations (*posho*): appeals for, 89; cut to force repatriation, 105; failure to provide, 145; inadequate, 94, 105; international control over, 181; lack of, 100; need for, 105–7; phasing out, 127; and perceived refugee privilege, 108–9; refusal to provide, 95; trading, 85, 185; withdrawn for noncooperation, 93, 99–100, 130

Rassemblement Démocratique Rwandais (RADER), 131

Refugee (Control) Act (1965), 115, 117, 127–28, 130

refugee camps: administrators, 99–101; agency within, 91–92, 99–100; aid agencies in, 179, 181, 188, 201; attacks on Rwanda; and bureaucracy, 90, 92, 98; Burundian, 161, 165–66, 169–70; and citizenship, 19; competing sovereignties in, 8, 13, 19, 128; control of, 99, 102, 170, 194; creation of, 1; and designation of refugee status, 3, 6, 9, 108, 110, 154, 179, 194; elites in, 181; food resources in and around, 186; and fuel resources, 170–71; and humanitarian crisis, 196; and identity, 7, 108, 156; international funding of, 98, 101, 109, 140, 165, 174, 179, 189, 194; local leaders in, 99, 133, 170; local staff in, 186; management, 160, 173–74; markets, 181, 185; and military training, 170, 187; overcrowding in, 160, 169–70, 180; and privileged status, 19, 110, 154; and repatriation, 188–89, 198; resistance to, 90–91, 98–100, 102, 184; sanitation in, 166, 169; security in and around, 169, 181–82, 184, 188; and segregation, 108, 110; state-sanctioned, 94, 102; Tanzanian control of, 128, 186; and Tanzanian socialism, 87; temporality of, 90; violence associated with, 177, 179–81, 185, 189; and *ujamaa* villages, 140; water in, 165, 169, 172, 175, 184, 186; and weapons, 180. *See also* Benaco; Chabalissa II; Muyenzi; UNHCR

Regional Commissioner (RC), 123, 126, 154

Regional Trading Corporation (RTC), 146

relief. *See* humanitarian aid

repatriation: army involvement in, 188; due to lack of aid, 165; eventual, 53; feared, 188; forceful, 159, 189–91, 200; lack of, 188; to manage noncooperative refugees, 129; as nonviable option, 153; opportunities for, 187; peaceful, 93; planned, 163–65, 169, 195; and refugee permits, 129, 154; repercussions of, 189; and Rwandan attacks, 188; and Rwandan politics, 93; as solution to refugee problem, 12, 159, 165, 169, 190; suspended, 165; voluntary, 105, 160, 164, 169, 176, 198–99

Index · 309

resistance: active, 61; by marginalized people, 147–49; to development, 111; efforts to quell, 113, 129; to humanitarian aid, 13; imaginary, 64; passive, 61; as political activism, 134, 194; to settlement, 111; smuggling as, 148; to *ujamaa*, 87, 139

Rhodesia, 124

riots, 67, 99, 181

roads: access to, 64, 91, 143–45, 170, 181–82, 187, 198; dangers on, 179; improvements to, 50, 54, 91, 189, 191, 199; international funding for, 119, 121, 135; Karagwe–Ngara, 200; lack of, 65, 88, 99; lack of funding for, 88; Mpanda–Mwesi, 125; poor quality of, 62, 69, 99; Rusumo–Ngara, 200

robbery, 179–80, 184

RODESO, 190

Ruanda-Urundi: Belgian control of, 32–33, 35, 40, 42, 46, 51, 79; borders of, 23–25, 34–39, 41, 44–45, 54–55, 65, 81–82; camps along the border of, 51, 54; coffee production in, 62, 65; creation of, 37; and Hamitic hypothesis, 40; and illegal trade, 65; laborers from, 44–45, 56; migration from, 40, 44–45, 50–52, 54, 56, 82; nation building in, 97; political violence in, 81, 97; relationship to Ngara, 10, 18, 25, 38, 41, 50–51, 54–55, 82

rural areas: agricultural development in, 69, 142; identity politics of, 139; and international experts, 61; poor residents of, 59, 142; resistance in, 139; support for organizations, 66–67; and TANU, 68; *ujamaa* villages, 142. *See also* poverty

Rusumo: and aid agencies, 179; border crossing, 159, 197; bridge, 1, 162, 166–67, 180; and EAC, 26, 197; Falls, 83, 159; and genocide, 162, 166, 179–80, 193; and repatriation into Rwanda, 188. *See also* Rusomo Falls Hydroelectric Project

Rusumo Falls Hydroelectric Project, 197

Rwandan civil war, 1, 161, 163, 165

Rwandan Patriotic Front (RPF), 160–62, 188–89, 199

Ryckmans, Pierre (Governor-General of Belgian Congo, 1934–1946), 38

salt, 146–47, 185

sanitation, 165–66, 169, 190

Scalettaris, Giulia, 13

Schneider, Leander, 59

science, 60–61, 72. *See also* modernity

Scott, James, 133, 147, 149

second economy. *See* informal economy

security: camp, 181; concerns, 162; conflicts over, 97; deterioration of, 169, 187; economic, 145, 149; food, 186, 194; forces, 67, 78; as fundamental need, 191; material, 178; measures, 128, 183; physical, 93, 178; psychological, 93; responsibility for, 101; territorial, 5; threats, 186

sedentarization, 152

self-governance, 25

self-help, 69, 73, 80, 87–88, 97–98, 109, 120, 126

self-reliance, 87, 140–42, 144, 149, 152

self-rule, 33, 40, 60–61, 66, 68

settlements; and aid organizations, 103, 201; alteration of landscape, 80; authority within, 96, 101, 106; beside rivers, 83; borders of, 80, 100, 103; and citizenship, 152, 154; containment of refugees, 80; control of, 115, 128, 135; and definition of refugees, 108; as development villages, 87; dispersal from, 102, 170; forced into, 100, 154; internationally funded, 87, 156, 172; Kanyina 1, 92; labor migration from, 107; land shortage in, 102; lessons from, 111; Mbuba 1, 92; permanent, 90; placement of, 80, 103, 164; refusal to move, 99; refusal to stay, 92; scholars living in, 93; splitting up refugee leaders, 92; and *ujamaa*, 152

settler, 12, 89, 106, 108, 118, 121, 126

shamba, 16–17, 45, 51, 57, 88, 98, 144, 199

Shanga, 145, 186

shelter, 88, 95, 167–68, 180, 186, 188

Sijaona, Lawi (Tanzanian Minister of State), 121

Singida, 164

Sisal Labor Bureau (SILABU), 55

sleeping sickness, 55, 73

smuggling, 59, 65, 71–72, 74, 149, 155

soap, 147, 185

socialism: African, 97, 106, 141, 150, 157, 202; in Arusha Declaration (1967), 142, 151; and Tanzanian citizenship, 141, 155; ideas, 80; reluctance toward, 157; Tanzanian, 68, 87, 111, 141, 149

310 · Index

Sokoine, Edward (prime minister of Tanzania, 1977–1980, 1983–1984), 149–50
South Africa, 163
sovereignty: changing, 37; and citizenship, 195, 202; competing, 8, 19, 113, 115, 194; as ideal, 8–9; political, 201; respect for, 84; as set of claims, 9, 13, 113; state, 94, 128; Tanzanian, 115, 156, 195; territorial, 9; threatened by realities, 8; unequal, 9, 134–35; and UNHCR, 12
Soviet Union, 60–61, 85–86
soya beans, 107
squatters, 47–48
stability, 36, 78, 80, 87, 134–35, 153, 197
Stockwell, Roy Zandemar (British officer), 81, 83
structural adjustment programs, 157, 161
sugar, 17, 147, 149
sweet potatoes, 107

Tabora, 119, 123–26, 129, 131, 198
Tanganyika African National Union (TANU): and African empowerment, 66; development agenda, 67–68; and end of chiefly tribute, 97; failure of, 68; and independence, 67; and nation building, 68; and perceptions of territory, 87; popularity of, 66–68; priorities of, 69; and rural development, 69, 87
Tanganyika Christian Refugee Service (TCRS): Aantjes, Jaap, 190; aid projects, 107, 118; and division of aid responsibility, 101, 106, 110–11, 117–18, 125, 133, 164, 167, 173–75, 177; failures of, 111, 120, 126, 159; Farquharson, George, 119, 121; and food rations, 127, 130, 160; Franzen, Charles, 183; and fuel rations, 170–71, 173; global reputation of, 118, 121, 173; Laiser, Isaac, 107; local reputation, 125, 133, 159, 181, 187; and LWF, 119, 121, 190; Mezza, Lazarus, 188, 190; motivations of, 106, 174–75; Neldner, Brian, 125, 130, 201; Njunde, Cassius, 126; Norredam, Jorgen, 119, 121, 124–26; origins of, 105; pivot to development work, 163–64, 167, 189; and politics of refugee aid, 110, 160, 163–65, 168, 177, 182, 187, 189; and refugee relations, 120, 130, 134, 163, 165, 167, 188, 194; and refugee resettlement, 123–24,

165, 169–70, 188; Simeso, Admasu, 166–68, 174, 176, 193; staff issues, 121, 126, 181–83; Staub, Bernhard, 163, 165, 168, 172–73, 182, 189; Jones, Ted, 172, and *ujamaa*, 122; and UNHCR, 124–25, 127, 133, 135, 163–65, 171, 173–74, 182, 189; and water resources, 172, 184; Waters, Tony, 166
Tanganyika Rifles, 107
Tanganyika Tobacco Board (TTB), 71–72
Tanzania Immigration Act (1973), 154
taxation: and chiefly governance, 49; and citizenship, 9; and colonization, 43, 45, 48–49; and decolonization, 73; evasion, 149; and migration to Buganda, 50; and migration to Uganda, 57; and native authorities, 49; as state building, 41; tax base, 12
technology: and colonial project, 31, 62; communication, 168; and conflict between aid agencies, 173; creating solutions to agriculture problems, 39, 58, 61; and development, 61; expense of, 72; to fight poverty, 142; and mandate system, 25; and model farms, 62; preferred over local knowledge, 60; and refugee problems, 87, 133; resistance to, 61, 64, 66; TANU attempts to implement, 69; and *ujamaa* villages, 140
theft: creative, 158, 191; and conflict between locals and refugees, 185–86; of drugs, 72; of fuel, 170–71; motivations for, 186, 191; as obstacle to humanitarian aid, 171; and perceptions of otherness, 110; prevention of, 171, 180
tobacco: colonial introduction, 70; and conflict over techniques, 72; cooperative unions, 71; corruption and, 71; disappointment in cultivation, 70–71, 88; efforts to expand cultivation, 71–72; failure to export, 71, 88; illegal trade in, 72, 88; marketing boards, 70–72; and pestilence, 72; production levels, 70–71; state–supported cultivation, 70, 88; widespread cultivation of, 70. *See also* Nyamirembe Native Tobacco Board; Tanganyika Tobacco Board (TTB)
trade liberalization, 157
transnational aid, 3, 84, 195, 202
transportation, 50, 100, 107, 118, 126, 170

Index · 311

Treaty Concerning a Modification of the Boundary between Tanganyika Territory and Ruanda-Urundi (1934), 37

Tripp, Aili Mari, 150

troublemakers, 79, 92, 98–100, 107

trusteeship: Belgian Trust, 82; British Trust, 82; sacred trust, 25, 32, 37; territories, 37, 39; Trusteeship Council (TC), 37

tsetse flies, 73, 87–89

Turnbull, Richard (Governor of Tanganyika, 1958–1962), 67

Tutsi: and Burundian politics, 31, 120, 162, 164–65; attempted coup in Burundi (1993), 162, 165; colonial definitions of, 34–35, 39–40, 42, 83; commission of genocide against Hutu in Burundi (1972), 164; continuation of genocidal violence against in refugee camps, 179, 186, 188; and desire to restore monarchy, 79, 81, 97; economic status of, 93; and feudalism, 47; first wave of Rwandan exiles (1959–1964), 79, 83, 160; genocide against (1994), 162, 180–81; and Hamitic hypothesis, 28, 40, 47, 79, 83; and imagined Rwandan nation, 116; labeled as *inyenzi*, 79; massacres in Burundi, 165; military training in exile, 82, 160; and native authorities, 39; perceptions of superiority, 28, 31, 34–35, 40, 42, 47, 79, 83, 93; raids into Rwanda, 79, 120, 160; and regional migration, 83; relations with Hutu, 47, 79, 83, 161–62, 164; reluctance to embrace agriculture, 85; and Rwandan civil war, 160–61; and Rwandan Patriotic Front (RPF), 160–61, 188; and Rwandan politics, 31, 79, 81, 120, 161; second wave of Rwandan exiles (1994), 162, 179–80; threats to, 118; as victims of violence as refugees, 179, 186, 188; villainization of, 161; working with Belgian colonizers, 40, 47, 79. *See also* inyenzi; Rwandan Patriotic Front (RPF)

Twining, Edward (Governor of Tanganyika, 1949–1958), 67

Uganda: borders of, 34, 36, 45, 54; as British protectorate, 44, 54; and canalization of migrants, 53; coffee production in, 62; and coffee smuggling, 65; colonial concerns over refugees in, 81; condition of Rwandan refugees in, 86; and East African regional ties, 151; efforts to control migration to, 51, 54, 56, 62; labor migration to, 45, 48–52, 56–58, 62–63, 65, 69, 73, 83, 88; refugee migration into, 91, 196; refugee preference for, 132; refugee raids into Rwanda from, 105; regional links, 24; settlement in, 50; as staging ground for Rwandan Patriotic Front, 160–61; and Tanganyikan tobacco exports, 71; and UNHCR efforts in, 135; violence against Rwandan refugees in, 153; war with Tanzania (1978–79). *See also* Rwandan Patriotic Front (RPF)

uhujume (sabotage), 149–50

ujamaa vijijini (*ujamaa* in the villages), 142

ujamaa villages: and cash crops, 145; failure of, 157; and moral citizenship, 152; motivations behind, 142; movement to and from, 141, 142, 144–45; refugee exclusion from, 151; Rwandan refugees in, 140, 151–52; and trade, 146; transition of refugee settlements into, 16, 140

UN Security Council, 8, 11

Union Nationale Rwandaise (UNAR), 93, 131

United Nations High Commissioner for Refugees (UNHCR): accountability of, 12, 86, 94; Aga Khan, Saruddin (UNHCR Deputy High Commissioner), 103–4; in Burundi, 95, 100, 120–21; camps in Congo, 121–22; choice of settlement location, 16, 77, 120, 140, 164; debates over refugee services, 106–7, 129–32, 153, 160, 163, 174, 176; de Bosch Kemper, G., 127, 130–31; and development of refugee solutions, 87, 130, 132, 140, 152, 163, 169, 174, 176–77, 195; and development of work in Tanzania, 11; failures of, 105, 110–11, 120, 135, 169; formation of, 11; funding for refugee efforts, 101, 118–19, 134–35, 155–56, 160, 165, 173, 182, 186–87, 189; goals of, 84, 86, 115, 131, 168, 172, 174; Gussing, Nils, 132; initial involvement with Rwandan refugees, 101; international reputation, 85–86, 105, 114, 118–19, 152–53; internal functions of, 14, 117, 160; involvement in decolonization process, 85–86; Jaeger, Gilbert, 121; Jamieson, Thomas, 129; Kohaut, R.C., 132; Kuijpers, Armond, 117–18; and local

312 · Index

access to refugee services, 125, 160, 169, 172, 176, 185, 189, 198; mandate of, 12, 106, 116, 119, 127, 160, 193, 201; and Mwesi airlift, 122–23; oversight responsibilities, 101; policing function of, 12, 128–29, 163, 181, 184; politics of, 114–17, 119, 125, 127–28, 130, 134, 200; Pryce, Colin, 182; and Radio Kwizera, 187; and refugee permits, 128–29, 131; refugee transfers to second asylum nation, 117–18, 120–21, 123; refusal to relocate refugees, 113, 132; and regulation of African borders, 7, 41, 114, 128, 153; relations with refugee leaders, 79, 113, 115, 127, 130–33, 135; relationship with ws-lwf, 106, 119–20, 122; relationship with Tanganyikan Christian Refugee Service (tcrs), 12, 106, 111, 117, 120, 123–24, 127, 130, 159–60, 163–65, 167, 170–74, 182, 189; relationship to Tanzanian government, 101, 106, 110, 117–19, 121, 129–31, 140, 153, 164, 181, 188, 198; as a state, 12, 128; and state sovereignty, 12, 128, 134, 153, 155, 188; tensions between expatriate and local staff, 124, 167, 182–83; tensions with local authorities, 125, 133, 182, 184–85; tensions with other agencies, 96, 110–11, 160, 163–65, 171–74, 182; tensions over refugee designation, 123, 155–56, 193; treatment of expatriate staff, 183; and use of local resources, 184–86, 189. *See also* Mwesi Highlands Refugee Settlement
United Nations Visiting Mission (1954), 37, 66
United States, 15, 60, 85–86
Uyui Prison, 129

voluntarism, 142
voluntary repatriation. *See* repatriation

wage economy, 40, 44
wage labor, 43–44
wageni (guests), 108
wahujume (selfish traders), 140, 149, 155
wakimbizi (those who run), 108, 110–11, 195
water production, 92, 170, 172–73
water sanitation, 10, 17, 88, 108, 151, 165–66
water supply, 92, 107, 146, 171
watoro (those who flee justice), 108
Watutsi/Watusi. *See* Tutsi
weapons, 31, 142, 147, 179–80
West Lake Province (wlp), 77–78, 83–84, 87–88
West Lake Region (wlr), 89, 91, 98, 103, 107, 109
Whitaker, Beth, 178
women; affected by inflation and illegal trade, 185, 198; and rape, 180, 185; reluctance to speak about experiences, 17; struggles with men's labor migration, 65
World Bank, 157, 197
World Food Program (wfp), 185–86, 189, 198
World War I, 10, 24–25, 32, 35, 85
World War II, 11–12, 34, 37, 60–61, 74, 85, 127, 202

Yeld, Rachel (Oxfam), 99–100

Zaïre. *See* Congo
Zanzibar, 87, 117, 124

Index · 313